Macro and Micro Policies for More Growth and Employment

Symposium 1987

Edited by Herbert Giersch

Institut für Weltwirtschaft an der Universität Kiel

Routledge
Taylor & Francis Group
LONDON AND NEW YORK

First published 1988 by Westview Press

Published 2018 by Routledge
52 Vanderbilt Avenue, New York, NY 10017
2 Park Square, Milton Park, Abingdon, Oxon OX14 4RN

Routledge is an imprint of the Taylor & Francis Group, an informa business

CIP-Titelaufnahme der Deutschen Bibliothek

Macro and micro policies for more growth and employment:
symposium 1987 / Inst. für Weltwirtschaft an d. Univ. Kiel. Ed.
by Herbert Giersch. - Tübingen: Mohr, 1988
  ISBN 3-16-345395-3 brosch.
  ISBN 3-16-345396-1 Gewebe
NE: Giersch, Herbert [Hrsg.]; Institut für Weltwirtschaft <Kiel>

ISBN 13: 978-0-367-00350-0 (hbk)
ISBN 13: 978-0-367-15337-3 (pbk)

CONTENTS

Preface

Major industrial countries have shown strikingly different performances
in recent years. Between 1982 and 1987, employment in the United States
and Japan increased by 13 and 6 per cent respectively but only by
2 per cent in Western Europe. While unemployment rates in America and
Japan are presently almost as low as they were in the late 1970s when
the cyclical position was about the same, they are double as high as
they were then in Western Europe. Correspondingly, GNP growth in
Western Europe was low by past and international standards.

Economists have offered different explanations relating to different policy
paradigms. In planning our traditional Kiel Week Conference, we wanted
to look at them more closely in an attempt to find out where the disagreement has its roots. The conference took place at the Institut für
Weltwirtschaft on June 24-26, 1987. This volume presents the papers,
the comments, and summaries of the subsequent discussions.

The conference started off with the pros and cons of rules for the conduct of monetary and fiscal policy. Opponents argued that rules - especially for monetary targeting - had failed because of drastic changes
in the velocity of circulation, particularly in the United States. In
Western Europe, these rules were to be held responsible for the high
unemployment: discretionary policies to boost demand would have been
superior.

Proponents of rules insisted that the best contribution to be expected
from macroeconomic policies was that demand should expand predictably
along a noninflationary growth path. A rule for monetary policy in the
United States designed to neutralize shifts in velocity was presented. Its
supporters argued that slow growth and high unemployment were supply-
side problems to be tackled by measures on the micro level.

The other side made the point that expansionary monetary and fiscal
policies, even if not called for as a causal therapy, would help to allevi-
ate the problems on the supply side if there were any. Several investi-

gations to support this position were submitted. The "output gap" hypothesis for Europe was criticized for crucially depending on doubtful estimates of potential output and trend productivity. The conjectures focussing on "hysteresis" and "efficiency wages", though not so clearly relating to the macroeconomic demand/supply dichotomy and hence less controversial, received due attention. But their policy implications were seen to be similar to those of the output-gap explanation: give a boost to demand and trust that labor markets will take care of themselves in the course of the expansion.

Sceptics, notably from Europe, thought that there was more to it and that there was therefore more to be done. After all, America and Europe had been hit by the same supply shocks, and monetary policy had been directed at reducing inflation on both sides of the Atlantic. What then accounts for the fact that, during the recent recovery, unemployment in the United States declined to pre-recession levels, but remained high and even increased in Western Europe? The difference was seen - by some, though not all - in the operation of the labor markets: flexibility in the level and structure of real wages on one side of the Atlantic, substantial rigidities of a legal and institutional nature, including corporatist rigidities, on the other. A case study for West Germany drew attention to dismissal protection, unemployment compensation, well-meant social policies, subsidies to ailing industries, and protective measures which turned out to be barriers to entry both for new firms and for the unemployed. In these circumstances, measures to stimulate overall demand would, by themselves, not make the system more flexible though prosperity might facilitate legislative action towards more openness and deregulation.

The question what international coordination could contribute to achieving, faster growth and lower unemployment without more inflation was behind two related topics. The first related to the proposal of targeting exchange rates between the United States, Japan and Western Europe; those who raised objections implicitly argued that targeting monetary growth and letting exchange rates fluctuate freely would be a safer way to achieve price level stability as a sound basis for a better growth performance. The second topic was the general issue of policy coordination.

While there was no dispute about the advantages of coordination in the supply of genuine public goods, disagreement prevailed about the coordination of monetary and fiscal policies. Some participants suspected substantial costs of coordination, well above the possible benefits predicted by the game-theoretic approach, if policymakers did not know the true model, as must be presumed, if they erred on the inflationary side, and if rational economic agents were quick to discover a miscredited strategy and to anticipate undesirable outcomes.

On this as well as other topics it became clear once more that conferences such as this tend to be more productive in raising than in answering questions, but productive they nevertheless are.

The Institut für Weltwirtschaft is indebted to the participants for their papers and comments. Credit is due to Joachim Scheide for helping to prepare the conference and writing the summaries of this volume; Dietmar Gebert and Fiona Short deserve acknowledgement for their editorial efforts. Finally, the Institut would like to thank the City of Kiel, the Landeszentralbank Schleswig-Holstein and the Dresdner Bank for their hospitality.

Kiel, July 1988   Herbert Giersch

I

Jean Waelbroeck

Macroeconomic Issues for Europe in the 1980s: Can the NAIRU Be Tamed?

1. World-Wide Risks

In this paper, I intend to focus on the macroeconomic issues that confront this continent, and view problems of other areas from this perspective. This is a Eurocentric perspective: it does make sense in terms of the preoccupations of this conference, insofar as the continuing failure of Western Europe to generate jobs is the most serious economic issue of this decade. An improved European growth performance, on the other hand, could make a major contribution to improved world prospects, whether by:

- helping the United States to cope with its current deficit and to reduce its budget deficit without triggering a recession;

- helping developing countries to resume satisfactory growth; or

- making it possible for Japan to head off the worrisome wave of protectionism which is affecting its exports both to the United States and to the European Community.

Such a European recovery seems unlikely at the present time. From a European perspective, the main risks in mid-1987 are indeed on the negative side, in comparison with a recent period when Europe did poorly, in spite of an external environment that was on the whole quite favourable. The high dollar, that had opened up markets in the United States and reduced competition from US firms elsewhere, has been replaced by a realistically-priced currency which, if current efforts to stabilize it remain unsuccessful, could become substantially undervalued.

The US boom, that in three months will be the longest period of sustained expansion in US history, has helped European exporters up to now, but at some point a recession will take place. With the current trade policy stance of Congress and a weakened US Presidency, a sudden recession could destroy the uneasy truce that has so far held back the danger of a trade war. There is also the vaguer risk that the decapitalization of US business in recent years, as a result of the take-over craze, could heighten the economy's vulnerability to a downswing. It had been possible until quite recently to pretend not to see that major developing country debtors defaulted on their debts some years ago, but this is now too obvious to deny. This has implications for the balance sheets of the world banking system and, more importantly, cuts off for some time a useful channel for capital flows that has helped to sustain overall economic growth. Oil prices, that had dropped markedly, have now bottomed out, and in fact the shock of another price explosion is not to be excluded as a result either of a short-run disruption of supplies in the Gulf, or of the energy shortage which experts have long insisted will hit the world in the long run, because of the poor success of oil exploration in the last two decades.

2. What's Wrong, Indeed If Anything?

In contrast with the pessimism of this introduction, it is interesting that Western Europe has fared better than is usually thought, during a recession that is now fourteen years old. Both statistical data and plain walking in the streets confirm that standards of living have been high and rising. Since the first oil shock of 1973, per capita GNP has risen as quickly in the United States (before the shock, Europe was doing better). High unemployment cannot but have led to misery which, in the absence of reliable data, has been reflected mainly in the quite notice-able increase in begging (1), but, thanks to the social security system, the social situation is less explosive than could have been feared.

_____

(1) Less harassing, however, in the experience of a frequent trans-atlantic traveller than in US cities.

The era of stubbornly upward-creeping real wages is over, except possibly in Britain. Phillips curve estimates such as those of Gordon [1987](1) give adequate fits, but it is important to be aware that wages did not come down spontaneously in response to labour market disequilibria: they were levered down by governments, sometimes with a helping hand from union leaders, in the hope that restoring profits would make European economies dynamic again. The "wage gap" that fed so much policy writing some years ago is however largely a thing of the past.

It appears to be true that productive capacity would soon be exhausted by an economic expansion, according to data from the European Community Business Tests that suggest that capacity utilization is close to the levels reached before the second oil shock (2). Would production bottle-necks prevent a recovery? Not if it is sufficiently gradual to allow capacity to adjust: but this would require fresh investment. It would be highly dangerous to adopt policies of deficit spending that would destroy the saving which, if demand recovered, economies would need to recover fully.

Would investors be willing to increase capacity if demand rose? The restoration of profits is a first reason to be optimistic in this respect. Not only has the incentive to invest been improved, but retained profits have traditionally played a large role in financing so-called "productive" investments. The channels through which capital is supplied have also become more efficient; the Eurobond and Eurocurrency markets have not only grown in size, but also in the flexibility which lenders and borrowers may desire as to currency exposure, horizon, and time profile of interest payments. Real rates of interest do, it is true, remain at historically high levels, but after years of low investment, there should be a back-log of unrealized investments that are profitable at those rates. The rough doubling of stock market prices has in any event sharply raised the market assessment of the net worth of firms that is reflected by Tobin's Q, and this also should encourage plant expansion. Finally,

---

(1) Cf. also his contribution to this volume.
(2) This data and other more informal sources also suggest that an expansion would soon produce shortages of skilled workers.

there is money. That a large supply of equity capital is available is witnessed both by the success of large privatization operations in Britain and France, and by large takeover bids in the former country. Submarkets that specialize in venture capital have likewise grown swiftly. So why are things not better?

There is in Europe a widespread conviction that recovery is impossible. Any significant expansion of production, it is thought, would quickly lead to a return to stagflation. And indeed, despite dismal GNP forecasts that are 1 per cent below the rate of growth that is compatible with zero growth of unemployment, the forecasts collected in a recent compilation of private forecasts [Economic Forecasts, 1987, p. 21], as well as those of the BIS and the OECD, suggest that a moderate rebound of inflation may take place.

Current macroeconomic models, on the other hand, imply that there is room for expanding production, and that the impact on inflation would be quite moderate. Belief in models is at a low ebb in the policy-making world. And it is indeed true that this evidence must be qualified by the observation that practically all the data is drawn from observations for years when contraction, not expansion, was observed. The "insider-outsider" model that is widely invoked these days to account for Europe's labour market problems does imply a response of wages to changes in employment that is quite non-linear, and may well be asymmetric. It is quite reasonable, therefore, that a great deal of attention is being paid to Great Britain's current experience, as a test case of whether expansion without inflation is feasible. It is worrisome that the quite mild upswing in that country has not only prevented the sharp deceleration of inflation that has taken place elsewhere, but appears to be worsening the trend of both wages and consumer prices.

Last, but definitely not least, unemployment - 11 per cent at the end of 1986 - is still on a rising trend that has not been interrupted since the beginning of the recession. In no country has it fallen significantly (1).

_____

(1) The marked improvement that has taken place in Britain appears to
    be due to a change in labour regulations, the improvements in

3. The Fuzziness of the Data

A cautionary note on data is in order before going on. There is significant uncertainty about where Europe stands today.

I mention only in passing the black economy that by moderate estimates may amount to 5 per cent of GNP and more according to more imaginative ones. Where this output is in the data is unknown - the undeclared book-keeper is somewhere in value added, the undeclared wallpaper-hanger is not - unless the statistics office has brought in his earnings through some rough adjustment of the data. The resulting uncertainty may affect estimates of the rate of growth of GNP, and certainly affects the data on income distribution by type of earner.

How savings have evolved is also questionable. It has been argued that the excessive fiscal prudence of European governments has prevented a recovery in output. Judgment on fiscal policies depends however on whether debt service is adjusted to take account of the impact of inflation. If the need for such an adjustment is accepted, it turns out that major countries, such as France, Britain, and the Federal Republic of Germany, have had substantial budget surpluses in recent years, and the deficits in such countries as Ireland, Italy, and Belgium become less frightening. On the other hand, as a result of national accounts identities, it must also be accepted that if public dissaving is adjusted downwards, so should private savings be, yielding a drastically modified picture of the evolution of thrift. The available pool of saving would be considerably smaller than is generally thought, calling for prudence in diverting scarce private saving to the funding of government deficits.

The unemployment figures, finally, are more and more "just a number", the evolution of which has no very clear meaning. They are consciously biased on the low side by numerous measures that aim at making them

_____

Belgium and in the Netherlands are even more the result of changing regulations than of any change in the underlying pattern of steady increase. The drop in the Federal Republic of Germany may be genuine but is slight. I abstract here from the see-saws of unemployment in Sweden that are a (highly interesting) special case.

look better, such as extensions of military service or of the school age, early retirement, the reclassification of older workers or long-term unemployed as pensioned or incapacitated, and so on. There are those who register for unemployment benefits but are not really looking for work, whether women who wish to look after their children, young people taking time off for the sake of leisure and sometimes for study, and the long-term unemployed who no longer try to get work. There are the true illicit workers: it is surprisingly easy to get such jobs on a full-time basis, and they offer quite high incomes. There are also the professional unemployed, who earn more than fully occupied workers by adding some illicit earnings to their jobless benefits. The boom in part-time work hides many who would like to work full time, but can not get the jobs they want. Are the many workers in retraining, in Sweden and elsewhere, genuinely studying, or just looking for a "better dole"? And finally, there is the growing number of workers who have been pushed off the unemployment rolls either, as in France, because they have been unemployed for longer than is allowed, or because through some foolishness, they have infringed some regulation, and have lost the right to benefits.

4. Policy Options

a. The Public Finance/Monetary Policy Conundrum

Here, the analysis is standard.

The US balance-of-payments deficit is about right, given the budget deficit that reflects the country's inflexible fiscal stance (both roughly $100 billion higher than before the Reaganomic tax cuts). So far, that deficit has largely been financed by capital exports from Japan, and by the saving released by the reduction in developing countries borrowing.

As stressed by McKinnon recently in the Financial Times, the indicated remedy is monetary expansion (1). His conclusion is perhaps too sweeping. Japan, for example, may wish to resort to deficit spending to absorb a structural oversupply of domestic savings, which has accounted for its balance-of-payments surplus. Reducing this surplus might lessen foreign protectionist pressures. Developing countries have little scope for expansionary monetary policies. For Europe, McKinnon's conclusion is however valid. In addition to his arguments, policy-makers in Europe will keep in mind that, should demand increase significantly, substantial amounts of capital will be needed to fund the increase in capacity required. For this reason also, monetary expansion that stimulates investment is preferable to deficit spending that will crowd it out.

In fact, for this one time policy has moved in the right way. The motivation was perhaps not what is should have been. Monetary expansion was desirable to boost demand, and indirectly to support the dollar: the desire of governments to support the dollar, recently restated in the Louvre Agreement, has led to monetary expansion that has substantially exceeded the Bundesbank's targets in particular (2). In a system that has only one degree of freedom, it does not matter that a side objective is inappropriately made into a primary target, if the primary target variable is moved in the right direction.

That the system has but one degree of freedom is however a fact that macroeconomic theory should recognize explicitly. Fiscal policy is largely beyond the control of policy-makers, whether in the US, or in Europe: increasing expenditures or cutting taxes is all too easy, but the reverse

---

(1) Which may, according to standard analysis, again call for some loosening of monetary policy in the United States also in order to offset the deflationary impact in that country of easier money policies in Europe.
(2) The Bundesbank has expressed strong dissatisfaction with this over-shooting of money targets. However, what matters is that the needed monetary expansion has taken place, and that whatever it pretends to wish, the Bank has let it take place.

process entails enormous difficulties, as the groups that are affected by taxes and expenditure link elbows to preserve their benefits (1). Fortunately, it is monetary, not fiscal expansion that is required at the present juncture, despite what the BIS report of 1987 advises.

b. The Wandering NAIRU and the Macroeconomic Employment Contract

It is trivial that demand expansion would bring about recovery if prices and wages could be kept under control. The basic problem is that the "non-accelerating inflation rate of unemployment" (the NAIRU) is, or is judged to be, close to the current very high unemployment levels. If that is true, so that any reduction in unemployment brings about an acceleration of inflation, it would seem indispensable to add the real wage to the armoury of the macroeconomic policy-maker. And, indeed, recent history suggests that there is scope for manipulating this variable, either directly by wage freezes or income policies of the Swedish type, or indirectly by deindexation. Or, even more speculatively, by schemes such as those that Layard [1982] and Weitzman [1984] have proposed (2).

It will however be argued that, although policies of rolling back real wages have been used successfully in recent years in many countries, more of the same is not a viable option today. These policies have made sticky wages come unstuck, they have been the modus operandi of a Phillips curve response that would not come by itself. They would not work in today's circumstances.

It must be realized that the cut that would be needed to reduce un-employment decisively would be quite large. Both casual observation and

---

(1) It is true that, as in the Netherlands in the last few years, a national consensus may be reached that makes cutbacks in expenditures possible. That does not change the fact that fiscal variables are far harder to modify than monetary ones.

(2) Richard Layard proposed introducing a special levy, taxing at a high rate wage increases that exceed a norm set by the government. Martin Weitzman proposed that the wages of workers should include a substantial profit-sharing component set in relation to profit.

econometric estimates suggest that the real wage elasticity of labour demand is at most around unity. Halving today's 11 per cent rate of unemployment would therefore require a substantial reduction in the living standard of workers. Because of perverse short-term effects that reflect the fact that wage earners spend their incomes more quickly than their employers, the ensuing increase in employment would come slowly, making this policy unpalatable from the political point of view (1).

Most fundamentally, cutting real wages by fiat will not work if workers perceive that their bargaining strength makes it possible for them to get more than what politicians ask them to be content with. This is true even if national union leaders give their assent to the wage cut. Real wage cuts could be enforced when real wages were so high that, in Belgium, for instance, the corporate sector lost money for two years in succession. Today, with booming stock markets and profit rates that have returned to the levels of the beginning of the recession, measures to cut wages would, as happened at the end of the Labour government headed by Callaghan, trigger a rash of wildcat and other strikes, unless as a more likely outcome, employers turned out to be smart enough to concede gracefully the wage increases which their workers would other- wise wring out of them.

The wage is a price, it reflects market forces like any other prices, and cannot be changed arbitrarily. The rate of interest also is a price. It can be changed because, if need be, more money can be printed. Work- ers cannot be printed.

The wandering NAIRU cannot be brought down by legislation: only changes in the structure of labour markets can reduce it. What needs to be adjusted is a balance of power that has shifted decisively in favour of workers, as a result of the sweeping institutional changes that took place almost everywhere in Europe in the late 1960s and in the first half of the 1970s.

---

(1) As was clear both in the Dutch and the Belgian experiments with this policy variable.

There is where the Layard [1982] and Weitzman [1984] schemes strike the right note: it is the institutional changes that have shifted the balance of power between employers and employees that are at the root of the trouble, and what they propose to change is institutions. By focusing attention on an elegant panacea that has little chance of being implemented, these proposals have however diverted attention from a more practical examination of the causes of stagflation.

To characterize the basic idea that will be put forward, I shall use the term "national employment contract" to designate the wide variety of formal and informal arrangements that regulate labour markets at the national level. The choice of this term underlines the analogy between these rules and the microeconomic contracts that guide labour relations at the firm level. It also reflects the dependence of these arrangements on a complex process of bargaining, as social groups interact through the national political process.

Recent labour market theory has stressed that microeconomic employment contracts are to a significant extent implicit [cf. Azariadis, 1975; Baily, 1974]. This is also true of the "national employment contract". Its basis is social law, but how this is implemented depends significantly on the precedents and traditions of the courts, and on the pressure of public opinion, that makes unenforceable legal provisions that the public feels are not fair.

The theory of implicit contracts emphasizes that, because unemployment arrangements tend to be lasting ones, labour contracts involve more than just setting the price for labour. They involve complex arrangements which also determine the variance of that price, given the uncertainty about states of the world over the period of the contract. Because, for various reasons, workers have a greater aversion to risk than their employers (1), it is profitable for the latter to assume more than their share of the expected risks, in exchange for a lower expected wage. In effect, employers intervene as risk insurers, receiving a premium that is

---

(1) The risk aversion of workers could stem from their poorer access to insurance and credit markets.

equal to the reduction of the expected wage that workers forego in exchange for a reduced economic risk.

Such a view of labour markets, focused on the relation between employers and individual workers, may be adequate in the United States context where, except in the smokestack industries and the public service, labour unions have lost most of their influence. In this continent, however, unions are too important for their role to be overlooked. They are, and this is what the public mainly sees, the agents of workers in negotiations about labour contracts. But they are also key agents in the political process. Every social democrat party is supported by a strong and influential trade union wing; Catholic parties, where they are strong, are likewise connected to Christian unions, so that there are many countries, including my own, where no government is thinkable that does not view with sympathy the wishes and perceptions of that group.

Why should unions offer wage concessions to obtain the employers' agreement to clauses that enhance the economic security of workers, if they can make the government compel firms to obey the clauses? Security can be made into a public good that does not have to be bought. In fact, by making workers more secure, it strengthens their bargaining power: instead of having to be paid for by lower wages, economic security makes it possible to wring more concessions from employers (1).

The system of social laws that has thus arisen is one of the attractive features of European society. A frequent comment of visitors from this continent to the United States is an expression of shock at the areas of poverty and derelict housing in that country, which hardly exist except in the South of this continent. The national unemployment contract ac-

---

(1) Implicit contract theory has become unpopular as an explanation of wage rigidity as economists realized that in an Arrow-Debreu equilibrium under uncertainty, it is obvious that on grounds of Pareto optimality, risks will be transferred optimally from risk averse agents to less risk averse ones, but that this will not cause involuntary unemployment. The argument is of course not applicable if, thanks to the political power of unions, they are able to make security into a public good.

counts for much of the difference. As will be argued, it may also account for Europe's failure to create the jobs that its people need, in contrast with the United States' brilliant performance in this respect.

What are the main components of this "national employment contract"? Its details vary between countries, but there are broad similarities between the systems that exist throughout the continent.

- Typically, about a third of wages is "socialized", i.e. redistributed as pensions, health insurance, and other social benefits.

- Minimum wages tend to be high and effectively enforced.

- Unemployment benefits are substantially more lasting and attractive than in the United States.

- Severance pay may amount to several years of wages for older workers with substantial seniority.

- Firing workers is usually subject to quite strict legal provisions to ensure that no unfairness is involved (1).

- Almost everywhere, finally, European governments have proved willing to grant large subsidies to firms suffering from economic difficulties, to prevent them from closing down (2).

How does the contract contribute to stagflation?

It does play a role in enabling unions to win strikes, through legal provisions and customs that enable them to enforce the loyalty of workers. Labour legislation implemented by Mrs. Thatcher's government

(1) The paper by Soltwedel and Trapp in this volume contains a remarkable summary of the rigidities that result from the regulation of Germany's labour market. In Portugal, firing a worker is even unconstitutional. In France, job cuts were, following a rule established by a right wing government, subjected for about ten years to an "autorisation administrative" that, at least for large firms, was granted only after much delay, and only to firms that could convince the authorities that their situation was desperate. In Italy, redundant workers are shifted to a "Cassa d'Integrazione", which maintains their pay at the government's expense; they have to be the first to be rehired if the firm increases employment again.
(2) In my country, according to calculations by the National Bank, these amounted to 8 per cent of GNP in 1985.

in Britain has drawn attention to key issues, such as union shops, the right of union leaders to undertake industrial action without consulting their members, their ability to coerce workers into refusing to go back to work.

The authority of unions also has less obvious origins. In Britain and elsewhere, shop stewards often have enough control over the daily operations of production facilities to make life miserable for workers who do not support their initiatives, and to affect the earnings of their fellow workers. In Belgium, union dues are paid by employers in some industries, and unions are the only effective purveyors of unemployment insurance (1). The law, or custom, may provide unions with the means to increase the cost of strike to the employer, and reduce that borne by the workers. Are the former allowed to lock out workers if, by a clever design of the pattern of strikes, a firm or an industry is immobilized by closing down a few key facilities? If such a lock-out is permitted, are the workers affected entitled to unemployment benefits (2)? Is secondary picketing allowed? Is it acceptable to call on the police to help strike-breakers enter production facilities? On such matters, current ethics and the force of public opinion may be as important as the law, and there is in practice a great deal of fuzziness about which acts committed during a strike are likely to lead to prosecution. Can workers in a video cassette or a cheese factory steal the inventory and sell it in support of their strike? In order to avoid the penalties that would result from late delivery, can a firm use a helicopter and a few strong men to recover from its own factory finished pieces of equipment which strikers have impounded?

What is at issue in those examples is the (negative) short-term costs of strikes to employers and workers. It is not surprising, given the newsworthiness of strikes, that this aspect of the role of unions has at-

---

(1) This can also be obtained directly from the government, but the delays are such that it is much preferable to obtain support from one's union.
(2) In most public service strikes, it is usual for a large majority of workers to declare that they could not enter their place of work, entitling them to draw their full salary.

tracted a good deal of attention. There is reason to think, however, that although winning strikes is important, the key causes of stagflation lie deeper, and it is at this deeper level that the role of the macroeconomic employment contract is crucial.

To underline the fact that it is wrong to focus too much on the role of unions, I will show how stagflation may occur even though workers do not bargain collectively. Recent work on the efficiency wage theory of wages [Stiglitz, 1984] has emphasized that, because poor performance cannot be detected with certainty, employers are able to secure good performance from their workers only because they can threaten to fire the workers who are caught shirking (1). Since shirking is more agreeable than working hard, it is necessary to offer wages and working conditions that are substantially more attractive than those which dismissed workers could get elsewhere. The "national employment contract" obviously encourages wage creep. By making dismissal difficult and costly, it reduces the probability of being fired if shirking is detected, and thus increases the premium that must be offered to deter shirking. Unemployment and redundancy benefits improve the alternatives that are open to a dismissed worker. To obtain good performance, therefore, employers have to offer wages that look quite attractive to unemployed workers: involuntary unemployment will arise even if unions do not strive to keep wages above the equilibrium level. As the expected income of a dismissed worker depends on what he can hope to earn elsewhere, a leap-frogging process may get under way, which provides a possible explanation of stagflation (2):

Implicit contracts theory accounts for only part of the truth. It is obvious that, in addition to the individual bargaining that it describes, there is also collective bargaining. Unions remain very strong throughout Europe; in some countries (mine, for example), union participation has continued to rise throughout the recession.

---

(1) For jobs higher up in the jobs hierarchy, promotion may serve to reward a good performance, as firing sanctions a poor one.
(2) It has been argued that technological change has increased the proportion of jobs where the productivity of workers is hard to observe, and that this may be one of the explanations of stagflation.

Our next task is thus to examine how union power affects wages, and how this power is influenced by the national employment contract. Here, any analysis must take account of the fact that strikes are comparatively rare, amounting everywhere today in Europe to less than 1 per cent of working hours. In fact, their frequency has fallen sharply during the last decade. Most of them are trivial; they last a few days, perhaps a few hours only. Production shortfalls are quickly made up, and part of the lost earnings are made up by overtime. The strikes could be regarded as a kind of ritualized combat, that is very rarely pushed to the point where serious harm is inflicted on either party.

In fact, agreement is reached in the vast majority of cases by a process of consensus that involves a good deal of haggling but where the key points are not as rule in great doubt, as they reflect decision rules that are carried over tacitly from one agreement to the next, and the parties' understanding of what agreements arrived at in other firms suggest is the normal type of settlement at any point in time. Cooperative behaviour of this type, because it avoids the costs of recurrent strikes, is obviously one that both parties should try to sustain. The low frequency of strikes shows that they do succeed in this.

There are however a few cases each year where a strike really hurts and decides something, because a principle is involved. For the employer, the outcome may be bankruptcy or the need to reduce production sharply; for labour, it may be the unpredictable consequences of a damaging defeat, as a myriad of comfortable tacit agreements are wiped out by a triumphant management that is eager to make the investment in winning the strike pay off. Most important of all is the signal which is sent to agents in the rest of the economy that a principle that had been followed in collective bargaining is no longer sacrosanct.

In spite of their small number, it is those strikes that matter. It is not because it is ritualized that combat is unimportant. When David faced Goliath, only one man died, but Israel was saved.

What are these key conflicts? In recent years, they have often involved firms that are in trouble. Should their workers accept wage cuts, or should they (as has almost invariably happened on this side of the Atlantic) restrict themselves to accepting cost-cutting measures? Is it prudent for workers in firms that are going through a bout of prosperity to attempt to skim those momentary profits by wildcat strikes?

It is in these crucial marginal cases that the national labour contract may often tilt the balance in favour of labour. Reference has been made above to the tactical aspects of strikes: primary and secondary picketing, the use of violence to prevent resumption of production or to make it possible, and other equally telegenic matters. Of more fundamental importance are the less spectacular strategic factors about which we know much less. Tactical aspects are dominant during a strike, but before the strike starts, the strategic ones dominate. Workers worry about more than losing their income for an indeterminate period of time, they are also concerned about weakening a firm for whom most of them hope to work for many more years. What if the boss were not lying when he asserted that the strike and/or the concessions demanded would prove so damaging that the work force would have to be cut back sharply?

Workers know that unions have misjudged the situation often in this long recession, and firms have been damaged or destroyed. If this should happen, each one wonders whether his employer will be bailed out long enough out by subsidies to make it possible to get another job without suffering unemployment. Could it turn out that the firm will not be able to meet severance pay obligations? Will he lose part of his pension rights? How do unemployment benefits compare to his wage, how long will they last? If he is an older worker, and feels that he has little chance of finding alternative employment, can he expect that an early pension will be offered to him by the government that minimizes the cut in standard of living which closing down a plant would cause (1)?

Do workers who envisage industrial action have to fear the competition of outsiders? In Europe, there is almost no precedent for this: the Wapping

---

(1) And sometimes in fact improves it. In my country, for example, the combination of an early pension and the part-time work that is allowed can be more profitable than full-time work.

conflict between Ian Murdoch and the printers' union is the only case that I know where this has happened in a major company. This record is sustained by a prevailing ethic that deems "fire one bunch and hire another" - tactics to be reprehensible - but the ethic would quickly crumble if such tactics were to prove quite profitable. They cannot be if, as in many countries, wages are set on an industry basis, and the scales that are negotiated between employers and workers are sanctioned by legal provisions that protect them from being undercut.

Often, the protection of insiders is indirect. In the United States, deregulation has enabled new airlines, using less well paid staff, to compete with existing airlines: in Europe, such competition is not allowed. Similarly, low cost mini-mills in the steel industry (usually paying lower wages) have everywhere received far less than their share of government subsidies, and have been prevented from expanding and thus threatening jobs in large plants where pay is higher.

5. Macroeconomic Policies for the Late 1980s: The Key Issues

Macroeconomic policy-making in Western Europe is conducted under the spectre of stagflation. Inflation is not high any more in most countries, but policy-makers remember strongly the dismay they experienced as the rate of increase of prices and wages failed to respond to a rise in un-employment that seemed boundless. Academics are adventurous souls and some, most prominently the members of the CEPS Macroeconomic Policy Group (1), have had the courage to advocate a boost in demand as the way out of the recession. Support for such a policy is negligible outside the ivory tower.

If the fear of escalating inflation could be shown to be unreasonable, recovery would not be hard to bring about. Even if government shirked away from deficit spending, remembering the severe budgetary problems

(1) The composition of the Group varies. For a collection of papers during its most Keynesian incarnation, cf. Blanchard et al. [1986].

of countries which allowed the fiscal situation get out of control, monetary policies could be used to expand demand. Real rates of interest are so high that Europe is very obviously not in a monetary trap. In fact, after a prolonged period of low investment, and given the scope for labour saving which modern electronic provide, there is good reason to think that a very large investment in physical capital would be needed to restore full employment.

The trap in which Europe is caught is a social trap, from which it will not be easy to escape.

The macroeconomic employment contract which shelters citizens to an unprecedented extent from economic and other risks has been a remarkable achievement. It is extraordinary that it has spread so well the burden of very high rates of unemployment that deep poverty remains quite rare. Conquering microeconomic risk has however created a perhaps graver macroeconomic one. The provisions of the employment contract are so effective that only extremely high rates of unemployment are able to avoid accelerating inflation. Thus, measures that seemed well meant and generous have paradoxically compelled governments to adopt macroeconomic policies that condemn broad groups to the demoralization of unemployment. The young and the unskilled, with rates of unemployment ranging between 20 and more than 40 per cent, are the main victims of this situation.

It is not certain that Europe can escape from the trap. The national employment contract is highly appreciated, its effectiveness in spreading the burden of unemployment over the whole population is obvious to all. It is equally obvious that, in the depressed conditions of today, removal of this safety net would cause unacceptable misery: the patient would die before he is cured. No politician stands a chance of election who announces that he plans to eliminate significant pieces of the relevant legislation.

And yet, something must be done to bring down the NAIRU, to restore the forces that made it possible in the past to reconcile full employment and price stability. The economic cost of today's unemployment is huge.

Its long-term social implications are even worse, as it leaves tens of millions of men and women with no alternative but to settle into and organize their lives as the parasites of their compatriots.

What changes of the national employment contract seem possible?

The first and foremost change is to stop the practice of slowing the death of enterprises through subsidies, and granting older workers generous early pensions. I do not believe that Weitzman's profit-sharing economy will come into being, but Europe needs a loss-sharing one: workers in dying firms and in dying industries must accept wage cuts to save their firms, and to recreate incentives to move labour into profitable industries. Subsidies, to the extent that they are still given out, should be conditional on wage cuts.

It should also be made harder for firms to pass on higher wage costs to their clients via higher prices. The best way to do so is to make demand more elastic through less protection. Three decades after the Rome Treaty came into force, an extraordinary variety of comfortable arrangements continue to partition the European community into twelve national markets. This raises the NAIRU. By making it too easy to raise prices, these trade barriers enable employers to yield too easily to wage demands. The European Commission's plan to unify the internal market by 1992 would, if implemented, help to establish a greater degree of competition. Whether the plan will be successful is not clear at present: it is the meat of tomorrow. The Commission's current enthusiasm for supporting internal price-rigging cartels by anti-dumping and unfair trading duties is, however, the poison of today.

The legislation that embodies the national employment contract cannot and should not be torn down, but it should be reformed extensively. How this needs to be done varies substantially between countries, as risks that are well insured in one are poorly insured in the next. The conceptual background of such a reform should be a grid of the risks and options that determine the lives of workers, representing the state space that is relevant to workers. Its dimensions should be such factors as age, sex, employment status, health and other disabilities, education and other training, wage level. It would help to focus on such issues as, for example, is the wage-spread large enough to provide the incentives to acquire skills? What is the differential between wages and unemployment benefits, both for low and for better-paid workers? Are the benefits offered to young workers too high? Are unemployment benefits too close to the minimum wage? Do poverty traps exist so that some categories of workers would lose money by accepting a job? What about the bankruptcy traps that appear to exist, since combinations of redundancy benefits, early pension, and the permission to work given to pensioned workers (1) are, in some cases, so profitable that some of the workers have reason to hope that their firm dies?

Politicians are inveterate plagiarists, everywhere there has been talk of reforming taxation along the lines of the recent US tax law. What is far more urgent is the rationalization of the complex system of laws that preserve citizens from economic risks. Such a reform would be far more useful than a fiscal one, and would in addition make a significant contribution to social justice. Social and labour legislation is however extraordinarily diverse, with for example laws that date back to the nineteenth century, important rights and obligations that are entangled in a jungle of decrees and administrative circulars, and so on. The reform would not be easy to design or implement.

Should not employers be tougher? Is it not after all their job to keep the NAIRU in check by pitting outsiders against insiders? Is it an accident that in Britain, real wages continue to rise worryingly, in spite of very high unemployment, when it turned out that its entrepreneurial class was so flabby that it took a South African, an American, a Canadian, an Indian, and an Australian to bring unions to heel in the automobile, steel, coal, shipbuilding, and newspaper industries (2)? That the De Benedetti, Prodi and Agnelli, who revived Italian big business, were found readily at home may explain the country's remarkable resilience in

---

(1) Or the opportunity that they have of working illicitly.
(2) Too many third generation businessmen? Or, as our chairman might suggest, three decades of Keynesian dolce vita?

recent years (1). Could it be that what Europe needs is more of the nasty men which the French like to castigate as "patrons de choc".

One final remark: the national employment contract is to a significant extent implicit, like the one which exists at the firm level. Most of the reforms suggested in this paper can be implemented without passing any law. There is no legal obligation for governments to grant subsidies or early pensions, or for the European Commission to slap anti-dumping duties on outside competitors whose only crime is to be efficient. No laws were broken when major public sector unions in Britain were made to stop abusing the public purse, or when the "march for work" in Torino permitted the rebirth of Fiat. What is needed is the support of public opinion, an understanding that adjustment is unavoidable and that competition should be nurtured. And fortunately, public opinion has moved so sharply that all through the continent, we see socialist governments adopt as a matter of course measures that yesterday's right wing ones would not have dared to envisage. Neil Kinnock, had he been elected, would have proved more hard-headed than Ted Heath in 1974.

Thus, I shall end on a note of hope. Europe is closer than is generally thought to the time when, thanks to supply-side policies that are tough enough, confidence in price stability is restored leading voters to support once again demand expansion. When that day comes, Europe's governments will implement at last the two-handed approach that is needed to end the recession.

Bibliography

AZARIADIS, C., "Implicit Contracts and Underemployment Equilibria". Journal of Political Economy, Vol. 83, 1975, pp. 1183-1202.

BAILY, Martin J., "Wages and Employment under Uncertain Demand". The Review of Economic Studies, Vol. 41, 1974, pp. 37-50.

(1) The rate of unemployment remains statistically high. In view of the prevalence of cheating, facilitated by the size of the country's "illicit economy", this rate is not a valid indicator of labour market slack.

BLANCHARD, Olivier, Rudiger DORNBUSCH, Richard LAYARD (Eds.), Restoring Europe's Prosperity. London 1986.

BOLTHO, Andras (Ed.), The European Economy: Growth and Crisis. Oxford 1982.

DAHRENDORF, Rolf, Europe's Economy in Crisis. London 1982.

ECONOMIC FORECASTS, Vol. 4, May 1987, p. 21.

GORDON, Robert J., "Productivity, Wages, and Prices Inside and Outside of Manufacturing in the US, Japan, and Europe". European Economic Review, Vol. 31, 1987, pp. 685-732.

LAYARD, Richard, Is Incomes Policy the Answer to Unemployment? London School of Economics, London 1982, unpublished manuscript.

STIGLITZ, George, Theories of Wage Rigidity. National Bureau of Economic Research Working Papers, 1442, 1984.

WAELBROECK, Jean, "The SPELC: A Tale of Post-War Western Europe". The World Economy, Vol. 6, 1982, pp. 409-420.

WEITZMAN, M.L., The Share Economy. Cambridge, Mass., 1984.

Comment on Jean Waelbroeck, "Macroeconomic Issues for Europe in the 1980s: Can the NAIRU Be Tamed?"

William A. Niskanen

In my role as a discussant, I will follow the usual practice of expressing my own views without much reference to the paper presented. In this case, I have few reservations about this practice, because I did not have an opportunity to read the paper prior to its presentation.

For the United States, the major macroeconomic conditions of the 1980s were wholly unanticipated at the beginning of the decade. Among the more important of these unanticipated conditions were the following:

- the high level and unusual variability of real interest rates;

- the rapid increase in the real foreign exchange value of the dollar through February 1985 and its subsequent decline;

- the rapid decline in the US foreign account balance;

- the high rate of US domestic investment in the 1983-1984 period and its subsequent decline; and

- the decline in money velocity since 1981.

For this conference, the more important issue is whether we understand these conditions even now.

The conventional explanation attributes the first three conditions (interest rates, the exchange rate, and the foreign account balance) to the rapid increase in the US federal budget deficit. This explanation is plausible, broadly shared, and, I believe, wrong - or, at least, incomplete. Consider the following empirical observations:

- the variability of real interest rates has been unrelated to the relative federal deficit;

- the dollar peaked in early 1985, although the deficit continued to increase through 1986;

- the simple relation between the foreign account balance and the budget deficit has often been negative; in other words, the US often had a foreign account surplus when the budget deficit was at its highest;

- most importantly, the combination of high real interest rates and strong US domestic investment in the 1983-1984 period indicates that, at least for these years, real interest rates were high primarily because of an increased demand for investment rather than a reduced net supply of saving.

A better explanation of the first four conditions, I believe, must account for the substantial changes in the taxation of business investment in this period. The 1981 tax legislation in the US dramatically reduced the effective tax rates on new business investment. The 1982 legislation substantially increased these rates. The several tax reform proposals beginning in late 1984 would have further increased these rates. And the 1986 tax legislation now makes the effective tax rate on business investment higher than in 1980.

My interpretation of this evidence is that the growing federal deficit may have contributed to the high level of interest rates, but that the variability of real interest rates and the exchange rate were primarily due to changes in the US taxation of business investment in addition to the normal effects of cyclical conditions. In addition, the US foreign account balance is more closely related to the sum of domestic investment and the budget deficit; the substantial decline in this balance since 1982 is not due to a continued increase in the relative budget deficit but to the fact that the budget deficit did not decline as usual during the recovery years.

One lesson that we should learn from this experience is that the budget totals convey very little useful information about the effects of fiscal policy on the economy. The details are important. A wide range of economic conditions is consistent with the same budget totals, and vice versa, depending on the tax rates that are implicit in the spending programs and the tax code.

On the final condition: in retrospect, I believe, there should have been no "velocity puzzle". The econometricians substantially misled us, by focusing primarily on the sample of postwar data, to believe that most of the increase in velocity through 1981 was some unexplained trend and that the interest elasticity of the demand for money was very low. The decline in velocity since 1981, I believe, is fully explained by the decline in market interest rates, the increase in deposit rates authorized by deregulation, and the substantial increase in unrealized financial wealth not included in national income. The decline in velocity also has another important implication - suggesting that the increase in the deficit had no effect on total demand; if the Keynesians are right, the growth of money velocity should have increased relative to the prior trend rather than declining from the prior average 3 percent annual growth to the average 2 percent annual decline since 1981.

The major lessons of this period for economists are the following:

- the effects of fiscal policy on the economy depend primarily on the details of the budget and the tax code;

- the effects of fiscal and monetary policies in an open economy are often very different from those in a closed economy; and

- a little more humility would also be appropriate.

II

Bennett T. McCallum*

The Case for Rules in the Conduct of Monetary Policy: A Concrete Example

1. Introduction

The purpose of this paper is to provide a nontechnical but reasonably up-to-date description of the case for rules, as opposed to discretion, in the conduct of monetary and fiscal policy. Special attention will be paid to the current state of macroeconomic theory and to the experiences of developed economies in the postwar (i.e., post-World War II) era. A specific rule for monetary policy is proposed and some evidence regarding its potential effectiveness is reported.

2. Basic Considerations

The first thing that needs to be emphasized is that the issue of rules versus discretion is not the same as the issue of activist versus non-activist policy. That a policy rule can be activist - i.e., can be one that adjusts the value of a policy instrument in response to prevailing economic conditions - is a sufficiently elementary point that it has been clearly expressed in the widely used undergraduate macroeconomics text-book of Dornbusch and Fischer [1984] for almost a decade (1). Yet it

---

* The author is indebted to A. Meltzer for helpful suggestions.
(1) The example provided by Dornbusch and Fischer [1984, pp. 342-343] is a policy rule that sets the money-stock growth rate equal to

needs to be emphasized, as leading economists (1) and policymakers - see, e.g., Volcker [1983] - continue to argue in a fashion that muddles together the two distinct issues, and sometimes even proceeds as if rules could be discredited in general by listing disadvantages of a particular type of rule that calls for a constant growth rate of the monetary stock.

What then *is* the nature of the rules versus discretion distinction? It is I think widely agreed among macroeconomic researchers that the crucial distinction is the one illustrated in the seminal paper of Kydland and Prescott [1977](2) and elaborated upon by Barro and Gordon [1983a]. But precisely how to characterize this distinction is not so clear. Many economists use the term "precommitment" to describe policymaking by rules (3), and often continue by discussing the difficulty or impossibility of achieving precommitment. Now, the context of monetary and fiscal policy, it would appear that literal and full precommitment is in fact virtually impossible. But it is not impossible for a monetary authority to select policy actions that conform to the "rule" sequence in the Kydland-Prescott example, so it must be concluded that precommitment cannot be the crucial characteristic. Instead, policymaking according to a rule exists when the policymaker chooses not to attempt optimizing choices on a period-by-period (or case-by-case) basis, but chooses rather to *implement* in each period (or case) a formula for setting his instrument that has been designed to apply to periods (cases) in general, not only the one currently at hand. Thus the policymaker's efforts toward optimization enter in the *design of the formula* utilized, not in the actions selected in each period (4).

4.0 + 2(u - 5.0), where u is a recent unemployment rate. Both u and the (annualized) money-stock growth rate are here measured in percentage points.

(1) Tobin [1983] recognizes the analytical validity of the distinction, but refuses to accept it as a practical matter.

(2) Which constitutes an application to macroeconomic policy of a point developed previously by Kydland [1975].

(3) Examples are Barro and Gordon [1983b] and Grossman and van Huyck [1986].

(4) This characterization is consistent with Friedman's [1962, pp. 239-241] analogy to the constitutional protection of free speech.

To provide an example of this distinction, and also to begin our discussion of the *advantage* of rule over discretion in the context of monetary policy, let us briefly review the basic model laid out by Kydland and Prescott [1977]. In this setup, the monetary authority's objectives are represented by a loss function in which the arguments are the squared deviations of unemployment and inflation from values determined by considerations of allocational efficiency (1). It will simplify matters without distortion of the argument, however, simply to take the loss function to be decreasing in the current money-growth *surprise* (since unanticipated money growth reduces unemployment) and increasing in the square of money growth itself (since money growth induces inflation)(2). There are also discounted values of similar terms for all future periods, but for present purposes these can be ignored. If, with this objective function, the monetary authority were to adopt a policy *rule* by choosing among constant money growth rates, it would recognize that with moderately rational agents the surprise values will average zero whatever his choice; thus the chosen money growth rate would be zero. For the same reason, moreover, an *average* growth rate of zero would be implied by

---

(1) Our conclusions will depend upon the plausible assumption that deviations of inflation from the optimal rate are increasingly costly at the margin; use of the squared deviation reflects that requirement in a tractable manner. The unemployment term is of the form $(u_t - k\bar{u}_t)^2$ with $\bar{u}_t$ the natural-rate value of u_t and with $k < 1$. The latter condition expresses the assumption that the monetary authority's target value for u_t is below the natural rate. Barro and Gordon [1983a] interpret this as reflecting some externality and consequently claim that there is no discrepancy between the policymaker's objectives and private agents' preferences. The analysis would remain the same, however, if the $k < 1$ condition were interpreted as merely reflecting a desire by the policymaker for an excessively low rate of unemployment. Indeed, all that is necessary is that the policymaker values marginal reductions of unemployment in the vicinity of its natural-rate value.

(2) In the cited literature, "money growth" and "inflation" are often used interchangeably. In my opinion, it is preferable to think in terms of money growth as unemployment is in fact more closely related to money than price level surprises. In addition, inflation actually responds to money growth only slowly, so current money growth affects expectations of future inflation. Recognition of this point overturns the argument of Grossman and van Huyck [1986] to the effect that the Kydland-Prescott setup is misspecified.

the optimal choice of a (possibly activist) rule when a broader class of rules is considered.

But suppose that, instead, the authority executes policy in a period-by-period or discretionary manner, i.e, by selecting each period's money growth rate on the basis of a fresh optimization calculation. Then in each period the prevailing *expected* money growth rate is taken by the authority as a given piece of data - a new "initial condition". The current surprise then appears to the authority to be under its control, so the loss-minimizing choice of the current money growth rate is that value which just equates the marginal benefit of surprise money growth to the marginal cost of money growth *per se*. With the objective function as described, this seemingly optimal value will clearly be positive. But since moderately rational private agents will come to understand this process, their expectations regarding money growth will be correct on average. Thus, the surprise magnitude will be zero on average, over any large number of periods, even though the magnitude within each period is under the control of the monetary authority. Consequently, there will on average be on benefit - no extra employment - materializing from surprises. On average, then, the discretionary regime will feature more money growth (i.e., inflation) but the same amount of surprise money growth (i.e., unemployment) as with a well-designed rule base on the same objectives. Thus the objectives will be more fully achieved with the adoption of a rule than with period-by-period attempts at optimization.

It should be noted that the foregoing line of argument does not require that the economy actually be one in which monetary surprises induce temporary output and employment gains. Nor is it necessary that private sector expectations are fully rational. What is required is that the monetary authority *believes* that unusually rapid monetary growth will induce output/employment gains and that expectations are rational enough to avoid any permanent bias. Also, the economy must be one that satisfies the weak version of the natural rate hypothesis (1): output and employ-

_____

(1) For additional discussion of related issues, including reputational models, see McCallum [1987]. Alternative surveys are provided by Barro [1986] and Cukierman [1986].

ment must be independent over long spans of time of the economy's average inflation rate.

To this point it has been argued that the conscientious attempt to avoid both inflation and unemployment will lead to an excessive amount of the former, with no reduction in the latter, when monetary policy is conducted in a discretionary manner. Is there any empirical evidence to suggest that this theoretical proposition is in fact descriptive of the workings of actual central banks and actual economies?

To my mind, the most impressive evidence in this regard comes from a straightforward examination of the postwar inflationary experience of the industrialized nations of Europe and North America. Specifically, price levels now are in all these national several times as high as they were in 1950. Even in Germany the value of the currency is now less than a third of its 1950 level, while the comparable magnitude is less than one tenth for France, Italy, and the United Kingdom. (A few figures are reported in Table 1.) While there have been no episodes of extremely rapid inflation, price levels have risen steadily and substantially. The relevant question is, therefore: Why has the experience been one of *positive* inflation in most years in all of these countries? The populations, governments, and central banks of these nations do not *enjoy* inflation - indeed, they regard it as something positively undesirable on its own. Also, there is little reason to believe that the policymakers in these

Table 1 - Consumer Price Indices, Post-World War II

	CPI level in		Ratio
	1950	1985	
Belgium	30.1	140.5	0.214
France	15.6	157.9	0.099
Germany	39.2	121.0	0.324
Italy	13.9	190.3	0.073
Netherlands	23.9	122.7	0.195
United Kingdom	13.4	141.5	0.095
United States	29.2	130.5	0.224

Source: IMF [various issues].

Table 2 - Wholesale Price Indices, Pre-World War I

Year	Belgium	Britain	France	Germany	United States
1776	.	101	.	.	84
1793	.	120	.	98	100
1800	.	186	155	135	127
1825	.	139	126	76	101
1850	83	91	96	71	82
1875	100	121	111	100	80
1900	87	86	85	90	80
1913	100	100	100	100	100

Source: Mitchell [1978]; US Bureau of the Census [1975].

nations are of the opinion that there is any *permanent* stimulative effect on employment or output of positive inflation rates. They know that employment and output growth were not enhanced by the inflation and rapid money growth of the 1970s. So why have price levels not moved downward about as often as upward, leaving current prices about the same as in 1950?

My suggestion, of course, is that the Barro-Gordon theory (1) provides an answer to these questions, namely, that discretionary policymaking has been exercised in the postwar era by central bankers who wish to avoid inflation but who also have employment or output concerns. The plausibility of this suggestion is enhanced, I believe, by a comparison of the postwar experience with that of an earlier era in which monetary policy was circumscribed by formal rules. Here the reference is, of course, to the period before World War I, when the countries under discussion maintained commodity-money standards. As all readers probably know, price levels at the start of World War I were roughly the same as they had been in the mid-1800s - or the late 1700s, before the start of the Napoleonic Wars. (A few relevant figures are reproduced in Table 2.)

---

(1) While the model outlined above was developed by Kydland and Prescott [1977], its use as a *positive* theory of policy behavior was pioneered by Barro and Gordon [1983a].

3. A Specific Rule for Monetary Policy

Instead of continuing the discussion of rules versus discretion in the abstract, let us now turn to the consideration of a specific rule for the conduct of monetary policy. Examination of a concrete proposal should help to reveal weaknesses in the rule-based approach, if they exist, or to attract support for the rule, if its desirable properties are convincingly impressive.

In previous works, I have emphasized four principles that should be respected in the design of a monetary rule [McCallum, 1984; 1985], which are as follows. Firstly, the rule should dictate the behavior of a variable that the monetary authority can control directly and/or accurately. To specify behavior of some magnitude that is not itself controllable - such as the M1 measure of the money stock, for instance - would be to leave the task of rule design seriously incomplete. Secondly, the rule should not rely in any essential way upon the presumed absence of regulatory change and technical progress in the financial industry. While these processes may not produce as much turmoil in the future as they have in the recent past, it would be unsafe to presume that they will not be present again to a significant extent. Thirdly, neither money stock or (nominal) interest rate paths are important for their own sake. They are relevant only to the extent that they are useful in facilitating good performance in terms of inflation and output or employment magnitudes. Fourthly, a well-designed rule should recognize the limits of macroeconomic knowledge. In particular, it should recognize that neither theory nor evidence points convincingly to any of the numerous competing models of the interaction of nominal and real variables. The economics profession does not have a reliable quantitative or even qualitative model of aggregate supply (or "Phillips Curve") behavior. In other words, the profession does not have accurate knowledge of the way in which changes in nominal GNP will be divided, on a quarter-to-quarter basis, between real output growth and inflation (on this topic again, cf. McCallum [1987]). Thus any rule whose design depends upon some particular model of that devision warrants very little confidence.

In one of these earlier papers [McCallum, 1984], I proposed in quali- tative terms a rule that respects all four of these principles. My proposal began with the specification of a target path for nominal GNP that grows evenly at a prespecified rate that equals the economy's pre- vailing long-term average rate of real output growth. For the US, the appropriate figure is about 3 percent per year. Since this magnitude will be virtually independent of monetary policy over any extended period (say, 20 years or more), keeping nominal GNP growth at the appropriate value - henceforth assumed to be 3 percent per year (1) - should yield approximately zero inflation over any such period. Furthermore, the pre- vention of fluctuations in nominal GNP growth should help to prevent swings of real output from its trend path (2). While some output fluc- tuations would continue to occur even with a perfectly smooth growth path for nominal demand, they would probably be as small as can feasibly be obtained, given the absence of a reliable Phillips curve model.

To complete the rule, an operational mechanism must be specified for keeping (nominal) GNP growth close to the prespecified 3 percent growth path (3). My 1984 suggestion was to adopt as an instrument the mon-

---

(1) Specification of the trend value of real output growth is, of course, part of the rule's specification. It should be based on the economy's actual real growth record over the past several decades and should be changed very infrequently - say, one every ten years. Any error in setting this rate will obviously lead to an error of equal per- centage magnitude (but of opposite sign) in the inflation rate in- duced by the rule. Fortunately, the conceivable magnitude of such errors is quite small - probably less than 1 percent per year - for developed economies.

(2) The workings of the rule are independent of the currently-prominent issue concerning the nature of output trends. Thus the target path for nominal GNP should be set to grow at the value γ whether real output growth occurs according to $y_t = \alpha + \gamma t + \varepsilon_t$ or to $y_t - y_{t-1} = \gamma + \varepsilon_t$. (Here ε_t denotes white noise.)

(3) By virtue of its emphasis on this operational mechanism, the current proposal is quite different from other schemes involving "nominal GNP targeting" such as those of Gordon [1985], Hall [1983], and Taylor [1985]. This difference is clearly exemplified by Gordon's [1985, p. 77] reference to "controlling growth in nominal GNP ... *rather than* controlling the monetary base"(my italics). Much of Gordon's discussion, incidentally, is concerned with a difficulty not elsewhere discussed in the present paper, namely, that of *starting up* a rule like [2] from initial conditions with nominal GNP growth

etary base, a variable that can be accurately set on a day-by-day basis by the central bank of any political entity with a floating exchange rate. Specifically, the rule "would adjust the base growth rate each month or quarter, increasing the rate if nominal GNP is below its target path, and vice versa" [McCallum, 1984, p. 390].

The algebraic form implicit in this description is as follows, where b_t = log of monetary base (for period t), x_t = log of nominal GNP, and x_t^* = target-path value for x_t:

$$[1] \quad \Delta b_t = \Delta b_{t-1} + \lambda_1 (x_{t-1}^* - x_{t-1}), \, \lambda_1 > 0$$

In this formula, the magnitude of λ_1 would have to be chosen so as to (i) provide adequate responsiveness of base growth to departures of x_t from its target path but (ii) without inducing dynamic instability of the type that can prevail when feedback effects are too strong. Presuming this value is satisfactorily chosen, one attractive feature of the scheme summarized in [1] is that it would automatically adjust the b_t growth rate, in a fashion that would yield zero inflation on average, in response to alternations in base "velocity" stemming from technical or regulatory changes. Even in the face of drastic changes of this type it would remain true that an increase in Δb_t would be expansionary, and a decrease contractionary, in terms of aggregate demand - and more knowledge than that is not required for the appropriate type of adjustment.

I have recently become persuaded (1), however, that a somewhat different specification would have better properties. Instead of [1], then, I would like to propose the following rule for quarterly adjustments:

---

substantially different from 3 percent. In this regard, my own in-clination would be to begin with a path that adjusted gradually toward the 3 percent figure, attaining the latter after (say) three years. Another objective of Gordon's is to argue the desirability of *final sales* over GNP as a nominal demand variable; I have no desire to quarrel with that argument.

(1) In part by discussions with Allan Meltzer.

$$[2] \quad \Delta b_t = 0.00739 - (1/16)[x_{t-1} - x_{t-17} - b_{t-1} + b_{t-17}]$$
$$+ \lambda_2(x^*_{t-1} - x_{t-1}), \; \lambda_2 > 0$$

Here the constant term 0.00739 is simply a 3 percent annual growth rate expressed in quarterly logarithmic units, while the second term subtracts from this the growth rate of base velocity, calculated as an average over the previous four years (1). Finally, the third term adds an adjustment in response to departures of GNP from its target path. Again the only parameter value to be determined is that for the response coefficient, in this case denoted λ_2. Again it is possible to induce dynamic instability by setting the value of λ_2 too high. But as the response is now applicable to Δb_t rather than its change, $\Delta b_t - \Delta b_{t-1}$, the danger of instability is lessened. My proposed value for λ_2 is 0.25, which implies an extra 1 percent base growth per *year* for each 1 percent deviation of nominal GNP from its target path.

4. Properties of the Proposed Rule

To determine how this rule would work, one needs to experiment with it. Since experiments with actual economies can be very expensive to the societies involved, such experimentation needs to be done with a model. The problem, of course, is that there is no agreement as to the appropriate model. My conjecture, however, is that rule [2] with $\lambda_2 = 0.25$ will perform well for a wide variety of quantitative models of developed market economies such as the US, the UK, Germany, Italy, France, or the Netherlands. Let me immediately be clear, however, about what is here meant by the term "perform well". Specifically, the criterion involves only the time path of nominal GNP; as we do not know how changes in GNP will be divided among inflation and output growth, the rule should not be judged on the basis of any particular model's predictions in that regard. Subject to that stipulation, it is my

---

(1) Note that $x_{t-1} - x_{t-17} - b_{t-1} + b_{t-17} = \sum_{j=1}^{16} (\Delta x_{t-j} - \Delta b_{t-j})$.

conjecture that application of the rule [2] in place of actual historical policy would yield simulated nominal GNP paths that are smoother than those actually experienced (1), as well as implying growth at noninflationary rates. This type of result will be obtained, I believe, whether the models utilized are constructed along Keynesian or classical lines provided that they are not strongly inconsistent with the natural-rate hypothesis.

Such simulations with a wide variety of models have yet to be conducted. But I can report results based on two extremely simple models that are merely atheoretic regressions of nominal GNP on past values of itself and values of the monetary base (2). The first such model, pertaining to the US economy for 1954.I-1985.IV, consists of the following estimated regression equation:

[3] $\Delta x_t = 0.00749 + 0.257 \, \Delta x_{t-1} + 0.487 \, \Delta b_t + e_t$
$\qquad\;\; (0.0021) \quad (0.079) \qquad\quad (0.121)$

$\qquad R^2 = 0.23 \quad \hat{\sigma} = 0.010 \quad D.W. = 2.11$

Here, e_t denotes the residual, i.e., the estimated disturbance, for period t. Simulated values for b_t and x_t have been calculated for 128 periods by means of [2] and [3], with initial conditions corresponding to 1954.I and with e_t residual values fed in each period as shock estimates. This procedure is analogous to one stochastic simulation of [2] and [3] with shocks drawn from a population with mean 0 and standard deviation 0.010.

Results of this simulation exercise are shown in the figure, where TAR denotes the target path x_t^*. Clearly the rule induces x_t to follow the target path quite closely. To put this behavior into perspective, the

---

(1) Here, I am assuming simulations that feed in random errors of the same magnitude as seem to occur in actuality; cf. the discussion below.
(2) Since drafting this paper, I have also obtained results for a model that consists of a 4-variable vector autoregression (VAR) system, the variables being four lags each of the 90-day treasury bill rate and the logs of real GNP, the GNP deflator, and the monetary base. The RMSE value with $\lambda_2 = 0.25$ in rule [2] is 0.0219, almost the same as for model [4].

Table 3 - Simulation Results for Alternative Rules

Policy	RMSE	
	Model [3]	Model [4]
1. Eq. [2], $\lambda_2 = 0.25$	0.0197	0.0217
2. Actual historical	0.7711 (0.0616) (a)	0.7711 (0.0616) (a)
3. $\Delta b_t = 0$	0.2258	0.2302
4. $\Delta b_t = -0.0041$	0.0358	0.0391
5. Eq. [2], $\lambda_2 = 0$	0.0499	0.0502
6. Eq. [1], $\lambda_1 = 0.02$	0.0424	0.0671

(a) This is RMSE relative to fitted trend rather than target path.

result of this simulation is compared with simulations using alternative policy rules in Table 3. There the first numerical column reports root-mean-squared-error (RMSE) values - i.e., square roots of the mean over 128 simulated quarters of the squared deviations of x_t from x_t^*. The RMSE value of 0.0197 in line 1 indicates that the root-mean-squared deviation of nominal GNP from its target path is roughly 2.0 percent under rule [2], since log deviations are approximately equal to percentage deviations divided by 100. That figure can be compared with a RMSE value of about 22 percent when the policy rule is one that sets the monetary base growth rate at zero throughout the period (line 3). This surprisingly high magnitude obtains because base velocity has grown enough during the 1954-1985 period that no growth in the base would have permitted a significant amount of inflation (1)! The base growth rate needed to yield zero inflation - literally to yield 3 percent nominal GNP growth - with model [3] is $\Delta b_t = -0.0041$ (i.e., about - 1.6 percent per year). With that rate held constant for 128 periods, the RMSE is about 3.6 percent (see line 4), which is only about twice as large as

---

(1) That this is the case can be seen from the model reported in [3]. Setting both Δb_t and e_t at zero for all t yields $\Delta x_t = 0.00749 + 0.257$ Δx_{t-1}, which has a steady-state value of $0.00749/(1-0.257) = 0.0100$. Thus with zero base growth, nominal GNP would grow at about 1 percent per quarter or 4 percent per year. With 3 percent per year real GNP growth, we would then have about 1 percent per year inflation.

38

Simulation Results for 1954-1985 with Policy Rule [2] and Model [3]

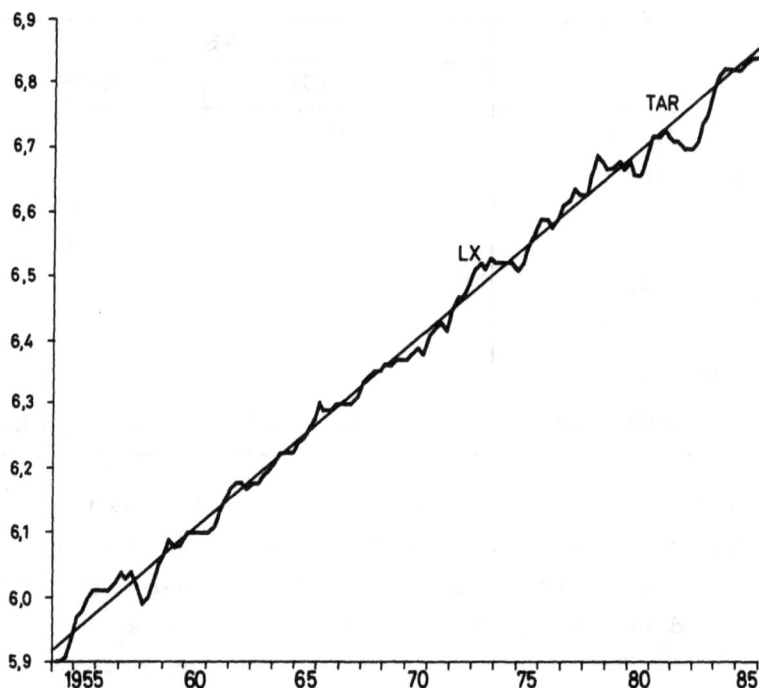

Note: The target path TAR increases by 0.00739 each quarter, starting from the actual value of 5.909 for 1953.IV. Here 5.909 = log 368.3, while 368.3 is nominal GNP measured in billions of dollars (annual rate, seasonally adjusted).

with policy rule [2]. But it is important to recognize that the correct constant value of Δb_t embodied in the "rule" of line 4 could not have been known ex ante, before the experience of 1954-1985 had been accumulated, for it is calculated on the basis of model [3](1). By contrast, our preferred rule [2] is not based on any parameter estimated in the model.

In response to the last claim, it could be said that - while not precisely based on model [3] - the parameter value $\lambda_2 = 0.25$ in rule [2] is to some extent based on ex post knowledge. Consequently, it is of interest to know how rule [2] would perform with different values used for λ_2 - in particular, with $\lambda_2 = 0$. Results for that case, which corresponds in spirit but not in detail to the rule proposed by Meltzer [1984; 1986], are

---

(1) Specifically, by solving $\Delta x = 0.00749 + 0.257 \, \Delta x + 0.487 \, \Delta b$ for Δb with Δx set equal to 0.00739.

reported in line 5. There we see that performance is less good than in line 1, but still rather impressive. Shifting λ_2 in the other direction, to a value of 0.5, yields results (not tabulated) that are even better than in line 1. Also reported in Table 3 is one result pertaining to the policy rule [1], which I had previously proposed. Specifically, line 6 shows that with $\lambda_1 = 0.02$ the RMSE would be about 4.2 percent, which is not too bad. But using instead $\lambda_1 = 0.05$ would result in explosive fluctuations.

Finally, the foregoing RMSE figures can be compared to those that actually were obtained during 1954-1985, i.e., with actual Federal Reserve policy. Because of the substantial amount of inflation that occurred, the RMSE value is enormous in comparison - the value is 0.7711, over 30 times as great as in line 1. Perhaps more interesting, however, is the extent of actual nominal GNP *variability* about its (inflationary) trend path. Consequently, the RMSE value for x_t relative to a fitted linear trend is also reported in line 2. That value is 6.2 percent per period, somewhat higher than in lines 5 and 6, and just over three times as great as in line 1. Thus, the first-column indications of Table 3 are that our proposed rule would not only prevent inflation but also yield less variability in nominal GNP growth than actual Fed policy.

The foregoing estimates are all predicated, however, on the "model" of GNP behavior given in [3]. The extreme simplicity of this specification arguably tends neither to favor nor harm the simulated performance of our rule [2]. But there is one aspect of specification [3] that is questionable and that works in our favor - namely, the inclusion of the current-period value of Δb_t as an explanatory variable. To some extent the estimated effects, a critic might claim, could be due to the sample-period response of Δb_t to Δx_t, rather than the causal direction presumed in [3]. Consequently, results are reported in column two of Table 3 for simulations like those of column one except that the "model" is as follows:

[4] $\Delta x_t = \underset{(0.0020)}{0.00506} + \underset{(0.083)}{0.199} \Delta x_{t-1} + \underset{(0.127)}{0.529} \Delta b_{t-1} + e_t$

$R^2 = 0.23 \quad \hat{\sigma} = 0.010 \quad DW = 2.05$

Here, *none* of the current-period connection between Δb_t and Δx_t is attributed to the direction going from policy to GNP. This specification should be expected to sharply deteriorate the rule's performance, as it introduces a full two-quarter lag between target departures $x^*_{t-1} - x_{t-1}$ and corrective effects.

Indeed, as an inspection of Table 3 will readily indicate, the performance of rules [2] and [1] both deteriorate. The former remains superior, nevertheless, to any of the other possibilities considered, and continues to yield substantially less GNP variability than observed in actual US experience. Since there is probably some within-quarter response of Δx_t to Δb_t in actuality, this brief investigation suggests results intermediate to those of columns one and two. For rule [2], they are clearly excellent.

5. Criticisms

At this point, it will be useful to consider some possible objections that might be raised by critics. Three that will be discussed in turn pertain to (i) the Lucas critique, (ii) the natural-rate hypothesis, and (iii) our neglect of open-economy considerations.

With respect to (i) the point is, of course, that the parameters of our models [3] and [4] might change with an alteration in policy from that actually experienced to that of the hypothesized rules. Since these "models" are not structural, this objection is in principle correct. I would suggest, however, that the Lucas critique is much more important quantitatively for equations relating real to nominal variables - e.g., Phillips curves - than for ones relating nominal demand to nominal policy variables. If this conjecture is correct, then [3] and [4] should be virtually immune to the critique, as it has been found to be rather hard to detect empirically even in Phillips-curve relations [cf., e.g., Gordon and King, 1982].

Next, there is the issue of the natural-rate hypothesis, which has recently come under attack as a result of extremely high and persistent European unemployment rates (cf., e.g., Fitoussi and Phelps [1986]; Blanchard and Summers [1986]). But in the context of the present discussion, the issue is not whether unemployment promptly reverts following a shock to some "natural" level, but whether the trend growth rate of real output is essentially independent of monetary policy. If the recent experience is thought to provide evidence against this relevant proposition, it is unclear how the posited relationship would go. Proponents of the notion that nominal demand behavior affects the trend output rate usually hypothesize a positive relationship, i.e., that real output growth is stimulated by more rapid growth of nominal demand. But in fact nominal GNP growth has been *more* rapid in Europe during the 1970s and 1980s than is was during the 1950s and 1960s (1), yet it is the more recent period that has featured high unemployment and reduced real growth.

Finally, let us briefly address the issue of how our proposed rule should be modified to take account of open-economy considerations, i.e., large import and export sectors. With regard to this, the relevant principle to keep in mind is that the most constructive thing that monetary policy can accomplish is to induce nominal aggregate demand to grow smoothly and at a noninflationary rate. Thus, the only modification required to our rule is the possible replacement of nominal GNP with some other measure of nominal aggregate demand. My first inclination would be to use real GNP multiplied by the consumer price index. But the main point is that steady growth in some such aggregate constitutes a more reasonable objective for the monetary authority than either maintaining a fixed exchange rate or following a target path for any measure of the money stock. These are variables that are neither instruments nor ultimate targets. While the same is true of nominal aggregate demand, it is a magnitude that is more closely related to output and inflation variables - which are ultimate targets.

---

(1) For Europe as a whole, nominal GDP grew at an average rate of 14.8 percent over the 1955-1969 period and 24.6 percent over that of 1969-1983 [IMF, various issues].

6. Conclusion

Let us now conclude with a brief summary of the foregoing argument. The paper begins by reiterating that a policy rule can be activist; the distinction between rules and discretion depends upon the stage at which optimization calculations enter the policy process - in the design of a formula (rule) to be implemented each period or in each period's (discretionary) selection of a policy action. Next, the Kydland-Prescott [1977] example is used to illustrate the tendency for discretionary monetary policy to produce more inflation than would result from a rule with no additional employment obtained in compensation. Then a specific monetary rule is proposed, one that sets the monetary base - a controllable instrument - each period in a manner designed to keep nominal aggregate demand growing smoothly at a noninflationary rate. Some simple simulations are conducted which suggest that this rule would have worked well in the US, over the 1954-1985 period, if it had been in effect. The basic idea is that, since economists do not understand how nominal demand changes are divided between inflation and output growth, the most useful thing that monetary policy can accomplish is to keep nominal demand growing smoothly at a noninflationary rate. This can apparently be achieved well by means of a rule such as the one proposed.

Bibliography

BARRO, Robert J., "Recent Developments in the Theory of Rules versus Discretion". The Economic Journal, Vol. 95, 1985, Supplement, pp. 23-37.

--, David B. GORDON [1983a], "A Positive Theory of Monetary Policy in a Natural Rate Model". Journal of Political Economy, Vol. 91, 1983, pp. 589-610.

--, -- [1983b], "Rules, Discretion, and Reputation in a Model of Monetary Policy". Journal of Monetary Economics, Vol. 12, 1983, pp. 101-121.

BLANCHARD, Olivier J., Lawrence H. SUMMERS, "Hysteresis and the European Unemployment Problem". In: Stanley FISCHER (Ed.), NBER Macroeconomics Annual 1986. Cambridge, Mass., 1986, pp. 15-78.

CUKIERMAN, Alex, "Central Bank Behavior and Credibility: Some Recent Theoretical Developments". Federal Reserve Bank of St. Louis Review, Vol. 68, 1986, pp. 5-17.

DORNBUSCH, Rudiger, Stanley FISCHER, Macroeconomics. New York 1984, 3rd. Edition.

FITOUSSI, Jean Paul, Edmund S. PHELPS, "Causes of the 1980s Slump in Europe". Brookings Papers on Economic Activity, 1986, pp. 487-513.

FRIEDMAN, Milton, "Should There Be an Independent Monetary Authority?" In: Leland B. YEAGER (Ed.), In Search of a Monetary Constitution. Cambridge, Mass., 1962, pp. 219-243.

GORDON, Robert, "The Conduct of Domestic Monetary Policy". In: Albert ANDO, Hidekazu EGUCHI, Richard FARMER, Yukata SUZUKI (Eds.), Monetary Policy in Our Times. Cambridge, Mass., 1985.

--, Stephen R. KING, "The Output Cost of Disinflation in Traditional and Vector Autoregression Models". Brookings Papers on Economic Activity, 1982, pp. 205-272.

GROSSMAN, Herschel I., John B. van HUYCK, "Seigniorage, Inflation, and Reputation". Journal of Monetary Economics, Vol. 18, 1986, pp. 21-31.

HALL, Robert E., "Macroeconomic Policy under Structural Change". In: Industrial Change and Public Policy. A Symposium sponsored by the Federal Reserve Bank of Kansas City, 1983.

KYDLAND, Finn E., "Noncooperative and Dominant Player Solutions in Discrete Dynamic Games". The International Economic Review, Vol. 16, 1975, pp. 321-335.

--, Edward C. PRESCOTT, "Rules Rather than Discretion: The Inconsistency of Optimal Plans". Journal of Political Economy, Vol. 85, 1977, pp. 473-491.

INTERNATIONAL MONETARY FUND (IMF), International Financial Statistics. Washington, D.C., various issues.

McCALLUM, Bennett T., "Monetarist Rules in the Light of Recent Experience". The American Economic Review, Vol. 74, 1984, pp. 388-391.

--, "On the Consequences and Criticisms of Monetary Targeting". Journal of Money, Credit and Banking, Vol. 17, 1985, pp. 570-597.

McCALLUM, Bennett T., "Inflation: Theory and Evidence". In: Benjamin M. FRIEDMAN, Frank HAHN (Eds.), Handbook of Monetary Economics. Amsterdam 1987.

MELTZER, Allan H., "Overview". In: THE FEDERAL RESERVE BANK OF KANSAS CITY, Price Stability and Public Policy. Kansas City, 1984, pp. 209-222.

--, "Limits of Short-Run Stabilization Policy". Economic Inquiry, Vol. 25, 1987, pp. 1-14.

MITCHELL, Brian R., European Historical Statistics 1750-1970. New York 1978.

TAYLOR, John B., "What Would Nominal GNP Targeting Do to the Business Cycle?" In: Karl BRUNNER, Allan H. MELTZER (Eds.), Understanding Monetary Regimes. Amsterdam 1985, pp. 61-84.

TOBIN, James, "Monetary Policy: Rules, Targets, and Shocks". Journal of Money, Credit and Banking, Vol. 15, 1983, pp. 506-518.

UNITED STATES OF AMERICA, BUREAU OF THE CENSUS, Historical Statistics of the United States. Washington, D.C., 1975.

VOLCKER, Paul A., "Statement Before the House Committee on Banking, Finance, and Urban Affairs". Federal Reserve Bulletin, Vol. 69, 1983, pp. 617-621.

Alan S. Blinder

The Rules-versus-Discretion Debate in the Light of Recent Experience

1. Introduction

The rules-versus-discretion debate has been raging for more than fifty years now - with no end in sight. Positions and arguments, however, have changed over the years, under the joint influence of evolving economic doctrines and changing real-world events. I argue in this short paper that, for both these reasons, the pendulum is now - or rather should now be - swinging back toward discretion.

2. Defining the Issue

Before proceeding, it is important to clarify the questions that are being asked. To do so, I begin with a homely example far removed from economics, but which makes the nature of the rules-versus-discretion controversy transparent while leaving its resolution appropriately murky.

The question is: should you tinker with the thermostat in your home? We all know the right answer. If you want to maintain a fixed household temperature and the thermostat is working well, there is probably no reason for human intervention. In fact, by fiddling with the settings, you are liable to do more harm than good. But if the thermostat is malfunctioning, you can probably improve matters by using your own best judgment to adjust the controls. However, if your choice is between a malfunctioning thermostat and turning control over to you four-year-old, you may think twice before opting for human discretion. It depends on how badly the thermostat is working - and on how reliable your child is! Finally, if your preferred temperature changes from time to time, a thermostat with a fixed setting will not serve your well.

Each of these obvious points has a counterpart in the context of stabilization policy. If the macroeconomic servo-mechanism works expeditiously to cure recessions and end inflations, then the case for government intervention is weak. This, of course, was the classical view of the economy; and in recent years it has enjoyed a revival in my country. In Europe, where it takes quite an imagination to see the macroeconomic thermostat at work, the argument against discretionary policy now takes a different form: that stoking the boiler no longer produces heat.

On the other hand, if the economy's self-correcting mechanism is ineffective or nonexistent, then well-conceived government policies offer the prospect of genuine improvement. That, of course, is the Keynesian position; and I will have more to say about it later.

The difficult questions come when we must choose between a poorly-functioning economic servo-mechanism and a government which may be neither competent nor entirely trustworthy. Thus the questions are clear. It is only the answers that elude us. If we want to know whether discretionary policy is likely to outperform fixed rules, we need to know:

(i)   How effective is the macroeconomic servo-mechanism? Or, looked at another way, how much good could be done by an omniscient and benevolent government? As I will note shortly, opinions on this question have changed dramatically over the years - and should be changing once again.

(ii) How good a job can we expect from real governments, which are certainly not omniscient and may not be totally benevolent? This question, of course, is timeless and transcends economics. In the specific context of stabilization policy, the answer hinges both on the state of economic knowledge and on possible conflicts between what is economically right and what is politically expedient.

Table 1 illustrates the possibilities. Those who are optimistic about the economy's ability to right itself and pessimistic about the likelihood of beneficial state intervention (upper right-hand box) will probably ad-

Table 1

Government Economy	Competent honest	Incompetent dishonest
Highly self-regulating	?	rules
Not self-regulating	discretion	?

vocate rules. Certainly, if the macroeconomic servo-mechanism works promptly and the government is controlled by charlatans or fools, any reasonable person will favor rules over discretion. The new twist in this argument, suggested first by Kydland and Prescott [1977] and developed by Barro and Gordon [1983], is the idea that even a knowledgeable government intent on serving the public interest may systematically do the wrong thing. I shall discuss that presently.

By contrast, those who see the market economy as unstable and who believe in - or, perhaps, hope for - wise government decisions (lower left-hand box) often advocate discretionary policy. The hard choices come in the impure cases. For example, what if the economy is reasonably stable, but government economic managers are expert and trustworthy (upper left-hand box)? Can they improve on market outcomes? This possibility seems to have attracted precious little attention - perhaps because it is so removed from reality. The focus of the debate, instead, has been on the lower right-hand box - the case where the economy has a tendency toward instability, but the government is ignorant, incompetent, or politically motivated. That is the case on which I will concentrate.

We also need to clarify what is meant by the world "rule". Table 2 provides the relevant two-way classification. In principle, a rule can be complicated and based on numerous contingencies. For example, the instruction "Make money grow at 4 percent per annum, plus 1 percent for each percentage point of unemployment above 5 percent, minus 1/2 percent for each percentage point of inflation above 2 percent, minus 1/4 percent for each $10 billion of current account deficit ..." can be thought of as a rule. It is the kind of "reaction function" that comes out

Table 2

	Contingent	Noncontingent
Based on outcomes	discretion	price stabilization rule nominal GNP rule
Based on instruments	Tinbergen-Theil "reaction functions"	k-percent rule

of the Tinbergen-Theil approach to optimal policy (lower left-hand box). I think, however, that most people find it more natural to think of complicated lagged feedback rule like this as rough characterizations of discretionary policy. The distinction between discretion and complex rules with many contingencies is for philosophers, not economists. To qualify as a rule by my (economist's) definition, there must be few or no contingencies (lower right-hand box). Milton Friedman's famous k-percent rule for the money supply is the best known and clearest example.

The second distinction is between rule that apply to instruments that the authorities control (either directly or indirectly) versus rules that apply to outcomes which the authorities can influence, but not control. An example of the former is, again, Friedman's constant money growth rule and variants thereon. An example of the latter is instructing a central bank to manipulate its instruments as necessary to achieve price stability - and nothing else (upper right-hand box). Nominal GNP rules also fall in this category.

There are advocates of each sort of rule. The argument for instrument-based rules is based on accountability. Only instruments, not outcomes, are directly controlled by the state and hence government officials can be held accountable for their handling of instruments like the money supply, but not for what happens to outcomes like inflation. Thus those, like Friedman, who feel it important to monitor the performance of the authorities are led to favor instrument-based rules. For example, McCallum [1984, p. 125] notes that "it is crucial ... that the rule be ... specified in terms of a controllable instrument variable, in order to minimize possible self-deception. Adoption of an intermediate target variable, be it Ml or nominal GNP, does not constitute adoption of a rule".

The argument for rules based on outcomes, of course, is that these are the things of ultimate concern to people. No one really cares about the money supply; but people are directly concerned about inflation, un-employment, real GNP growth and the like. A rule for the money supply, even if scrupulously adhered to, may do more harm than good if the linkages from money to important economic variables are obscure and unreliable.

I would like to point out an irony here. One of the traditional arguments for rules is that we really do not understand the inner workings of the economy very well, and so are better off not tampering with the eco-nomic machinery. In reality, however, such ignorance severely undercuts the case for instrument-based rules. For if we do not understand how changes in the money supply affect inflation and unemployment, or if the linkages from money to ultimate economic variables are fragile and ephemeral, then it is unlikely that we can design a money supply rule that we would really want to live with. Such a rule would be like stubbornly holding a fixer rudder in a stormy and unpredictable sea. Under such conditions, most ships will do better with even a modestly competent helmsman.

This is much more than a debater's point. Recall that is was in October 1979 that the Federal Reserve Board announced its putative conversion to monetarism and that changes in the American financial system forced the Fed to revise its definitions of the money supply several times during the early 1980s. What if it had been serious about achieving a constant money growth rate? Between December 1980 and December 1982, the old definition of Ml *declined* at a 1.3 percent annual rate. Had we locked in to, say, a 4 percent growth rule for old Ml in 1980, the economy would have been awash in liquidity in 1982 (1). On the other hand, the new definition of Ml rose at a 7.6 percent annual rate during

---

(1) I, personally, would have counted that a plus. But many monetarists think otherwise.

that period. Had we applied the 4 percent growth rule to new M1, much tighter credit conditions would have strangled the economy and deepened the recession. And I can hardly imagine the sorry state of the US economy today had the authorities limited money growth to 4 percent per year - instead of the 14 percent average growth we have experienced over the last two years. A similar story could be told for Great Britain, where strict monetarism - had it really been practised - would have been even more catastrophic than the policies that were followed. This is one of several recent events which have pushed the pendulum back toward discretion.

Thus, I cannot disagree more with Barro's [1985, p. 33] opinion that "a workable monetary rule would seem to entail settling on some definition of money ... *Ex ante*, the precise definition of money may matter little. Yet it is important to stick with the chosen definition in order to avoid discretionary behaviour" (1). Of course, Barro's concern was to limit the freedom of action of policymakers while mine is to stabilize the economy. The two objectives are rather different. As someone once remarked, it inspires more awe than confidence to watch a central bank resolutely follow a straight line to oblivion.

Outcome-based rules are less subject to this objection. If, for example, the central bank is instructed to stabilize the price level, shifts in the relationship between money and prices will make its job more difficult. But they will not lead the bank systematically astray. If it finds that people suddenly crave larger money balances, it can make the money supply grow faster without violating its rule. Similarly, a central bank targeting the growth rate of nominal GNP would wind up conducting a countercyclical policy if a drop in aggregate demand caused real GNP growth to slow.

But outcome-based rules have two drawbacks. First, the performance of the government becomes harder to monitor. If OPEC quadruples the price of oil and inflation rises, shall we declare that a central bank following a

---

(1) In fairness to Barro, he favors an outcome-based rule for the price level rather than a money supply rule. Nonetheless, he prefers a money supply rule to discretion.

price rule failed in its mission and throw rascals out? Surely the central bankers will claim, with some validity, that rising oil prices made it more difficult to achieve zero inflation - and perhaps it would not have even been sensible to try.

This last remark leads to the second problem with outcome-based rules. The concerns of the body politic are multi-faceted and not describable by a single target variable. That makes it difficult to formulate a simple rule for policymakers to follow. For example, the nominal GNP rule implicitly weights the real growth and the inflation rate equally, which does not accord with my sense of relative costs. It is also particularly unforgiving when an adverse supply shock (which may do nothing to nominal GNP growth) hits. But once "rules" start involving many outcome variables and/or numerous contingencies, they start resembling the directives that, e.g., the laws of the United States give to the Federal Reserve Board and the President; that is, they describe a regime of pure discretion (upper left-hand box).

Complexity poses problems for advocates of rules that are subtle and deep. If there are (explicit or implicit) costs of decisionmaking and numerous relevant contingencies, some of which have very low probabilities of occuring, it is surely not rational to specify and agree upon a detailed rulebook covering all contingencies. The costs of doing so are simply prohibitive. But that, of course, means that policymakers must wind up retaining some discretion, at least to deal with "unusual" events. Now a problem arises. When the "state of nature" is revealed, someone must decide whether it is one of those rare states in which the authorities are entitled to exercise discretion or one of the common states in which it must stick to the rule. Who will do this? We know, of course, that decisionmakers always think that the circumstances they have to deal with are special.

The upshot of all this is that I am not setting up a straw man when I treat the word "rule" as synonymous with "simple rule". The essence of the argument for rules is that they must be simple to be effective. Advocates of rules certainly see it that way (see, for example, Barro [1985]). Thus, in what follows, I shall treat the two left-hand boxes in

Table 2 as representing discretion and the two right-hand as representing rules - generally rules based on a single variable.

3. A Brief History of the Debate

Before Keynes, the rules-versus-discretion debate hardly existed because few economists saw any rationale for what we now call demand
management, nor had any idea how to accomplish it.

In the classical view, employment and production were strongly self-
regulating and the income-velocity of money was more or less fixed. That
created a tight link between money and prices which was institutionalized
by the gold standard - which can be thought of as a rule for manipulating the money supply to stabilize the price level. Of course, price
stability required discretionary adjustments of the money supply when
the rules of the gold standard game were not or could not be followed.
Friedman and Schwartz [1963] can be read as testimony to the fact that
this job was not done at all well in the United States. Figure 1 shows
the result: the price level in the US fluctuated dramatically during the
1869-1939 period, albeit without any pronounced upward trend. During
the pre-Keynesian period, few governments say output stability as their
responsibility; that was believed to be the province of the market.

The worldwide depression of the 1920s and 1930s shook people's faith in
the economy's self-regulating properties, and *The General Theory* provided both a diagnosis of the problem and a cure. In the Keynesian
view, which gradually became predominant, natural economic forces would
not be relied upon to maintain high employment - certainly not in the
short run, and perhaps not even in the long run. While Keynesian
economics maintained the classical link from money to prices, it loosened
the link considerably. Keynesians saw a rise in the money supply as
partly absorbed in higher output and partly absorbed in lower velocity.
Only what was left over could push up the price level.

Figure 1 - Implicit Price Deflator, 1869-1939 (1982=100)

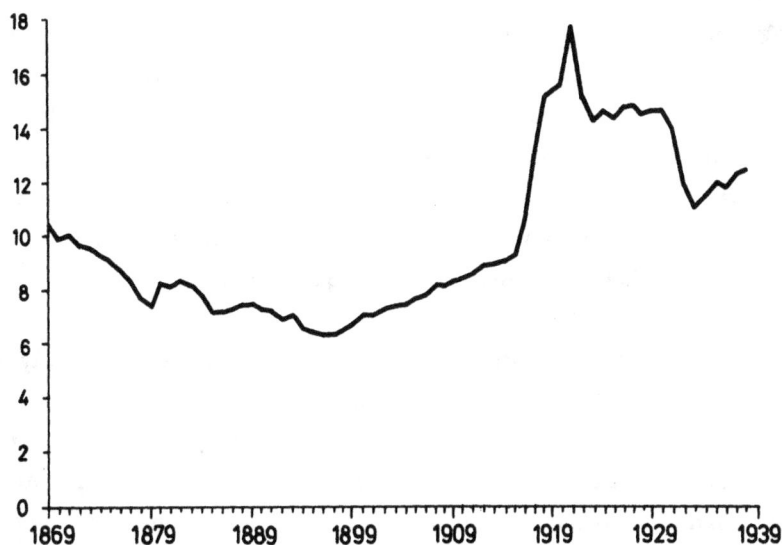

Influenced by Keynesian ideas and, perhaps even more, by the ascend-
ance of the liberal view of the state as a beneficent guarantor of social
well-being, governments around the world came to accept responsibility
for achieving and maintaining high employment - in word, if not in deed.
A simple, and probably naive, chain of logic underpinned the adoption of
discretionary demand management policies:

(i)   Government is an appropriate instrument for the amelioration of
      social ills.

(ii) The economy will not perform well if left to its own devices.

(iii) The government understands the problem and knows how to
      ameliorate it.

In each of these three respects, the Keynesian interlude differed from
both its classical antecedents and the challenges that were soon to come
from monetarists and classical revivalists.

Monetarists argued that the economy's self-correcting mechanism was far
stronger than Keynes thought - perhaps not in the very short run, but
certainly in the medium run. Hence, given the limits imposed by eco-

nomic ignorance and the inevitable delays in the policymaking process, there was little hope that even a capable and well-meaning government could do much to enhance output stability. How much less, then, could be expected from an incompetent or perverse government? The wisest course of action, monetarists insisted, was to return to the classical frame of mind and concentrate on stabilizing inflation by stabilizing money growth. Hence the emphasis on Friedman's constant-money-growth rule, which is designed to produce zero long-run inflation, not to iron out cyclical fluctuations in either prices or quantities.

This change in attitude was driven not only and perhaps not mainly by economics. Political philosophy played a prominent role. Monetarists rejected the liberal view of the state, replacing it by conservative distrust of concentration of power. To them, the words of Lord Acton rang truer than the words of Lord Keynes. Since politicians could not be counted on to do "the right thing", it was better to tie their hands with fixed rules.

The monetarist case for rules was built on three pillars, each of which denies one of the links in the Keynesian chain of logic.

(i)   The state cannot be trusted to pursue the public interest.

(ii)   The economic servo-mechanism works efficiently.

(iii)   Our knowledge of the economy is imperfect.

I will argue below that the second of these three pillars is very weak indeed. But who can deny that the other two contain important elements of truth? Yet ignorance, as I argued earlier, probably does not call for rules - and certainly not for instrument-based rules like Friedman's. And the idea that society should take important economic decisions out of the hands of politicians strikes many people as profoundly undemocratic. Into whose hands should we put them?

All this adds up, at least in my mind, to a very weak case in favor of rules and against discretion. Hence, it is significant that the latest arguments for rules take a different tack entirely. Unlike the monetarist arguments, they are based on neither the ignorance nor the knavery of government officials. In fact, the new classical theory assumes that everyone (including the government) knows how the economy operates and that the government's objectives are the people's objectives. Nonetheless, some new classical theorists argue that, unless the central bank is committed to a fixed rule, it will systematically err in the direction of excessive inflation. The essence of the argument is that optimal policy may not be consistent over time: even a well-meaning government may find it tempting to promise one thing and then do another.

4. Reneging, Credibility, and Reputation

Once again, a homely example will help both explain the problem and point toward a resolution, before we get enmeshed in details.

Course examination are stressful experiences for students and teachers alike. We use them both to rank students and to make sure they master the course material. To most educators, the latter is by far the more important purpose. But the learning objective does not require that the examination actually be given. It is enough to announce the examination, let students prepare for it, and then call it off at the last minute. In a real sense, everyone would be better off if the examination were cancelled. Thus it superficially seems to be the right thing to do. Yet it is rarely done, and for good reasons. Teachers know that this trick can only be pulled off once or twice. After that, students would cease believing the threat and would no longer study for examinations. And that would be a real loss to both faculty and students.

Notice the obvious but important point that neither ignorance nor incorrect objectives play any role in this example. An omniscient and benevolent despot presiding over the last year of the human race really would cancel examinations. It's the optimal thing to do. The problem arises from taking a short-sighted perspective. It is cured by showing proper concern for the future consequences of current actions.

The analogous problem in stabilization policy is as follows. Modern macroeconomic theory generally that there is a short-run tradeoff between inflation and unemployment, but no long-run tradeoff. I will question this assumption shortly; but, for the moment, let us accept it. If so, a rise in inflation caused by expansionary monetary or fiscal policy reduces unemployment only transitorily. This gives the authorities the following choice, which is not unlike that facing the schoolteacher. If they stimulate the economy now, unemployment will be lower for a time. Not only the government, but also the people will benefit from this. but a temporary economic boom will build in a higher inflation rate for the future, which no one wants. If expectations are rational, the government cannot reduce unemployment permanently by, say, printing money faster. Nonetheless, the government always has a temptation to stimulate the economy to secure the short-run gains of lower unemployment - and the temptation grows stronger the shorter the time horizon. For example, a democratic government on the eve of an election may find the temptation irresistible.

Notice the parallels to the examination problem. The problem is not a failure to pursue the public interest nor ignorance of how the economy works, but rather shortsightedness. If this really were the last year of mankind, the optimal policy would indeed be highly stimulative. Just as in the examination example, the need to preserve their reputations for the future is what restrains policymakers.

Now let us relate this to the rules-versus-discretion debate. One way to solve the problem of dynamic inconsistency is to use fixed rules to precommit decisionmakers to follow policies that serve long-run objectives. Thus teachers can be ordered by their deans to give final examinations in all courses, or central banks can be compelled by law to limit money growth to the long-run growth rate of real GNP, as Barro and Gordon [1983] recommend (1). In some cases, precommitment by law might be optimal. For example, patent laws guarantee temporary monopolies to

---

(1) Actually, in Barro and Gordon's [1983] model, the inflation rate is under the central bank's control; and they advocate a rule setting the inflation rate to zero every period. In the real world, this seems out of the question.

inventors even though society would reap greater benefits by allowing free access to inventions. We do so to encourage more innovation.

But rigid precommitment is not always the best strategy. Consider another well-known example of dynamic inconsistency: reactions to floods. Society would rather people did not build homes on flood plains, for rescue and rebuilding operations after floods are expensive. So it makes sense to announce that anyone who builds there does so at his own risk. However, land is cheap in a flood plain; so some people, believing that a merciful government will bail them out, build there anyway. Now the river overflows its banks, and the people who live in the flood plain wind up on their roofs calling for help. Should the government follow the dynamically consistent policy, to wit, let them drown? Few societies deem that an appropriate response. Instead, governments not only rescue the people, but often provide them assistance in rebuilding. Is that right or wrong? If the answer is unclear, society may want to maintain flexibility - that is, *discretion* - to deal differently with different situations.

Another example where societies have opted for discretion is in the issue of capital levies. The easiest and least painful way for a government to raise revenue is to expropriate existing wealth. But if this is known to be the government's tax policy, capital accumulation will be stifled and economic growth will be ruined. So, even without legal compulsion, governments of market economies generally adhere to an *unwritten* law that prohibits capital levies. (Note, by the way, that it is an unwritten law.)

Or do they? Think again. Many capitalist countries occasionally enact windfall profit taxes - as my own did on the oil industry when OPEC's actions swelled their profits in the 1970s. It is also common to enact tax changes that reduce property values. For example, when the Reagan administration eased the tax burden on new corporate investments in 1981, it tacitly reduced the capital values of old ones. Similarly, the reduction in US personal income tax rates in the 1980s reduced the values of many tax deductions that had bee capitalized into asset values. All such policy changes amount to small-scale capital levies and are, in a sense, dynamically inconsistent. Yet, if done in moderation, they are apparently acceptable and do no grievous harm to capitalism. Knowing where to draw the line is what I mean by exercising discretion.

But suppose we are determined to achieve dynamic consistency. Rules are not the only way to do it. In fact, the examination problem is not solved by laws ("precommitment"), but rather by building and maintaining a reputation. Students do not expect teachers to renege on their pledges to give an examination because they have not reneged in the past. Similarly, a government convinces business, labor, and consumers that it is serious about fighting inflation by actuailling fighting it. Our own former Federal Reserve Chairman, Paul Volcker, is a prime example of what I mean. Early in his tenure as Federal Reserve chief, he identified the campaign against inflation with monetarist operating procedures. But, once his credibility as an inflation fighter was established, he was able to renounce monetarism in 1982 without spooking the financial markets.

Similarly, the Bundesbank does not adhere to any fixed rule for monetary policy. In fact, according to Schlesinger [1984, p. 100], it follows precisely the year-by-year approach that Barro and Gordon say must lead to excessive inflation: "the Bundesbank has thus adopted a pragmatic attitude: It relates what is does to the initial conditions and the climate of expectations in which its monetary policy has to be applied ... Year for year, the Bundesbank derives its monetary growth target from two basic components: assumed growth in production potential and so-called unavoidable price rise".

It is hard to imagine a clearer description of a purely discretionary regime, and Schlesinger [1984, p. 100] has "great difficulty in seeing how any other course could possibly be taken". Yet no one doubts the Bundesbank's anti-inflationary zeal.

A government that looks ahead and values its reputation will be loath to reach for short-run gains that may come at the expense of long-run costs. Neither Volcker nor Schlesinger do so. However, periodic elections pose a problem for the reputational solution to the dynamic inconsistency problem, for they have a way of shortening political time horizons. Politicians, we know, sometimes act as if time ends at the next election. Such behavior is considered shortsighted and unstatesmanlike, and no one is surprised when it leads to poor policies.

Simple ideas like these do not require equations for their explication. Nonetheless, they have been complexified and rendered mathematically in recent macroeconomic literature, which builds on the work of game theorists like Friedman [1971] and Kreps and Wilson [1982], amongst others. This work highlights the crucial difference between finite and infinite horizons, which is related to the distinction I have just made between farsighted and shortsighted behavior.

If the central bank's reputation as an inflation fighter is a zero-one variable, as in Barro and Gordon [1983] - which seems to be a uniquely bad way to model it - then a finite horizon will destroy the reputional equilibrium. The reason is simple. There is no sense in investing in reputation in the last period; the only sensible strategy is to push un- employment as low as possible along the short-run Phillips curve. But since rational people understand this, reputational considerations carry no weight in the next-to-last-period, and so on. The low-inflation solution therefore unravels, and we get high inflation instead of these models. Four or five year election intervals seem to make the finite horizon problem highly pertinent. This point is related, of course, to the political business cycles literature.

The remedies to this conundrum are painfully obvious. Firstly, if there is no known "last period", then there is no unraveling. That may be one reason why most societies take control of the money supply - or at least direct control - out of the hands of politicians. Central bankers who are politically independent, or at least serve long terms, are naturally more farsighted than politicians who must frequently stand for reelection. Secondly, when reputation is not a zero-one variable, but rather an asset that can be augmented or drawn down, equilibria with low inflation can emerge. Who doubts that this is the more realistic way to model reputation?

Since the central ideas really are simple, I find no purpose in either recounting or criticizing the details of any of these game-theoretic models of credibility and reputation. The conclusion of this latest round of the rules-versus-discretion debate, it seems to me, amounts to saying that it is better to have farsighted decisionmakers rather than short-sighted ones. Stated in this way, the conclusion is (a) obvious and (b) strikingly similar to the earlier monetarist distrust of politicians.

5. How Good Is the Servo-Mechanism?

I do think it possible to read the recent record as strong evidence that politicians are becoming more farsighted. Indeed, some might claim the reverse. (My own view is that nothing much has changed in this regard.) And, given the doctrinal controversies that have left macro-economics in a shambles, I would not argue that we know a lot more today about how the macroeconomy works than we did 15 years ago (for example, cf., Blinder [1986]). Thus, if any of the three pillars supporting the monetarist argument for rules has been shaken in recent years, it must be the one of the economy's self-regulating properties.

That is indeed the case. But, unfortunately, economic theory and economic reality have marched off in opposite direction. As I noted earlier, the revival of classical economic theory brought with it a renewed faith in the macroeconomic servo-mechanism and an enhanced skepticism about discretionary stabilization policy. At the same time, however, Western industrial countries have experienced their most prolonged unemployment problems since the depression of the 1930s. The US has probably turned in the best unemployment performance over the past dozen years (cf., Figure 2). But even in my country the unemployment rate has remained above 6 percent continuously since late 1979. This is a rate we once associated with recession troughs. In Germany, where the unemployment rate never exceeded 1.3 percent between 1960 and 1973, it has been above 4 percent since 1981 and above 7 percent since 1983. In the United Kingdom, where unemployment rates in the 2-3 percent range

Figure 2 - Unemployment Rates in Industrial Countries, 1960-1985 (percent)

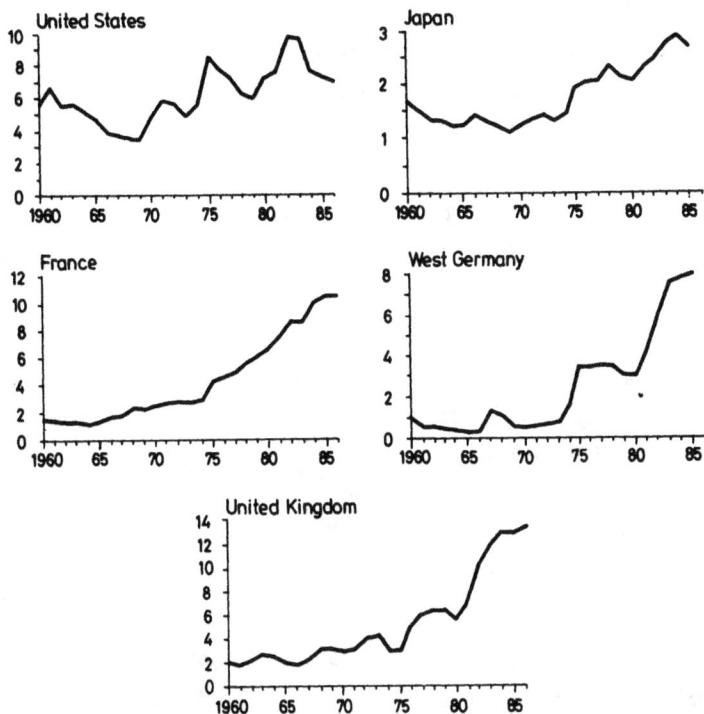

were once common, unemployment has exceeded 10 percent since 1981. In France, unemployment has increased every year since 1973, rising from under 3 percent to over 10 percent. I could go on and on, for it is much the same all over Europe. Even Japan has witnessed a near tripling of its (low) unemployment rate, with no signs of reversal.

All this has an eery resemblance to the sorry experience of the industrial world in the 1930s. And, just as it did then, accumulating evidence is making it harder and harder to accept economic theories that emphasize a strong tendency of industrial economies to return to a normal or "natural" rate of unemployment. Indeed, it is more than a little mystifying that the new classical approach to macroeconomics caught on in this environment.

The facts, it seems to me, speak unequivocally against the view that the Western economies have strong, reliable servo-mechanisms pulling them toward their natural rates of unemployment. But, as the joke says, an economist is someone who sees that something is true in practice and asks if it can true in theory. So this view will not carry the day in academic circles until we have a well worked out *unnatural* rate theory in which an economic boom can bring on *permanently* low unemployment and a recession can leave unemployment *permanently* high.

This we do not yet have. But some provocative and important work by Lindbeck and Snower [1986] and Blanchard and Summers [1986] is pointing us in that direction. In insider/outsider models, insiders may have the power to block the adjustment to lower wages and higher employment that is the essence of the macroeconomic servo-mechanism. They may, for example, protect their own jobs and high wages by refusing to cooperate with new workers or refusing to let them in the union. Rather than risk industrial strife, employers may refrain from cutting wages and eschew hiring new workers. So wages remain high despite high unemployment and outsiders are frozen out.

Now, if a cutback in aggregate demand (an unanticipated cutback, for new classicals) leads to a recession, some of the insiders will lose their jobs, transforming them into outsiders with no effective voice. The remaining insiders adopt a bunker mentality, seeking to protect themselves from wage cuts. So the new, lower level of employment becomes the norm. Any time aggregate demand falls, the unemployment rate ratchets up again. Within limits, there is no tendency for unemployment to return to any "natural" rate. Instead, the system has hysteresis. All this rings alarmingly true as a description of Europe since 1974. Even if the hysteresis theory is not literally true, the data (cf., Figure 2) certainly suggest that any tendency to return to a fixed natural rate of unemployment must be agonizingly slow.

But, of course, the hysteresis mechanism works in both directions. If the economy expands and new jobs are created, some of the outsiders become insiders and the natural rate of unemployment falls. Therein lies the important and obvious implication of hysteresis theories for the rules-versus-discretion debate. If the economy will not cure unemployment on its own, while spurts in demand (within limits) lead to long-lasting - perhaps even permanent - employment gains, then even a slothful, mildly incomponent and politically-motivated government with meagre understanding of the economy can probably improve matters by expanding aggregate demand when unemployment is high. Isn't that just what Keynes said governments should do?

Bibliography

BARRO, Robert J., "Recent Developments in the Theory of Rules versus Discretion". The Economic Journal, Vol. 95, 1985, Supplement, pp. 23-37.

--, David GORDON, "Rules, Discretion and Reputation in a Model of Monetary Policy". Journal of Monetary Economics, Vol. 9, 1983, pp. 101-121.

BLANCHARD, Olivier J., Lawrence H. SUMMERS, "Hysteresis and the European Unemployment Problem". In: Stanley FISCHER (Ed.), NBER Macroeconomics Annual 1986. Cambridge, Mass., 1986, pp. 15-78.

BLINDER, Alan S., "Keynes after Lucas". Eastern Economic Journal, Vol. 12, 1986, pp. 209-216.

FRIEDMAN, James W., "A Noncooperative Equilibrium for Supergames". The Review of Economic Studies, Vol. 38, 1971, pp. 1-12.

FRIEDMAN, Milton, Anna J. SCHWARTZ, A Monetary History of the United States, 1867-1960. Princeton, N.J., 1963.

KREPS, David, Robert WILSON, "Reputation and Imperfect Information". Journal of Economic Theory, Vol. 24, 1982, pp. 253-279.

KYDLAND, Finn W., Edward C. PRESCOTT, "Rules Rather Than Discretion: The Inconsistency of Optimal Plans". Journal of Political Economy, Vol. 85, 1977, pp. 473-491.

LINDBECK, Assar, Dennis J. SNOWER, "Wage Setting, Unemployment, and Insider-Outsider Relations". The American Economic Review, Vol. 76, 1986, pp. 235-239.

McCALLUM, Bennett T., "Credibility and Monetary Policy". In: THE FEDERAL RESERVE BANK OF KANSAS CITY (Ed.), Price Stability and Public Policy. Kansas City 1984, pp. 105-128.

SCHLESINGER, Helmut, "The Role of the Central Bank in Achieving Price Stability: An International Perspective". In: THE FEDERAL RESERVE BANK OF KANSAS CITY (Ed.), Price Stability and Public Policy. Kansas City 1984, pp. 97-103.

Comments on Bennett T. McCallum, "The Case for Rules in the Conduct of Monetary Policy: A Concrete Example" and on Alan S. Blinder, "The Rules-versus-Discretion Debate in the Light of Recent Experience"

Robert J. Gordon

An attempt to absorb the two papers by Blinder and McCallum reminds me of dinner at an old-style French restaurant where there is too much butter and cream. In the case of these papers there are too many stories and too many footnotes, without enough of an attempt to focus on central issues.

Of the two papers, that by McCallum appeals to me most. Here we have a specific proposal, rich in details with which one can grapple and quibble. I find Blinder's paper to be rather limited and old-fashioned in its interpretation of the stabilization policy debate. In particular, his paper does not recognize the convergence between monetarists and Keynesians that has occurred through the mutual acceptance of nominal income targeting by many on each side; nominal income targeting simultaneously satisfies the desire of monetarists for a nominal anchor, while pleasing Keynesians through the avoidance of the difficulties caused for pure monetary rules by the instability of velocity.

M c C a l l u m ' s proposal is very close to one I made in a paper written four years ago [Gordon, 1985]. The acceptance of nominal GNP targeting by many economists of a Keynesian persuasion has, as I suggested, fundamentally altered the dialogue between Keynesians and monetarists. I'll begin by repeating my own proposal and then contrast it with McCallum's, to bring out to good and bad parts of both his proposal and mine. With that common background, since McCallum and I are quite close, the differences with Blinder will emerge clearly.

1. Why Nominal GNP Targeting?

McCallum's case for nominal GNP targeting is based on a dislike of inflation, dramatized by his table showing how much prices have gone up in the postwar period. But this does not explain why he prefers nominal GNP targeting to targeting the price level itself. Let's step back and assess the arguments for targeting real income, nominal income, and the price level. The argument against targeting real income, as well as anything else real like employment or unemployment, is twofold. First, we do not exactly know the natural level of output or employment, and if we guess wrongly in an optimistic direction, we will build in an inflationary bias to the system. Second, if there is a supply shock that reduces natural real GNP, a policy that targets real GNP as if nothing had happened will be inflationary - the implied monetary accommodation of supply shocks is particularly dangerous in the presence of even partial wage indexation. I agree with McCallum that we need a nominal anchor to keep the price level from running away.

Why nominal GNP instead of the price level? Here again the issue revolves around supply shocks, taking the form either of oil price changes, autonomous wage movements, or changes in the underlying rate of productivity growth. With price level targeting, the monetary authority is required to "extinguish" any adverse supply shock, forcing 100 percent of the economy's adjustment to take the form of a drop in real output. With nominal income targeting, the monetary authority automatically splits the difference, allowing half of the impact of the supply shock to fall on lower real output and the other half on a higher aggregate price level. In Hall's [1984] variation of nominal income targeting, a formula makes the price response 75 percent and the output response 25 percent, instead of the arbitrary 50-50 required by straightforward nominal GNP targeting. While my compassionate heart is sympathetic to Hall's variation, I think it is too difficult to implement and too prone to an automatic inflationary bias, so, like McCallum, I'll stick to unadorned nominal GNP as the target.

A complete list of possible targets would also include interest rates and the money supply. Objections to interest rate targeting have been familiar since Friedman's Presidential Address and do not need to be repeated here; objections to money-supply targeting center on serially-correlated movements in velocity. Such velocity movements have been so important in the US that they have essentially destroyed the monetarist case for monetary rules and have forced the monetarists to jump on the nominal income bandwagon already crowded with Keynesians.

There is a legitimate question as to whether nominal GNP targeting should be called rules or discretion. Here, Blinder's distinction between outcomes and instruments is useful. Nominal GNP targeting involves a rule for an outcome without specifying whether it is to be achieved with a rule for an instrument, or with discretion involving which instruments are to be used, and how. McCallum's so-called rule is sufficiently complicated to verge on discretion, and I'll suggest later that the empirical basis for his particular formulation is much weaker than he admits.

2. Implementation of Nominal GNP Targeting

Several aspects of my proposal are different from McCallum's, and as such, raise issues that others may want to address. First, much of the quarter-to-quarter variation in nominal GNP growth reflects the high variance of inventory changes. A feedback rule like McCallum's will cause policy to be too activist, since policy will be forced to respond to inventory fluctuations that are inherently transitory. A better target is nominal GNP minus inventory change, which in the US we call "nominal final sales" (henceforth abbreviated to "NFS").

Second, there are inevitable lags in the response of NFS to monetary policy. My proposal attempts to minimize the lags by calling for the targeting of a NFS forecast, rather than actual NFS. Thus, in McCallum's formula, monetary policy would respond not to the gap between actual NFS and target, but between forecast and target. My version has the advantage that it maximizes the use of available information. If the most recent actual value of NFS is low because of some reason that forecasters believe to be transitory, monetary policy would not respond. But if on the basis of current information forecasters believe that NFS will be low over the next year, whatever the current value, then monetary policy would respond. My specific proposal is to target on the deviation between the NFS target (specified in levels to avoid "base drift") and a four-quarters-ahead forecast. Exactly whose forecast should be used, and whether the central bank should use a secret internal forecast or publicly-available information, are details that need not concern us here.

I doubt if McCallum would disagree violently with NFS, and perhaps not with forecasts. Where we have our major disagreement is with his choice of the monetary base as his only instrument to achieve the nominal GNP target. In my 1985 paper [Gordon, 1985], I went considerably further than he has in testing for the relative significance of interest rates, the monetary base, and the money multiplier in explaining the time path of nominal GNP, using the vector autoregressive framework for econometric estimation. In my case, I tried to minimize the force of the Lucas critique by doing the estimation for three separate nine-year periods, dividing the full interval between 1953 and the Fed's regime change in 1979.

My results are striking, and completely at variance with his. First, there was no significant causal role for the monetary base in explaining NFS in either the 1950s or 1970s. Even in the 1960s, when NFS growth and base growth accelerated together, there is no significant role for the base. In fact, feedback from NFS to the base in the 1960s is stronger than feedback from the base to NFS.

For those not convinced by econometric evidence, the raw data may be more interesting. The Fed has already managed to stabilize the base in two quite different periods and yet has failed miserably in stabilizing NFS. For instance, between 1954 and 1971, the four-quarter rate of change of the monetary base never fell below 0.1 percent nor rose above 2.2 percent in any single quarter. The same narrow range was maintained between 1971 and 1979, when four-quarter base growth never fell below 6.6 percent nor rose above 8.9 percent. Even though base growth was essentially trendless over the whole of the 1970s, the core inflation rate moved from around 5 percent in the early 1970s to almost 10 percent at the end of 1980.

The only monetary variables having significant explanatory power for sales growth are the Treasury bill rate in the 1950s and the multiplier in the 1970s. Other work I've done suggests that after 1979 the Treasury bill rate reemerged as the main significant monetary variable, primarily moved by the connection between high short-term interest rates in early 1981 and the subsequent collapse of the economy in 1982. The conclusion is that McCallum's rule is vulnerable to the Lucas critique: manipulating the monetary base is likely to be far less potent in controlling nominal GNP than his results suggest. My approach to nominal GNP targeting would be to use the latest information in deciding which monetary variable to adjust when nominal GNP growth deviates from target; today I might adjust short-term interest rates, in other eras the monetary base. Alan Blinder would be quite right to describe my approach as "instrument discretion to achieve an outcome rule".

My other serious objection to McCallum's paper involves his preference for zero inflation. McCallum has an attitude toward the existing research on inflation behavior which I would call "aggressively agnostic". We know a lot more about inflation behavior, particularly for the US, than he allows. The first thing we know is that inflation behavior in the US is dominated by inertia. Today's inertial inflation rate inherited from the past is about 4 percent. Suddenly to adopt a NFS rule compatible with zero inflation would subject the economy to a massive deflationary shock. A long and costly period of low output and high unemployment would result. I do not regard the welfare costs of 4 percent inflation to be worth serious discussion, and would recommend an alternative nominal GNP target. If the economy is presently operating at close to the natural rate of unemployment, as most people think is true for the US, then the NFS growth target should be set at the growth rate of natural real GNP plus the inherited (inertial or core) inflation rate. This amounts almost exactly to Schlesinger's quotation in Blinder's paper, that the central bank should target potential output growth plus "unavoidable inflation", except that my version of nominal GNP targeting would not budge in the face of an adverse inflationary supply shock, while Schlesinger might adjust his definition of what is "unavoidable" in this case.

There remains the issue of the open economy. In my view, monetary and fiscal policy provide the government two instruments to control two targets, NFS and the exchange rate. As a practical matter, I think that fiscal policy is too difficult to adjust in the US system to be used for the short-run control of NFS, and so the role of fiscal policy must be directed to the exchange rate. Ronald McKinnon [1984] would assign the instruments in the opposite direction, as would a recent proposal by Marcus Miller and John Williamson [forthcoming]. My conclusion, however, reflects the central worldwide consensus of economists and policy-makers, that for its massive current account deficit the US has only its own fiscal deficit to blame, and a properly-managed fiscal policy would have avoided much or most of the international imbalance.

I have directed most of my attention to McCallum's paper, since it contains the greatest overlap with my own work. There is space for only a few remarks on the paper by B l i n d e r. Much of Blinder's paper reviews elements of the monetarist-nonmonetarist debate, which are familiar from many textbooks, including his own. One of these elements is his 2 by 2 matrix setting out the properties that lead economists to prefer rules or discretion. I would arrange the matrix somewhat differently, as follows:

	Views about self-correcting properties of private economy	Views about efficacy of government stabilization policy
Monetarists (rules)	optimistic	pessimistic
Nonmonetarists (discretion)	pessimistic	optimistic

The advantage of this setup is that it clearly pinpoints as the major difference between monetarists and nonmonetarists a differing locus of optimism and pessimism. Monetarists are optimistic about the ability of the private economy to remain at some sort of equilibrium or natural rate without government intervention, while they are pessimistic that government intervention can do more good than harm. Nonmonetarists, or "activists", believe the reverse, that the private economy has a tendency to remain away from equilibrium for a period of time measured in years rather than months, and that government intervention can push the economy in the right direction back toward equilibrium.

Blinder does not ignore nominal GNP targeting entirely, but gives it short shrift by saying that it is too tough in response to adverse supply shocks. He would do well to cite Hall's proposal which is precisely along these lines, and to include in his defense of discretion how he would limit the extra inflation that would result from his accommodating stance, particularly in the presence of wage indexation. By failing to pursue the implications of nominal GNP targeting, Blinder misses not only the convergence of monetarist and nonmonetarist views, but also fails to note that some of the episodes in which he recommends discretionary action would be handled automatically with nominal GNP targeting.

A good example of this is Blinder's discussion of high unemployment in Europe as evidence of the dubiousness of self-correction and the need for discretionary policy. One must agree with his stress on the eerie similarity of Europe today to the US of the 1930s, when the downward pressure of economic slack on wage and price changes seems likewise to have disappeared. In my own paper at this conference, I find substantial evidence of economic slack in most European countries and room for expansionary policy. Yet one interpretation of Europe's problem is that policymakers, particularly the Bundesbank, *have failed to keep nominal GNP growing on target*. With inflation slowing down year-by-year in Germany, France, and Italy, and with the real growth rate stuck in the mud, it is obvious that nominal GNP growth has been allowed to decelerate steadily. Policymakers following either McCallum's plan or mine would have been required to pursue an aggressive monetary and/or fiscal expansion to avoid this slowdown in nominal GNP growth. Let Blinder call that discretion if he wishes, but for me it qualifies as operating by a rule.

And, as one last point, Blinder's discussion of Europe includes the sentence, "the US has probably turned in the best unemployment performance over the past dozen years" (p. 60). Whatever happened to Austria, Sweden, Switzerland, and Japan?

Bibliography

GORDON, Robert J., "The Conduct of Monetary Policy". In: Albert ANDO et al., Monetary Policy in Our Times. Cambridge, Mass., 1985, pp. 45-81.

HALL, Robert E., "Monetary Strategy with an Elastic Price Standard". In: FEDERAL RESERVE BANK OF KANSAS CITY, Price Stability and Public Policy. Kansas City, 1984, pp. 137-159.

McKINNON, Ronald I., An International Standard for Monetary Stabilisation. Institute for International Economics, Washington 1984.

MILLER, Marcus H., John WILLIAMSON, "The International Monetary System: An Analysis of Alternative Regimes". European Economic Review, Vol. 32, 1988, forthcoming.

Pascal Salin

The papers by Alan Blinder and Bennett McCallum contribute greatly to a clarification of the debate on rules versus discretion. In the present comment, we begin with the problem of defining rules (Section 1). We believe that general rules of conduct ought to be added to the debate and we develop their role in the field of policy design (Section 2). We then discuss the problem of optimum and stabilization (Section 3) and we end with a discussion of "instrument-based rules" versus "outcome-based rules" (Section 4).

1. Definition of Rules

Alan Blinder rightly stresses that one cannot discuss the issue of rules versus discretion without making clear distinctions between different sorts of rules. The distinctions he proposes are useful. Thus, he stresses the differences between simple rules and complex rules (the working of which depends on the existence of contingencies) and the differences between rules concerning instruments and rules concerning outcomes.

I certainly agree with Alan Blinder's view according to which there is no big difference between discretion and complex rules and, therefore, I agree with him when he defines "rules" as "simple rules".

Alan Blinder prefers discretion to rules, outcome-based rules to instrument rules. Bennett McCallum prefers instrument rules to outcome-based rules and both of them to discretion. However, both of them over-look a more fundamental distinction, the one made by Friedrich Hayek [1968; 1973] between rules of just conduct and commands, i.e., rules commanding a result. In my opinion, in the discussion of rules versus discretion, one has to add this distinction between rules of just conduct and rules imposing a result.

In fact, the classification ought to be the following:

1 Rules of just conduct
2 Rules of result (specific commands)
  2A simple rules
    a instrument-based rules
    b outcome-based rules
  2B complex rules (close to 3-discretion)
3 Discretion

Alan Blinder's preferences would rank as follows: 3, 2Ab, and 2Aa. Those of Bennett McCallum would be: 2Aa, 2Ab, 2B, and 3. Mine would be: 1, 2Aa, 2Ab, 2B, and 3. Thus, the ranking of Bennett McCallum is a partial ordering of a wider class of possibilities. Although I prefer to consider this wider ordering, I share Bennett McCallum's view and, therefore, I shall not comment much on his paper. However, even if I mostly agree with his general approach, I wonder if the specific rule he is proposing can be classified in the category of "simple rules" which he favors in principle.

Rules of just conduct are rules which specify the general behavior of individuals - as regards, for instance, the implementation of contracts - without caring about the specific outcome of the interplay between individuals in the framework of these general rules. On the contrary, all the rules examined by Alan Blinder and Bennett McCallum are rules which require a specific result, considered as desirable by the policy-maker or, more generally, by the one who designs the rules. For instance, as regards the rules referred to in Table 2 of Alan Blinder's paper, one has to give a precise value either to instruments or to outcomes. To take a precise example, the Milton Friedman rule of constant monetary growth, which makes a specific result mandatory, can be considered a "constructivist" rule.

What could be a rule of just conduct in the field of macroeconomic policy? First-best solutions would imply, for instance, currency competition, i.e., rules according to which anyone has the right to issue a currency and anyone has the right to use the currency he desires: or institutional limits to taxation and to regulations so that no one could be arbitrarily deprived of his property, and so forth.

Unhappily, we live in a second-best world and we have, anyhow, to design rules for policy. Nowadays, the production of money is monopolized by the State, there is an unlimited power of governments to create legislation, and so forth. The most important problem, then, is to determine whether some sort of contractual rule can be reintroduced into the system. We shall return to this problem later on.

2. Some General Considerations on Rules of Just Conduct

In any institution there are rules (or principles for policy and action). In a firm, for instance, there are more or less implicit internal rules of organization. Besides, the firm chooses to give specific information to consumers about the characteristics of the product it obtains, thanks to its more or less efficient organization. But the firm does not try to define the production policy which can be "optimal" for the consumers. It tries to know what the consumers desire without caring about *why* they desire such or such commodity. In other words, firms do not mind about the preference functions of the consumers and the possibility of their reaching an optimum.

If we try to evaluate optimal solutions in the production of money and in macroeconomic management, it is because we implicitly assume that stabilization policy and/or money creation are public goods: some phenomena, such as externalities or natural monopolies, make it inefficient to rely on market forces to reveal optimal solutions. Moreover, it is also implicitly assumed that public goods have to be produced by the government.

In my opinion these proposals are wrong: there is no discrepancy between the individual and the "social" optimum in the production of money or stabilization services [cf., Salin, 1988], we cannot know the preferred positions of the individuals and, therefore, we cannot define an optimum from outside in an a priori way: and even if there were an argument for considering money production and stabilization as public goods, it would not imply that they had to be produced by the government, since individuals are able to produce public goods in an efficient way. Therefore, when trying so-called optimal rules for monetary policy or stabilization, we are only the more or less passive victims of the pretence of knowledge.

Let us take, as an example, one of the usual justifications for public monopolization of a production, that of the "natural monopoly". In fact, we do believe that "natural monopolies" do not exist [Lepage, Salin, 1987]. But, let us assume anyhow that they can exist. In such a case, it is usually said, the monopolization of production by the government makes it possible to oblige the monopolist producer to behave *as if* there were competition. But, how can we define competition, how can we know the results which would be obtained from competition and the free working of the market forces? In fact, competition cannot be defined by its results (the number of producers, the prices, and so on) but, only by its process. In particular, competition implies the definition of property rights and the enforcement of contracts. And one cannot admit that those who signed a contract can change the contract in a discretionary way: there is a contradiction between contract and discretion.

Therefore, if it is assumed that the monopolization of an activity - the production of money or stabilization services - makes it possible for the government to behave as if there were competition, this would imply that the government follows rules, as competition does (definition of property rights and enforcement of contracts). In that sense, it is contradictory to favor public monopolization and public management on the one hand, and discretion on the other. Thus, even in the second-best world of a public monopoly in the production of money and stabilization services, rules are better than discretion.

3. Optimum and Stabilization

The comparison made by Alan Blinder with the thermostat is an interesting one. But it is misleading in several respects:

First, it implies a constant, well-known mechanism: the thermostat is built by an engineer and, if it works well, which one may assume, it gives the correct answer to the stimulus. But the working of a society cannot be understood so precisely and easily.

Second, the production function may be more complex than it appears in the example given by Alan Blinder. For instance, wearing a sweater is a substitute for choosing a higher temperature on the thermostat. Thus, even from an individual point of view, there is not one unique solution to obtain the optimal - individually-desired - temperature.

Third, the thermostat is intended to help reach an individual target - the temperature desired by its owner - and it is managed by the owner. Problems begin to appear when other people interfere in the process, for instance the four-year-old child in the example, since he may not have the same knowledge as his father of the working of the thermostat. But Alan Blinder ought to add that a further problem arises if even the child has its own target for temperature and it is different from the one desired by his father. A problem of collective decision then arises. It can be solved only by a proper definition of property rights: the owner of the thermostat has control over its working, but if he freely decides that his son should share the property right of the thermostat in some proportion, rules have to be defined to obtain a satisfying collective arrangement and to avoid a situation of perpetual conflicts, with the father and his son continuously modifying the thermostat, in a *discretionary* way, in order to reach their own preferred temperatures. Similarly, from an economic policy point of view, social disorder would emerge from the generalized discretionary behaviour from all the members of society. What is termed "discretionary stabilization policy" is in fact a situation where citizens follow rules and the people "who own the government" behave discretionarily - as does the father with his thermostat.

The problem with stabilization policy is that those who decide on the policy are not mainly those who bear the consequences. And no one knows the "optimal temperature" desired by all the members of society. It is a fallacy to pretend to create an "optimal" policy without first solving the problem: who has the right to do what? (For instance, to raise taxes, to change the growth rate of money, and, therefore, the value of money, and so forth.)

Similarly, Bennett McCallum quotes the approach of Kydland and Prescott, according to which "the monetary authority's objectives are represented by a loss function ... in order to get allocational efficiency" (p. 28). But which are the goods to be allocated? They are goods which belong to specific individuals. These goods do not have to be allocated. Their owners make the necessary decisions and the only problem is one of producing the information which is relevant to them. Now, one could ask how to produce "optimum" information, which means the information desired by individuals, when they are arbitraging with other goods and services. As for any other good, getting "optimal" information is the result of individual choices and it can be done efficiently only by defining property rights on information. Thus, when money is nationalized and monopolized, it is impossible to evaluate the information desired by money-holders on the quality of money. In short, one cannot speak of "optimum" without determining whose optimum, for optimum is an individualistic concept. Moreover, any optimum is ever-changing due to changes in preferences, information and/or technology.

The authorities are not the owners of the resources they pretend to allocate. Nor are they the owners of the unemployment rate or the inflation rate they pretend to stabilize. Concepts such as social optimum or macroeconomic stabilization are meaningless, since optimum and stabilization are individualistic concepts. In fact, we cannot define an optimum without making reference to the people who act and who think.

Everyone is stabilizing his own situation at any given time, taking account of his ever-changing preferences. Individuals choose what they consider the optimal amount of information.

Stabilization is not a public good, not more than the market, the working of which is the outcome of the free interplay between individuals who accept some general rules of just conduct. Similarly, the case against macroeconomic stabilization is exactly the same as that against planning. Both destroy precisely the information which would be necessary for individuals to make their own stabilization policies and their own planning.

If information is "given" in a discretionary way by the government, it cannot be optimal for those who really decide. As for any other production of goods, the best way to bring information to people is through the contract, which makes it possible for anyone to know how his co-contractor will behave. Therefore, the problem is not only to decide between rules and discretion but also, if one is in favor of rules, to distinguish between "contractual rules" and "noncontractual rules".

Even in a second-best world, with, for instance, the nationalization of money and regulations, contractual rules can be introduced. Let us take an example in the field of taxation. Alan Blinder accepts small changes in taxes. In other words, he justifies discretion by the fact that the nature of government activity is discretion. The law of contract would not allow such discretionary and unforeseeable changes: new taxes or higher tax rates ought to apply only to activities which do not exist yet and not to existing activities, the environment of which is thus modified with possible dramatic consequences.

Considering the problem of contracts makes clearer a point made by Bennett McCallum according to which "literal and full precommitment is in fact virtually impossible" (p. 27). In fact, it depends on the nature of the precommitment. If it concerns the behavior of the government (which it must) and not the result it has to obtain, precommitment is possible. When two individuals agree on a contract, they are not committed to the result of the contract (it can be good or bad *ex post*), but they are committed to do exactly what is specified by that contract.

Usually, when agreeing on a contract, a seller does not promise a precise result or even a certain degree of satisfaction to the buyer. He just promises to deliver a specific good or to carry out a specific order. He commits himself to his own behavior and not to the result of his behavior. On the contrary, politicians tend much too often to "promise" specific results (for instance a low rate of unemployment or a low rate of inflation) and they embark into a discretionary policy, instead of promising to behave in some specific way and to apply well-specified rules, for instance, to maintain the price of the national currency in terms of gold, to index the currency or to limit the long-run growth rate of the quantity of money to a pre-specified level.

The distinction between simple and complex rules, made by Alan Blinder, seems to be an important one. However, when the "rule" consists of defining a specific result of the policy (for instance, a specific inflation rate or a specific unemployment rate) one can question the fact that it is labelled as a "rule". It is a (more or less believable) promise; it is not a rule of conduct.

Under a contractual approach of economic policy, the problem is quite different: individuals can understand even complex rules if they feel concerned. For instance, they can understand a complex indexation system, if they consider it important to maintain the purchasing power of their wealth, whereas a "rule" compelling the government to obtain specific values for the balance of payments or the rate of unemployment, and implying precise and complex definitions of these objectives, may not be understandable and relevant for the citizens. But politicians are inclined to choose such artificial and meaningless concepts as objectives for economic policy. And they can reach them, if one does not consider the opportunity cost of the necessary policies. On the contrary, in a free market, the seller tends to give guarantees concerning the characteristics and qualities of the goods he sells, without referring to the results and satisfaction the buyer obtains from using them: someone who sells a hammer does not guarantee you will not get hurt.

The stabilization is not compatible with discretion and it is not even compatible with noncontractual policies (which may be fallaciously called "rules"). Instability in regulations or taxation result from the non-contractual nature of relations between the government and citizens. It explains why the state, in modern times, is the main source of instability, although it pretends to pursue stabilization policies. And, contrary to many other risks in life, one cannot insure oneself against the risks from a *discretionary* economic policy, for instance, an increase in taxes!

To evaluate institutions or policies, one is tempted to consider the results they produce and to subscribe to institutions and policies or to reject them according to one's subjective appreciation of the results. However, the evaluation ought to be made in terms of principles and not in terms of (subjectively appreciated) results. For instance, patent laws must exist, not because they are "socially useful", but because they are coherent with principles concerning property rights. And the outcome happens to be beneficial to all people.

One could say the same for a system of rules such as the gold standard. According to Alan Blinder, the gold standard can be thought of as a "rule for manipulating the money supply to stabilize the price level"

(p. 52). I should not interpret it in that way. It is rather a rule *for not manipulating the money supply*. Alan Blinder does not see the true nature of this rule because he forgets the existence of rules of conduct (category 1 in our classification above). The working of the gold standard is the (unintended) outcome of contracts - i.e., of property rights - between the issuer of the currency and the holder (who exchanged gold against currency). A contract guarantees the purchasing power of a fiat money in terms of gold. Meanwhile, it gives information to the users of the currency: people know what they get in terms of gold for the notes they have. Finally, but less importantly, it happened in history that the gold standard made relatively stable prices possible. Thus it cannot be said, contrary to Alan Blinder's assertion, that "discretionary adjustments of the money supply" had to be made "when the rules of the gold standard were not or could not be followed" (p. 52).

Similarly both Alan Blinder and Bennett McCallum seem to admit that people would benefit from a temporary increase in employment founded on illusions. It reflects, in fact, the fallacy of a macroeconomic approach. Unemployment is not an interesting target in an individualistic approach. One cannot evaluate the loss due to unemployment or the gain due to more employment. Both Alan Blinder and Bennett McCallum assume that more employment - due to surprises and short-run illusions - can be considered as gains. This is wrong, since it means that people would choose to work less than they actually do, if information were better, i.e., if there were fewer surprises.

The whole profession of economists is erring when it refuses to come back to such principles. Let me be frank: there is a vested interest for economists in refusing this step towards principles, since their usefulness as specialists and holders of specific knowledge would diminish. There may be more than merely an illusion in producing sophisticated models which aim at letting people believe it is possible for a government or, even, a collusion of governments, to obtain optimal stabilization. And there may be some blindness in the incapacity to see the real consequences of so-called stabilization policies in the present century. Recognizing the principles and accepting the abandoning of the pretence of knowledge, some economists might consider it their duty to transform themselves into politicians to try to explain and to apply these principles, instead of being *"experts"* for politicians and the public opinion.

Going back to the present institutional arrangements; from the previous arguments, there are some other reasons for preferring rules to discretion. Let us take the specific problem of economic stability. According to Alan Blinder, the Friedman rule cannot iron out "cyclical fluctuations", which is consistent with his assumption that "the economy has a tendency toward instability" (p. 47). But he does not explain what he means by instability and why the "economy" is inherently instable. This assumption is debatable, but, anyhow, we do not know the influence of a lot of variables on economic instability and, therefore, we cannot lay the foundations for a discretionary policy.

One may desire, for instance, to stabilize the inflation rate, i.e., the rate of change of a given price index. However, there are continuous changes in relative prices and each of us has his or her own price index. We cannot define price stability very precisely and the rate of price stability desired by each of us may be quite different. If there is competition in the production of currencies, each producer can define his production policy. And each of us can choose the currency which corresponds better to his or her own definition of price stability. There is no necessity to give an a priori definition of price stability in general. When there is a monopoly in the production of money, we have to refer to a general concept of "price stability" in order to design the production policy of the monopolist, but we do not know to what extent it corresponds with what all individuals consider as price stability.

However, *if* the government has monopolized the use of an instrument - for instance money - rules are better than discretion. Let us compare the two cases:

- Discretion: as the knowledge concerning possible links between money creation and, for instance, prices, employment or growth is not very sound, even competent and honest governments cannot obtain very satisfactory results.

- Rules: let us assume, for instance, that there is a monetary rule (predetermined growth rate of some monetary aggregate). Even if they cannot forecast the results of a specific policy (any more than the monetary authorities under a discretionary policy), at least in the short or medium term, the users of money know the rule and the future path of the relative scarcity of money. And they make adjustments to accommodate for the unknown part of the relation between money creation and their own price index or other variables which are relevant to them. There are techniques to cover oneself against risk and, anyhow, the individuals know better than any one else their desired inflation rate or their propensity to accept risk. In other words, the main problem is not to obtain a given macroeconomic result, but to give reliable information to individuals who are making their own stabilization policy, and to introduce something similar to a contract (fixed price or predictable price of the currency).

According to Alan Blinder his concern is to "stabilize the economy", but what does this mean? Is there such a thing as *the* economy? And what does he want to stabilize in the "economy"? Should we decide to stabilize inflation or unemployment or any other macrovariable?

4. Instrument-Based or Outcome-Based Rules

We stressed in our previous discussion that policies have to be evaluated according to two criteria: the extent to which they are respectful of property rights and their capacity to give reliable information. A contractual approach seems to be consistent with both criteria. It is therefore quite obvious that instrument-based rules are preferable, since a contractual approach is easier for instruments than for outcomes.

Let us take the example given by Alan Blinder in which people suddenly hold larger money balances: according to him, outcome-based rules are better, since the central bank can evaluate the situation and, for instance, accelerate the creation of money to compensate for the larger desired balances. But which rate of money creation ought the central bank to choose? Is the change in the money velocity transitory or not? What is the lag between money creation, inflation, inflationary expectations and the changes in the velocity of money? Is there a risk inducing cycles in money creation? These are some legitimate questions which need precise answers.

The mere choice of a constant rate of inflation as a policy target can be questioned. In fact, if the velocity of money decreases, it may be for an unknown reason. To decide to create money is also to decide that the banks will grant more credits, which may cause undesirable changes in interest rates. The instability in money creation, in response to the (desired) changes in the velocity of money introduces instability in credit conditions. In Alan Blinder's example, there are, in fact, at least three possible targets: stability of inflation, of the velocity of money, of credit and interest rates. If free to choose, people may prefer to get stability in credit conditions and to make some arbitrage between instability in inflation and instability in the velocity of money.

Rules can concern only the things and decisions on which an individual or an institution has legitimate control. Once more, we meet property rights. All institutions need rules, but rules are related to their decisions concerning what they have to manage. The inflation rate does not "belong" to the central bank and the monetary authorities and therefore one cannot ask them to give precise determined values. What belongs to them is either the monetary base (because they have monopolized it), or the quantity of money (because they own the brand of the currency). Thus, monetary authorities could be asked not to reach a given inflation rate, but rather either to limit the quantity of money (or the monetary base) or to give some price guarantee concerning the assets they produce directly or indirectly.

Alan Blinder proposes that the central bank should increase M, as a countercyclical policy, if there were a drop in the real rate of growth of GNP and if there were a nominal GNP target. But we do not know the reason for the drop and the acceleration of money creation may have adverse effects on real growth, with disequilibrating consequences. The pretence of knowledge is always present.

According to Alan Blinder, the fact that we have not much information on the precise links between instruments and important variables, such as inflation or unemployment, makes a plea for discretion, since what is desired is the outcome and this one cannot predict precisely. However, the outcome of a discretionary policy is even less predictable.

As a concluding comment, I should be inclined to agree with the principles proposed by Bennett McCallum, in particular his first principle, namely that "the rule should dictate the behavior of a variable that the monetary authority can control directly and/or accurately" (p. 32) and the fourth principle, according to which a rule might be compatible with the state of knowledge. But I should not agree with the two other principles, for instance the idea that money stock or interest rates are not important for their own sake, but only in relation with inflation and unemployment. The reasons should be clear from our previous discussion.

Bibliography

HAYEK, Friedrich, The Confusion of Language in Political Thought. Institute of Economic Affairs, Occasional Papers, 20, London 1968.

--, Law, Legislation and Liberty. Vol. I: Rules and Order. London 1973.

LEPAGE, Henri, Pascal SALIN, La Libéralisation des Télécommunications. Paris 1987.

SALIN, Pascal, "Macro-Stabilization Policies and the Market Process". In: K. GROENVELD, J. MUYSKEN, J.A.H. MAKS (Eds.), Economic Policy of the Welfare State and the Market Process, Success or Failure. Amsterdam, forthcoming.

Joachim Scheide

Has the case for rules really been discredited by recent experience? The easy answer would be: we don't know because rules have never been tried. To judge the desirability or quality of specific rules by looking at the American experience of the early 1980s does not seem to be appropriate. In this period, the American authorities tried to tackle two enormous problems created, to a large extent, by government policies: they were fighting inflation and reducing regulations in financial markets at the same time. It is true, as Alan Blinder has argued, that there was much uncertainty about which of the M's should be used as targets; but neither this uncertainty nor the fact that definitions changed are by themselves arguments against monetary targeting or monetarist rules. Nor is there unambiguous evidence that the demand for money, applied to a consistently-defined measure of money, has become unstable in this period. Thus, the precondition for the monetarist prescription has not been damaged.

Fixed rules for the money supply, such as the k-percent rule, have been criticized on various grounds; this is taken up in Bennett McCallum's paper. He argues that the distinction should not be made between fixed rules and discretion, but rather between precommitment and discretion. If we look at other countries, it is a well-understood practice that the k-percent rule has to be adjusted under certain conditions. Alan Blinder quotes Helmut Schlesinger and claims that also the Bundesbank opposes rules. But that reading is different from that which I would suggest (we should not take the sentence about pragmatism too seriously, because it is nothing but the excuse for discretionary behavior in the presence of "unusual circumstances"): Schlesinger defines just that procedure which is usually followed in West Germany when the monetary target is set for the coming year. The Bundesbank estimates the growth rate of permanent output (potential as opposed to actual output) and of permanent velocity (as opposed to short-run fluctuations of velocity); finally, in times of positive inflation, a reduction of the "underlying rate" of inflation is planned. So, if there is any new evidence or information on any of these underlying factors, the k-percent rule will be revised - as, among others, Milton Friedman has always suggested. The only problem is, of course, that the Bundesbank has, in most cases, not followed the announced path. As much of the work at the Kiel Institute shows, monetary policy has been unstable and has therefore contributed to cyclical fluctuations and persistent inflation. But the Bundesbank has been *relatively* successful, i.e., the performance has been worse in many other countries.

Governments or societies do not like inflation, nor would they want to produce it deliberately. However, as the work of Kydland and Prescott as well as Barro and Gordon has shown, there is always an incentive for governments to cheat. This analysis is one way to explain why we have persistent inflation in industrial countries even with benevolent governments. What are the alternative explanations? Should we only rely on supply shocks or wage-push mechanisms in order to explain the trend of the rising price level?

The rule proposed by Bennett McCallum is, just as the k-percent-rule, directed at price level stability in the medium run. We may discuss the properties of alternative rules - such as the price level rule (especially with respect to the different reactions to supply shocks, and so on). But this simple rule seems to have a tremendous advantage over the policies actually pursued over the past 30 years in the United States - and, one can guess, in other countries as well. This is demonstrated by the simulations which give us an idea what would have been achieved by strict adherence to that rule: first, fluctuations in nominal GNP as well as real GNP would have been reduced drastically, therefore major recessions would have been avoided (how should advocates of discretion not like this result?); and second, there would have been no sustained inflations or deflations but rather a stable price level over the medium run.

This rule, just like other rules of this sort, implies that excessive wage increases are not accommodated and that firms are not bailed out. Instead, it improves the basis for calculations. It does not produce price surprises and therefore - as many believe - does not trigger persistent business cycles. The benefit, the "free lunch", of this policy would have been not only more stable, but possibly even higher growth, if we believe not only in some empirical evidence, but also in the views of several schools of economic thought, including the Austrian view, for example. Someone who does not accept a rule like the one suggested would have to argue that the employment or growth performance could have been better with discretionary policies.

In the debate on rules and discretion, the case for one or the other is often supported by analogies; some are helpful, some are misleading. Alan Blinder uses the analogy of the reaction to floods, which is taken from Kydland and Prescott; it describes that it would make sense to set up a rule which is in the interest of society. If the government cannot guarantee that everybody will always be saved should there be a flood, it is better to enforce a rule saying that nobody should live in such an area. The equivalent issue in stabilization policy is that, since the monetary authorities cannot manipulate employment or prevent unemployment in the medium run, it would only be honest not to promise more than they can achieve.

The record of monetary policy in stabilizing employment and the price level is not satisfactory, to say the least. To some, like Alan Blinder, the costs of inflation are minor if compared to output losses stemming from fighting inflation. But is that really the issue? Do we really have the choice along the Phillips curve? If we follow the assignment theorem, we can argue that monetary policy has a comparative advantage in achieving price level stability. It should therefore concentrate on that and leave other targets for different instruments of policy. Such an assignment can, of course, be disputed; but it follows from the notion of the natural rate of unemployment or the neutrality of money in the models like the one underlying Bennett McCallum's rule.

There are, of course, major differences in philosophies about the - as Alan Blinder calls it - servo-mechanism of the private economy, and here the divergencies are probably greater than in the debate whether we should have rules or discretion, or, in fact, these divergencies are *the* reason for Blinder not accepting rules. Bennett McCallum takes the natural rate as given - or, to put it more bluntly, the level of unemployment the private sector wants - and he believes in a rapid adjustment to that rate after a shock or, at least, he believes that we don't have enough knowledge to guarantee a faster adjustment.

Alan Blinder argues that the view "of the economy's self-regulating properties" (p. 60) has been shaken in the last 15 years. What is the evidence for this? He looks at the currently observed unemployment rates and sees that they are much higher than before and often higher than in previous recession troughs. Does this mean that the diagnosis about the causes for unemployment is also straightforward, that just from looking at these rates we have to conclude that unemployment today has resulted from a continued shortage of demand? I think exactly what needs to be explained is why is it that, over the past 15 years, the unemployment rate observed at business cycle peaks has increased from one cycle to the next.

Over the past 15 years, there has always been the claim that special circumstances exist, and this notion was not confined only to policy-makers. We had the inflation round starting in the early 1970s, the oil price shock, the recession; then the recovery had to be sustained by locomotive policies. We got the same once again, inflation plus oil plus recession; all events were calling for discretionary actions just as they are now.

Some differences between the views can be illustrated in terms of the Phillips curve (cf., figure). Alan Blinder suggests a demand boost which will - as he quite carefully states - perhaps even lead to permanent employment gains. This is a very honest statement. I assume that his diagnosis with respect to West Germany's Phillips curve would be that there is indeed an exploitable tradeoff. In the present debate on the international coordination of economic policy, West Germany is usually viewed as *the* candidate for more demand stimulation. Indeed, it seems, that we can observe a negative slope if we connect the period of the early 1970s with the current year. However, the trend of unemployment has almost continuously moved upward. There was only one exception, namely in 1978/79, when unemployment declined slightly. We can very well remember the discussion at that time. West Germany was said to have ample capacity to expand without any serious danger of inflation.

West Germany's Phillips Curve, 1960-1987

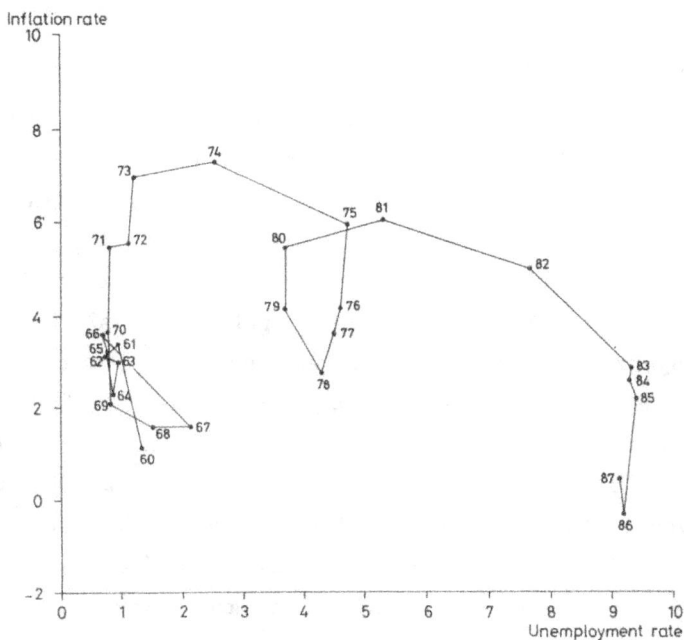

Unemployment was much higher than before (about three or four times as high as in the beginning of the 1970s), so there was - supposedly - room for a decline. The vote was then - as it is now - for more monetary stimulus and expansionary fiscal policy. This policy was indeed pursued in Germany and in other countries. In Germany, the unemployment rate went down by much less than the proponents of expansion had expected. Above all, the price paid for this policy experiment was very high: inflation went up in Germany and other countries, and the worldwide boom contributed to the explosion of raw material prices. It is true that we can never be certain what the level of the natural rate of unemployment is; but we can say that we would have fared better in practically all countries with a rule like the one suggested here, i.e., we would have had no sustained inflation and therefore most likely no severe recession in the 1980-1982 period. We would possibly all agree that that would have been an achievement unless someone wants to argue that unemployment would be even higher today if we had followed a rule that was designed to avoid overexpansion and inflation.

As a final remark, I would like to question the relevance of the rigidity hypothesis. The papers presented at this conference make very different statements about the evidence. Maybe wage and price rigidity is one argument Alan Blinder has in mind when he refers to the "malfunctioning" of market forces. I don't want to discuss the flexibility of wages in the US - we have observed nominal wages falling in several areas of the economy. West Germany seems to be different, as are other countries in Western Europe. In 1986 and 1987, we could observe increases of real wages to the order of 3 to 4 percent each year, the highest increases over the past ten years or so. This happened in spite of the record-high unemployment. Now, what is the rigidity in this? What adaptive wage-setting process has led to such high increases? One could possibly argue that wages are not flexible enough downward at the beginning of a cyclical downturn. But we are now in the fifth year of recovery with still high unemployment figures, and wage increases have not been adjusted downward but are going up. Who has forced the unions and employers to do so? The same puzzle applies to relative wages. In 1987, wages have been increased nationwide by some 4 percent, no matter whether a particular sector is booming or close to bankruptcy, no matter whether it is a region with 4 percent or 15 percent unemployment. This may sound rigid, indeed, but there is no reason why this should be so. And if we complain about this rigidity, we should argue that wage negotiators should consider the market signals and the different situations in their firms, sectors or regions. If we're pessimistic about the success of such advice, I cannot understand why we should be so optimistic that this "malfunctioning of the market process" can be overcome by more monetary expansion.

Leland B. Yeager

B e n n e t t M c C a l l u m points out how much price inflation countries in the free world have suffered since World War II and asks whether it, instead of approximate price-level stability in the long run, has lastingly benefited output and employment. He is doubtful. Before World War I, he reminds us, money units were defined in gold, and without obvious damage to production and employment.

Gold may not have provided an ideal definition (I happen to think we could do better nowadays), but at least it was a definition; it served to limit the range and changeability of expectations. Nowadays, in contrast, participants in sensitive markets, notably the foreign-exchange market, must eagerly watch each day's economic and political news and must not only form their own interpretations of it but must also be concerned with what other people's interpretations are likely to be. No wonder quasi-speculative capital movements are as volatile as they are, and, in consequence, exchange rates also.

It is an absurd system in which no rules exist to enable people confidently to predict the future purchasing power of money. Money's value simply emerges as the by-product of the monetary authorities' doing whatever seems best to them month by month and day by day. It is an absurd system in which the Federal Reserve in the United States gets badgered daily with diverse unsolicited advice in Business Week and the Wall Street Journal by such people as Alan Blinder, Paul Craig Roberts, Irving Kristol, Milton Friedman, and miscellaneous editorial writers.

McCallum's question whether the inflation bias of free-world economies has lastingly benefited production and employment, together with the implications that a reasoned answer would carry for policy from now on, should have been a main focus of our discussions. Yet Alan Blinder and Willem Buiter and any other advocates of discretionary demand management in our midst managed to avoid facing that question squarely. Framing policy for the long run is evidently foreign to their way of thinking. They want to deal with each situation as it arises, using the best theory and all relevant information then available, accepting some rise in prices when it occurs as a by-product of measures thought likely to expand production and employment on particular occasions. The long-run consequences for the price level evidently should not, in their view, be a focus of policy decisions and the choice of institutions.

In presenting his case for discretionary management, A l a n B l i n d e r points out an irony. One traditional argument for rules is that we economists and policymakers do not understand in detail how the economy works, so we are better off not tampering with it. Yet such ignorance undercuts the case for rules concerning the exercise of policy instruments. How could we know enough to frame a rule sound enough to stick with through thick and thin? On the other hand, Alan Blinder - and later on, Willem Buiter as well - pays some attention to the credibility of economic policy. He also takes some swipes - justified swipes, I think, and more of them in the American Economic Review, May 1987, than in his conference paper - at the new classical (macro)economics of Robert Lucas and company.

I'll express one quibble. Blinder says: "[T]he idea that society should take important economic decisions out of the hands of politicians strikes many people [evidently including himself] as profoundly undemocratic. Into whose hands should we put them?" (p. 54). That question should bring to mind arguments in favor of institutions that largely leave decisions in the hands of ordinary people trading in markets, institutions under which decisions need not be made by politicians or central bankers or other government officials. Incidentally, we should beware of the tacit idea that since democracy, more democracy is better. That idea suggests approval of increased intervention by democratic government, that is, by government. But no such inference in favor of governmental activism follows from the proposition that democracy is the least bad method of choosing and monitoring a country's rulers.

From the conference papers and sessions, informal conversations, and earlier reading, I can guess at some possible ways of arguing that accepting an inflation bias can promote output and employment even in the long run. Efficiency-wage and hysteresis effects might enter into the argument. Policymakers might tolerate wage pushes and even support them with expansionary demand policies in the hope that higher wages would somehow improve the efficiency of labor. Nutrition and health care might figure in one possible channel of cause and effect. Higher wages might give workers a greater stake in holding their jobs and so discourage shirking. Policymakers might hope that the employment effects of expansionary monetary policy would prove more than temporary. Employment creates human capital: being employed enhances a worker's employability. Furthermore, if macroeconomic policy can expand the in-group of actually employed workers even only temporarily at first, then, by that very token, the group of workers both interested in the wage moderation conducive to their keeping their jobs and in a position to negotiate that moderation expands. (Contrast the situation in which a shrunken group of jobholders cares little about how their high-wage policies deprive outsiders of jobs.) A policy of tolerating moderate inflation might thus be thought conducive to avoiding either more severe inflation or heavy unemployment or both.

More plausible, perhaps, are arguments centering around supply and demand shocks. Suppose a crop failure or OPEC predation or the like boosts an important range of prices. Other prices, being sticky for various readily-understandable reasons, will not promptly go down enough to keep the average price level constant. A similar point holds when a major shift in the pattern of demand boosts some prices: other goods *from* which demand has shifted may not promptly fall in price enough to hold the average price level steady. Monetary policy tight enough to force some prices down and keep the average level steady after all would depress production and employment as a side effect. Policy might better, on this theory, simply tolerate the rise in the price level caused directly by the shock in question. One might hope that the rise might later be reversed by *favorable* supply shocks, by different demand shifts, by the usual uptrend in productivity, or even by gradual erosion of the downward stickiness of prices that had not been shocked upward. A policy of tolerating or accommodating upward price pushes in the short run might thus be compatible with average price stability in the long run. But if the fortunate reversals did not occur, or not in sufficient degree, then the monetary policy aimed at maintaining production and employment in the face of short-run shocks would result in a long-run inflationary bias. A resolutely anti-inflationary policy would impair production and employment in the short run and, since the long run is a series of short runs, impair them in the long run also.

Along lines like these, then, one might conceivably argue that an inflation/unemployment tradeoff exists even in the long run. I should have liked to hear the argument developed explicitly at the conference, subjected to critical examination, and refuted if it is wrong. (Attempts to refute the tradeoff argument would surely invoke the expectations bred by chronic inflation and the consequent dissipation of the "real" benefits sought by accommodating or expansionary monetary policies.) But, as I said before, thinking about long-run trends and consequences appeared uncongenial to the conferees advocating discretionary demand management; they preferred to focus on what policy would be best in the short run in each particular episode or set of circumstances.

Summary of the Discussion by Joachim Scheide

One issue in the discussion was whether we should consider equation [4] in Bennett McCallum's paper as a structural or as a reduced-form representation of the economy. If the equation is structural, the expected coefficient for the impact of the monetary base on nominal GNP should be *one*. If, however, the equation is not structural, the question arises whether it can be used for simulation. In fact, equation [4] is not structural; it was stressed again that the relationships between nominal variables (e.g., monetary base and nominal GNP) were not as sensitive to the Lucas critique as the relationships between nominal and real variables (e.g., monetary base and unemployment); therefore, the simulations were still a good exercise. Nevertheless, if this kind of study is undertaken with many different models and if in all of them we get "good behavior" in the sense defined in the paper, we would have substantial, though not conclusive, evidence for thinking that this kind of rule would work well.

How much weight should be put onto the two final targets, real output growth and inflation? For example, some participants were obviously prepared to opt vote for a different ratio than the 50:50 implied by the

McCallum rule. It was also argued that this particular rule aimed at something which *did not matter*; according to this opinion, the authorities should aim at ultimate targets - such as real GNP - and use whatever indicators they may have (nominal income may be one of them) to get inferences about the ultimate target. Also, some felt that mono-target policy determination was not appropriate; since there are several targets and several instruments, they would prefer a more complex model to optimize than the two-equation-model used in Bennett McCallum's paper. The argument against the notion that "nominal GNP does not matter" was that what one really wants to do is to make a rule work on something that gets as close as possible to the things that matter. To go beyond targeting nominal GNP one would have to have an accurate understanding of precisely how changes in nominal GNP are going to split themselves up between changes in output and changes in inflation on a, say, quarter-to-quarter basis. Since such knowledge does not exist, it was argued that this was the right place to stop going down that line of thought.

As to the inflation target, it would, of course, be clear that at times of high or even moderate inflation, the rule would not be devised to stop inflation at once but to grind it down over a period of three years or so.

A further issue of the discussion was whether the monetary base could really be considered an appropriate instrument for stabilizing nominal GNP growth. What about using interest rates instead? The fact that the link between the monetary base and nominal GNP was quite weak in, for example, a four-variable vector-autoregression system (real GNP, price level, monetary base and nominal interest rate) did not mean, however, that the monetary base could not have a stabilizing influence. The reason for the rather loose relationship was simply that the standard errors in those vector autoregressions are fairly high. It was suggested that nominal interest rates should not be used as instruments because one does not know by simply looking at them whether they are high or low; such uncertainty would not exist for the judgement on the growth of the monetary base.

The difference between the proposed rule and a price level rule was stressed by several participants. In their opinion, a policy following McCallum's rule had the advantage that it would not react to an adverse supply shock with monetary tightness. This, however, would be required according to a price level rule, and the effect would be that the negative short-term real effects of a real shock on the economy would be exaggerated. In the McCallum rule, the supply shocks would be allowed to work through changes in the price level; in the medium run, however, inflation would not be affected.

What are the general characteristics of policy rules, and how can they be made effective? An important problem for policymakers is, of course, that at certain in - periods, policy options that have sub-optimal consequences in the long run (time inconsistency) may become optimal. The analogy of the *flood*, as described in Alan Blinder's paper, raises the problem of "moral hazard": if the government were to intervene and pluck those people off the roofs who insited on building their houses in endangered areas, their behavior would indeed be encouraged. This is one of the crucial issues in the rules-versus-discretion debate and finds its parallel in, for example, stabilization policy when the central bank has to decide whether it should accommodate excessive wage increases.

If it is so hard for governments to resist "short-sighted" actions, should their hands be tied? Should rules become a part of the constitution? The problem arises, of course, that rules especially on stabilization policy are not widely accepted; and since such rules may always be improved, it would be very difficult if not impossible to devise a rule that is simple and correct. What is negarded as a correct rule exactly depends also, of course, on someone's view as to how the economy works. If the economy is inherently unstable, it would be necessary for the government to change its policy parameters very often and sometimes drastically in order to stabilize economic activity. Some argued that, in such a case, simple rules might prove too rigid. One way to get around that problem might be to ensure that the right persons are in the right positions. However, who are the right persons?

III

Robert J. Gordon*

Wage Gaps versus Output Gaps: Is There a Common Story for All of Europe?

1. Introduction

a. The Issues

Books and papers attempting to explain high European unemployment have become a growth industry of their own. For almost every country in Europe, estimates are available that decompose the post-1970 rise in unemployment between demand and supply factors. Several ambitious studies attempt such a decomposition for a large number of countries (especially those of Bean et al. [1986], Bruno, Sachs [1981; 1985], Sachs [1979; 1983], and Bruno [1986]). Many others (in particular those published in Economica 1986) carry out this task for a single country. The consensus of this literature is that much of the rise in unemployment in Europe has been caused by supply factors, in the sense that the natural rate of unemployment or "NAIRU" has increased by half or more of the total percentage point rise in actual unemployment. There is much less consensus regarding the nature of the supply problem. Several papers by Bruno and Sachs blame an increase in the "wage gap", that

* This research has been supported by the National Science Foundation and the German Marshall Fund. Discussions with Gregory Chow were helpful in developing the tests of aggregation across national boundaries in Europe. I am particularly grateful to Daniel Shiman for his tireless and talented research assistance in creating the data bank, running the regressions, and converting piles of computer printout into legible tables.

is, an index of labor's income share, while other authors (especially Bean et al. [1986]) go beyond the endogenous wage gap to deeper structural factors, such as an increasing generosity of unemployment benefits, increasing skill and location mismatch in the labor market, "labor militancy" due to increased union power, an increasing tax "wedge", an absence of "corporatism", and other factors.

As its title suggests, this paper is about two aspects of the supply-demand dichotomy, wage gaps and output gaps, for eleven European countries both individually and collectively (for comparative purposes the US, Canada, and Japan are included as well). For each country, we calculate new measures of the wage gap and ask whether, even if one is willing to waive the theoretical objections to the concept, there is any evidence that wage gaps in individual European countries have increased enough to explain higher unemployment. Furthermore, we develop new measures of the output gap for each country, using econometric wage and price adjustment equations, and employing the two hypotheses that "natural output" evolves as a trend between benchmark years and alternatively according to the "hysteresis" hypothesis as a moving average of actual output.

The case for supply-side unemployment in Europe has often been based on alleged differences in the dynamics of wage and price adjustment between Europe and the US. Since the articles of Sachs [1979] and Branson and Rotemberg [1980], Europe has been said to exhibit "real wage rigidity", leading to an increase in the wage gap in the wake of a productivity growth slowdown, while the US has been said to exhibit "nominal wage rigidity" that makes its aggregate supply curve relatively flat and opens the way for vigorously stimulative aggregate demand policies. The present paper builds on a companion study [Gordon, 1987] that rejected the transatlantic real versus nominal rigidity distinction in light of econometric evidence that, for Europe as a whole (an aggregate of 11 countries), nominal wage and price adjustment coefficients are similar to those in the US and that, furthermore, Europe's uniqueness consists not of real wage rigidity but rather too much real wage flexibility at the time of the famous wage "explosions" of the late 1960s.

b. The Research Agenda in This Paper

That study looked at the behavior of an eleven-country aggregate called "Europe" but did not ask whether its bold aggregation was legitimate. This paper takes the next essential step and inquires into differences among the 11 countries. Does the apparent similarity of dynamic wage and price behavior in Europe and the US extend to all 11 countries, or are there systematic differences between the four low-unemployment countries (Austria, Belgium, Sweden, and Switzerland) and the remaining high-unemployment nations? The common approach of other comparative studies is to estimate equations for each country, one at a time, without ever inquiring whether differences among countries are statistically significant. This paper makes a start at asking a new and interesting question: is it necessary to divide econometric wage and price equations into compartments corresponding to national boundaries, or rather can the 11 countries be aggregated into a small number of subsets or even into one grand European aggregate? And if there are subsets of countries that accept aggregation or, more formally, "pooling" in a statistical sense, do the pooled subsets have any common features along the dimensions of high unemployment, hysteresis, or corporatism?

The companion paper [Gordon, 1987] treated only a European aggregate in order to allow space to investigate differences in behavior between the manufacturing and nonmanufacturing sectors in the European aggregate, the US, and Japan. This paper goes further by treating the 11 European countries individually at the sacrifice of dropping the manufacturing-nonmanufacturing distinction, treating only the entire economy without any sectoral disaggregation. Like the other study, this paper not only estimates new wage and price equations but also, in light of the central role of productivity growth in the interpretation of wage gaps and real wage behavior, estimates new econometric productivity equations that decompose observed productivity behavior among cyclical effects, real-wage substitution effects, and underlying secular trend effects. The estimated secular trends, in turn, are not forced to be constant over the postwar period but rather are allowed to change both after 1972 and after 1979.

While wage, price, and productivity equations have been estimated by numerous authors, the research undertaken here is unique in its data base, econometric specification, and testing of aggregation across European national boundaries. Almost all previous studies in this area have used data that are inconsistent by sector, leading to regressions in which the wage rate in the manufacturing sector is related to employment or unemployment in the aggregate economy (1). Yet, in 1984, manufacturing value added was only 24 percent of total output in the US and 29 percent in Europe. In contrast, this study is based on a consistent data base in which time series for 14 countries over the 1961-1984 interval have been developed for the aggregate economy. The data series available for all 14 countries include such variables as real value added, the value added deflator, compensation per hour, employment, and hours per employee (2).

A further innovation in the data base corrects an error in previous measures of the wage gap or "labor's share". While employment and hours data include not only employees but also the self-employed, the income of the self-employed is included in the official OECD national accounting system as part of capital's "operating surplus" rather than as part of the income of labor. When the income of the self-employed, which the OECD calls "household entrepreneurial income" is added to the compensation of employees and treated as part of labor's income share, the secular increase in labor's share in Europe and Japan, to which Bruno and Sachs have previously called attention, disappears almost entirely (3). Rather than criticizing the concept of the wage gap upon which

---

(1) All studies using the LSE Centre for Labour Economics data bank, including Newell and Symons [1985], Grubb [1986], and Bean et al. [1986], are guilty of mixing manufacturing wage data with data on aggregate employment or unemployment. That data bank contains no data at all on wages for the aggregate economy, only for the manufacturing sector.
(2) The 14 countries are (in the order listed in Table 1) the US, Canada, Japan, France, Germany, Italy, the UK, Austria, Belgium, Denmark, the Netherlands, Norway, Sweden, and Switzerland. Countries included in the LSE Centre for Labour Economics data bank, but excluded here, are Australia, Finland, Ireland, New Zealand, and Spain.
(3) As far as I can tell, only Sachs [1979] makes an explicit adjustment for self-employment income. Since he does not present estimates of labor's share with and without the adjustment, it is not clear whether his adjustments are larger or smaller than mine.

previous investigators have based their claim that much European unemployment is "classical", this paper shows that the properly-measured
wage gap shows little if any secular increase not just in the US, but
also in Japan and in most European countries.

The econometric specification builds on my own past research for the US
and differs markedly from most other work on these issues. Since observed unemployment rates incorporate both cyclical demand fluctuations
and a secular increase due to some variety of supply factors, raw unadjusted unemployment rates are an illegitimate measure of demand
pressure. Or, stated another way, it is inconsistent to start out a study
treating the raw unemployment rate as a measure of cyclical pressure,
which implies that the natural rate of unemployment is constant, and
finish up a study concluding that the natural rate of unemployment has
risen substantially (1). Yet to impose some decomposition between the
demand and supply components of unemployment *ex ante* in order to
construct an unemployment-based cyclical measure presupposes an answer
to the basic question that all such studies are attempting to address. To
avoid this pitfall, in this paper the measure of cyclical variability that
enters the productivity, wage, and price equations is not the level of
unemployment but rather sectoral output detrended by the "trends-
through-benchmarks" method (the "output gap"). All equations are
estimated in first differences rather than levels in order to avoid
spurious correlations among variables (especially productivity and the
real wage) that display common changes in trend. Special attention is
given to the response of real wage changes to the productivity growth
slowdown that has occurred everywhere, an issue that is ignored in the
majority of studies that include only a single constant term in equations
explaining wage changes, and yet is essential in testing the hypothesis
that real wage growth in Europe was too "rigid" to respond to the post-
1973 productivity growth slowdown. Wage and price equations are based
on the assumption of disequilibrium labor market adjustment, in contrast

---

(1) The studies that erroneously treat unadulterated unemployment rates
    as cyclical variables in wage or productivity equations include Sachs
    [1983], Bruno and Sachs [1985], Blanchard and Summers [1986],
    and Bean et al. [1986].

Table 1 - Standardized Unemployment Rates for Selected Years

	1961	1972	1979	1984
United States (a)	6.4	5.5	5.8	7.4
Canada (a)	6.5	6.2	7.4	11.2
Japan	1.2	1.4	2.1	2.7
11 European countries, of which:	1.7	2.7	4.9	9.6
France (a)	1.4	2.7	6.0	9.7
Germany	0.3	0.8	3.2	8.6
Italy	5.1	6.3	7.5	10.2
United Kingdom	2.2	4.3	5.6	13.2
Austria	1.9	1.2	2.1	4.1
Belgium	2.1	2.7	8.2	14.0
Denmark	2.0	0.9	6.1	10.1
Netherlands	0.5	2.2	5.4	14.0
Norway	1.8	1.7	2.0	3.0
Sweden	1.4	2.7	2.1	3.1
Switzerland	0.0	0.0	0.4	1.1

(a) Because of recessions in the US and Canada in 1961, and a dip in French output in the early 1960s, 1964 is chosen as the benchmark year for these three countries.

Source: For Switzerland and Denmark, 1972 and 1979: OECD [1984; 1985b, p. 28]. For other countries for 1972, 1979, and 1984: OECD [1985a, Table R12]. For all countries for 1961: OECD [1971, Table 10].

to some work (especially Newell and Symons [1985]) based on a market-clearing interpretation.

This paper takes the "output gap" (the log ratio of actual real GDP to "natural" real GDP) as the basic measure of cyclical demand pressure and measures "natural" real GNP by trends through the benchmark years 1961, 1972, and 1979, with the 1972-1979 rate of growth extrapolated to 1984. By taking 1979 as a benchmark year in which natural real GNP is assumed to be equal to actual real GNP (with a zero output gap), this paper *accepts in advance the proposition that the natural rate of unemployment has increased and provides no explanation at all for this increase*. This evident in Table 1, which displays standardized unemployment rates for each country for the benchmark years 1961, 1972, and 1979. Since we assume that cyclical demand pressure was zero for all countries in 1979, we assume that between 1972 and 1979 there were major unexplained increases in the natural unemployment rate for France, Germany, Belgium, Denmark, and the Netherlands. Lesser but nontrivial increases in the rate occurred in Canada, Japan, Italy, the UK, and Austria. The natural rate assumed in 1984 cannot be read from this table; in the concluding section of the paper a calculation is provided that works backward from out measure of the output gap to arrive at a measure of the natural rate of unemployment for each country in 1984.

c. Themes That Emerge

The most interesting new result in this paper is that national boundaries within Europe are no longer relevant when studying wage behavior. In a step-by-step test of pooling across pairs of European countries, and then alternative pairs of country groups, we find *no single case* in which a regression pooled across country boundaries fits worse (using the usual 5 percent significance criterion) than regressions estimated for separate members of each pair. These results raise serious doubts about a large segment of the literature on high European unemployment, particularly those papers which attribute low unemployment in some countries to "corporatist" wage-setting institutions, and those which blame excess real wage increases in some countries for their high unemployment.

Confirming my recent work, the results cast doubt on most of the contrasts between US and Europe that have received heavy emphasis in previous research, not only for the aggregate of 11 European countries studied in Gordon [1987], but also for most individual European countries. With the single exception of the UK, there is no evidence to support Sachs' [1983] claim that productivity in Europe is "classical", varying countercyclically. Furthermore, there is remarkably little evidence of greater nominal wage flexibility in Europe than in the US, or of greater real-wage rigidity in Europe.

The apparent consensus that European real wages are excessive is simplistic; in 1984 the wage gap (an index of labor's share on a 1972 base) for an aggregate of 11 European countries was as low as the US wage gap and lower in Germany, Italy, the Netherlands, and Norway. There is absolutely no relation across European countries between those that have high unemployment in the 1980s and those that exhibit high wage gaps. The highest wage gaps adjusted for estimated productivity trends are all in low-unemployment countries, Japan, Austria, and Switzerland.

The wage and price equations estimated in the paper address the common distinction between real-wage rigidity in Europe and nominal-wage rigidity in the US (see especially Branson and Rotemberg [1980]). We find that the bulge in the wage gaps of Europe and Japan in the 1970s is not due primarily to a failure of real wages to decelerate in response to the post-1973 productivity growth slowdown, but rather results to a large extent from episodes of autonomous "wage push" in Europe in the late 1960s and in Japan during 1973/74. In this sense, real wages in Europe and Japan were *too flexible, rather than too rigid.*

The paper also reveals an interesting dichotomy between large and small countries within Europe. There is little degenerate behavior evident in the statistical evidence for the large countries - no countercyclical productivity behavior that would suggest a deterioration in productivity gains in response to a future output stimulus (except in the UK); no evidence of substantial excessive real-wage changes between the mid-1960s and mid or late 1970s; and no evidence of a substantially steeper aggregate supply curve that would inhibit policymakers from administering a demand stimulus. But several small countries exhibit signs of excessive real-wage increases through the late 1970s, followed by a rapid readjustment since then. The paper points to, but does not solve, a puzzle in the high "wage-gap" indexes of some small countries that have relatively low unemployment (especially Austria and Switzerland) in contrast to the relatively low level of wage-gap indexes in other high-unemployment countries, especially Germany, Italy, and the Netherlands.

2. The Data Base, the Productivity Trend, and the Wage Gap

a. The Data Base for Fourteen Countries

Most comparative econometric studies of wage and employment equations have indiscriminately mixed data on the hourly wage rate for the manufacturing sector with economy-wide data on unemployment and/or output (1). The work of Artus [1984] is almost unique in developing a consistent data base for manufacturing, and this paper builds on his research by developing an analogous data base for the aggregate economy. The aim of the data compilation is to develop consistent series on value added, the value added deflator, compensation, employment, and hours per employee. These series allow the calculation of all of the variables that matter for a study of productivity, wage, and price behavior. Average labor productivity is real value added per labor hour, the wage rate is compensation per labor hour, and the wage gap is the nominal wage rate, divided by the value added deflator, divided in turn by average labor productivity. Because the real product wage relevant for the hiring decisions of business firms is expressed at factor cost, i.e., net of indirect taxes, special care has been taken to achieve a consistent set of net-of-tax product price deflators at factor cost.

The aggregate data are developed here from published OECD series, together with a crucial unpublished series on aggregate hours per

---

(1) The LSE data base, as described by Grubb [1986], contains hourly earnings only for manufacturing, and not always on a consistent base. Data for Australia and Norway are for males only, data for the US include production workers only, data for Austria, Belgium, Denmark, and Sweden include mining, data for Belgium includes transport, and data for Spain include all industries.

employee (1). A unique feature of the data base is the explicit treatment of self-employment income. Previous studies have included in indexes of labor's income share and the "wage gap" only the compensation of employees. But the income of the self-employed consists mainly of labor income and should also be included rather than hidden, as at present, in the OECD's umbrella capital income measure called "the operating surplus". This is particularly important in this study, which measures the wage rate as compensation per hour. Since measures of employment and total hours include the self-employed, so should the measure of compensation. Thus, our measure of total compensation adds the OECD measure of "household entrepreneurial income" to employee compensation.

Potential defects in these procedures may be enumerated briefly. The use of compensation per hour to represent the wage rate has the advantage that separate wage-rate series can be developed for the aggregate, manufacturing, and nonmanufacturing sectors, but has the disadvantage that any compensation per hour series displays cyclical fluctuations created not by changes in the "pure" wage itself, but also by changes in the fraction of hours paying overtime rates, and by changes in the interindustry mix between high and low-wage activities. While my past work on US wage behavior has been based on an hourly-earnings index, adjusted for shifts in overtime and the interindustry employment mix, such indexes are not available for other countries, and thus the need for consistency requires use of an unadjusted compensation per hour series for each country and each sector. The addition of self-employment income to employee compensation also raises issues that

---

(1) This unpublished series was provided by John Martin of the OECD. All other series for the aggregate sector were obtained from an OECD PC data diskette. The manufacturing data were transcribed manually from printouts provided by the IMF in May, 1985 and include manufacturing value-added deflators, output, compensation, employment, and hours for the fourteen countries identified in footnote 2 on p. 100. The compilation of the manufacturing data is described in the data appendix of Artus [1984]. A critical step in the development of the data base was the location of data on the absolute value of each variable (particularly nominal output, nominal compensation, and labor hours) for the aggregate economy in 1972, in order to allow subtraction of manufacturing values from aggregate values to obtain the needed residual values.

require further research, including the separation of the labor and capital components of entrepreneurial income.

b. Untangling the Productivity Trend

We need to identify secular trends in productivity growth for five purposes. First, measures of the "wage gap" should be corrected for cyclical variations in productivity, relating the level of real wages to the secular trend in productivity. Second, identifying the concept of "real-wage rigidity" in a dynamic wage-change regression cannot be accomplished without some measure of "rigid relative to *what?*". Third, most evidence for the US suggests that prices are set relative to "trend unit labor cost", that is, wages divided by the trend in labor's average product, rather than relative to actual unit labor cost. Fourth, the cyclical productivity regressions developed in this section also allow us to assess the effect or real-wage movements on the demand for labor and on labor's average product. Fifth, our equations allow us to assess the claim by Sachs [1983, p. 281] that "in Europe (but not in Japan) the overall effect of a sustained rise in unemployment is to raise productivity relative to trend". His claim that labor productivity varies countercyclically in Europe contrasts with the standard assumption in the US that productivity varies procyclically.

c. Specification of the Productivity Equations

The basic specification relates the log ratio of hours to trend output ($N_t - Q^*_t$) to the log output ratio ($Q_t - Q^*_t$), representing the cyclical effect of output on hiring decisions; to the real-wage defined relative to the underlying productivity trend $[(W_t - P_t) - \theta^*_t]$, which could differ from zero as a result of excess growth in the real wage; and to the productivity trend itself (θ^*_t). Defining all upper-case letters as logs of levels, we can write:

[1] $$(N_t - Q^*_t) = A + \phi(Q_t - Q^*_t) - \sigma(W_t - P_t - \theta^* t) - \theta^* t$$

where A is a constant. Note that [1] adds a cyclical effect to a standard static labor-demand function in which labor hours depend on the real wage and labor-augmenting technical progress. The trend in [1] picks up the effects of growth in the capital-labor ratio and of changes in other inputs.

When [1] is rewritten as an equation for the average product of labor (Q/N), we can interpret the parameter ϕ as indicating the effect of cyclical movements in the output ratio on labor productivity:

$$[2] \quad (Q_t - N_t) = -A + (1-\phi)(Q_t - Q^*_t) + \sigma(W_t - P_t - \theta^* t) + \theta^* t$$

If the parameter ϕ is unity, then a permanent increase in the output ratio has no impact on actual labor productivity, whereas a value of ϕ below unity implies a permanent productivity gain ("short-run increasing returns") and a value of ϕ above unity implies a permanent productivity loss ("short-run diminishing returns"). Thus the Sachs phenomenon of countercyclical productivity movements in Europe requires an estimated value of $\phi > 1.0$.

d. Theoretical and Actual Wage Gap Indexes

We note that [1] allows us to define a wage-gap concept adjusted not just for cyclical effects but for the endogenous reponse of productivity growth to excess growth in the real wage. Defining θ as the log level of labor's *actual* average product and θ^* as the growth rate of the *trend* in labor's average product, we can write the actual wage-gap index (WG_t) as $W_t - P_t - \theta_t$ and the adjusted wage gap index (WG^*_t) as $W_t - P_t - \theta^* t$. Using these definitions, we can rearrange [2] to obtain:

$$[3] \quad WG_t = A - (1-\phi)(Q_t - Q^*_t) + (1-\sigma)(WG^*_t)$$

This expression places an interesting perspective on the interrelationships between real-wage behavior, productivity growth, and the wage-gap index. If the elasticity of labor input with respect to the excess real wage (σ) in [1] is unity, then [3] shows that the excess real-wage growth "pays for itself" by boosting *actual* productivity enough to keep the actual wage gap index ($WG_t = W_t - P_t - \theta_t$) unaffected. Only if the elasticity (σ) is less than unity is excess real-wage growth manifested in an increase in the observed actual wage-gap index.

e. Estimation of the Labor Input Equations

Equation [1] could be estimated either in levels or in growth rates. Initial testing indicated that the growth rate specification is superior, avoiding the serial correlation that occurs with the level specification for some countries. Allowing for lags and a post-1972 break in the productivity growth trend, [1] becomes:

$$[4] \quad (n - q^*)_t = \sum_{j=0}^{1} \phi_j (q-q^*)_{t-j} - \sum_{k=0}^{1} \sigma_k (w-p - \sum_{i=0}^{1} \theta^*_i)_{t-k} - \sum_{i=0}^{1} \theta^*_i$$

where θ^*_0 is the 1964-1972 productivity trend and θ^*_1 is the 1973-1984 productivity trend. To unscramble the productivity trends from the estimated regression, run:

$$[5] \quad (n - q^*)_t = \sum_{j=0}^{1} \phi_j (q-q^*)_{t-j} - \sum_{k=0}^{1} \sigma_k (w-p)_{t-k} - \sum_{i=0}^{1} \alpha_i + \epsilon_t$$

where α_0 is the constant term (= 1.0 for 1964-1984) and α_1 is a dummy variable (= 0 for 1964-1972 and = 1.0 for 1973-1984). Then the productivity trend terms are defined as:

$$[6] \quad \theta^*_0 = -\alpha_0/(1-\sum_k \sigma_k); \quad \theta^*_1 = -(\alpha_0 - \alpha_1)/(1-\sum_k \sigma_k)$$

In preliminary tests, an additional productivity term (α_2 = 1.0 for 1980-1984) was entered to test for the significance of a second growth slow-down after 1979, but this term was uniformly insignificant in the presence of the real-wage variable. With the real-wage variable omitted, α_2 was significant for several countries, as discussed below in connection with Table 4.

Table 2 - Equations Explaining Annual Change in Hours Relative to Trend Output Growth $(h_t - q^*_t)$, 1964-1984

| | Sum of coefficient on current and one lagged change in | | Constant (trend) terms | | | | |
| | output ratio | real wage | 1963 -1984 | 1973 -1984 | $\bar{R}^2$ | S.E.E. | D.-W. |
	(1)	(2)	(3)	(4)	(5)	(6)	(7)
United States	0.86**	-0.22	-1.70*	0.92	0.82	0.78	2.17
Canada	0.86**	-0.62**	-1.33*	0.51	0.84	0.84	2.50
Japan	0.36*	-0.46**	-4.98**	3.11**	0.91	0.78	2.36
11 European countries, of which:	0.78**	-0.44**	-2.81**	0.99**	0.92	0.37	2.20
France	0.86**	-0.68**	-1.71**	0.42	0.92	0.53	1.33
Germany	0.91**	-0.53**	-2.31*	0.51	0.81	0.78	2.47
Italy	0.58**	-0.47**	-3.10*	1.37	0.81	0.92	2.06
United Kingdom	1.13**	-0.01	-3.39**	1.11	0.71	1.29	2.66
Austria	0.71**	-0.41*	-3.62**	1.75**	0.75	0.94	2.25
Belgium	0.79**	-0.63**	-1.79**	0.34	0.87	0.80	1.81
Denmark	0.75*	-0.77**	-0.73	0.095	0.60	1.60	2.05
Netherlands	0.60*	-0.51**	-2.17	0.23	0.68	1.04	2.15
Norway	0.40	-0.22	-3.31**	-0.13	0.02	1.50	1.83
Sweden	0.69**	-0.24	-3.76**	2.36**	0.79	0.89	2.11
Switzerland	0.89**	-0.59**	-1.81	1.28**	0.95	0.55	2.33

Note: * indicates significant at the 5 percent level; ** at the 1 percent level.

f. Estimated Productivity Equations

Results for the productivity regression equations are presented in Table 2 for the fourteen countries, with the countries listed in the same order as Table 1 (North America and Japan at the top, followed by the four large European countries and then the seven small European countries). All sums of coefficients on the output ratio are between zero and unity except for the UK, indicating almost uniformly procyclical behavior of productivity. Only the UK exhibits a countercyclical effect; the US, Canada, France, Germany, and Switzerland exhibit a mildly procyclical effect, and there are strongly procyclical effects in Japan, Italy, and all of the small European countries except Switzerland. The bottom line for a GNP-weighted aggregate of all the 11 European countries displays the interesting result that the labor-hoarding (or procyclical productivity) phenomenon is somewhat more important in Europe than in the US, directly contradicting Sachs' [1983] results.

The real wage elasticities have the correct negative sign and are statistically significant in all the countries but the US, the UK, Norway, and Sweden. Most of the elasticities are in the vicinity of -0.5, indicating that an increase in wages relative to the productivity trend, for whatever reason, boosts productivity by enough to offset about half but not all of the resulting upward pressure on the wage gap (recall that an elasticity of -1.0 would be required for the wage gap to be unaffected by an acceleration of wage growth relative to trend productivity growth). It seems ironic, in light of the emphasis placed on real-wage substitution in the labor market by British authors, including Bean et al. [1986] and Newell and Symons [1985], that the country with the least evidence of a real-wage effect is the UK. There seems to be no connection between the real-wage elasticity and the post-1970 rise in unemployment. Relatively high elasticities are found for countries with high unemployment rates in the 1980s (France, Germany, Italy, Belgium, Denmark) and low unemployment rates in the 1980s (Japan, Austria, Switzerland). Interestingly, the elasticity for Europe as a whole is almost indentical to that in Japan.

The productivity trend terms displayed in Table 2 are the α coefficients that must be unscrambled, using [6], to reveal the underlying structural productivity trends (θ^*). As displayed in Table 2, the productivity coefficients are useful mainly as an indication of the statistical significance of the post-1972 slowdown in productivity growth. Somewhat surprisingly, the slowdown terms in column (4) of Table 2 are significant only for Japan, Austria, Sweden and Switzerland. For all the other countries except Norway, the slowdown terms have the correct positive sign but are insignificant at the 5 percent level.

Table 3 - Contribution to Fitted Values of Productivity Growth of Trends, Real-Wage Effect, and Cyclical Output Ratio Effect for Selected Intervals, 1964-1984

	1964-1972				1972-1979				1979-1984			
	trend	real wage	output ratio	total	trend	real wage	output ratio	total	trend	real wage	output ratio	total
	(1)	(2)	(3)	(4)	(5)	(6)	(7)	(8)	(9)	(10)	(11)	(12)
United States	2.18	0.04	0.00	2.22	1.00	-0.05	-0.03	0.92	1.00	-0.27	-0.06	0.66
Canada	3.52	0.19	-0.01	3.69	2.18	-0.81	-0.02	1.34	2.18	-0.72	-0.23	1.22
Japan	9.25	-0.56	-0.39	8.29	3.47	0.48	-0.03	3.92	3.47	-0.54	-0.01	2.91
11 European countries, of which:	4.98	0.17	-0.06	5.08	3.22	0.14	0.01	3.38	3.22	-0.77	-0.41	2.04
France	5.40	-0.04	-0.01	5.35	4.08	0.19	-0.02	4.25	4.08	-0.87	-0.39	2.82
Germany	4.91	0.17	-0.04	5.04	3.66	0.10	0.02	3.78	3.66	-1.36	-0.18	2.11
Italy	5,81	0.32	-0.10	6.02	3.23	-0.08	0.03	3.18	3.23	-1.09	-0.89	1.26
United Kingdom	3.76	0.08	-0.08	3.76	2.53	-0.05	0.02	2.50	2.53	-0.07	0.19	2.65
Austria	6.09	0.06	0.06	6.20	3.14	0.76	0.00	3.90	3.14	-0.78	-0.55	1.80
Belgium	4.90	0.55	-0.04	5.41	3.97	0.57	0.50	4.55	3.97	-1.24	-0.34	2.40
Denmark	3.11	1.70	-0.26	4.55	2.70	0.82	0.02	3.54	2.70	-1.63	-0.15	0.93
Netherlands	4.46	0.92	-0.04	5.34	3.99	0.43	0.01	4.43	3.99	-3.08	-0.15	-0.16
Norway	4.27	0.35	-0.05	4.58	4.43	-0.13	0.00	4.30	4.43	-1.06	-1.07	2.13
Sweden	4.96	-0.27	-0.39	4.30	1.85	0.16	0.17	2.17	1.85	-0.78	-1.25	0.84
Switzerland	4.39	-0.14	-0.08	4.17	1.29	0.89	0.43	2.22	1.29	0.20	-0.23	1.64

Table 3 presents an extremely interesting decomposition of the fitted values of *actual* growth rate of productivity in three periods (1964-1972, 1972-1979, and 1979-1984), subdividing the growth rate that the Table 2 equations explain into three sources, (i) underlying trend, (ii) contribution of real wage changes (the $w-p - \Sigma \theta^*_i$ term in [4]), and (iii) the contribution of changes in the output ratio. The total shown in columns (4), (8), and (12) is for the fitted value of the equations from Table 2. Recall that the post-1972 trend effect is the sum of columns (3) and (4) in Table 2, with the signs reversed, as written out in [6].

The countries can be divided into groups, according to the main sources of changes in observed productivity growth. The first group consists of those countries in which the observed slowdown in productivity growth after 1972 is mainly explained by the underlying trend term: the US, Japan, the UK, Austria, Sweden, and Switzerland. For the second group of countries the 1972-1979 slowdown is mainly explained by the trend term, but a further large slowdown in 1979-1984 is explained by a slowdown in real wage growth (Canada, France, Germany, Italy, Belgium, Denmark, the Netherlands, Norway, and Sweden). Further large contributions of the output ratio after 1979 occur in Italy, Austria, the Netherlands, and Norway.

For Europe as a whole, *all* of the slowdown in productivity growth after 1979 is attributed to the real-wage and cyclical effects. The US had less of a real-wage effect after 1979, both because the coefficient on real wages is smaller in Table 2, and because the slowdown in real-wage growth was less dramatic than in Europe. For Japan, the dominant fact is the slower post-1972 trend, and the real-wage effect is relatively minor, contributing a positive half percentage point in 1972-1979 which was reversed in 1979-1984.

g. Trends in Output, Productivity, and Hours

Table 4 brings together the *assumed* trend growth rates of output (based on the benchmark years 1961, 1972, and 1979, as explained above) with estimated trend growth rates of productivity. Unlike those

Table 4 - Growth Rates in Trend Output, Output/Hour, and Hours for Selected Intervals, 1960-1984

	1960-1972			1972-1979			1979-1984		
	output	output/ hour	hours	output	output/ hour	hours	output	output/ hour	hours
	(1)	(2)	(3)	(4)	(5)	(6)	(7)	(8)	(9)
United States	3.66	2.11	1.55	3.00	0.88	2.12	3.00	1.73	1.27
Canada	5.28	3.49	1.78	3.89	1.35	2.54	3.89	3.44	0.44
Japan	4.34	8.91	0.43	4.11	3.82	0.29	3.92	3.06	0.86
11 European countries, of which:	4.35	5.09	-0.73	2.74	3.39	-0.65	2.74	3.74	-1.00
France	5.23	5.30	-0.07	3.37	4.16	-0.79	3.37	5.24	-1.87
Germany	4.26	5.16	-0.90	2.62	4.04	-1.43	2.62	3.55	-0.93
Italy	5.02	6.41	-1.39	3.17	3.07	0.10	3.17	3.26	0.10
United Kingdom	2.73	3.75	-1.02	2.31	2.22	0.09	2.31	4.39	-2.08
Austria	4.75	6.03	-1.28	3.16	3.62	-0.46	3.16	3.41	-0.25
Belgium	4.73	5.13	-0.40	2.68	4.40	-1.72	2.68	4.22	-1.54
Denmark	4.29	4.32	-0.03	2.11	3.13	-1.01	2.11	2.32	-0.20
Netherlands	4.73	5.33	-0.60	2.92	4.50	-1.58	2.92	2.28	0.64
Norway	4.21	4.41	-0.20	4.67	4.30	0.37	4.67	4.21	0.45
Sweden	4.05	4.59	-0.55	2.07	2.09	-0.02	2.07	1.53	0.54
Switzerland	4.44	4.12	0.32	0.11	2.21	-2.10	0.11	0.25	-0.15

displayed in Table 3, the productivity trends in Table 4 are obtained from estimates of [4] in which the real wage effects are omitted. These trends can be interpreted as incorporating a cyclical adjustment but no decomposition of the portion of the productivity trend attributable to real wage movements. When [4] is reestimated without the real wage variable, the third dummy variable representing the post-1979 slowdown becomes significant only for Germany, the Netherlands, Switzerland, and the aggregate of the 11 European countries. (Tables showing these regression results with the third dummy variable have been omitted to save space.)

The purpose of Table 4 is to shed some light on the sources of the divergent movements of European unemployment rate from the unemployment rates of the US and Japan. The counterpart of rising unemployment is, of course, slow or negative growth in labor hours. Obviously some part of the European unemployment problem results from output falling below trend, with log output ratios in Europe for 1984 of -8.8 percent, as compared with -5.3 percent in the US and an assumed ratio of zero for Japan. Within Europe, the largest negative output ratios were for the Netherlands (-13.2 percent) and France (-11.5 percent).

Leaving aside questions of utilization, however, it is also possible to look at the implications for labor hours of the underlying trends in output and productivity. Taken together, the output and productivity growth trends imply trends for labor input, shown in columns (3), (6), and (9) of Table 4. Aggregate European trend hours fell in all three periods. However, the European aggregate disguises divergent hours trends among the 11 countries for the 1979-1984 period, ranging from +0.64 percent in the Netherlands to -2.08 percent in the UK.

Table 4 places an interesting perspective on the US phenomenon of rapid hours growth. Part of the US difference from Europe stems from a lower decline in hours per employee (at a rate of about -0.25 percent per year as contrasted with -0.9 percent per year since 1972). However, most stems from faster employment growth. One can view the US's success in achieving rapid employment growth, however, as the counterpart of its dismal productivity record. One can calculate that if the US had achieved the existing growth rate of output in 1979-1984 but had combined it with European trend productivity growth, the US would have had 8 percent fewer hours of labor input, or *9 million additional unemployed* (ignoring effects on labor force participation and hours per employee).

h. Implied Measures of the Wage Gap

We now turn to the estimates of the wage gap. For this purpose we return to the productivity growth trends from [4], which includes changes in the real wage as a determinant of the growth rate of hours relative to output. In Table 5a we display the actual wage-gap index (WG_t), or $W_t - P_t - \theta_t$, which is simply a calculation from the data of an index of labor's share (including self-employment income) and which does not rely

Table 5a - Wage Gap Based on Actual Productivity (1972 = 1.0)

	1963 (1)	1966 (2)	1969 (3)	1972 (4)	1975 (5)	1978 (6)	1981 (7)	1984 (8)
United States	0.979	0.983	1.009	1.000	0.987	0.987	0.963	0.948
Canada	0.996	0.987	1.003	1.000	1.017	0.984	0.971	0.954
Japan	1.040	1.016	0.974	1.000	1.081	1.050	1.008	1.010
11 European countries, of which:	0.985	0.987	0.979	1.000	1.032	1.018	1.011	0.985
France	1.008	0.990	0.991	1.000	1.028	1.024	1.024	1.007
Germany	0.981	0.991	0.974	1.000	1.003	0.999	0.990	0.949
Italy	0.960	0.957	0.964	1.000	1.035	0.999	0.990	0.983
United Kingdom	0.976	0.980	0.966	1.000	1.069	0.990	0.974	0.950
Austria	1.006	1.020	1.011	1.000	1.082	1.116	1.115	1.066
Belgium	0.982	0.996	0.975	1.000	1.031	1.041	1.037	1.005
Denmark	0.950	0.988	0.993	1.000	1.066	1.043	1.060	0.990
Netherlands	0.936	0.972	0.984	1.000	1.055	1.015	1.000	0.943
Norway	0.927	0.934	0.970	1.000	1.036	1.040	0.896	0.860
Sweden	1.025	1.029	1.018	1.000	0.993	1.061	0.991	0.915
Switzerland	1.012	1.003	0.985	1.000	1.038	1.033	1.037	1.041

on any regression estimates. This is compared in Table 5b with the adjusted wage-gap index (WG^*_t), or $W_t - P_t - \theta^* t$, that is, the real wage divided by the productivity trend estimated in Table 2 and displayed in Table 3.

The raw data in Table 5a will astonish readers of previous studies by Bruno and Sachs and others. Since the European unemployment problem emerged after 1972, the wage-gap index is expressed as 1972 = 1.0 (as compared to a base of 1965-1969 for Bruno and Sachs [1981]). Of the 112 wage-gap indexes displayed in Table 5a, only *two* are greater than 1.10, and these are both for Austria, one of the low-unemployment countries. Such high-unemployment countries as the UK, Belgium, Denmark, and the Netherlands display relatively small increases in the actual wage gap (WG_t) index in Table 5a. Of particular interest are the 1984 data: only three countries have 1984 wage gap indexes on a 1972 base equal to

Table 5b - Wage Gap Based on Trend Productivity (1972 = 1.0)

	1963 (1)	1966 (2)	1969 (3)	1972 (4)	1975 (5)	1978 (6)	1981 (7)	1984 (8)
United States	0.976	1.015	1.024	1.000	0.981	0.989	0.959	0.926
Canada	1.001	0.997	0.998	1.000	0.982	0.949	0.885	0.861
Japan	1.107	1.044	1.029	1.000	1.120	1.079	1.033	1.014
11 European countries, of which:	0.972	0.978	0.976	1.000	1.033	1.032	0.995	0.936
France	1.018	1.016	1.001	1.000	1.049	1.041	0.978	0.957
Germany	0.957	0.976	0.980	1.000	1.016	1.026	0.973	0.891
Italy	0.958	0.965	0.979	1.000	1.007	0.980	0.952	0.879
United Kingdom	0.959	0.955	0.936	1.000	1.019	0.982	0.964	0.935
Austria	0.998	1.000	1.000	1.000	1.105	1.130	1.128	1.035
Belgium	0.913	0.936	0.921	1.000	1.110	1.098	1.073	0.996
Denmark	0.826	0.870	0.964	1.000	1.053	1.103	1.069	0.969
Netherlands	0.836	0.876	0.942	1.000	1.115	1.057	0.916	0.786
Norway	0.909	0.911	1.007	1.000	1.034	1.024	0.840	0.759
Sweden	1.070	1.051	1.051	1.000	1.019	1.067	0.988	0.891
Switzerland	1.039	1.012	0.982	1.000	1.080	1.086	1.126	1.130

or greater than 1.01, and these are all low-unemployment countries, Japan, Austria, and Switzerland!

The adjusted wage gap (WG^*_t) in Table 5b displays the familiar "hump-shaped" time path, with a peak for most countries in 1976 or 1978, and a marked decline from 1978 to 1984. The only three countries with a 1984 wage-gap index greater than 1.00 are the same three low-unemployment nations, Japan, Austria, and Switzerland. While the adjusted indexes support the previous research of Bruno and Sachs that has shown a substantial increase in wage gaps between the mid-1960s and mid-1970s, there are numerous interesting differences with the Bruno-Sachs esti-mates. These are summarized in Table 6 which compares the 1966-1975 wage-gap increases from Tables 5a and 5b with the most recent adjusted wage gaps published by Bruno [1986, p. S40] and also Bruno's adjusted wage-gap indexes in 1976 with ours in 1975, both unadjusted and ad-

Table 6 - Wage Gaps, 1975-1976

	1975	1975	1976
	Gordon unadjusted (1966 = 1.0)	Gordon adjusted (1966 = 1.0)	Bruno adjusted (1965 = 1.0)
United States	1.004	0.967	1.027
Canada	1.030	0.985	1.053
Japan	1.064	1.073	1.157
11 European countries, of which:	1.046	1.056	1.115
France	1.038	1.032	1.079
Germany	1.012	1.041	1.108
Italy	1.081	1.043	1.168
United Kingdom	1.091	1.067	1.132
Austria	1.061	1.105	-
Belgium	1.035	1.185	1.275
Denmark	1.079	1.210	1.157
Netherlands	1.085	1.273	0.908
Norway	1.109	1.135	1.168
Sweden	0.965	0.970	1.010
Switzerland	1.035	1.067	-

justed. Looking first just at the comparison of the unadjusted and adjusted wage-gap indexes from Tables 5a and 5b, we note that the productivity adjustment does not make much difference except for the three small European high-unemployment countries, Belgium, Denmark, and the Netherlands. Here, in Table 6, there are huge increases in the wage gap during the 1966-1975 period once the productivity adjustment is applied. We note in Table 2 that these countries all have relatively large elasticities of labor hours to excess growth in the real wage, and so the relatively small increases in the unadjusted wage gap (WG_t) occur because excess wage increases "pay for themselves", raising productivity enough to create only a minimal increase in the wage gap.

The differences between our adjusted wage-gap indexes in Table 5b and Bruno's measures of the same concept display an important difference.

For North America, Japan, and all the large European countries our 1966-1975 increases are all lower than his 1965-1976 differences. Our average index for North America and Japan is 1.008 compared to his 1.079; our average for the four large European countries is 1.046 compared to his 1.122, Only for the small European countries are his estimated 1965-1976 differences larger; our average index of 1.155 can be compared to his of 1.104. This discrepancy is almost entirely due to the Netherlands. If our estimate for the Netherlands is substituted for his, his estimated 1965-1976 index becomes 1.177.

It is beyond the scope of this paper to search in detail for the sources of the discrepancy between these estimates and Bruno's. I would specu-late that the sources involve three areas: (i) Bruno and Sachs in the past have used data from a secondary source, the US BLS, rather than creating their own series from primary national accounts data; (ii) we include self-employment income as part of labor's share, and it is not clear that Bruno and Sachs do so (1); and finally (iii) our post-1972 estimated productivity growth rate trends may be more rapid than those used by Bruno (2).

Table 5b raises difficult substantive questions for proponents of the hypothesis that European unemployment is classical, in the sense that real wages are excessive as measured by the adjusted wage-gap index. None of the four large European countries seems to have experienced a marked increase in the real wage relative to the underlying productivity trend, yet all have experienced high unemployment in the 1980s. As early as 1981, before wage rates could have been held down substantially by negative demand pressure, all four large European countries ex-hibited adjusted wage-gap indexes below 1.00 on a 1972 base.

---

(1) As noted above, there is a reference to the issue of self-employment income in Sachs [1979], but the description is too vague to deter-mine whether his procedures are comparable to ours. The topic is not addressed in Bruno [1986].
(2) My published comments on Sachs [1983] contain a critique of the methods used to estimate cyclical productivity effects and pro-ductivity trends.

The most promising evidence in Table 5b for the wage-gap proponents is the very large 1966-1975 increases exhibited by the three European countries which are both relatively small and which have experienced relatively high unemployment in the 1980s, Belgium, Denmark, and the Netherlands. But this in itself is puzzling. Why should high unemployment be caused be high real wages in small countries, when unemployment is almost as high in large European countries without excessive real wages?

Further questions are raised by the dramatic nose-dive of the wage-gap indexes from 1978 to 1984 in every country, on both an adjusted and unadjusted basis. As our estimated wage equations suggest below in Table 8, there are positive effects of demand pressure on real wages, so that much of the decline in the wage gap in the 1980s can be attributed to negative output gaps (i.e., an actual unemployment rate above the natural unemployment rate). But then this interpretation is completely inconsistent with the "hysteresis" hypothesis recently advanced by Blanchard and Summers [1986] and others. If the natural unemployment rate has marched upward in tandem with the actual unemployment rate, as suggested by the hysteresis hypothesis, then there was *little or no output slack in 1984*, and hence *no explanation* for the rapid downward adjustment of real wages relative to productivity that has occurred in the 1980s. Our interpretation, developed more formally below, is that there has been plenty of slack, and that wage gaps have collapsed as a direct result of output gaps.

Looking just at the wage-gap indexes for the US, Japan, and the aggregate of all the 11 European countries, it is hard to see how the minor differences in these indexes could be responsible for the substantial differences among the three economies in the evolution of unemployment rates since the 1960s. Comparing 1963 and 1984, the US and European adjusted wage-gap indexes in Table 5b are basically identical, and the 1979-1984 decline of 6.3 percentage points in the US was actually less than that of 9.6 percentage points in Europe. The Japanese story seems to have been one of a jump in the wage-gap index as a result of the 1973/74 wage push, followed by moderation that returned the index almost to its 1972 value by 1984.

3. Wage and Price Equations

a. Developing an Econometric Specification

In previous research [Gordon, 1985; 1987], I have shown how a dynamic disequilibrium wage adjustment equation of the expectational Phillips curve type can be derived from static labor supply and demand equations, together with the hypothesis that wages adjust to eliminate any gap between labor demand and supply at a speed that is proportional to the size of the gap (1). The wage-change equation based on this formulation is joined by a price mark-up equation that sets the level of the product price equal to a weighted average of trend unit labor cost and import prices, with an allowance for a cyclically sensitive mark-up. A third equation, called the "reduced-form", is specified as the solution when the wage-change equation is substituted into the first-difference form of the mark-up equation. The model is specified without any lagged wage terms in the wage equation, and so the rate of wage change is "solved out" in the reduced form, which includes lagged price change terms as well as all the other variables that appear in either the wage-change or mark-up equations.

Rather than repeat that theoretical analysis, this paper moves directly to the econometric specification, based on a dynamic theoretical equation that relates the change in wages relative to trend productivity to (i) the expected rate of product price inflation, (ii) the log output ratio, (iii) the change in import prices relative to the domestic GNP deflator, (iv) the total rate of change in three tax rates (indirect, income, and payroll), and (v) a "wage push" factor defined in the theoretical analysis as the difference between the rate of change of the "aspiration" wage demanded by workers and the growth rate of productivity relevant for price-setting (the θ^* term estimated in Table 2 above). The following section sets out the main decisions that are made in converting the theoretical model into an econometric specification.

---

(1) For an alternative formulation that derives a Phillips curve wage equation based on the hypothesis that the rate of change of wages is a linear function of the gap between lagged labor demand and supply, see McCallum [1974a; 1974b].

(i)   Basic format: All equations express every variable (other than the log output ratio variable) as first differences of logs.

(ii)   Expected price change: The expected inflation term is proxied by two lags on the annual change in the value-added deflator. Two lags appear to be sufficient to explain the wage changes without including a third or further lags, while the "zero" lag (current price change) is excluded to avoid simultaneity and identify the wage and price equations (i.e., the current change in unit labor cost is entered into the price mark-up equations, but the current change in price is not entered into the wage equations). This treatment reflects the (structural) assumption that wages can influence prices within the current year more than prices can influence wages, and the high degree of simultaneity between annual changes in wages and prices is attributed to the price-setting process (1). The theoretical wage equation calls for the expected price change term to enter with a unitary coefficient; the wage equations are estimated below with the sum of coefficients on the two lagged price change terms both estimated freely and also constrained to equal unity.

(iii)   Demand pressure variables: It has been customary in previous studies to designate the unemployment rate or its inverse as the sole demand pressure variable. However, in theory it is not the level of the unemployment rate that matters, but rather the excess demand for labor, which should be measured as the *deviation* of the actual from the natural unemployment rate. If the natural unemployment rate has risen, as seems to have occurred in most countries, the use of the unemployment rate to measure excess demand introduces measurement error. The procedure used here is to take advantage of the regular "Okun's Law" relationship observed in many countries [Gordon, 1984; Hamada and Kurosaka, 1984] in the form of a high negative correlation between the log

---

(1) For a discussion of alternative methods of imposing structure on wage and price equations within this context, see Blanchard [1986]. In some of his quarterly wage equations Blanchard imposes the structural assumption that the coefficient on the current price change in the wage equation cannot be higher than a specified amount, e.g., 0.3.

ratio of actual to "natural" output (log Q - log Q*) and the deviation of the actual from the natural unemployment rate. The required natural output series consists of exponential trends running between the benchmark years of 1961, 1972, and 1979, with the 1972-1979 trend extended to 1984 on the assumption that most countries were operating below natural output after 1979 and hence that not benchmark year is available for the 1980s (1).

(iv) Tax rates: Three tax rates are available for each country, indirect, payroll, and income. There are insufficient degrees of freedom to include all three tax change terms in annual equations for the short 1964-1984 interval. Instead, the rate of change of the total indirect, payroll, and personal tax rates is entered as a single variable. The change in the total tax rate (t^T) is calculated at an annual rate over two years, rather than one year, to allow for lags without using up an extra degree of freedom.

(v) Wage push or real-wage rigidity: The theoretical wage change equation allows for the possibility that the "aspiration" real-wage rate rises more rapidly than the rate of productivity growth (θ^*) relevant for price setting; this could reflect either real wage stickiness in response to a slowdown in productivity growth, or an autonomous episode of "wage push" that is not captured by the other terms in the wage equation.

The real-wage rigidity or wage-push effect, which we can call the "excess change" in the real wage, is measured by a set of dummy variables. These appear in the specification of the wage equation below in [7], designated by the notation D_{it}. The first of such dummy variables (D_{1t}) is simply a constant term for the full sample period. The theoretical specification contains no constant term (since the log output ratio is defined as zero when there is no demand pressure that would make trend

(1) Exceptions to this procedure are that 1984 is used as a benchmark year for Japan to take account of highly different growth rates of output during 1979-1984 in manufacturing versus nonmanufacturing. Also, since 1961 was a recession year in North America, the first benchmark is 1964 in Canada and the US, and also in France. The 1961-1964 growth rate of natural output for these countries is assumed to be equal to the observed 1964-1972 growth rate.

unit labor cost - the dependent variable - differ from expected product price inflation). Thus a significant positive value for the constant term would indicate that, on average over the sample period, the change in the real-wage rate is larger than the trend growth rate of productivity, after taking account of the effect of the other variables in the equation (the log output ratio, the relative import price change, and tax changes). Additional dummy variables are also entered for the 1973-1984 (D_{2t}) and 1980-1984 (D_{3t}) periods to test for the excess change in the real wage during different intervals of the sample period. The sum of the constant and the 1973-1984 dummy indicates for the 1973-1979 period the excess change in the real wage (measured as an annual rate of change), while the sum of the constant, the 1973-1984 dummy, and the 1980-1984 dummy indicate the excess change for the 1980-1984 interval. This interpretation of the excess change in the real wage requires that the sum of coefficients on the lagged product price change terms (p_{t-1} and p_{t-2}) is constrained to equal unity. The wage equations are estimated both with and without the set of constants and dummy variables.

In previous research on European wage setting behavior, Nordhaus [1972] identified a "wage explosion" in the late 1960s, and this episode of autonomous wage push was confirmed later by Perry [1975] and Gordon [1977]. To isolate this episode, an additional dummy variable is included in the European wage equations, defined as 1.0 for the years 1968-1970 and 0.0 otherwise. While there have been no wage explosions in the US, the time paths of wages and prices were displaced by the Nixon wage and price controls period in 1971/72 and subsequent post-controls "rebound" in 1974/75. This displacement is captured by a single dummy variable defined as 1.0 in 1971/72, -1.0 in 1974/75, and 0.0 otherwise. The fit of the Japanese wage equations is markedly improved when the period 1973/74 is treated as a period of wage explosion in that country, captured by a dummy variable equal to 1.0 for 1973/74 and 0.0 otherwise.

For Europe, wage-push and controls dummy variables have been defined as follows. For Germany and Italy, there is a single dummy variable equal to 1.0 in 1970 and 0.0 otherwise, to take account of the wage push that occurred during the 1969/70 period (often described as the 1969 "hot autumn" in Italy). In France there is one dummy variable defined as 1.0 during 1968, the year of the general strike and the Grenelle Agreement (and 0.0 otherwise), and a second dummy variable defined as 1.0 during 1982, the year most affected by the Mitterand wage-push policies. The UK is by far the most complicated to handle, particularly in annual data. Following our previous work, we treat the 1970 wage explosion as a rebound from the previous period of "restraint" and define a dummy variable equal to +1/3 in 1967-1969 and -1 in 1970; the second UK dummy variable required at the time of the 1976-1978 "social contract" is defined as +1/2 in 1976/77 and -1/2 in 1978/79.

b. Summary of the Specification of the Wage and Price Equations

The preceding discussion suggests the following wage equation, in which the dependent variable is the rate of change of trend unit labor cost:

$$[7] \quad w_t - \overset{*}{\theta}_t = \alpha_{11} p_{t-1} + \alpha_{12} p_{t-2} + \alpha_{20} \hat{Q}_t + \alpha_{21} \hat{Q}_{t-1} + \alpha_3 (p^F - p)_t$$

$$+ \alpha_4 (t^T)_t + \alpha_5 D^{WP}_t + \delta_0 D_{0t} + \delta_1 D_{1t} + \delta_2 D_{2t}$$

Here Q_t is the output ratio, t^T_t is the change in the total tax rate, D^{WP}_t is the wage-push or controls dummies, and the dummy variables designated D_{it} measure the presence of excess real-wage change for the 1964-1984, 1972-1984, and 1980-1984 periods. The inclusion of the lagged as well as current output ratio term allows the effect of aggregate demand to enter either as a level effect, rate of change effect, or both. In Table 8 below this specification of the wage-change equation is estimated first with the D_{it} terms omitted and with the coefficients on the lagged price terms freely estimated, and then a second time with the D_{it} terms included and the constraint imposed that $\alpha_{11} + \alpha_{12} = 1.0$.

The wage-change equation is supplemented by an equation that explains changes in the value added deflator, based on the mark-up hypothesis, which can be estimated in the straightforward form:

$$[8] \quad P_t = \beta_{10}(w-\theta^*)_t + \beta_{11}(w-\theta^*)_{t-1} + \beta_{20}\hat{Q}_t + \beta_{21}\hat{Q}_{t-1} + \beta_3(p^F-p)_t$$

$$+ \beta_4(t^T)_t + \beta_5 D^{WP}_t$$

The wage-push/controls dummy variables are entered exactly as in the wage equations. In the case of Europe and Japan, the coefficient β_5 might be negative if an autonomous wage push squeezed profit margins, while in the US that coefficient could have either sign since, since the 1971-1972 controls program applied to price mark-ups as well as wage rates.

The final equation to be estimated is the reduced form that results when the theoretical wage-change equation is substituted into the price-mark-up equation. To simplify the presentation of the reduced form, the complex set of lagged coefficients is relabelled (e.g., $\gamma_{11} = \beta_{10}\alpha_{11}$), and several lagged terms that are indicated by the substitution are dropped to save degrees of freedom:

$$[9] \quad P_t = \gamma_{11}P_{t-1} + \gamma_{12}P_{t-2} + \gamma_{20}\hat{Q}_t + \gamma_{21}\hat{Q}_{t-1} + \gamma_3(p^F-p)_t + \gamma_4(t^T)_t$$

$$+ \gamma_5 D^{WP}_t + \delta_0 D_{0t} + \delta_1 D_{1t} + \gamma_2 D_{2t}$$

Notice that the productivity trend term (θ^*_t) drops out of the reduced form, but included are the three dummy variables (D_{it}) that measure the presence of excess real-wage change for the 1964-1984, 1972-1984, and 1980-1984 periods. The reduced form price change equation [9] is estimated first with the D_{it} terms omitted and with the coefficients on the lagged price terms freely estimated, and then a second time with the D_{it} terms included and the constraint imposed that $\gamma_{11} + \gamma_{12} = 1.0$. If any of the three δ_i coefficients were significantly positive, this would indicate that excess real-wage change created an acceleration of inflation, and indirectly an increase in the natural rate of unemployment.

c. Means and Standard Deviations

As a preliminary to presenting the estimates of the wage and price-mark-up equations, Table 7 presents sample means and standard deviations of the main variables for the periods before and after 1972. Without describing all the figures in detail, several generalizations are evident from an inspection of the table. First, rates of change of trend unit labor cost and of the GNP deflator are relatively similar in each period for each country, reflecting the absence of any major change in the adjusted wage-gap indexes. Second, both wage changes (net of productivity growth) and inflation rates are higher in the second period than the first, with the notable exceptions of Germany and the Netherlands (for wage change), and Switzerland (for inflation).

The third observation is that the log output ratio for most countries is positive in the first period and negative in the second (with a close similarity between the US and the European aggregate). Fourth, the relative price of imports was strongly negative in the first period for all countries, helping to contribute to low inflation and low unemployment, while the reverse was true everywhere but in Austria, Norway, and Switzerland in the second period.

d. Equations for Wage Change

We now turn to estimates of the equation for wage change, specified as in [7] above. For variables where a string of lagged values is entered, only the sum of coefficients is exhibited in Table 8, as in Table 2 above.

Two estimates of the wage equation are presented in Table 8 for each country. The first omits the "excess real-wage-growth" dummy variables and freely estimates the coefficients on lagged price change. The second includes the dummy variables and constrains the sum of coefficients on lagged price change to be unity, so the dependent variable is in the form of real-wage growth adjusted for the estimated productivity trend.

Table 7 - Sample Means (and Standard Deviations) for Selected Series
and Periods

	1962-1972				1973-1984			
	trend unit labor cost	infla-tion	output ratio	import defl.	trend unit labor cost	infla-tion	output ratio	import defl.
	(1)	(2)	(3)	(4)	(5)	(6)	(7)	(8)
United States	3.65 (1.38)	3.43 (1.51)	1.06 (2.34)	-0.85 (2.08)	6.16 (1.69)	6.81 (1.89)	-3.20 (3.60)	3.65 (11.19)
Canada	3.38 (1.90)	3.35 (1.16)	0.24 (1.30)	-1.83 (1.34)	7.49 (3.40)	8.74 (2.99)	-2.50 (5.72)	0.48 (5.70)
Japan	4.37 (1.44)	5.14 (1.00)	3.10 (2.36)	-5.02 (3.17)	5.86 (7.11)	5.73 (5.25)	1.82 (1.82)	3.49 (17.92)
11 European countries, of which:	5.02 (1.79)	4.67 (1.45)	0.54 (0.72)	-3.13 (1.23)	8.21 (2.70)	8.78 (1.97)	-2.44 (3.74)	2.07 (8.19)
France	4.61 (1.96)	4.65 (1.37)	-0.83 (0.68)	-2.55 (3.14)	9.51 (2.76)	9.86 (1.74)	-2.78 (4.45)	1.69 (10.07)
Germany	4.44 (2.53)	4.04 (1.98)	0.13 (1.68)	-4.15 (2.50)	3.41 (2.55)	4.35 (1.37)	-3.08 (3.40)	2.15 (7.14)
Italy	6.19 (3.43)	4.95 (2.12)	2.80 (1.90)	-3.12 (1.74)	14.06 (2.70)	15.17 (2.65)	-2.02 (4.60)	3.56 (13.81)
United Kingdom	5.15 (3.59)	4.93 (2.17)	0.93 (1.10)	-1.53 (3.31)	11.26 (5.69)	11.81 (5.67)	-2.87 (4.80)	2.22 (9.84)
Austria	4.10 (1.72)	4.16 (1.52)	-2.60 (1.51)	-3.81 (3.78)	5.99 (3.89)	5.73 (1.49)	-1.74 (3.33)	-0.61 (4.99)
Belgium	4.53 (3.51)	3.99 (1.31)	-0.20 (1.24)	-3.52 (2.29)	6.44 (5.09)	6.69 (2.62)	-0.82 (3.96)	2.97 (6.87)
Denmark	8.25 (3.09)	6.74 (1.15)	1.76 (1.78)	-4.61 (2.52)	8.86 (4.22)	9.18 (1.89)	-2.33 (2.27)	1.68 (8.14)
Netherlands	7.79 (2.67)	5.69 (2.30)	-0.56 (1.81)	-4.54 (2.67)	4.04 (6.10)	6.02 (2.56)	-2.98 (5.75)	2.05 (8.20)
Norway	6.26 (2.40)	5.08 (2.48)	0.61 (1.12)	-3.83 (1.51)	6.86 (3.34)	8.81 (2.50)	-2.87 (4.24)	-1.18 (5.59)
Sweden	4.05 (1.69)	4.76 (1.58)	2.83 (1.65)	-2.77 (1.97)	8.44 (3.27)	1.86 (1.86)	-0.53 (2.61)	2.75 (7.65)
Switzerland	4.75 (2.76)	5.15 (2.13)	1.69 (1.91)	-2.71 (2.49)	5.38 (3.18)	4.37 (2.50)	1.70 (4.12)	-1.56 (9.54)

Table 8 - Equations for Annual Change in Trend Unit Labor Cost ($w_t - \theta^*_t$), 1964-1984

	Sum of coefficients		p^F-p	t^T	Constant (trend) terms			Controls and wage-push dummies	$\bar{R}^2$	S.E.E.	D.-W.
	inflation	output ratio			1964-1984	1973-1984	1980-1984				
	(1)	(2)	(3)	(4)	(5)	(6)	(7)	(8)	(9)	(10)	(11)
United States	1.06**	0.50**	0.04	0.03	-	-	-	-2.47	0.77	0.93	2.59
	1.00(a)	0.59	0.02	-0.29	0.28	0.63	0.42	-2.24	0.77	0.93	2.78
Canada	0.87**	0.25	-0.07	0.53	-	-	-	-	0.63	2.09	2.15
	1.00(a)	0.43	-0.09	0.37	-0.47	-0.68	1.85	-	0.56	2.27	2.15
Japan	0.70**	0.31**	-0.00	0.69	-	-	-	13.84**	0.95	1.17	2.56
	1.00(a)	0.40	-0.01	-0.31	-2.01	-0.93	-1.54	14.78	0.92	1.49	2.37
11 European countries, of which:	1.10**	0.65**	0.10*	-0.84	-	-	-	2.61**	0.82	1.19	1.72
	1.00(a)	0.60	0.09	-1.09	0.46	1.06	-0.94	2.80	0.83	1.15	1.67
France	1.16**	0.77**	-0.03	-1.13*	-	-	-	4.43*(b)	0.72	1.85	1.78
	1.00(a)	0.61	0.03	-1.24	-0.80	-1.32	-2.00	3.64(c)	0.76	1.74	1.86
Germany	0.91**	0.37**	0.00	0.35	-	-	-	5.52**	0.66	1.50	2.06
	1.00(a)	0.22	0.05	-0.04	0.11	0.01	-1.72	6.28	0.64	1.55	2.26
Italy	1.01**	0.54*	0.60	-0.05	-	-	-	1.01	0.70	2.83	1.96
	1.00(a)	0.88	0.01	-0.12	-1.21	1.82	1.72	0.61	0.68	2.91	1.67
United Kingdom	0.90**	0.59*	0.10	0.29	-	-	-	-4.24(d)	0.63	3.39	1.94
	1.00(a)	0.77	0.10	-0.14	0.37	-0.72	1.46	-4.21(e)	0.56	3.74	1.93
Austria	1.11**	0.37*	0.18*	0.87	-	-	-	-	0.67	1.83	1.98
	1.00(a)	0.51	0.25	0.48	2.19*	-1.32	-0.76	-	0.73	1.65	2.24
Belgium	1.17**	0.72*	-0.03	-1.06**	-	-	-	-	0.67	2.46	1.76
	1.00(a)	0.59	0.02	-4.58	5.66**	-1.30	-5.37*	-	0.86	1.58	0.91
Denmark	1.22**	1.14**	0.06	-2.51	-	-	-	-	0.25	3.23	1.54
	1.00(a)	0.64	0.09	-2.72	2.70	-0.70	-2.75	-	0.19	3.35	1.60
Netherlands	0.78**	0.39	-0.08	1.48	-	-	-	-	0.53	3.55	1.24
	1.00(a)	-0.04	0.12	0.03	3.23	-3.25	-6.11	-	0.57	3.37	1.67
Norway	0.76**	0.21	0.08	1.37	-	-	-	-	0.27	2.51	1.53
	1.00(a)	0.31	0.08	0.99	-0.50	-0.48	-0.99	-	0.05	2.86	1.68
Sweden	0.75**	0.30*	0.09	0.42	-	-	-	-	0.53	2.37	2.00
	1.00(a)	0.83	-0.04	-0.20	-2.60	3.39	-1.45	-	0.65	2.05	2.96
Switzerland	0.89**	0.22	-0.07	0.02	-	-	-	-	0.05	2.93	1.53
	1.00(a)	0.36	-0.05	-2.07	0.44	2.56	-4.88	-	0.11	2.83	1.54

(a) Sum of coefficients constrained to equal unity. - (b) Coefficient of second control dummy is 5.62*. - (c) Coefficient of second control dummy is 6.14**. - (d) Coefficient of second control dummy is -9.40*. - (e) Coefficient of second control dummy is -8.68. - * indicates significant at the 5 percent level, ** at the 1 percent level.

In the first unrestricted version of the wage equation, presented as the first line of each pair, some of the coefficients on lagged inflation are below unity and some are above. If "excess real-wage growth" occurs but no dummies are included, then the excess growth in the nominal wage rate relative to price change is likely to be picked up by a coefficient of greater than unity on the price change variable. This occurs in the US, France, Austria, Belgium, Denmark, and the European aggregate.

The coefficients on the output ratio are generally positive and highly significant, supporting the Phillips-curve hypothesis of a relation between the *change* in the wage rate and the *level* of a cyclical variable. Note that, because the current and one lagged output ratio term are included, the specification could reveal either a "level effect" (a positive sum of coefficients) or a "rate-of-change effect" (a positive current coefficient followed by an equal and negative lagged coefficient, with a zero sum of coefficients). The sum of coefficients on the output ratio is insignificant in both versions of the wage equation only in Canada, the Netherlands, Norway, and Switzerland. For all countries, however, the coefficient has the expected positive sign.

An important finding is that the slope of the Phillips curve for the US is very similar to that for the European aggregate. The countries with the most flexible wages in response to business-cycle fluctuations in output (when one examines the average output ratio coefficient in the two lines of Table 8) are France, Italy, the UK, Belgium, and Denmark. The theme in the literature supporting a greater degree of wage rigidity in the US than in Europe or Japan is not supported here. The output response of wage rates is actually greater in the US than in either Japan or Germany.

The wage equations also include the change in the real import price and in the total tax rate. The import price terms have the correct positive sign more often than not but are generally insignificant, except in Austria and the European aggregate. The tax terms often have the incorrect (negative) sign, with no significant positive coefficients. There are significant negative coefficients in France and in the restricted version for Belgium. Thus, these results deny the existence of a significant "tax-push" effect that is responsible for driving up real-wage rates and in this sense conflict with the hypothesis advanced by Tullio [1987] and with results of Knoester and van der Windt [1985].

Column (8) of Table 8 displays the coefficients on the wage push, controls and "incomes-policy" dummy variables. Where blanks are shown, no such dummies are defined. Two dummies are defined for France and the UK, as indicated in the note to Table 8. The dummies are significant and

have the correct sign for Japan, France (except first dummy in the restricted equation), Germany, and Europe. Only the second UK ("social-
contract") dummy is significant, and then only in the unrestricted
version. To interpret these coefficients, they imply as an example, that
in the 1973-1974 period wage rates in Japan increased 14 percent more
per year than can be explained by the other variables. The US wage-
controls dummy variables have the right sign and magnitude suggested
by previous research but are not significant.

The second line of each pair of results displays a version of the wage
equation in which the sum of coefficients on lagged inflation is constrained to be unity, and the "excess real-wage-growth" dummy variables are included (see columns (5), (6), and (7))(1). These coefficients
are almost all insignificant, except for a large positive coefficient for
1964-1984 in Austria and Belgium, and a large negative coefficient in
Belgium for 1979-1984. These results suggest that there is no statistical
evidence to support any generalization that European real-wage increases
were excessive over the post-1972 period when unemployment increased,
except for the isolated wage-push episodes shown in column (8), most of
which refer to the pre-1972 period. Also important for the interpretation
of the European unemployment problem is the absence of a significantly
positive coefficient for 1980-1984, as would be required to confirm the
hypothesis that high unemployment in Europe did not hold down wage
changes as much as would have been predicted from pre-1980 behavior.
The interpretation of the 1980-1984 period receives more attention in our
discussion of the "hysteresis" hypothesis below.

e. Aggregation Tests: Is Europe One Country?

Throughout its history, Europe has been plagued by national boundaries. The Common Market and the EMS have made important progress in

---

(1) In the wage equation with the constant terms of columns (5)-(7)
    excluded, the restriction is accepted by a conventional significance
    test at the 5 percent level for all countries but Japan and Denmark.
    In the reduced-form equations presented in Table 12, the restriction
    is accepted for all countries but Japan.

knocking down national boundaries in the economic, if not the political, sphere. Table 9 suggests that national boundaries within Europe also play little role in one specific area of economics, the dynamics of wage behavior.

Each aggregation test consists of a comparison of the fit of separate wage equations (corresponding to the unrestricted wage equations displayed as the first line for each country in Table 8) for a pair of countries with a pooled-wage equation containing all of the same observations for each country but forcing all coefficients in each country (except on country-specific wage-push variables) to be the same (1). Each aggregation test results in an F-test which indicates whether there is any significant deterioration in fit when two countries are pooled.

24 lines are displayed in Table 9, the first 23 for various combinations of European countries and the last for a comparison of Europe and the US. For every combination within Europe, there is no significant deterioration in fit when two countries or groups of countries are pooled. We start by grouping the small European countries, Austria plus Switzerland ("AS"), Denmark plus Norway ("DN"), and Belgium plus the Netherlands ("BN"). Further groupings in lines 4 through 6 suggest that all seven countries can be aggregated into one country called "Small". Lines 7 through 9 achieve a grouping of the four large countries called "Large", and line 10 indicates that the two pseudo-nations "Small" and "Large" may be grouped together into "Europe".

Several alternative schemes for aggregating the countries are presented in the bottom section of the table. Lines 11 and 12 indicate that the four low-unemployment small countries (Austria, Norway, Sweden, and Switzerland) may be successfully aggregated into a country called "Low", and line 13 suggests that the three high-unemployment countries

---

(1) If there are 21 observations for Austria and 21 observations for Switzerland, then the pooled regression contains 42 observations. However, care is taken to make sure that lagged values for observation 22, Switzerland in 1964, refer to Switzerland in 1963 and not Austria in 1984! Note that the D_{it} dummy variables are not included, since the wage equation used in the aggregation tests is the unrestricted version from Table 8, while the D_{it} dummy variables are meaningful only in the restricted version.

Table 9 - Chow Tests of Aggregating European Countries Using Separate
and Pooled-Wage Equations

Countries or aggregated groups compared in tests	Resulting aggregation	F-test	(degrees of freedom)	Significance level
1. Austria + Switzerland	→ AS	1.13	(6,32)	0.37
2. Denmark + Norway	→ DN	1.88	(6,32)	0.11
3. Belgium + Netherlands	→ BN	1.88	(6,32)	0.12
4. DN + SD	→ SC	1.20	(6,32)	0.33
5. AS + BN	→ TT	0.44	(6,32)	0.84
6. TT + SC	→ Small	2.02	(6,32)	0.09
7. France + Germany	→ FG	2.33	(6,29)	0.06
8. FG + Italy	→ CE	0.75	(6,28)	0.61
9. CE + United Kingdom	→ Large	0.96	(6,28)	0.47
10. Small + Large	→ West Europe	1.86	(6,29)	0.12
11. AS + NO	→ L1	1.03	(6,32)	0.43
12. L1 + SD	→ Low	1.99	(6,32)	0.10
13. BN + DK	→ High	1.96	(6,32)	0.10
14. Low + High	→ Small	2.07	(6,32)	0.08
15. France + Italy	→ FI	1.87	(6,29)	0.12
16. France + United Kingdom	→ FU	0.77	(6,28)	0.60
17. Germany + Italy	→ GI	0.50	(6,30)	0.80
18. Germany + United Kingdom	→ GU	1.89	(6,29)	0.12
19. Italy + United Kingdom	→ IU	2.35	(6,29)	0.06
20. Small + France	→ SF	2.08	(6,30)	0.09
21. Small + Italy	→ SI	0.38	(6,31)	0.88
22. Small + Germany	→ SG	1.39	(6,31)	0.25
23. Small + United Kingdom	→ SU	1.56	(6,30)	0.19
24. West Europe + US	→ NA	3.11	(6,30)	0.017

(Belgium, Denmark, and the Netherlands) may be aggregated into a
country called "High". Furthermore, "Low" and "High" may be aggregated together.

Alternative combinations of the large countries are presented in lines
15-19. Together with the combinations on line 7, all possible permuta-
tions of the four large countries pass the aggregation test. Similarly,
the group of small countries can be aggregated with any one of the four
large countries, as shown on lines 20-23, or with the group of large
countries, as shown on line 10. Of all these tests, only that for France

plus Germany (line 7) and for Italy plus the UK (line 19) come close to failing the aggregation test at the five percent significance level.

While these tests "knock down" national boundaries within Europe, they do not manage to span the Atlantic Ocean, for the final aggregation test of Western Europe and the US fails at almost the one percent level. This occurs, despite the apparent similarity of the US and Europe equations in Table 8, because of the higher import price coefficient for Europe and, more importantly, because of a different pattern of lag coefficients on inflation and the output ratio.

f. Unemployment as an Alternative Explanatory Variable

An unusual feature of this paper is the use of detrended output (the "log output ratio") as the only measure of demand pressure on wage and price changes. How would the wage equations be affected if the log output ratio were replaced by the unemployment rate? Since the definition of the output ratio involves defining the amount of demand pressure in a benchmark year as equal to zero, the specification of the wage equation requires excluding a constant term. The dummy variables in columns (5)-(7) of Table 8 test the explicit hypothesis that, relative to the output ratio, real wages increased faster during specified periods than is justified by productivity growth. However, when the unemployment rate replaces the log output ratio, the value of the unemployment rate is positive rather than zero in a benchmark year, requiring that a constant term be included.

Table 10 exhibits four columns of results for the wage equations of Table 8, estimated alternatively with the current and lagged value of the log output ratio and of the unemployment rate. For each version Table 10 displays the sum of coefficients on the demand variable, the significance level of the sum of coefficients, the significance level on a test that excludes the demand variable entirely from the equation, and the standard error of estimate of the overall wage equation. The specification of the wage equation used for these tests includes the three constants of Table 8, columns (5)-(7), but omits the restriction that the sum of the

Table 10 - Comparison of Using Output Ratio versus Unemployment in Wage Equations 1963-1984

	Output Ratio				Unemployment			
	sum of coeffs.	sig. level sum	exclude	S.E.E.	sum of coeffs.	sig. level sum	exclude	S.E.E.
	(1)	(2)	(3)	(4)	(5)	(6)	(7)	(8)
United States	0.55	0.00	0.00	0.83	-1.43	0.00	0.00	0.91
Canada	0.50	0.09	0.17	2.09	-1.57	0.05	0.13	2.05
Japan	0.28	0.26	0.35	1.30	0.12	0.98	0.86	1.40
11 European countries, of which:	0.57	0.01	0.01	1.03	-1.23	0.00	0.01	1.01
France	0.46	0.05	0.01	1.39	-2.02	0.00	0.00	1.09
Germany	0.29	0.18	0.21	1.46	-0.48	0.18	0.30	1.50
Italy	0.77	0.06	0.07	2.68	-2.52	0.08	0.11	2.77
United Kingdom	0.50	0.35	0.01	2.76	-1.06	0.14	0.26	3.78
Austria	0.51	0.10	0.24	1.71	-1.90	0.07	0.17	1.66
Belgium	0.58	0.03	0.09	1.61	-0.63	0.09	0.13	1.65
Denmark	0.27	0.77	0.85	3.44	-0.59	0.30	0.07	2.84
Netherlands	0.04	0.91	0.97	3.16	-0.27	0.58	0.71	3.07
Norway	-0.02	0.94	0.97	2.54	-0.44	0.85	0.96	2.54
Sweden	0.61	0.19	0.40	2.07	-0.41	0.78	0.89	2.20
Switzerland	0.67	0.08	0.17	2.68	-6.33	0.10	0.10	2.57

lagged price terms equals unity. The inclusion of three constants allows the natural unemployment rate to increase over time and thus satisfies the previously stated objection to the use of the "raw" unemployment rate as a measure of demand pressure. As shown in Table 10, for several countries the standard error of estimate of the wage equation is lower (i.e., better) with the unemployment variable than the log-output-ratio variable (Canada, France, Austria, Denmark, the Netherlands, Switzerland, and the European aggregate).

Interestingly, this test again reveals a difference between the large and small European countries. Overall. the large countries seem to exhibit a greater degree of significance for either demand variable than do the smaller countries, where none of the significance levels in columns (3) and (7) falls below (i.e., is better than) the 0.05 level. The weak significance of *both* the output ratio and unemployment variables for the European aggregate suggests that the insignificance of either demand variable for the small European countries may reflect noisy data. Perhaps the most important result is that for the European aggregate, the coefficients and significance levels of both the output ratio and unemployment rate are basically identical to the equivalent figures for the US.

g. Mark-Up Price Equations

To complete the estimation of the wage-price model, Table 11 reports estimates of the price mark-up equation in the form [8] above. To review, the mark-up equation is specified in first difference form. The inflation rate is regressed on the change in trend unit labor cost (current and one lag), the output ratio (current and one lag), the current rate of change of relative import prices, the two-year change in the total tax rate, and the single dummy variable for wage push or controls. To validate the theoretical specification for the price equation in *levels* of a procyclically sensitive mark-up in *levels*, in an equation for the first difference of prices as in Table 11 the output ratio should enter as a first difference, that is, the coefficient on the current output ratio should be positive and on the lagged output ratio should be equal in absolute value and negative in sign.

The results appear to contradict the hypothesis of a procyclical price mark-up. Of the 14 lines in Table 11, seven indicate a significantly *negative* sum of coefficients on the output ratio (plus an eighth, the European aggregate), indicating a perverse Phillips-curve phenomenon that offsets part of the positive Phillips-curve effect in the wage-change equations. This result can be explained by some combination of measurement error and a substantive explanation. The measurement error, emphasized in Section 2 above, arises from the use of a wage index (compensation per hour) which reflects not just changes in wage rates but also the procyclical effects of overtime pay and of the changing mix of employment toward higher wage industries in boom times. If the measure-

Table 11 - Mark-Up Equations for Annual Change in Prices (p_t)

	Sum of coefficients on current and one lagged change in		p^F-p	t^T	Controls and wage-push dummies	$\bar{R}^2$	S.E.E.	D.-W.
	trend unit labor cost	output ratio						
	(1)	(2)	(3)	(4)	(5)	(6)	(7)	(8)
United States	1.01**	-0.15**	0.04	-0.06	0.45	0.94	0.58	2.29
Canada	1.11**	-0.05	0.18	-0.22	-	0.75	1.76	2.00
Japan	0.79**	0.22	-0.02	1.48**	0.63	0.86	1.45	2.05
11 European countries, of which:	0.97**	-0.22**	0.01	0.07	-	0.94	0.67	1.69
France	0.98**	-0.09	0.04	0.29	-1.67(a)	0.79	1.42	1.20
Germany	0.93**	-0.27**	0.05	-0.08	1.61	0.63	1.02	1.17
Italy	1.00**	-0.26**	0.06	0.18	1.11	0.95	1.34	0.94
United Kingdom	1.00**	-0.05	-0.04	0.03	2.46(b)	0.89	1.84	2.03
Austria	0.80**	-0.38**	-0.03	-0.05	-	0.39	1.33	1.50
Belgium	0.67**	-0.40**	0.23**	1.74**	-	0.83	1.00	2.00
Denmark	0.84**	-0.47**	0.02	0.72	-	0.42	1.53	0.91
Netherlands	0.81**	-0.30**	0.03	0.10	-	0.29	1.82	1.63
Norway	0.93**	-0.19	-0.01	-0.26	-	-0.16	3.36	1.42
Sweden	1.34**	-0.02	-0.11	-0.83	-	0.47	2.10	0.96
Switzerland	0.83**	0.09	-0.12*	-0.20	-	0.80	1.06	1.07

(a) Coefficient of second control dummy is -1.52. - (b) Coefficient of second control dummy is 1.67. - * indicates significant at the 5 percent level, ** at the 1 percent level.

ment error is all that is involved, then the cyclical responsiveness of wages is overstated in Table 8 and that of price mark-ups is understated in Table 11. Only the reduced-form equations in Table 12 provide an accurate indication of cyclical responses.

The substantive explanation suggests that in an open economy in which competition from abroad limits the short-run flexibility of prices, a demand expansion that raises the output ratio and the rate of wage change is reflected only partly in price change, resulting in a positive growth rate of the real wage. Such a result implies procyclical rather than countercyclical real-wage behavior, but refers to the rate of change of the real wage rather than its level. Seven sums of coefficients in column (2) of Table 11 are insignificantly different from zero, and in no case does this reflect any significant zig-zag from a positive to a negative coefficient, as would be implied by a rate-of-change effect of the business cycle on the *change* in the mark-up.

The other coefficients in Table 11 imply that the elasticity of price change to the change in trend unit labor cost is close to unity within the current and subsequent year. Import price changes are insignificant and/or have the wrong sign, except in Belgium. A positive and significant tax-push effect occurs only for Japan and Belgium. Finally, the wage-push and controls dummies are uniformly insignificant, indicating that for Japan and Europe the wage-push episodes raised wages but did not squeeze profits, leaving the mark-up unaffected.

h. Reduced-Form Inflation Equations

Together the wage and price mark-up equations imply the reduced-form equation for price change written above as [9]. This relates the current inflation rate to two lags of the inflation rate, the current and lagged output ratio, the current change in the important price, the two-year change in the tax rate, and the same wage-push and control dummies discussed before. Table 12 presents the results of estimating [9].

The reduced-form equation is critical for determining its natural rate of unemployment, as well as the overall nominal flexibility of an economy. Upward "wage-push" pressure working through positive coefficients on the D_{it} or D^{WP}_t dummy variables in the wage equation do not create inflation or imply an increase in the natural rate if the equivalent coefficients on D_{it} or D^{WP}_t are negative in the price mark-up equation. What matters are the net coefficients in the reduced-form equation. We return to the issue of the natural rate of unemployment below.

The reduced-form also is the final arbiter of nominal flexibility, since flexibility in the form of a high positive coefficient on the output ratio in the wage change equation means little if it is offset by a high negative

Table 12 - Equations for Annual Change in Value-Added Deflator (p_t), 1963-1984

	Sum of coefficients		p^F-p	t^T	Constant (trend) terms			Controls and wage-push dummies	$\bar{R}^2$	S.E.	D.-W.
	inflation	output ratio			1964-1984	1973-1984	1980-1984				
	(1)	(2)	(3)	(4)	(5)	(6)	(7)	(8)	(9)	(10)	(11)
United States	1.04**	0.26*	0.08*	-0.06	-	-	-	-1.49	0.86	0.88	2.50
	1.00(a)	0.33	0.07	-0.28	0.30	0.22	0.54	-1.55	0.85	0.90	2.68
Canada	0.98**	0.21	0.09	0.27	-	-	-	-	0.54	2.36	2.00
	1.00(a)	0.51	0.04	-0.43	0.79	-0.76	2.59	-	0.52	2.43	2.02
Japan	0.63**	0.45**	0.00	0.53	-	-	-	10.24**	0.88	1.32	2.56
	1.00(a)	0.32	0.00	0.96	-1.38	-2.67	2.25	11.91	0.77	1.86	2.05
11 European countries, of which:	1.06**	0.38**	0.09*	-0.58	-	-	-	2.12*	0.83	1.11	2.33
	1.00(a)	0.51	0.06	-0.71	0.07	0.82	0.63	2.25	0.83	1.10	2.12
France	1.08**	0.38*	0.02	-0.48	-	-	-	1.20(b)	0.74	1.57	2.11
	1.00(a)	0.44	0.01	-0.67	0.90	0.22	0.36	0.58(c)	0.75	1.55	2.12
Germany	0.93**	0.09	0.01	0.15	-	-	-	3.18*	0.52	1.18	2.37
	1.00(a)	0.27	-0.02	0.64	-0.27	0.39	1.15	2.75	0.48	1.22	2.14
Italy	1.01**	0.27*	0.12	0.18	-	-	-	1.79	0.87	2.04	2.44
	1.00(a)	0.75*	0.07	0.23	-2.10*	2.91*	1.55	1.90	0.90	1.82	2.15
United Kingdom	0.91**	0.55*	0.04	0.04	-	-	-	-1.52(d)	0.58	3.57	2.11
	1.00(a)	0.95	-0.01	0.08	-0.47	0.62	2.75	-1.66(e)	0.50	3.89	1.90
Austria	0.93**	-0.55	0.08	0.41	-	-	-	-	0.29	1.42	2.06
	1.00(a)	0.33	0.05	0.40	1.16	-2.20*	2.42	-	0.42	1.29	2.22
Belgium	0.85**	0.09	0.18*	0.87	-	-	-	-	0.49	1.70	1.88
	1.00(a)	-0.05	0.25	-1.57	2.72*	-1.51	-3.58	-	0.63	1.46	2.34
Denmark	1.04**	0.33*	0.00	-1.15	-	-	-	-	0.55	1.34	1.75
	1.00(a)	0.41	-0.01	-1.21	0.14	0.38	0.29	-	0.51	1.41	1.77
Netherlands	0.84**	0.04	0.00	0.67	-	-	-	-	0.13	2.01	1.56
	1.00(a)	0.21	0.01	-0.15	1.32	-2.23	2.36	-	0.11	2.04	1.80
Norway	0.93**	0.35*	0.09	0.33	-	-	-	-	0.03	3.07	2.03
	1.00(a)	0.88	0.17	0.07	0.10	-0.03	4.42	-	0.05	3.04	1.99
Sweden	1.18**	0.48**	-0.03	-0.69	-	-	-	-	0.61	1.80	2.03
	1.00(a)	0.93	-0.09	-0.68	-1.16	2.93*	1.38	-	0.70	1.58	2.13
Switzerland	0.85**	0.18	-0.14	-0.49	-	-	-	-	0.25	2.04	1.30
	1.00(a)	0.07	-0.12	-1.79	0.86	-0.15	-1.29	-	0.20	2.11	1.38

(a) Sum of coefficients constrained to equal unity. - (b) Coefficient of second control dummy is 1.96. - (c) Coefficient of second control dummy is 1.91. - (d) Coefficient of second control dummy is -6.74. - (e) Coefficient of second control dummy is -5.61. - * indicates significant at the 5 percent level, ** at the 1 percent level.

coefficient on the output ratio in the price mark-up equation. Column (2) of Table 12 indicates that there are significant Phillips-curve effects of the level of the output ratio in the reduced-form inflation equation (for either the first or second line of each pair) in eight of the 14 countries, plus the European aggregate. The only countries exhibiting wrongly-signed negative coefficients in either equation are Austria and Belgium. Comparing the US with Japan and the European aggregate, the sum of coefficients in the US is lower than in Japan and Europe for the unrestricted version, while both the US and Japan have lower sums of coefficients than Europe in the restricted version. Thus these results support the view that inflation is more responsive to demand shocks in Europe than in the US, but provide only mixed support to the common view that inflation is more responsive to demand shocks in Japan than in the US. In light of current policy debates, it is interesting that the results provide *no support at all for the view that inflation is more responsive to demand shocks in Germany than in the US.*

The other coefficients displayed in Table 12 can be compared with the parallel coefficients in Table 8 for the wage change equations. The coefficients on the relative import price change term are significantly positive only for the US, Belgium, and the European aggregate. The insignificance of the import price coefficients for Japan may reflect the much-discussed absence of manufactured imports.

The estimated controls coefficients in column (8) for the US aggregate economy are similar to those in my recent paper [Gordon, 1985] on the behavior of the US inflation rate in quarterly data, but in the present annual data are not significant. For Japan the 1973-1974 wage-push phenomenon was mostly, but not entirely, reflected in faster inflation, leaving the rest to be absorbed by a profit squeeze. In Europe the only significant wage-push coefficient in Table 12 is in the unrestricted equation for Germany, suggesting that in the other countries the significant wage-push effects caused a profit squeeze and did not cause faster inflation (when wages are solved out as in Table 12).

4. "Hysteresis" and the Natural Rate of Unemployment

a. The "Hysteresis" Hypothesis

The last set of regression results in the paper test the "hysteresis" hypothesis, which states that the natural rate of unemployment is "path dependent", that is, is not independent of the evolution of the actual unemployment rate but rather responds with a lag to the path of the actual unemployment rate. In this paper, which focusses on the equivalent concepts of the natural level of output and the log output ratio, the hysteresis hypothesis states that the natural level of output evolves not along a log-linear trend but with a lagged response to the actual path of output. If valid, this hypothesis would have the important policy implication that the output slump in Europe in the 1980s has reduced the natural level of output, gradually eliminating slack to the point that there is no longer any further downward pressure on wage changes.

Our test of the hysteresis approach can be illustrated in a simplified version of the wage equation included here for expository purposes only:

$$[10] \quad w_t - P_{t-1} = \alpha_0 + \alpha_{11}(Q_t - Q^*_t) + \alpha_{12}(Q_{t-1} - Q^*_{t-1})$$

$$= \alpha_0 + \alpha_{11}\Delta(Q_t - Q^*_t) + (\alpha_{11} + \alpha_{12})(Q_{t-1} - Q^*_{t-1})$$

where once again upper-case letters designate logs of levels, and both the current and one lagged value of the output ratio are included in the wage equation to accord with our basic specification reported in Table 8. The second line of [10] restates the role of the output ratio as entering through the current difference (Δ) and the lagged level.

Let us assume that the unobservable natural output level (Q^*_t) is some unknown weighted average of the linear trends of Table 4 (Q^T_t) and a hysteresis term (Q^H_t) equal to a four-year moving average of actual output:

$$[11] \quad Q^*_t = \Psi Q^H_t + (1-\Psi)Q^T_t$$

To identify the Ψ parameter, we substitute [11] into the *lagged level* term in [10], while assuming that in the difference term $Q^*_t = Q^T_t$. Rearranging, we obtain:

$$[12] \quad w_t - P_{t-1} = \alpha_0 + \alpha_{11}\Delta(Q_t - Q^T_t) + (\alpha_{11} + \alpha_{12})(Q_{t-1} - Q^T_{t-1})$$

$$- (\alpha_{11} + \alpha_{12})\Psi(Q^H_{t-1} - Q^T_{t-1})$$

The hysteresis coefficients (Ψ) listed in columns (1) and (3) of Table 13 are obtained by running the wage change equations from Table 8 and the reduced-form price change equations from Table 12 again with the addition of the lagged $(Q^H_t - Q^T_t)$ term. The term Q^H_t is defined as a trend adjusted, four-year moving average:

$$[13] \quad Q^H_t = [Q_t + (1+q^T_{t-1}) \, Q_{t-1} + (1+2q^T_{t-2})Q_{t-2} + (1+3q^T_{t-3}) \, Q_{t-3}]/4$$

where a lower-case q refers to the growth rate of the output trend for the year in question. The most important finding in Table 13 is that the hysteresis coefficients are insignificant at the five-percent level in the wage change equation in column (1), except for Austria, Belgium, and Switzerland, and in the reduced-form price change equation in column (3), except in Austria, Belgium, Sweden, and Switzerland. The fact that the hysteresis hypothesis is validated only for small European countries having both high unemployment (Belgium) and low unemployment (Austria, Sweden, Switzerland) seems to remove much of the "credibility" of the hysteresis hypothesis as an explanation of high European unemployment, particularly in the four large countries.

Another less formal test of the hysteresis hypothesis is implied by the dummy variables (D_{it}) in the reduced-form price equation. If the constant term for the 1980-1984 period is significantly positive, this means that the existing trend-based measure of the log output ratio predicts too little inflation during that interval, and that the "true" output gap is smaller. The statistical significance of such a shift effect cannot be read from the coefficients reported in Table 12, since all three D_{it} terms cover the 1980-1984 period. Instead, the identical equation was rerun with an alternative set of four dummy shift terms covering, respectively, 1963-1969, 1970-1974, 1975-1979, and 1980-1984.

The coefficients and t-ratios on these 1980-1984 dummy shift variables are shown for each country in columns (5) and (6) of Table 13. Positive coefficients are significant at the five-percent level only for Canada, Norway, and Sweden, and for no other country even at the ten-percent level. Only for Sweden do the two tests of hysteresis concur. We conclude that evidence supporting the hysteresis hypothesis is exceedingly weak, and that our trend-based output ratio series provides the most

reliable basis on which to base an estimate of the natural rate of unemployment.

b. Alternative Estimates of the Natural Rate of Unemployment

The estimates of hysteresis effects in Table 13 should be viewed as testing a very special and limited version of the hysteresis hypothesis. A
hysteresis coefficient equal to or close to unity means that wage and
price behavior is best explained by assuming that natural output follows
actual output with a short lag (i.e., the output gap disappears when
actual output grows at its trend rate, regardless at how low of high a
level). However, a hysteresis coefficient equal to or close to zero *does
not imply a constant natural unemployment rate*. Instead, the null
hypothesis of no hysteresis effect assumes that natural output grows
after 1979 at its 1972-1979 rate. Since the actual unemployment rate rose
from 1972 to 1979, the null hypothesis of no hysteresis allows the natural
unemployment rate to increase from 1972 to 1979 and, for most countries,
from 1979 to 1984 as well.

Any output gap estimate for 1984 (or any other year) can be translated
into an implied natural rate of unemployment by using Okun's Law,
which states that there is a regular relationship between the log output
gap $(Q_t - Q^*_t)$ and the unemployment gap $(U_t - U^*_t)$, where U_t and U^*_t
are the usual percentage rates not logs:

$$[14] \quad U_t = \sum_{i=1}^{4} \eta_i + \sum_{j=0}^{2} \mu_j (Q-Q^*)_{t-i} + \varepsilon_t$$

The first summation indicates that the level of the natural unemployment
rate (U^*_t) associated in a given time interval with the natural output
level (that is, a situation in which $Q_t = Q^*_t$) is estimated by the value
of one of four constants (η_i) applying to the intervals 1963-1969, 1970-
1974, 1975-1979, and 1980-1984. The second summation allows deviations
of the actual unemployment rate from the natural unemployment rate to
be explained by the current and two lagged values of the log output

Table 13 - "Hysteresis" Effects in Reduced-Form Price Equation and in Wage Equation

	Hysteresis coefficient (ψ)				Coefficient on 1980-1984 dummy	(t-ratio)
	wage equation		reduced-form price equation			
	ψ coefficient	(t-ratio)	ψ coefficient	(t-ratio)		
	(1)	(2)	(3)	(4)	(5)	(6)
United States	0.48	(1.57)	0.57	(1.13)	1.32	(1.32)
Canada	0.94	(0.98)	1.12	(1.97)	3.98	(2.22)
Japan	0.24	(0.32)	0.36	(0.70)	-1.83	(-1.27)
11 European countries, of which:	0.58	(0.98)	0.94	(1.78)	2.04	(1.26)
France	0.58	(0.94)	0.86	(1.32)	3.56	(1.50)
Germany	0.23	(0.20)	1.16	(1.44)	1.06	(0.94)
Italy	-0.66	(-0.31)	0.36	(0.26)	2.14	(1.39)
United Kingdom	0.84	(1.37)	0.94	(1.81)	2.83	(0.45)
Austria	0.94	(3.36)	1.28	(3.02)	0.08	(0.09)
Belgium	0.99	(2.57)	1.35	(2.52)	-1.53	(-1.07)
Denmark	-32.11	(1.55)	-1.50	(-0.59)	0.64	(0.40)
Netherlands	1.00	(1.41)	1.19	(0.78)	1.95	(0.78)
Norway	1.19	(1.85)	1.02	(0.97)	6.21	(2.36)
Sweden	0.17	(0.08)	0.81	(2.50)	3.43	(3.48)
Switzerland	1.34	(4.60)	1.28	(3.74)	0.21	(0.12)

ratio. The natural unemployment rate corresponding to a given value of Q^*_t (whether estimated by the trend or "hysteresis" moving-average method) can be calculated from [14] as:

$$[15] \quad U^*_{it} = \eta_i$$

Table 14 compares the actual 1984 unemployment rate with the two alternative definitions of the natural unemployment rate. The first, labelled "trend output", assumes that natural output grows from 1979 to 1984 at

Table 14 - Alternative Unemployment Concepts for 1984

| | Actual | Natural rate of unemployment | |
		based on trend output	based on hysteresis output
United States	7.4	4.0	6.8
Canada	11.2	7.5	9.7
Japan	2.7	2.7	2.8
11 European countries, of which:	9.9	6.2	8.9
France	9.7	6.7	8.6
Germany	8.5	4.5	7.3
Italy	10.2	9.3	10.1
United Kingdom	13.0	8.2	12.7
Austria	3.8	3.3	3.5
Belgium	14.0	14.1	12.9
Denmark	10.5	7.0	9.7
Netherlands	14.0	14.9	11.4
Norway	3.0	2.8	2.9
Sweden	3.1	2.8	3.5
Switzerland	1.2	1.5	1.2

its 1972-1979 trend. The second, "hysteresis output", assumes that natural output is a trend-adjusted, four-year moving average of actual output. The 1984 output gap is translated into an unemployment gap by running the regression in [14] above and then by using [15] to calculate the natural unemployment rate (U_t^*).

The most important conclusion in Table 14 is that the trend unemployment gaps are relatively large in France, Germany, and the UK. Combined with the low statistical significance of the hysteresis coefficient in Table 13 for these countries, this result suggests that there is substantial room for policymakers to stimulate aggregate demand without causing an acceleration of inflation. The marginal significance of the UK hysteresis term in the reduced-form price equation suggests that some weight should be given to the U^*_t estimate based on hysteresis output (12.7 percent), which indicates virtually no slack, and no room for demand expansion.

Another interesting result is that for all the seven small European countries, with the exception of Denmark, the trend and hysteresis versions of the unemployment gap are close to zero. Thus the low-unemployment countries (Austria, Norway, Sweden, and Switzerland) have low natural-unemployment rates by either the trend or hysteresis definition, and the high-unemployment countries (particularly Belgium and the Netherlands) have high natural-unemployment rates by either definition. For the small countries, then, not only are the hysteresis coefficients of Table 13 strongly significant for several countries, but the hysteresis hypothesis is supported in the broader sense that the *best estimate of the natural unemployment rate is whatever the actual unemployment rate happens to be.*

c. Wage Gaps with Zero Output Gaps

An important conclusion of this paper is that wage gaps in Europe have declined substantially since 1978 and are no greater than in the US. Some readers may react, "yes, but the wage gaps are low only because unemployment is high and has held down wages; with lower unemployment the problem of excessive real wages would return". *This view implicitly assumes that the actual unemployment rate has been sufficiently above the natural unemployment rate to exert downward pressure on wage changes.* Its quantitative significance can be assessed by using the wage change equations of Table 8 (second line of each pair) to calculate counterfactual rates of wage change on the assumption that the trend-based output gap was zero in every year from 1980 to 1984. The difference between wage changes calculated with the actual output gap and with the counterfactual zero output gap can be cumulated and converted into a counterfactual wage gap, as in Table 15.

Table 15 - Alternative Wage Gaps in 1984, with Actual Output Gap and with Counterfactual Zero Output Gap

	Wage gap based on trend productivity	
	with actual output (a) (1972=1.0)	with $Q/Q^N=0.0$ for 1980-1984
United States	0.93	1.10
Canada	0.86	1.03
Japan	1.01	1.02
11 European countries, of which:	0.94	1.06
France	0.96	1.05
Germany	0.89	1.08
Italy	0.88	1.16
United Kingdom	0.94	1.12
Austria	1.04	1.15
Belgium	1.00	1.10
Denmark	0.97	1.11
Netherlands	0.79	0.81
Norway	0.76	0.83
Sweden	0.89	1.00
Switzerland	1.13	1.01

(a) Taken from Table 5b, col. (8).

For every country but Switzerland, the counterfactual wage gap is substantially higher than the actual wage gap in 1984. For Europe as a whole, the wage gap is raised from 0.94 to 1.06. The difference is greatest for Italy, amounting to 28 percentage points. However, the calculation does not serve to reveal a "real-wage problem" in Europe as contrasted with the United States. The counterfactual 1984 wage gap in the US of 1.10 is actually higher than the figure of 1.06 for Europe. Furthermore, within Europe there is little relation between the counterfactual wage gaps and 1984 unemployment rates. Low-unemployment Austria's counterfactual wage gap of 1.15 contrasts with high-unemployment Netherland's counterfactual wage gap of 0.81.

5. Conclusion

This paper provides no explanation of high European unemployment. Instead, its results throw cold water on explanations in the previous literature based on high real wages in Europe, or on alleged differences in cyclical productivity, wage and price adjustment between Europe and the US. This dose of cold water comes in seven containers:

(i)   There is no evidence of countercyclical productivity movements in Europe, except in the UK. Actual productivity would temporarily increase faster than the underlying trend rate, rather than increasing slower than trend, in response to a demand expansion.

(ii)   After adjustment for the income of the self-employed, there is no evidence of excessive real wages in Europe. "Wage-gap" indexes on a 1972 base computed with either actual productivity or estimated trend productivity were almost identical in Europe to the values for the US in 1963 and 1984. The slight bulge in the European wage gap that occurred between 1974 and 1978 amounts to only about five percentage points over the US values.

(iii) There was indeed a real-wage explosion between 1966 and 1975 in three small high-unemployment countries (Belgium, Denmark, Netherlands). But the wage gap barely moved in the four high-unemployment countries (France, Germany, Italy, the UK), and in fact increased substantially less than in low-unemployment Austria. Thus the wage-gap concept is almost useless in providing an explanation of differences in unemployment experience *within* Europe.

(iv)   Further skepticism regarding the relevance of wage and price adjustment for the European unemployment problem is provided by aggregation tests. Tests for pooling of wage-change equations across national boundaries in Europe are accepted universally. There are no significant differences in wage behavior within Europe, except for country-specific instances of wage-push or incomes policies. Of 24 aggregation tests that are run and reported in Table 9, there is one single failure: the US wage equation cannot be aggregated with the pooled Western European equation. This result supports the view that the Atlantic Ocean is a valid boundary for comparative macroeconomic analysis while national borders within Europe are not, at least for dynamic wage behavior.

(v) While the US and European wage equations cannot be aggregated, most coefficients in the European wage equation are quite close to their counterparts in the US wage equation. In particular, there is no support for the proposition that the US is characterized by nominal-wage rigidity and Europe by real-wage rigidity. The degree of nominal-wage flexibility in Europe is about the same as in the US, and far from being too rigid, real wages in Europe were too flexible, jumping at the time of autonomous wage-push episodes in the late 1960s in France, Germany and Italy.

(vi) Just as the paper does not explain high unemployment in Europe, it does not deny that the natural unemployment rate compatible with a constant inflation rate has increased substantially since 1972 in every European country. However, output gaps in Europe are not zero. The econometric estimates imply that the unemployment rate could be pushed down by three percentage points, particularly in France and Germany, without causing an acceleration of inflation (holding constant real import prices). With falling real import prices in Europe, as has occurred and will continue to occur with a falling US dollar, there is even less reason to be concerned that an inflationary spiral would follow a stimulus to aggregate demand.

(vii) Some might argue that wage gaps in Europe in the 1980s have been pushed down by high unemployment and would bounce back if unemployment fell substantially. Indeed, we show that, for Europe as a whole, the wage-gap index would be 12 percentage points higher if output had continued to grow at its 1972-1979 trend rate. However, the claim that wage gaps have been held down by high unemployment and low output in the 1980s amounts to an acceptance of one of the major conclusions of this paper, as emphasized in the previous paragraph: Europe has experienced a substantial Keynesian output gap in the 1980s, and not all of the increase in European unemployment is "structural" or "classical" in nature.

150

Bibliography

ARTUS, Jacques, "The Disequilibrium Real Wage Hypothesis: An Empirical Evaluation". IMF Staff Papers, Vol. 31, 1984, pp. 249-302.

BEAN, Charles R., Peter R. G. LAYARD, Stephen J. NICKELL, "The Rise in Unemployment: A Multi-Country Study". Economica, Vol. 53, 1986, pp. S1-S22, supplement.

BLANCHARD, Olivier J., Empirical Structural Evidence on Wages, Prices, and Employment in the US. NBER Working Papers, 2044, Cambridge, Mass., 1985.

--, Lawrence H. SUMMERS, "Hysteresis and the European Unemployment Problem". NBER Macroeconomics Annual 1986, Vol. 1, 1986, pp. 15-77.

BRANSON, William H., Julio ROTEMBERG, "International Adjustment with Wage Rigidity". European Economic Review, Vol. 13, 1980, pp. 309-332.

BRUNO, Michael, "Aggregate Supply and Demand Factors in OECD Unemployment: An Update". Economica, Vol. 53, 1986, pp. S35-S52, supplement.

--, Jeffrey SACHS, "Supply versus Demand Approaches to the Problem of Stagflation". In: Herbert GIERSCH (Ed.), Macroeconomic Policies for Growth and Stability. Symposium 1979. Tübingen 1981, pp. 15-60.

--, --, The Economics of Worldwide Stagflation. Cambridge, Mass., 1985.

GORDON, Robert J., "World Inflation and Monetary Accommodation in Eight Countries". Brookings Papers on Economic Activity, Vol. 8, 1977, pp. 409-468.

--, "Unemployment and Potential Output in the 1980s". Brookings Papers on Economic Activity, Vol. 15, 1984, pp. 537-564.

--, "Understanding Inflation in the 1980s". Brookings Papers on Economic Activity, Vol. 16, 1985, pp. 263-299.

--, "Productivity, Wages, and Prices Inside and Outside of Manufacturing in the U.S., Japan, and Europe". European Economic Review, Vol. 31, 1987, pp. 685-733.

GRUBB, David, "Topics in the OECD Phillips Curve". The Economic Journal, Vol. 96, 1986, pp. 55-79.

HAMADA, Koichi, Yoshio KUROSAKA, "The Relationship Between Production and Employment in Japan: Okun's Law in Comparative Perspective". European Economic Review, Vol. 21, 1984, pp. 71-94.

KNOESTER, Anthonie, Nico van der WINDT, "Real Wages and Taxation in Ten OECD Countries". Institute for Economic Research, Erasmus University, Discussion Papers, 8501/GM, Rotterdam 1985.

McCALLUM, Bennett T. [1974a], "Money Wage Changes and the Excess Demand for Labour: International Evidence on a New Approach". Applied Economics, Vol. 6, 1974, pp. 205-213.

-- [1974b], "Wage Rate Changes and the Excess Demand for Labour: An Alternative Formulation". Economica, Vol. 41, 1974, pp. 269-277.

NEWELL, Anthony, James S. V. SYMONS, "Wages and Employment in the O.E.C.D. Countries". University College London Department of Political Economy, Discussion Papers, 85-24, London, September 1985.

NORDHAUS, William, "The Worldwide Wage Explosion". Brookings Papers on Economic Activity, Vol. 3, 1972, pp. 431-464.

ORGANIZATION FOR ECONOMIC COOPERATION AND DEVELOPMENT (OECD), Yearbook of Labor Statistics. Paris 1971.

--, Labor Force Statistics. Paris 1984.

-- [1985a], Economic Outlook. Paris, June 1985.

-- [1985b], Economic Outlook. Paris, December 1985.

PERRY, George L., "Determinants of Wage Inflation around the World". Brookings Papers on Economic Activity, Vol. 6, 1975, pp. 403-435.

SACHS, Jeffrey, "Wages, Profits, and Macroeconomic Adjustment: A Comparative Study". Brookings Papers on Economic Activity, Vol. 10, 1979, pp. 269-319.

--, "Real Wages and Unemployment in the OECD Countries". Brookings Papers on Economic Activity, Vol. 14, 1983, pp. 255-289.

TULLIO, Giuseppe, "Long-Run Implications of the Increase in Taxation and Public Debt for Employment and Economic Growth in Europe". European Economic Review, Vol. 31, 1987, pp. 741-774.

Sean Holly
Peter Smith*

Compositional Effects and Unemployment in the United States and Europe

1. Introduction and Background

In recent years, labour markets in the United States and Europe have performed rather differently, as can be seen in Figure 1. Whereas in the US unemployment in 1982 reached a peak of some 12 million, or 10.6 per cent of the labour force, and had fallen back to 8 million or 6.8 per cent by the end of 1986, unemployment in Europe, as a whole, has continued to rise. Among the major European countries during the 1980's, falls in unemployment have only been observed in the Netherlands and Belgium, the Nordic countries and for a period, in France and, more recently, in Germany, and during the second quarter of 1986 and into 1987 in the UK. The overall rate has continued to rise to 11.5 per cent in the EEC and 10.5 per cent in Europe as a whole. Employment growth has been similarly disperse. While employment has grown very strongly in the US since 1982, growth in Europe has been much slower. France and Germany had similar levels of employment in 1986 to those they had in 1980. In 1986, the UK was still some 2 per cent below the 1980 level. By contrast, employment in the US in 1986 was 10 per cent above the 1980 level.

Much of the debate in Europe about unemployment has focused on real wage or aggregate-demand explanations of unemployment. However, there is an alternative view which emphasises a number of sectoral aspects of the labour market. In particular, two main arguments have been used to

* The authors wish to acknowledge the assistance of Melanie Roberts in the preparation of this paper and the comments of their colleagues. The research was supported by the ESRC under grant no. B01250012.

Figure 1 - Employment and Unemployment

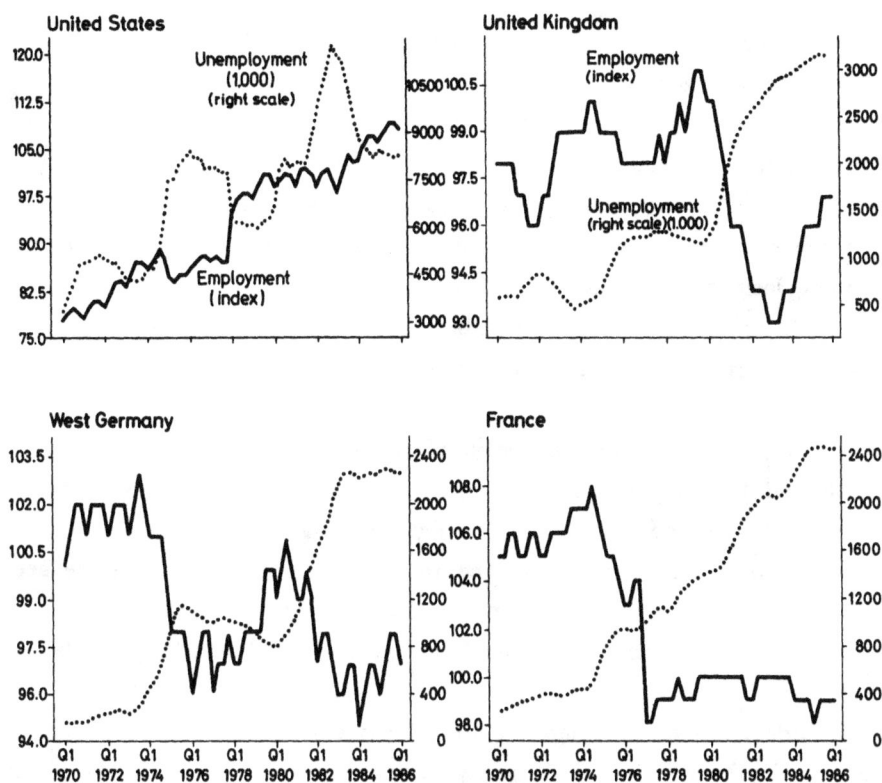

Source: OECD [various issues].

explain differences between the US and Europe. The first is that relative
wages in the US have been more variable than in Europe and that this
reflects the greater flexibility of the US labour market. This flexibility
has allowed sectoral growth in employment which would not otherwise
have taken place. The second argument points to the duration of unemployment and the observation that growth in the number of long-term
unemployed in the total has distorted the operation of the labour market,
especially in Europe. In this paper, we consider these two - possibly
complementary - hypotheses as a way of explaining why experience in
Europe has been so different from that in the US.

2. Relative Wage Variability and Employment

It is often argued that the labour market in the US is more flexible than that in Europe. One reason given for this is that in the US the coverage of collective agreements and the degree of unionisation is somewhat lower than in European countries. The corollary of this implied flexibility is that we would expect both wages and employment to vary more quickly when the economy is subject to shocks. As a causal influence, of course, we must look at the institutional arrangements and the shocks rather than look at relative wage variability on its own, since wages and employment are determined simultaneously.

First of all, we consider the comparative variability of relative wages in the US and UK. In the table, we present a measure of the variance of relative wages in the two countries. The working hypothesis is that relative wages are more variable in the US than in the UK. It can be seen that this is generally untrue for the period since 1971. However, this may tell us only a little about flexibility as the shocks hitting the labour market in the two countries may differ substantially. Shocks on the supply side have been dominated by oil price increases. On the demand side, shocks have originated mainly from changes in government policy and from overseas. Its more open character suggests that the UK economy would have experienced a greater number of shocks than the more closed US economy. The figures in the table, though incomplete, suggest, therefore, that we should be cautious when generalising about the degree of variability of relative wages.

One possible explanation for the relative variability of wages within a country is the level of inflation. If nominal and (expected) real wages are rigid we would expect inflation, both anticipated and unanticipated, to raise relative wage variability. Nevertheless, Hamermesh [1986] has examined the evidence for the United States and shown that higher inflation has tended to result in lower relative wage variability. His results suggest that anticipated inflation has little effect on dispersion. He concludes from these results that downward nominal or ex-ante real-wage rigidity is offset by other factors in the US. It could be, for example, that indexing increases when inflation uncertainty increases. This

Variance of Relative Wage Changes (a)

	1973	1974	1975	1976	1977	1978	1979	1980	1981	1982
US	1.66	0.50	2.01	3.23	1.51	1.02	0.45	1.14	0.99	3.70
UK	9.61	14.23	3.47	1.59	2.46	1.56	1.15	0.94	0.32	1.58

(a) Calculated as var $w_t = \sum_i (W_{it}/W_{it-1} - 1)^2 E_{it}$ where $W_{it} = w_i/\bar{w}$; w_i is the hourly wage rate in the i'th sector; $\bar{w}$ is the weighted average of wages among all i sectors; and E_{it} are the employment shares of the total of each of the i sectors.

Source: For the US - US Department of Labor [1987]; for the UK - Central Statistical Office, Databank.

indexing could be formally incorporated into wage settlements but in a less unionised economy such as the United States it could be organised on a less formal basis. These conclusions are somewhat tentative given that the methods used by Hamermesh have been subject to some persuasive criticism by Pagan [1984] among others. It would however be of interest to have comparative results for the United Kingdom.

While examination of the table does not suggest that variability has increased over time, there is evidence of continuing structural change in the labour markets of both the US and European countries. If we first consider just participation in the workforce, there have been a number of changes which indicate structural shifts in preferences and employment opportunities. The behaviour of participation rates for men and women for four countries are shown in Figure 2. There is evidence of a cyclical pattern in both rates. This is most marked in the UK where the female participation rate has varied by 4 per cent over as many years. It fell 2 per cent between 1980 and 1983 as a result of job losses. Many women, once they were made redundant, left the workforce. The tax and benefit system in the UK discourages married women from registering as unemployed. The increase in the participation rate from 1983 reflects growth in female part-time employment. Much of this has been in the service sectors. There is evidence that these trends have been followed to a lesser extent in other European economies. This has resulted in a

Figure 2 - Participation Rates (per cent)

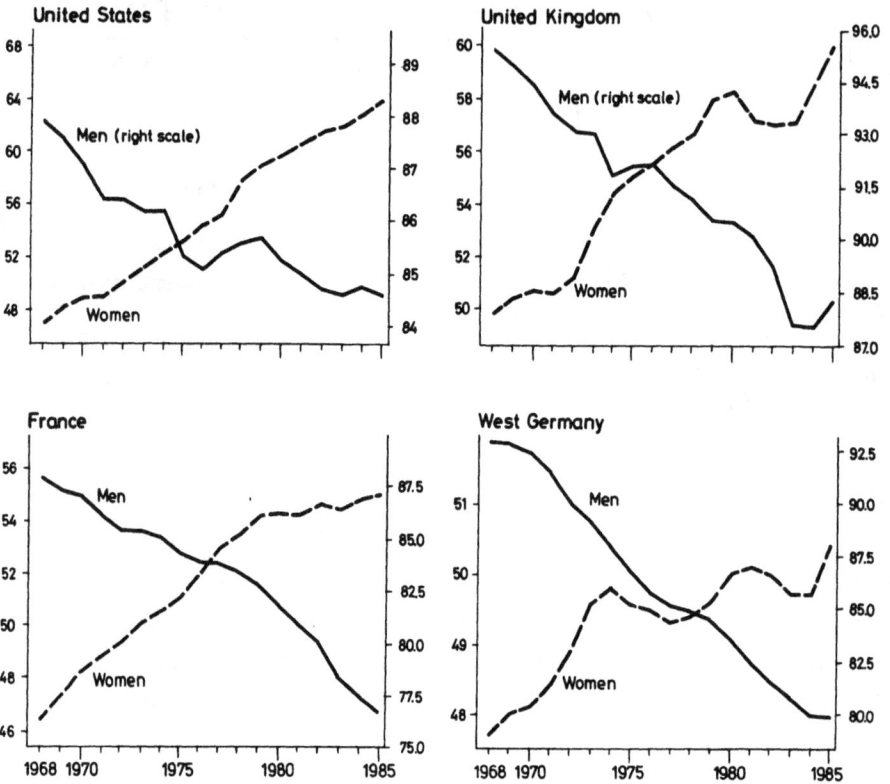

Source: OECD [1987].

period from 1983 onwards when employment and unemployment have risen simultaneously.

The interaction of relative employment and wage behaviour can be observed from the graphs in Figure 3, which demonstrate that much the same patterns of relative employment and wage growth have been observed in all countries. The figures show employment and wage growth relative to the manufacturing sector. In all four countries, the service sectors such as finance and retailing, along with other service industries, have been growing substantially. This reflects the secular movement of manufacturing production away from the US and Europe to other parts of the world, notably the Far East and South America. Relative earnings, however, have not followed the pattern of employment growth. Part of this can be attributed to productivity increases.

One novel explanation for why wage growth is so high in a declining sector such as manufacturing is given by Lawrence and Lawrence [1985]. They show that adverse shocks may in some cases lead to high wages where the wage is set by a monopoly union. In this case the union sets the wage on the basis of the derived elasticity of demand for the firm's output. If the inherited capital stock is quasi-fixed - despite being less productive - the elasticity of demand for labour will fall when there is excess demand and the wage will rise. This explanation is only relevant during the transition to lower employment and wages, but might help to explain why manufacturing wages have stayed high even though the sector is declining.

Other explanations rely on more traditional arguments, and attribute the differences in the behaviour of unemployment between Europe and the US to union/non-union differentials and employment legislation. A second form of explanation, with a more structural basis, concerns the way wages are fixed. Bargaining theories of the determination of wages go some way towards explaining why sector-specific shocks to relative wages can be offset. The dominant model of wage and employment determination in Europe appears to be the Nash model of wage bargaining with the additional assumption that employers determine the level of employment conditional on their expectation of the outcome of the wage bargain. The model is well described in Nickell and Andrews [1983], and elsewhere, and is sufficiently general to be able to incorporate the effects on wage relativities of a monopoly union as well.

In bargaining models of this kind, the union always considers outside wages, either when bargaining with the firm or when choosing its maximal point on the employment function if a monopoly [Oswald, 1981]. Outside wages represent both the welfare of members from previous periods who have lost their jobs and the wages of those competing for jobs with the union in any particular industry. Unemployment benefits perform much the same function for those who are currently unemployed.

Figure 3 - Relative Sectoral Employment and Earnings Development (a)

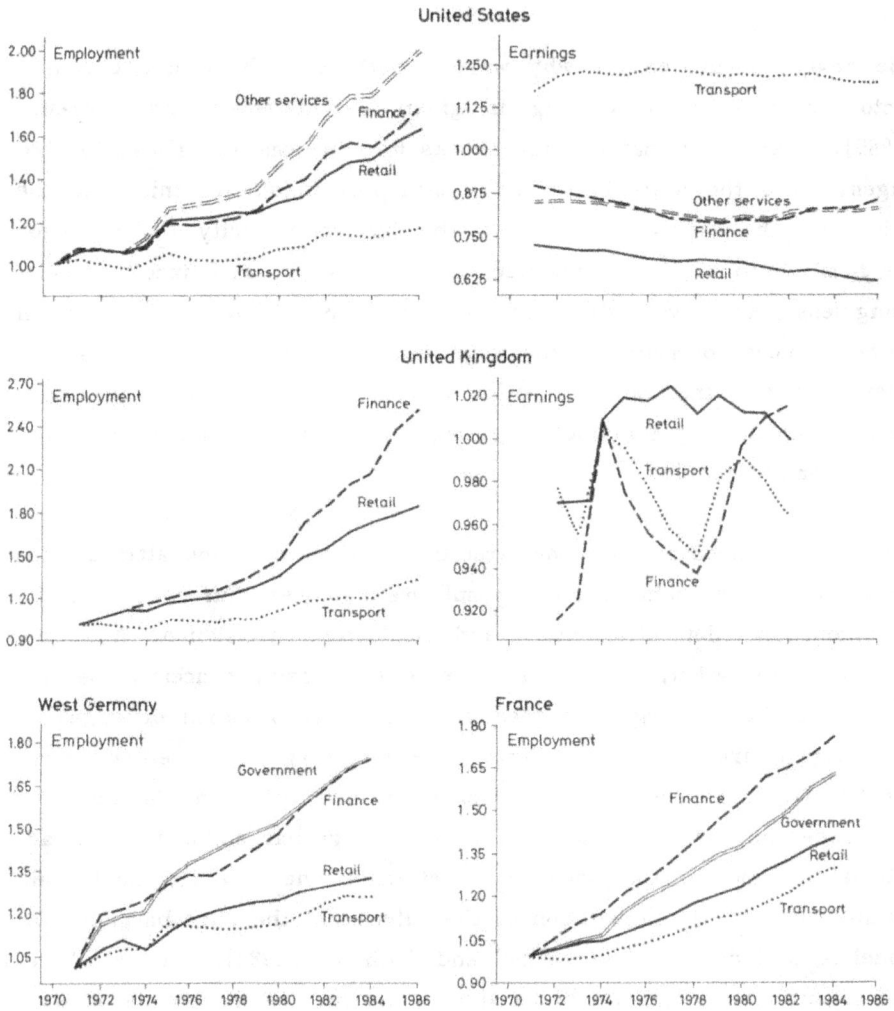

(a) All series relative to manufacturing levels. Employment series scaled, 1971 =1 except US, 1970 = 1.

Source: For the US - US Department of Labor [1987]; for the UK - Central Statistical Office, Databank; for France and West Germany - Statistical Office of the European Communities [1987].

We would expect that increases in outside wages or benefits would always raise the wages determined within the firm. This is because it raises the unions fall-back position in the Nash bargain and thus appears to strengthen the negotiating position of the union. It would then be the case that differences in the wage rise between sectors would tend to be reduced. To the extent that increased wages in one firm due to, say, a positive productivity shock are passed on to wage settlements in other firms, there is less variability between firms than would be the case in an atomistic labour market. This provides an alternative explanation for nominal and ex-ante real-wage rigidity to those described above. Nevertheless, wage differentials can be rigid both upward and downward, and further arguments are needed to ensure downward inflexibility. In practice, it may be that the union can introduce some uncertainty into wage negotiations by making comparisons with settlements which are higher than the average. The nature of wage bargaining in European countries makes application of these comparisons more likely than in a much larger, more atomistic labour market such as in the United States. In the UK for example something like three quarters of wages are covered by collective agreements. In the US, by contrast, coverage is less than one third for blue collar workers and nearer one quarter for workers as a whole. The conclusion is that wage bargaining between unions and firms encourages the reduction of differentials and that this might explain the lower dispersion of wages in Europe.

A second, increasingly popular group of models of union/firm wage bargaining considers the relationship between insiders and outsiders. The models of Blanchard and Summers [1987], for example, show that when the insiders dominate wage negotiations with firms, employment will tend to follow a random walk, since the utility of outsiders has no weight in the objectives of the union. This form of model suggests that the state of the labour market outside of the direct operation of the firm in question would have little or no effect on the wage outcome in the firm. Indeed the model in Solow [1985] demonstrates that, when the firm is subject to positive cyclical shocks, the union will aim to increase the wage paid to insiders rather than expand employment in order to reduce unemployment among the outsiders. These models, however, do explain why there may be a tendency for unemployment to remain high even when there is some expansion of aggregate demand. Thus they provide one explanation for the existence of hysteresis effects in the equilibrium level of unemployment which some think has characterised recent behaviour in European labour markets.

The empirical evidence on relativities in the UK is somewhat mixed. There does appear to be some evidence that settlements in the manufacturing sector lead those in the rest of the economy [cf., Holly, Smith, 1987]. The non-manufacturing sector in the UK is, on average, as covered by collective bargaining arrangements as manufacturing. Leading settlements in any pay round are mostly to be found in the manufacturing sector. In contrast, other work on relativities described in Foster et al. [1986] suggests that the public corporations lead the remainder of the public sector and that the private sector acts independently. Their results, however, do not suggest that manufacturing has led the wage round in the private sector.

Some indication of the degree of relative wage variation which might be neccessary to ensure more employment can be obtained from measures of structural mismatching. A study of the UK and some other industrialised countries by Jackman and Roper [1985] shows that structural mismatch has not risen appreciably since 1979. The indices they use are constructed by taking the variation in the absolute differences between the shares of each sector in total unemployment and its share of total vacancies. A further adjustment is made to offset the effects of neutral changes in aggregate demand. Industrial mismatching, as measured by their indices, after allowing for fluctuations in aggregate demand, increased somewhat during 1980, but other measures changed very little. They also found similar results when the analysis was conducted on a regional and occupational basis. When they examined data for France and West Germany, they obtained similar results with little evidence of structural mismatch.

These results suggest that, although the rate of industrial change is now more rapid, there is little evidence of a greater degree of structural imbalance.

We have examined a variety of evidence which suggests that there have been considerable changes in relative wages in the UK and other European countries as well as in the United States. In recent years, there has been a sharp structural change in the distribution of employment between sectors. Employment has grown rapidly in the service sectors compared with the manufacturing sector. However, unemployment in Europe has also risen sharply. We now turn to an alternative explanation for the pattern of unemployment in Europe which still stresses compositional effects but this time it is the nature of the unemployed themselves which is important.

3. The Causes and Effects of Long-Term Unemployment

The most significant compositional change among the unemployed has been a marked rise in those who have unemployed for more than one year. This can be seen by examining Figure 4 which shows the proportion of the total unemployed for more than one year. This has risen by a large amount in recent years in the four countries we examined. It is most noticeable among European countries, where figures of over 40 per cent for the last year are not uncommon. The contrast with the United States is stark. There the ratio has never risen above 12 per cent even though the pattern over time is somewhat similar to the European countries.

There is now a body of work which provides an explanation for why, firstly, the ratio has risen and secondly what effects a higher ratio has on the operation of the labour market. In Budd et al. [1985], it is shown that the observed rise in the UK ratio is consistent only with exit probabilities from unemployment falling as duration increases. Indeed, in the UK, the exit probabilities only fall significantly beyond one year. It is also shown that the reduced probability of leaving unemployment is due not only to less marketable workers being concentrated in the long-term pool (the so-called heterogeneity effect) but also and most importantly to the effects of unemployment itself (the state-dependence effect). Unemployment itself works in two main ways. Firstly, it affects human capital and the motivation for workers to search for a job and, secondly, there is greater discrimination by employers against those who have been unemployed for a great length of time. Firms may use the duration of unemployment as a signal for worker quality, which can be independent of other characteristics, and easily observed.

Figure 4 - Long-Term Unemployment as a Percent of Total Unemployment (a)

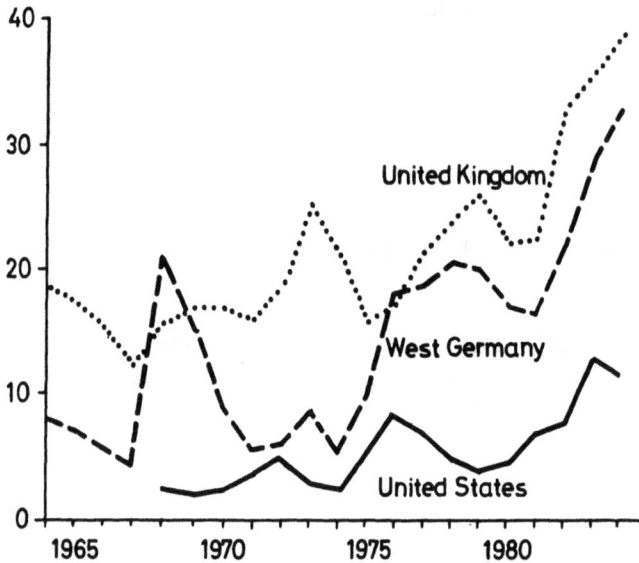

(a) Long-term refers to those unemployed for more than 12 months.

Source: OECD [various issues].

The second part of the analysis concerns the effects of this shift in the characteristics of the stock of unemployed on wage and employment determination. It appears that when bargaining for wages, unions and firms take less notice of the rise of the pool of the long-term than of the short-term unemployed in reaching settlements. It is perceived by them that the long-term unemployed do not represent competition for the jobs of those employed and therefore this group exerts no downward pressure on wage growth. Empirical work reported by Layard and Nickell [1986], Nickell [1987] and Budd et al. [1988] shows that the long-term unemployed have a negligible effect on real wages. Indeed it is hard to discriminate empirically between equations that include total unemployment and those which use only short-term totals. Coe [1988] has obtained similar results for other European countries. He does not find that the results are robust for the United States, though this may be because the ratio of long to short-term unemployment has not varied much in the US.

A second piece of evidence concerns the outward shift over time in the relationship between unemployment and vacancies (the U-V curve) that has been observed in some countries over recent years. Jackman et al. [1985] first pointed out that the relationship appears to have shifted out over time in the UK. This has had the result that the current level of vacancies is extremely high given the current level of unemployment. In Budd et al. [1987] it has been shown that the curve has also shifted out over time in West Germany. By contrast, it appears not to have done so in the United States. The steady-state U-V curve can be shown to be a simple function of net inflows to unemployment from the labour force, and the separations rate from employment and the level of search intensity of the unemployed or discrimination rate of employers.

Jackman et al. [1985] show that the only plausible explanation for this shift is a continuous fall over time in the average rate of search intensity. This can be given another interpretation by observing that the proportion of those with lower search intensities, or who suffer greater discrimination from employers, has risen over the same period. In Budd et al. [1985] some three quarters of the shift in the U-V curve since 1975 can be explained by the relative rise in the number who have been unemployed for more than one year.

4. Conclusions

In this paper we have considered a number of explanations for the con-trasting performance of Europe and the United States. Our evidence suggests that the differences between Europe and the United States can be attributed to a number of factors, some of which are compositional. In particular, if, due to a variety of institutional factors, labour markets do not respond as quickly as those in the United States, a shock to the European economies is more likely to raise the trend level of unemploy-ment because during the transition some of those who become unemployed will suffer sufficient damage to their human capital or become sufficiently discouraged that they become more likely to remain unemployed even after the economy has adjusted. Thus, even if a shock to the economy is entirely cyclical and does not require any structural adjustments in the form of changes in relative prices, there will be a tendency for the core of the unemployed to increase if there is a succession of adverse shocks which depress aggregate demand. Thus, the more flexibly the labour market can be made to work the less likely that those temporarily unemployed will fall over the threshold into more permanent unemployment. Equally, timely fiscal and monetary policies can help to offset the cyclical fluctuations in economic activity which create the conditions in which those made redundant because of a downturn in the economy drift into structural unemployment.

Bibliography

BLANCHARD, Olivier, Lawrence H. SUMMERS, "Hysteresis in Unemployment". European Economic Review, Vol. 31, 1987, pp. 288-295.

BUDD, Alan P., Paul L. LEVINE, Peter N. SMITH, Unemployment, Vacancies and the Long-Term Unemployed. Centre for Economic Forecasting, London Business School Discussion Papers, 154, London 1985.

--, --, --, "Long-Term Unemployment and the Shifting U-V Curve". European Economic Review, Vol. 31, 1987, pp. 296-305.

--, --, --, "Real Wage Adjustment and Long-Term Unemployment". In: Rod CROSS (Ed.), Unemployment, Hysteresis and the Natural Rate Hypothesis. Oxford 1988.

COE, David, "Phillips Curve Estimates Incorporating a Natural Rate with Hysteresis Effects". In: Rod CROSS (Ed.), Unemployment, Hysteresis and the Natural Rate Hypothesis. Oxford 1988.

FOSTER, Nigel, S.G. Brian HENRY, Chris TRINDER, Public and Private Sector Pay: Some Further Results. Centre for Labour Economics, London School of Economics, Discussion Papers, 267, London 1986.

HAMERMESH, Daniel S., "Inflation and Labour Market Adjustment". Economica, Vol. 53, 1986, pp. 63-73.

HOLLY, Sean, Peter N. SMITH, "A Two-Sector Analysis of the UK Labour Market". Oxford Bulletin of Economics and Statistics, Vol. 49, 1987, pp. 79-102.

JACKMAN, Richard, Stephen ROPER, "Structural Unemployment". Centre for Labour Economics, London School of Economics, Discussion Papers, 223, London 1985.

--, Richard LAYARD, Christopher PISSARIDES, On Vacancies. Centre for Labour Economics, London School of Economics, Discussion Papers, 165, London 1985.

LAWRENCE, Colin, Robert LAWRENCE, "Manufacturing Wage Dispersion: An End Game Interpretation". Brookings Papers on Economic Activity, 1985, pp. 47-106.

LAYARD, Richard, Stephen NICKELL, "Unemployment in Britain". Economica, Vol. 53, 1986, pp. S121-S169.

NICKELL, Stephen, Martyn ANDREWS, "Unions, Real Wages and Employ-ment in Britain 1951-79". Oxford Economic Papers, Vol. 35, 1983, pp. 183-206.

--, "Why Is Wage Inflation in Britain so High?". Oxford Bulletin of Economics and Statistics, Vol. 49, 1987, pp. 103-128.

ORGANIZATION FOR ECONOMIC COOPERATION AND DEVELOPMENT (OECD), Labour Force Statistics 1965-1985. Paris 1987.

--, Main Economic Indicators. Paris, various issues.

OSWALD, Andrew, "Trade Unions, Wages and Employment: What Can Simple Models Tell Us?". Oxford Economic Papers, Vol. 34, 1982, pp. 526-545.

PAGAN, Adrian R., "Econometric Issues in the Analysis of Regressions with Generated Regressors". International Economic Review, Vol. 25, 1984, pp. 221-247.

SOLOW, Robert M., "Insiders and Outsiders in Wage Determination". Institute for International Economic Studies, Seminar Papers, 323, Stockholm 1985.

STATISTICAL OFFICE OF THE EUROPEAN COMMUNITIES, Eurostat Review 1976-1985. Luxembourg 1987.

US DEPARTMENT OF LABOR, Employment and Earnings. Washington 1987.

Comments on Robert J. Gordon, "Wage Gaps versus Output Gaps: Is There a Common Story for All of Europe?" and Sean Holly and Peter Smith, "Compositional Effects and Unemployment in the United States and Europe"

Gerd Hansen

The paper by R o b e r t   G o r d o n is an interesting piece of work in several respects. It contains new ideas as well as new results. It is not possible to refer to all points made in the paper. Therefore, I would like to restrict myself to some critical remarks on his basic ideas.

It is the objective of the wage-gap concept to measure a *disequilibrium* real-wage rate and its effect on employment (or unemployment). The theory is designed to explain the observation that (especially in manu-facturing) the real-wage rate has grown faster than the productivity in several countries and therefore the labor income share has increased. The question arises if this observation is compatible with equilibrium changes in labor demand. The answer depends on the assumption with respect to technology and the definition of equilibrium.

Gordon starts out from the conditional labor-demand function resulting from a CES-production function with nonconstant returns to scale and labor-augmented technical progress. In log terms, this labor demand equation can be written as labor's income share S_L depending on output Q and the difference between real wage (w-p) and technical progress $\overset{*}{\theta} \cdot t$

[1] $S_L = A + (\phi - 1) Q_t + (1 - \sigma) [(w - p) - \overset{*}{\theta} \cdot t]$

with $\phi = (1 - \sigma + \sigma v)/v$; σ = elasticity of substitution i and
v = elasticity to scale.

The output variable disappears with constant returns to scale ($v = 1$).

There are three novelties in Gordon's approach:

(i) Instead of assuming long-run nonconstant returns to scale he allows only for short-run nonconstant returns to scale by substituting the output gap $Q-Q^*$ for output Q in [1]. This measures the required disequilibrium component in the time path of S_L.

From a theoretical point of view, the assumption is reasonable with respect to the fact that the rate of technical progress θ^* accounts for the long-run productivity increase. Long-run nonconstant returns to scale will measure the same shifts in the isoquants, if Q^* grows at a constant rate. But if normal output Q^* is a linear trend through all observations of output Q, one will get the same results by estimating the share equation with output Q instead of the output gap $Q-Q^*$.

Therefore, in order to make the approach useful, the equilibrium output path Q^* has to be defined in a different way. This is done by estimating Q^* from a benchmark-trend through 1961, 1972, 1979 which is extrapolated up to 1984. The implied assumption is that output (and unemployment) in these years is due to the natural rate – in all countries – and that changes in trend output Q^* after 1979 reflect changes in the natural rate. This is a rather strong assumption. One may ask how sensitive the estimates are with respect to this assumption. I would suggest to use at least for the purpose of comparison the much simpler equation with Q instead of $Q-Q^*$.

A second point is that Gordon's definition of normal output Q^* differs from full employment output calculated by means of the underlying production function. It seems to be better to calculate the wage gap from the first-order condition at full employment as well as the full employment output calculated from the production function [cf., Artus, 1984].

Furthermore, one may question the weak separability assumption with respect to materials and energy on the one hand and labor and capital on the other implied by the CES function for value added. Especially with respect to the energy price shock the elasticity of substitution may have changed.

(ii)   The second novelty is that Gordon allows for shifts in productivity growth after 1973 by introducing a dummy variable. This shift may again depend on his measure of the output gap.

(iii)   The third novelty is the fact that his calculation of the labor-income share includes the estimated income of the self-employed. In the official statistics, this component is part of the profit income. The wage-gap index based on actual productivity (= the labor income share index) given in Table 5a shows that there is only little variation in the labor share for most countries. The result that no wage gap is present in most countries depends mainly on this data set, because the observation the wage-gap approach tries to explain does not show up in the data.

The main shortcoming of the wage-gap concept lies in the unspecified labor supply. The wage-gap approach defines the equilibrium real-wage rate as a point on the labor-demand function only. The actual real-wage rate is *exogenous* and not determined on the labor market as it would be in the classical market-clearing approach. In that case, employment as well as real wages are simultaneously determined by exogenous variables affecting labor supply and labor demand such as - for example - the increase in the working population and labor participation which are important factors in Germany. Here, the labor force increased after 1979 by one million, the same as the increase in the number of unemployed.

Gordon refers to this subject in the second part of the paper by specifying a Phillips curve assuming that either nominal or real wage-rate changes eliminate the gap between labor supply and labor demand. But supply shocks from an increasing population and labor participation are *not* taken into account in his specification.

The main idea is to use the output gap instead of the unemployment rate as a measure of labor-market disequilibrium in order to avoid the assumption of a constant natural rate of unemployment. Later on, it is converted back by an Okun's law regression in order to calculate the natural rate of unemployment. The question is if this switching forth and back does really improve the results. A comparison with both measures of disequilibrium shows that, for most countries, the significance of the unemployment rate is still higher (see Table 10). For Germany, the long-run effect of the unemployment rate on wage is -0.48.

The effect of the output gap on real wages is smaller and, *more import-antly, it is offset* by the negative effect of the output gap in the mark-up price equation for Germany. The price/output-gap function for Germany is therefore horizontal. Nevertheless, Gordon uses these esti-mates to calculate a tremendous natural rate of unemployment. It is ob-vious that the horizontal Phillips curve does not fit the observed price/unemployment figures at least for Germany. The negative effect of the output gap on prices and its insignificance in the reduced form equation has to be explained.

In my opinion, it might depend on the fact that the mark-up is built on *normal instead of actual* unit labor cost, whereas in Germany increasing prices go along with decreasing capacity utilisation. On the other hand, lagged prices have a sum of coefficients near unity in the reduced-form price-equation which makes it rather difficult to calculate the long-run tradeoff between prices and output.

My last critical point refers to the aggregation of the European coun-tries. This is done in a step by step way controlling the Type I error on each of these steps. As a result, the overall aggregation may have a much higher Type I error as - for example - 5 or 10 percent. Further-more the result is not path independent. There should be at least a check of the overall significance at the end. I suppose that such a test will reject the aggregation.

I agree with the conclusion that the wage-gap concept is useless in pro-viding an explanation for unemployment, but *because of the missing labor supply shocks* and not because of the results given in the paper which are not shown to be robust with respect to the specific assump-tions and data. This is also supported by the range of different natural rates of unemployment and wage gaps given in Table 14 of the paper. The natural rate of unemployment for Germany is 4.5 percent or (under hysteresis output) 7.3 percent.

I like the paper by S e a n   H o l l y   and   P e t e r   S m i t h be-cause it looks more at the details of the unemployment problem. We have got more information on unemployment than just the rate of unemployment. Why do we not use this information? In this respect the paper goes in the right direction.

My first comment refers to the Table in the paper. Comparing these data with the following coefficients of variation, calculated by the US Bureau of Labor Statistics for 1975 and 1982, I would draw just the opposite conclusion. These differences probably refer to a different sectoral breakdown or a different weighting. But they have to be explained in any case.

Wage dispersion, 1975 and 1982 (US $)

	United States		United Kingdom		Germany	
	1975	1982	1975	1982	1975	1982
Mean	6.35	11.63	3.26	6.80	6.19	10.44
Standard deviation	2.32	5.48	0.61	1.85	1.19	3.06
Coefficient of variation	0.37	0.47	0.21	0.27	0.19	0.29

Note: The means, standard deviations, and coefficients of variation are computed using a sample of nine industries: apparel, textiles, iron and steel, motor vehicles, chemicals, leather, paper, electrical equipment, and electrical machinery.

Source: See Pauly [1985].

With respect to the explanation of high wages in declining industries, I believe that the main reason is that less productive workers (low-wage workers) are dropped out first, which changes the average wage. It is this structural change within declining industries which has to be analysed more carefully. Actually, trade unions still try to reduce the wage differentials, neglecting the fact, that this can only be done by reducing the (marginal) productivity differentials.

What is missing in the paper is an analysis of the employment effects of sectoral wage variability. The only work I know is a study by Pauly [1986] using the ARCH model to estimate the employment effects. His results show that the conditional variance of absolute wage increases have a significant effect on the rate of change of manhours in the respective sector relative to the average rate of change in manhours. But the effect of this variable on total employment is small compared with the total change of employment observed since 1980 especially in the US.

My last point refers to causes and effects on long-term unemployment. It is obvious that increasing unemployment cannot move along with a constant duration of unemployment. By definition the duration in months (= unemployed/exits from unemployment per month) is the inverse exit probability from unemployment per month. It is by definition and not by a causal relation that an increase in duration goes along with a decrease in the exit probability. To put this another way: increasing unemployment and constant duration are only compatible if the exit probability increases as fast as unemployment. Furthermore, it is not surprising that exit probabilities depend negatively on the duration of unemployment. This is not a causal relation but a spurious correlation. I suppose that one will find bad skills, regional immobility and so forth behind the different durations and exit probabilities. The relation between exit probabilities and duration is therefore not supposed to be constant over time. But if there is a certain duration which corresponds to significantly reduced exit probabilities, this provides good information to measure the natural rate of unemployment in a more sophisticated way.

Despite this criticism, I agree with the conclusion that the government should concentrate on reducing the number of long-term unemployed by improving skills and mobility and by stabilizing cyclical fluctuations by means of fiscal and monetary policies.

Bibliography

ARTUS, Jacques R., The Disequilibrium Real Wage Rate Hypothesis: An Empirical Evaluation. International Monetary Fund, Staff Papers, Vol. 31, 1984, pp. 249-302.

PAULY, P., Sectoral Wages and Employment: A Comparative Analysis for Germany and the U.S. Paper presented at the Annual Meeting of the German Statistical Society, Bonn, September 1985.

--, Wage Dispersion and Unemployment: Europe, Japan and the U.S. University of Pennsylvania, Discussion Papers, Philadelphia, April 1986.

Patrick Minford

I welcome, as always, R o b e r t   G o r d o n' s careful use of data and his irreverence towards accepted notions. His paper deals with a number of issues, including wage-gap measures, the growth of productivity, wage equations with associated measures of the natural rate of unemployment, and price equations. I have most to say about the third.

The wage gap literature attempts to estimate the gap between actual wages and "warranted" wages (i.e., those that would be consistent with full employment); this estimate is then used to explain actual unemployment. The idea is that, if economies are on their demand curves for labour, then unemployment will be explained by the wage gap; this is "classical" unemployment. It is possible they are *below* their demand curve, in which case unemployment is "Keynesian" and will not be explained by the wage gap. So the unemployment/wage-gap regressions test whether unemployment is classical or Keynesian.

The problems arise in measurement of the wage gap which is inherently difficult in the postulated disequilibrium world; both supply and demand curves, neither of which may be directly observed at any point in time, must be identified and estimated to find out both where the economy currently stands and its full employment equilibrium. The usual stopgap measure of the gap is the wage share in "full employment" GNP relative to some "normal" base year.

As Gordon notes, while the *actual* wage share will depend on the elasticity of substitution, the adjustment onto a full employment basis (which, in the Cobb-Douglas case, involves multiplying the actual wage share by the ratio of full employment productivity to actual productivity) can yield wildly different measures, even if one accepts that full employment productivity corresponds to "trend" productivity, which will not in general be the case when the trend in the natural rate is not towards full employment. Though much used, especially by Bruno and Sachs, the measure cannot substitute for a full model of the labour market; nor in any case does it shed any light on *why* wages are excessive, which is the major area of policy interest.

Gordon's examination of productivity behaviour is carried out in the course of establishing his wage-gap measures. His decomposition of productivity growth into output utilisation, wage-induced, and trend components is useful descriptive time-series work, as intended; understandably, the deeper issue of what triggers changes in trend productivity is not tackled here. The problem is that without such an identification the allocation of changes to trend and other factors is fairly arbitrary.

It is on the crucial wage equations that I have problems. Gordon starts from a disequilibrium dynamic wage adjustment equation; for excess demand he uses output deviations from trend instead of unemployment, in order to allow for changes in the natural rate. Apart from expected inflation, which he proxies by lagged inflation (in *annual* data), he postulates an ad hoc further adjustment mechanism in which labour market agents allow for changing import prices, tax rates, "wage push", and productivity growth.

While this is supposedly a disequilibrium adjustment equation, it is unclear why the adjustment paths of real wages should be affected by these factors. In particular "cost push" will surely add to disequilibrium and not be a factor affecting its rate of removal? In a disequilibrium framework real wages are supposedly being marked up or down by Marshallian sellers of labour who respond to excess stocks. This is not a bargaining model where unions and/or firms are setting real wages, nor a labour supply curve by atomistic workers (if so productivity should not enter). Yet somehow Gordon wants to incorporate elements from these other two frameworks into his wage equations; so he does it by a backdoor through this "adjustment" mechanism.

It seems to me that Gordon must have in mind essentially a bargaining framework much as in Bean et al. [1987]; the market is driving real wages towards some exogenously determined equilibrium real wage. But if it is, then the equation should contain a lagged real wage and the arguments of the equilibrium real wage level, so that it specifies a deterministic equilibrium.

Attempting to interpret the empirical results, I am first struck by how many dummies we have here. For wage/price controls this is fair enough; best practice, if not a counsel of perfection. But for wage push, widespread efforts have been made by now (see for example references in my comment on Holly and Smith on the following pages) to identify the constituent factors - unions, benefits, taxes and so forth. Why should we take Gordon's personal choice of dummies instead?

Secondly, the use of two years' lagged inflation in place of forward-looking inflation expectations seems indefensible; at the very least current inflation must influence current wage settlements. More generally, lag structures on inflation will shift around as regimes shift - notably the move from fixed to floating rates in the early 1970s.

All these difficulties make one sceptical of Gordon's empirical conclusions.

He finds the slope of the US and European Phillips curves (i.e., the coefficients on output deviations) very similar. Other studies have generally found Europe's real wages *more* responsive to cyclical variation than those in America - [cf., Grubb et al., 1982; Minford et al., 1986]. Gordon argues this is because his data are on economy-wide wages as opposed to the manufacturing wages generally used by others; in view of all the other differences in Gordon's specification and the well-known correlation between wages in different sectors, I am doubtful.

He finds that real wages were not generally "excessive" (this tallies with his earlier wage-gap analysis). But nevertheless he presents natural rates of unemployment, U^*, which have grown sharply. The two positions are contradictory. His test for excessive real-wage growth has low power, based as it is on dummies entered in the wage equation alongside all the other arbitrary elements of the specification. His estimates of U^* assume that $U = U^*$ when $y = y^*$; this is a frequent assumption but $U - U^*$ may lag well behind $y - y^*$. For the UK, I have found it does.

He finds no evidence of hysteresis. But again the test he uses has low power (he enters actual output in the equation to see whether trend output is following actual output) because of doubts over specification; in particular, the split time trends, calculated by the peak-to-peak method, already embody a response to actual output.

Gordon finally argues that even *nominal* wage rigidity is the same in Europe and the US, in spite of plenty of evidence that European in-dexation has produced rapid nominal wage adjustment, as compared with the US where contracts still seem to dominate. This peculiar result must be due to his exclusion of inflation from the equation.

Overall, Gordon has brought an interesting new data set to bear on an important area; this is very welcome. But his methods to date leave a lot of questions unanswered; and it is hard to regard the major empirical claims made in this work to date with anything other than scepticism.

The paper by S e a n   H o l l y and P e t e r   S m i t h examines two hypotheses: firstly, that lesser relative wage variability in Europe is a cause of its higher unemployment, and secondly that the long-term unemployed in the UK are "outsiders" who do not affect wage behaviour. The authors find no evidence for the first, but Phillips curves for the UK lead them to support the second and to advocate on this basis pol-icies of reflation "targeted" on the long-term unemployed.

In spite of the paper's professional execution, I found it superficial in its treatment of these hypotheses.

Illustration of Possible Developments in Europe

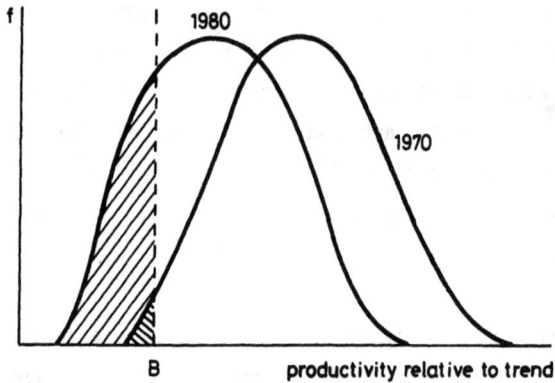

Take Europe's wage variability and unemployment. The authors seem to have missed the point of the argument which is that wage *differentials* have been narrowed - by government regulations, minimum wages, benefits, unions and so forth - and that this has raised unemployment at the bottom end of the labour market. Narrowing differentials would not obviously be associated with less relative wage *variability*, as interpreted in this paper; for example, differentials could widen smoothly in the US giving rise to little variability (or narrow with fluctuations in Europe giving more variability), nevertheless the cumulative US gap between top and bottom could increase substantially over a decade, say, relative to Europe.

What may well have happened in Europe is pictured in the figure, which shows a frequency distribution of the labour force across its marginal productivity (de-trended); B represents the level of social support benefits for the unemployed in terms of gross wage equivalent (i.e., it is the cost to an employer of hiring someone while giving him the same utility as he would have had, if unemployed on benefits). Those to the left of B will be long-term unemployed because their reservation wage, B, will exceed their marginal product. During the 1970s and early 1980s, Europe appears to have suffered a productivity slowdown, but growth in social support levels appears to have slowed *less*. Thus, the whole distribution has shifted leftwards, with B unchanged; long-term unemployment grows therefore. Also the wage differential narrows, since the lowest wage, B, is closer to the top wage in the distribution. Of course, the facts in each country differ (there is now a large literature explaining them; two examples are Minford et al. [1985] and Bean et al. [1987]); the figure is just an illustration of one possibility.

As for the US, it appears that B is of lesser importance, mainly confined to aid for families with dependent children which affects very low-income groups, particularly poor blacks. Consequently, while the US too has had a productivity slowdown, the position of B may not have shifted much to the right within the distribution. Instead of higher unemployment, we have seen an explosion in low-paid service employment as the rising labour force has driven wages down in services; aggregate real consumption wages in the US have been astonishingly static now for more than a decade.

Turning to the authors' second hypothesis, I would deploy the same analysis. The long-term unemployed are "outsiders" in the sense that they have withdrawn from active search. It is quite possible that they will not respond to temporary variations in real wages by entering the labour market; hence, a wage equation, or a Phillips curve relating expected real wages to unemployment, may well pick up no relationship with *their* unemployment or labour supply. So far so good; the authors, like many others, have picked up an empirical regularity.

But their policy deduction is invalid. "Targeted reflation" will not work unless it "targets" B. Yet that particular form of targetry is not to be found in this paper. Like so many well-meaning "liberals", they tiptoe round the offending central element and pretend it is not there; instead, they imply that the long-term unemployed just happen by hard luck to have become so and, that stroke of luck having occurred, they have thence become demotivated, lacking in human capital, and so on. Just trigger a reflation which, via public jobs say, employs them for a spell, and they will permanently return to the labour market at wages lower than B. But of course, given that because of long-term unemployment they are demotivated and have lower human capital, an employer may well offer wages quite a lot lower than B before he will take them on permanently: since they will reject such wages, they will return to unemployment after the public job programme, if indeed they exit from it at all during the reflation.

The authors' implicit story is optimistic and implausible. A sceptical economist, taught to assume that people pursue their private interests, should reject it and concentrate instead on politically feasible proposals to lower B; recent and proposed labour market policies in Britain (namely, "Restart", union laws, rent deregulation, rate reform) have precisely had this objective, contrary to some provocative remarks in this paper.

Bibliography

BEAN, Christopher, Richard LAYARD, Stephen NICKELL, "The Rise in Unemployment: A Multi-Country Study". In: Christopher BEAN, Richard LAYARD, Stephen NICKELL (Eds.), The Rise in Unemployment. Oxford 1987, pp. 1-22.

GRUBB, David, Richard JACKMAN, Richard LAYARD, "Causes of the Current Stagflation". Review of Economic Studies, Vol. 49, 1982, pp. 707-731.

MINFORD, Patrick, Paul ASHTON, Michael PEEL, David DAVIES, Alison SPRAGUE, Unemployment - Cause and Cure. 2nd edition, Oxford 1985.

--, Piere-Richard AGENOR, Eric NOWELL, "A New Classical Econometric Model of the World Economy". Economic Modelling, Vol. 3, 1986, pp. 154-174.

Summary of the Discussion by Joachim Scheide

Many of the comments focused on technical aspects whose solution was felt to be highly important for the interpretation of the empirical findings in both papers. One issue with respect to Robert Gordon's paper was how to identify shifts in the trend of output and productivity, because these estimates were essential to identify the output gaps. Some discussants raised doubts as to whether the trend of output, estimated for the 1973-1979 period, should be extrapolated until 1984. They pointed to other studies which identified a downward shift in the trend; the same applied to estimates of labor productivity. If there was indeed such a downward shift, the size of the output gaps estimated in the paper would have an upward bias; in turn, the judgement on the wage gap would be biased downwards because, given the high growth of productivity, the actual behavior of real wages would seem more moderate. The same would be true if the years chosen as benchmarks were exceptional in the sense of being peak years of the business cycle or of the inflationary process. A further issue was whether observed productivity could really be taken as a factor independent of wage behavior; high observed productivity growth might be misleading since it might only reflect a substitution away from labor induced by, for example, excessive wage increases.

All these problems would, of course, require much more complex studies, going more into detail on the production side as well as searching for appropriate wage equations. It was argued there was a trade-off between comprehensiveness and the degree of detail.

As regards the empirical research it was mentioned in the discussion, for example, that the focus on unemployment rates might be misleading at times when the growth of the labor force varies. Furthermore, unemployment rates may not tell us very much about the state of the economy and a look at employment rates instead was suggested; for example, the United States experienced a historical peacetime record with respect to the employment rate. The unemployment rate was an imperfect proxy, only loosely correlated with employment over time. Others were dissatisfied with the way of estimating potential output; they would have preferred some measure which was independent of the actual behavior of output.

In the discussion of the paper by Sean Holly and Peter Smith the problem of how to measure flexibility was raised. A country might achieve all the reallocations necessary for efficiency and full employment without any change in relative real wages if labor were homogenous and the mobility of labor were high. In this case, by looking at relative wages alone one would get an incorrect idea about the degree of flexibility. A similar fallacy might arise if we looked at the effects in different countries experiencing shocks: flexibility is something relative, i.e., it should be defined in terms of the magnitude of response of, for example, wage earners, relative to the magnitude of the shocks like the oil-price hike; therefore, if there were shocks with different magnitude, the outcome itself would not reveal any information about flexibility.

As to the example of long-term unemployment ("flowers on the shelf"), it was mentioned that there were different theories to explain the insider-outsider problem. One was the hypothesis of efficiency wages (put forward explicitly in Willem Buiter's paper) which stated that the wage was a signal of qualification and that, therefore, under certain circumstances, cuts in real wages were ineffective as an inducement for employers to hire more workers. Other theories stressed that it might be impossible to undercut existing wages due to union structures or that unemployment benefits may be high and prevent such moves by workers. All these theories needed to be tested, and then we might be better equipped to explain the existence of long-term unemployment.

With reference to the situation in the United States, where long-term unemployment was not such a big problem as elsewhere, the available evidence suggested that the reservation wage was determined more by the person's prior wage than by the nature of the benefit structure. Therefore, long-term unemployed consisted primarily of persons who were waiting to be reemployed in the sector with higher wages.

IV

Rüdiger Soltwedel

Peter Trapp*

Labor Market Barriers to More Employment: Causes for an Increase of the Natural Rate? The Case of West Germany

1. Introduction

Since the early 1970s the labor market situation in West Germany has deteriorated markedly. In 1986, total employment was about one million (4 percent) lower than in 1973; employment in the private sector even declined by some 8 percent. When the growth of the labor supply accelerated during the 1970s, due to demographic reasons and to higher participation rates of women, unemployment rose sharply. The number of workers registered as unemployed at the labor exchange increased from 273 thousands in 1973 to 2.2 millions in 1986. The unemployment rate (unemployed as a percent of the dependent labor force) went up from about 1 percent in the early 1970s to 9 percent in the mid-1980s.

The unemployment rate did not increase smoothly but jumped in two steps. In the recession of the mid-1970s it rose to 5 percent and in the early 1980s it moved to about 9 percent (Figure 1). This seems to suggest that the increase in unemployment was triggered off by the contractionary policies which led to the recessions. However, this cannot

---

* This paper draws extensively on the research undertaken at the Institut für Weltwirtschaft. Naturally, all errors and shortcomings in representing these research results are ours. An earlier version of this paper was presented by Rüdiger Soltwedel [1988] at the 1987 Carnegie-Rochester Conference.

182

Figure 1 – Unemployment Rate and Capacity Utilization in West Germany (in percent)

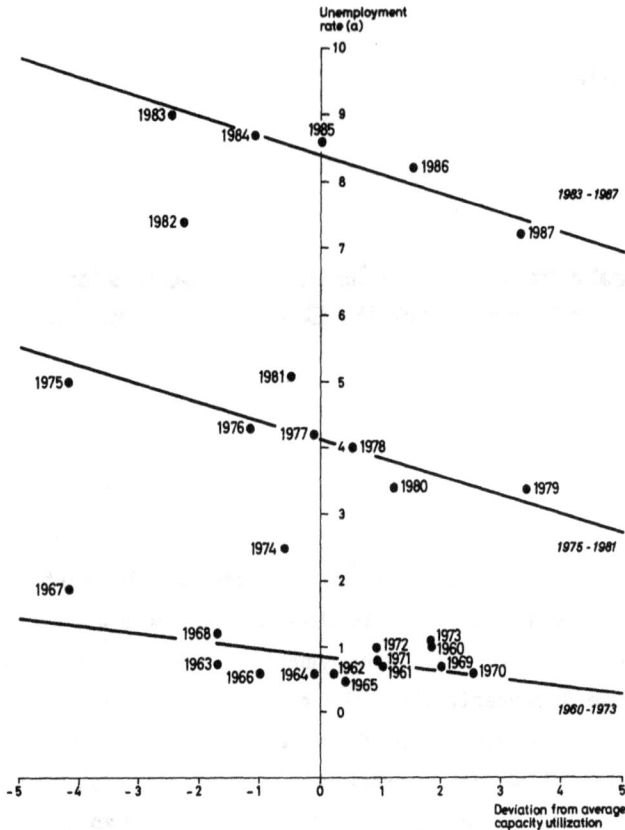

(a) Registered unemployed including one third of short-time workers.

Source: Own calculations.

explain why unemployment remained stubbornly high after the recession periods. In fact, after each recession demand picked up noticeably. At the end of the 1970s and since the mid-1980s capacity utilization in the overall economy has been about as high as it was at the beginning of the 1970s. Why did unemployment not fall to its pre-recession level in the course of the recovery? What is striking is that in spite of the sharp increase in unemployment real wages continued to rise at an annual rate of some 3 percent from 1973 to 1979. Only in the recession at the

beginning of the 1980s did real wages decline, but they started to increase again in 1984 regardless of the 2.2 million unemployed. It is also
worth noting that wage differentials between qualifications and regions
declined [Soltwedel, 1984; Gundlach, 1986], although unemployment
among less qualified workers was significantly higher than for skilled
workers and although regional differences between unemployment rates
became more pronounced. Why did wages not react to these imbalances?
What has prevented the wage structure from adjusting to the differences
in the development of labor supply and demand in regions and for
qualifications? Or, to put it more bluntly: why has there been no
efficient underbidding by the unemployed?

The hypothesis put forward in this paper is that the change from a full-
employment economy to a low-employment economy was brought about by
a fundamental change in the economic policy regime which started in the
second half of the 1960s. The policy aimed at providing greater equality
of opportunity for all citizens and at achieving more equality in income
distribution and more social security. The measures implemented for this
purpose actually reduced the incentives to work and to invest, distorted
the wage-setting process and resulted in an increase in the relative
price of labor and in a reduction of wage differentials. The institutional
set-up of the wage setting process protected insiders against outsiders'
wage competition. As unemployment increased, the government even
enhanced this protection. As a result of these policies, the natural rate
of unemployment in West Germany has risen dramatically over the last 15
years. The increase did not show up immediately because of the boom in
the early 1970s, but it became clearly evident when the economy moved
into the recession in 1974 and was re-inforced by the policy response to
the oil price hike.

The purpose of this paper is to analyze how labor-market regulations
and economic policies have influenced the wage formation process in West
Germany. All those measures are closely linked together, i.e., they are
complementary to each other, and it is not possible to quantify the effect
of one single measure. The policy-induced increase in rigidity in the
labor market has contributed towards keeping unemployment high in the
upswing from 1976 to 1979 and since 1983. As the attempts at increasing

employment failed, the government introduced other interventions. However, the results remained poor.

The first part of the paper contains a brief description of the new policy that began in the second half of the 1960s and of how the policy change affected the labor market. In the second part, an outline of the collective bargaining system in Germany is given and the effects of the policy change on wage bargaining are analyzed. After that, changes in the labor law, and in dismissal protection, and their effects on the hiring behavior of the firms are reviewed. In the final part of the paper, the development of business profits and of productive investment is analyzed. The evidence presented throughout this paper is descriptive rather than econometric and focuses on the institutional features of the West German labor market.

2. Policies for More Fairness and Equality

In the mid-1960s, there was a broad consensus in West Germany that, from a macroeconomic point of view, the distortions of the post-war period had been overcome. Production capacity had been reconstructed, supply bottlenecks, e.g., in housing or food supply, had been eliminated and the economy was operating at a very high level of employment. In achieving the economic miracle, which raised the standard of living in West Germany to an unprecedented level, the role of macroeconomic policy was rather limited [Paqué, 1987, p. 29]. The government relied mostly on the increase in incentives brought about by eliminating interventions: price controls were abolished, income tax rates were reduced, barriers to trade were removed, financial markets were liberalized and the currency convertibility was restored.

In spite of the success of this policy, there was widespread agreement in the 1960s that the government should assume a more active role in economic matters for two reasons:
- First of all, there was the feeling that, after the end of the reconstruction of the economy, a more active macroeconomic policy would be

necessary to maintain a high rate of growth and full employment because capitalist production of economic welfare in terms of income growth and high employment was considered to be inherently unstable. The recession of 1966/67 which led to a decline in real GNP for the first time after the war seemed to confirm this view. The Law to Promote Stability and Growth which was passed by Parliament in 1967 provided the government with the main instruments for macroeconomic interventions. Stimulatory monetary and fiscal policy proved to be so successful in overcoming the 1967 recession that the conviction that the government was able to ensure an appropriate GNP growth, a high level of employment and price stability became very strong. In 1970, the Chancellor Willy Brandt even proclaimed an unconditional "full employment guarantee" thus shifting the responsibility for labor-market developments from market participants to the government.

- Secondly, there was a consensus in society that the free-market economy, while producing a strong increase in overall prosperity, had led to an excessively uneven distribution of income and wealth. It was, therefore, considered to be the task of the government to take corrective action and to improve not only equality of opportunity but also equality of result. This was to achieve "social justice" and "social peace" which were regarded as important preconditions for political stability and sustained economic growth. Furthermore, production, employment, and investment should no longer be determined by a few capitalists but workers should participate in the decision-making process. "Daring more democracy" was the slogan coined by the Brandt administration. Consequently, the government embarked on a program of "internal reforms" designed to reduce income differentials, to improve social security, to provide entitlements for education and training, and to extend codetermination (Mitbestimmung) in large enterprises.

Despite (or because of) the social reforms, economic growth weakened and unemployment increased in the 1970s and in the first half of the 1980s. Predictably, the government blamed external developments, e.g., the oil price hike, volatile exchange rates, and high international interest rates for slow growth and high unemployment. In order to promote growth and employment, a large number of expenditure programs were adopted and subsidies were granted to ailing industries to prevent unemployment from rising further. As a consequence, public sector expenditures for most of the time rose faster than nominal GNP. In 1982, public expenditures amounted to almost 50 percent of GNP compared to 32.5 percent in 1960 and 38.6 percent in 1970.

In fact, the policies which had led to the increase in the public sector's share in overall economic activity aggravated the labor-market problems by inducing wage increases higher than the terms of trade-adjusted increase in productivity and by markedly reducing investment profitability. Thus, domestic policy reforms slowed down the growth of potential output and raised unemployment.

a. Social Policy

In the late 1960s, the welfare system in West Germany was already rather comprehensive. Nevertheless, the government decided that it was time to care more for those who had not fully participated in the economic miracle by providing protection against economic risks and giving more support to families. All measures under this policy label affected the labor market in one way or an other.

Since it is impossible to give a complete description of all measures that have been adopted since the late 1960s, only the most important areas will be mentioned. In total, public social benefits to private households rose from 18 percent of GNP in 1965 to some 27 percent in the period from 1975 to date. If the benefits paid by companies are taken into account, transfers to private households rose from 25 percent of GNP in 1965 to about 34 percent in the second half of the 1970s. These numbers may give an idea of the profound impact of the extension of social policy on the economy.

α. Unemployment Compensation

The unemployment insurance, which is compulsory for all employees, provides two kinds of compensations: unemployment benefits and unemployment aid. Generally, a worker who has paid unemployment contributions for a certain period of time is entitled to unemployment benefits for up to twelve months. In 1975, unemployment benefits were raised from 63 percent to 68 percent of the net earnings in the month preceding unemployment. The benefits are tax free and, up to 1982, they were calculated on the basis of net income earned including overtime payments. Since 1982, benefits have been slightly reduced. Overtime payments are no longer taken into account and unemployed without dependants receive only 63 percent of the net income. Elderly unemployed now can claim benefits for up to 32 months.

Unemployment aid is granted when unemployment benefits expire and no other income sources are available. In 1975, unemployment aid was raised from 53 percent to 58 percent of the net income earned in the preceding month. Payments to unemployed without children were cut to 56 percent in 1982. There is no time limit for the payment of unemployment aid. In addition to unemployment benefits or aid, households are entitled to other social benefits, e.g., rent allowances, if the family income is below a certain limit.

The annual income loss depends on the length of unemployment. For short periods of unemployment, the annual family income after tax can even be higher than when employed because of the progressivity of the tax schedule and because the family may be entitled to additional benefits at the lower taxable income [Fritzsche, von Loeffelholz, 1981].

In 1978, the effective income loss for the whole calendar year resulting from an unemployment period of three months amounted to roughly 4 percent for an unmarried income earner with an average income, and to about 6 percent for a married income earner [OECD, 1982]. The income loss was to the order of 12 percent in both cases when the unemployment period was six months, and when unemployment persisted for the whole calendar year, a loss of 32 percent was incurred. The changes in the unemployment insurance system implemented since 1982 have not fundamentally changed the picture.

β. Social Aid

Every household or person with inadequate sources of income is entitled to welfare payments (Sozialhilfe). The claim does not depend on previous social security contributions, tax payments or the willingness to work. Social aid is to ensure that everybody is able to afford a minimum standard of living. The level of assistance is determined by federal law and has frequently been changed; the municipalities have to grant and to finance social aid. The aid consists of monthly standard payments plus allowances for the rent and energy costs actually incurred plus irregular allowances for the purchase of big-ticket items (clothing, furniture, TV, and so on) which have been approved by the social office. The benefits are tax free. Welfare payments were raised markedly in the early 1970s. From 1969 to 1974 the monthly standard payments rose by 77 percent compared to an increase of the net income of a skilled worker of 52 percent In addition, social aid has been regularly adjusted to price-level changes and to the general increase in real incomes. Changes in the calculation procedures and in the price index used for the adjustment of social aid have resulted in an accelerated increase of entitlements in the mid-1980s.

Individual benefits depend on the size of the family, on the age of the children and on actual outlays for rent, energy and big-ticket items. Table 1 summarizes the typical assistance for a family of four (two adults, two children). From 1982 to 1986, the ratio of social aid (excluding irregular allowances) to the average net income of an employee rose from 73.7 to almost 78 percent (1). The difference between social aid and the net income that the recipients could earn in the labor market would probably be considerably smaller because their professional skills and abilities are usually below average.

The difference between unemployment compensations and the net income that could be earned in the labor market generally becomes smaller for

---

(1) The average income also includes the income of part-time workers. It is, therefore, lower than the average income of a full-time worker. On the other hand, actual social aid benefits are somewhat higher than shown in the table because irregular allowances are not included.

Table 1 - Social Aid and Net Earnings, 1982-1986

	1982	1983	1984	1985	1986
Standard allowances for social aid					
- father	338	342	351	371	389
- mother	270	274	281	297	311
- 1st child, 14 years	254	257	263	278	292
- 2nd child, 8 years	220	222	228	241	253
- total	1,082	1,095	1,123	1,187	1,245
Reimbursement for rent and energy	427	457	484	515	500
Total social aid payments					
- absolute figures	1,509	1,552	1,607	1,702	1,745
- in percent	73.7	74.2	75.7	79.0	77.6

Note: In percent of net monthly earnings per employee, including family allowances.

Source: Boss [1986a, p. 50].

the long-term unemployed. Thus, the incentives to take on a job do not increase when unemployment benefits expire. The increase of unemployment compensation is, therefore, likely to have produced more voluntary unemployment. Both unemployment compensation and social aid have reduced the supply of labor making it generally easier to enforce higher wage increases for all employees, especially for low wage earners. However, as the marginal product of less qualified workers did not rise correspondingly unemployment for this group increased sharply.

γ. Early Retirement

Since 1973, old age insurance has offered the possibility of early retirement (for men, 63 instead of 65 and, for women, 60 instead of 63) at an only slightly reduced pension. In addition, the government has encouraged early retirement contracts between unions and employees by sharing the cost burden. This was thought to give some relief to the labor market. Together with longer annual leave and the reduction of the weekly working time, early retirement has contributed to lower the supply of labor. However, instead of alleviating the labor-market problems, the reduction of the labor supply has increased the scarcity of skilled labor which is complementary to the employment of less qualified workers. At the same time, wage costs have increased as the cost of early retirement translated into higher retirement contributions. All in all, the shortening of the working time has reduced potential output and employment, as well as public sector expenditures, thus shifting the burden to those who are employed.

δ. Maternity Leave

The protection of women in the final weeks of pregnancy and in the post-natal period has been extended over the last years. In particular, the post-natal-leave period has been lengthened and financial support is offered to families. Employers have to keep the job open for the pregnant woman and to provide a temporary replacement. The increase in maternity leave has reduced the supply of labor and has raised companies' wage costs as well as the economy's social expenditures.

ε. Sick Leave

Up until 1970, sick leave arrangements for blue-collar workers were less generous than for white-collar workers. Since then, full earnings in the case of sick leave have also been granted to blue-collar workers. Studies show that the average sick rate of blue collar workers rose significantly after 1970 [Boss, 1986b]. The change in sick leave arrangements has increased moral hazard which is indicated by the fact that sick leave mostly occurs on Mondays and Fridays. The cost to employers for sick leave has risen from 1.7 percent of gross pay in 1966 to 6.3 percent in 1980 [Donges, Spinanger, 1983, p. 18]. Thus, the extension of paid sick leave has reduced the effective working time and increased overall wage costs for the firm.

b. Subsidies

Despite its public condemnation of subsidies German governments have given substantial support to specific industries. According to calculations carried out by the Institut für Weltwirtschaft based on a comprehensive definition of subsidies (financial assistance plus tax allowances) such payments to different economic sectors of the German economy have more than doubled from 1973 to 1984 [Jüttemeier, 1987]. Subsidies have risen at an average annual rate of about 7 percent compared to a growth rate of nominal GNP of about 6 percent In 1984, subsidies amounted to DM 120 billion; or 6.8 percent of GNP. The traditional recipients of sub- sidies were agriculture, coal mining, the federal railway system, and residential construction. However, in the course of the 1970s subsidies to many other branches expanded rapidly, e.g., to shipyards, the iron and steel industry, the airbus industry.

Public assistance to specific sectors has contributed to real wage rigidity. In particular, the response of wage determination to compet- itiveness problems has been very weak or even nonexistent, because both employees and unions rely on the government to intervene. Wage settlements for the ailing shipbuilding industry, for example, are the same as for the booming investment goods industries. Since ailing industries are often regionally concentrated, employment problems in those areas are aggravated. At the same time, there is no incentive for other companies to move into those regions because labor costs are kept at an artificially high level. The state-owned shipyard Howaldtswerke- Deutsche Werft AG (HDW) provided an extreme case of how public as- sistance can distort competitiveness and result in a waste of resources. While hourly labor costs (including overheads) at medium-scale shipyards which are privately owned and which receive a limited amount of subsi- dies amounted to DM 45-50 in 1984, wage costs at HDW were as high as DM 75-80. Because of the high wage level, HDW could attract qualified personnel more easily than its competitors. At the same time, HDW was able to underbid its competitors, not because its productivity was much higher but because it could rely on the tax payer to settle any losses [Jüttemeier, 1987, p. 21]. Krieger et al. [1985, p. 109] have provided evidence that the permanent subsidization of regionally-concentrated

192

Table 2 - Development of Subsidies, 1973-1985

Source	1973	1980	1984
Federal Government's Subsidy Report (a) (DM bill.)	41.7	65.3	74.5
Institut für Weltwirtschaft(b) (DM bill.)	56.9	102.7	120.0
- Subsidies (c) per employee (DM)	2,430	4,610	5,890
- in percent of GNP	6.2	6.9	6.8

(a) Financial assistance plus tax relief. - (b) According to the definition established by the US Congress [US Congress, 1972, p. 18]. - (c) Subsidies per person employed in the sectors subsidized.

Source: Deutscher Bundestag [1985]; Jüttemeier [1987].

industries (e.g., coal mining, shipbuilding) results in high wage standards for the whole region, thus impeding the regional restructuring process. Nearly all industries that pay higher wages than their competitive situation permits are heavily subsidized or to a large extent protected against internal and/or external competition [Witteler, 1986; Donges, Schatz, 1986].

c. Labor Market Policy

Intensive labor market policy was another factor inhibiting wage flexibility. The Labor Promotion Act of 1969 made provision for generous public support of training and education. The policy aimed at improving the qualification of non-skilled workers and at increasing the productivity of the work force. However, substantial above average wage increases for low income earners reduced the incentives to acquire higher qualifications. Later on, when unemployment started to rise, efforts were concentrated on providing training possibilities for the unemployed and offering wage subsidies to companies for taking on unemployed workers. No doubt, this policy was helpful in individual cases, but it could not cope with the unemployment problem. On the contrary, while confirming the existing wage structure which was not compatible with the differences in the marginal product of the work-force, this policy contributed towards increasing to the tax burden and deteriorated the incentive to work and to invest [Soltwedel, 1984].

d. The Increase of the Tax Burden

In order to finance the rapid expansion of public expenditures since the mid-1960s, taxes and social security contributions have been raised. Public sector revenues increased from some 34 percent of GNP in 1965 to 42.5 percent in the early 1980s. In particular, direct income deductions, i.e., income taxes and social security, rose strongly. The average tax burden of an unmarried skilled worker in the manufacturing sector increased from 31 percent in 1965 to about 48 percent in 1987. The marginal income tax rate of this worker was about 64 percent in 1987 (Table 3).

If wage earners had regarded the benefits provided by public sector spending on social purposes, subsidies, and labor market programs as additional income they would have accepted lower wage increases and a higher tax burden. The reduction of wages and the increase of the wedge between gross income and net income would have been the price for the welfare produced by the public sector. In addition, the policy change would have been less harmful for employment, if social minimum income had not been viewed as a substitute but as a complement to earned income and if this had induced wage policy to react in a flexible way to unemployment problems in specific regions and branches. Apparently this has not been the case indicating that the wage determination did not respond to the increase in unemployment as it should have done in a labor market functioning properly.

Table 3 - Income Taxation of Typical Households of Employees, 1982 and
1987 (percent) (a)

Type of household	Average tax rate	Marginal tax rate
	1982 (monthly earnings DM 3,000) (b)	
Single	45.7	60.5
Family with two children		
- 1 income earner	39.5	45.8
- 2 income earners	44.9	59.8
	1987 (monthly earnings DM 3,558) (b)	
Single	48.5	64.2
Family with two children		
- 1 income earner	39.2	47.1
- 2 income earners	46.6	62.8

(a) Income tax and social security contributions. Contributions in 1982
(1987): old age and disability insurance 18.0 (18.7) percent; health
insurance 12.1 (12.5) percent; unemployment insurance 4.0 (4.3) percent. - (b) Monthly earnings include employer's social security contributions.

Source: Boss [1987].

3. The Collective Bargaining System in West Germany

The labor market in West Germany has - by the public, by politicians,
by the courts, and even by economists - never been regarded as a
"normal" market-oriented subsystem of a competitive economy with individual freedom of contract and price (wage) flexibility as characteristic
features. The institutional framework of the bargaining system is laid
down in the Collective Bargaining Act (Tarifvertragsgesetz - TVG) of
1949, that has rather strong collectivistic traits (1). The TVG is based

(1) The most important provisions of the TVG already stem from an
agreement between the employers confederations and the labor unions
immediately after the revolution in November 1918. Since then, the
collectivistic bargaining procedure has not only been acknowledged
but accepted as the dominant principle.

on the constitutionally guaranteed individual freedom to form and join coalitions. These coalitions are entitled to contract on employment conditions in their own responsibility, i.e., independently of governmental interference (Tarifautonomie). On the side of the employees, only unions have the right to enter into collective agreements. On the side of the employers, every individual employer or the employers' confederation can make a contract with the relevant union.

There are 17 industry unions which are combined in the German Unions Association (Deutscher Gewerkschaftsbund - DGB)(1). Usually one union covers all employees in an industry and bargains with the employers' confederation or (seldom) with individual employers. Contrary to the situation in the United States, unions normally do not compete at the firm level for the representation of employees.

At present, the degree of unionization in the economy as a whole is about 41 percent. After a strong decline during the 1950s and stagnation during the 1960s, the degree of unionization started to climb after the early 1970s. The deterioration in the labor market conditions obviously did not make union membership less attractive (Figure 2). The degree of cartelization on the employers' side is even more pronounced: it is estimated by the Federal Confederation of Employer that in manufacturing and in the banking and insurance sector about 80 percent of the firms belong to an employers association, employing nearly 90 percent of the employees (2).

The wage bargaining process usually covers all firms of a distinct region, sometimes wage settlements are made on a nationwide level; but even when negotiations are regional, the results are often identical.

---

(1) Besides the DGB unions there are the German Salaried-Workers Union (Deutsche Angestelltengewerkschaft - DAG), the German Civil Servants Union (Deutscher Beamtenbund - DBB) and the small Christian Unions Association (Christlicher Gewerkschaftsbund - CGB).

(2) In wholesale, retail trade, and other service industries the degree of organization is markedly lower.

Figure 2 - Unionization in West Germany, 1951-1985

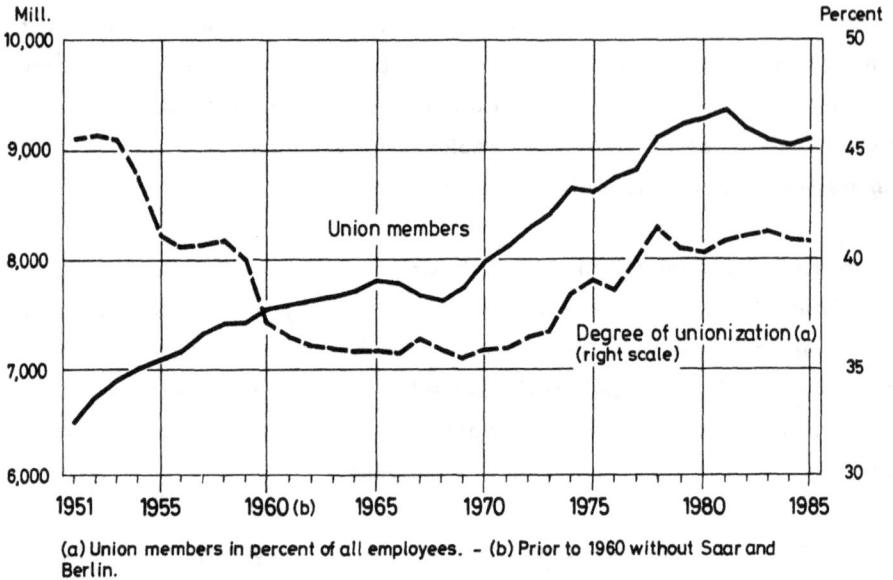

(a) Union members in percent of all employees. - (b) Prior to 1960 without Saar and Berlin.

Source: Statistisches Bundesamt [various issues]; own calculations.

The contracts are binding for all members of the employers' organization, companies normally making no distinction between union and nonunion workers. If an employer leaves the association before a new contract is signed, he still has to comply with the old contract unless he has explicitly denounced it. If he leaves the association after a new collective agreement has been signed, he is bound to satisfy the conditions of the new contract.

Any employer is free to offer better conditions than those laid down in the contract (Günstigkeitsprinzip), but he is not allowed to offer worse ones, except in those cases where this is explicitly provided for in the contract. There are, however, hardly any cases where the negotiating parties have weakened the character of the contract as a minimum condition. A voluntary renunciation of the contract on the part of the workers - to ensure endangered jobs - is usually illegal. Thus, the contracts constitute a norm that must be fulfilled even when the expectations (as regards sales and prices) on which the contract was based have changed significantly. As a result, a company that is faced with declining sales has to place the adjustment burden on employment:

- An individual employer who has run into difficulties may not lower contracted wages on his own even if his employees were to support such a "rescue operation". He has to ask his employers' association to renegotiate his individual case with the union. It is doubtful whether the rest of the cartel would allow marginal or even submarginal firms to continue to exist at somewhat lower costs than they have to pay. More likely, the intramarginal members of the cartel would prefer endangered firms go bankrupt. Concession bargaining as occurred in the United States is, therefore, not encountered in the industrial relations in West Germany.

- Since collective agreements are strictly binding, an employer who belongs to the cartel may also not hire an unemployed man at a wage below the contractual wage rate even if both would regard such contract as advantageous - it is illegal.

This collectivistic system has been justified - and that since the early 1920s - on the grounds that the provisions are necessary to avoid "wage dumping" (Lohndrückerei) and "dirty competition" (Schmutzkonkurrenz). This has been the standard argument, is still the prevalent opinion, and can be considered as the backbone of the German collectivistic labor law [Hueck et al., 1964, p. 254].

Another salient feature of the existing Collective Bargaining Act is that the contract between a union and an employers' association can be declared compulsory for the whole industry by the Federal Minister of Labor if one or (not seldom) both parties to the contract apply for it (1). Since most branches of the economy have a rather high degree of

---

(1) Such a declaration is conditional to a union or employers' association coverage of at least 50 percent of all employees in this industry and/or to the interest of the public, e.g., because otherwise wages would fall below some "socially acceptable" level. From the juridical point of view it is argued that this tool is necessary for those cases, where the power of the institutions is too weak to succeed. Then "the declaration of universal validity allows government to hasten to support the collective bargaining parties" [Herschel, 1983, p. 162 (translated by the authors)].

organization at least on the employers' side, only five to eight percent of all collective agreements are declared compulsory. This rather small fraction seems to suggest that one should not bother too much with this particular form of government interference.

During the last two decades, however, the number of these contracts has increased considerably. In 1968 only 173 contracts have been declared compulsory, since 1980 the number has hovered around 600. This development indicates that the quest for protection increases when economic activity is sluggish and when labor market conditions are getting worse. And the government is ready to provide this protection. The branches that usually apply for the contract being declared compulsory belong to the services sector and to several handicrafts (Table 4). They are rather labor-intensive and could normally absorb a relatively high proportion of unqualified labor.

To declare contracted wages as compulsory for complete branches deters potential entrepreneurs from starting a new business because they are legally forced to incur the same level of wage costs as the producers who are already in business. So the potential for start-ups is artificially reduced in branches where capital requirements and hence barriers to entry for newcomers are relatively low.

These remarks may suffice to show that the Collective Bargaining Law hampers or even prevents competition of outsiders (1). At the least, it delays wage adjustment where firms have run into difficulties and a quick reduction of costs is required. The expected outcome of the provisions of the law is that adjustment to shocks - oil price hikes, technological innovations, intensified international competition, unexpectedly volatile monetary and fiscal policies - will mainly take place in the form of employment changes.

---

(1) It lies in the logic of a system that protects rent maximizing by insiders to prevent the import of cheap labor; since the end of 1973, it has been forbidden to hire labor from outside the European Community (Anwerbestopp). Since the closure of the West German labor market, the foreign labor supply has declined from nearly 2.5 million in 1973 to less than 2 million during the 1980s.

Table 4 - Number of Collective Agreements Declared Compulsory for All Employers, 1968 and 1986

Industry	1968	1986
Agriculture, forestry	-	14
Stone, sand, and clay industry	26	70
Metal working (handicraft)	4	20
Textiles industry	2	43
Clothing industry	1	59
Paper and board processing	-	1
Wood processing	9	1
Food, drink, tobacco	6	42
Construction industry	44	148
Cleaning services	2	36
Wholesale trade	42	14
Retail trade	13	51
Traffic services	5	11
Hotels and lodging places	3	12
Journalistic professions, custody and other services	16	31
Total	173	563

Source: Bundesministerium für Arbeit und Sozialordnūng, unpublished material.

As a matter of fact, there have been and still are differences in contracted minimum wages between industries and regions. But they have shown a strong tendency of levelling off until the mid-seventies and no differentiation occurred thereafter:

- In the investment goods industries (the largest fraction of the economy covered by a single union) regional differences in minimum wages have nearly been eliminated: the hourly wage of skilled workers showed a spread of some 15 percent in 1968 and declined to close to zero in the mid-1980s (Table 5). The regional divergence in 1968 was even greater than the mere figure suggests, since in most regions there were (at

Table 5 - Minimum Wages in Investment Goods Industries in West Germany, 1968 and 1985 (DM per hour)

	Skilled workers' wage		Lowest wage		Highest wage	
	1968	1985	1968	1985	1968	1985
Schleswig-Holstein	3.92	11.56	2.84	9.48	5.20	15.37
Hamburg	3.89	11.56	2.92	9.48	5.18	15.37
Lower Saxony	3.47	11.50	2.57	9.32	4.62	15.30
Lower-Weser Area	4.04	11.56	3.03	9.42	5.37	15.37
North Rhine-Westphalia	3.94	11.56	2.88	9.48	5.24	15.37
Hesse	3.75	11.56	2.81	9.36	4.50	15.37
Rhineland-Palatinate	3.65	11.56	2.65	9.36	4.85	15.37
North Württemberg-North Baden	3.92	11.56	2.94	9.42	5.29	15.60
South Württemberg-Hohenzollern	3.85	11.55	2.89	9.42	4.79	15.31
South Baden	3.60	11.53	2.70	9.42	4.79	15.31
Bavaria	3.46	11.56	2.53	8.79	4.15	15.37
Saar	3.71	11.56	2.89	9.48	4.45	15.37
Average	3.77	11.55	2.80	9.37	4.87	15.37
Spread (DM)	0.58	0.06	0.50	0.69	1.22	0.30
(percent)	15.4	0.5	17.8	7.4	25.1	2.0
Standard deviation	0.18	0.02	0.15	0.18(a)	0.37	0.07
Coefficient of variation	4.9	0.2	5.3	1.9(b)	7.7	0.5

(a) Without Bavaria: 0.05. - (b) Without Bavaria: 0.6.

Source: See Table 3.

least) two local wage categories depending on the density of population in the region of the place of work; these categories were eliminated in 1974/75.

- The (relative) minimum wage for unqualified labor was raised considerably in several branches up to the mid-1970s. Since that time, the pace of reducing wage differentials has decreased strongly, but, apart from construction, there has been no reversal in the trend to less wage differentiation (Table 6). However, the development of contrac-

Table 6 - Skill Differentials in Minimum Wages in Selected Industries in West Germany, 1960-1985

		1960	1970	1975	1985
Iron and steel	a	74.2	80.0	81.5	81.5
(North Rhine-Westphalia)	b	100.0	107.8	109.8	109.8
Metal manufacturing	a	70.2	75.0	80.0	82.0
(North Rhine-Westphalia)	b	100.0	106.8	114.0	116.8
Chemical	a	71.6	78.5	85.0	85.8
(North Rhine-Westphalia)	b	100.0	109.6	118.7	119.8
Paper	a	71.4	83.5	89.0	89.6
(Schleswig-Holstein, Hamburg, Lower Saxony)	b	100.0	116.9	124.6	125.5
Ceramic	a	74.9	81.9	84.3	85.1
(North-West Germany)	b	100.0	109.3	112.6	113.6
Construction	a	87.6	90.9	90.9	82.7
(North Rhine-Westphalia)	b	100.0	103.8	103.8	94.4
Printing	a	61.0	65.0	71.6	74.0
	b	100.0	106.6	117.4	121.3
Woodworking	a	75.1	78.1	82.1	85.0
(North Rhine)	b	100.0	104.0	109.3	113.2

Note: Line a indicates lowest wage as a percentage of skilled workers' wages. Line b: 1960=100.

Source: See Table 3.

tual minimum wages is understating the levelling process of the employment costs for different qualifications. Collective agreements on the payments of fixed wage components for saving schemes (vermögenswirksame Anlage) increased in coverage and amount. An additional levelling effect resulted from the strong increase in paid annual leave, especially for the lower income and age brackets; in 1985, the average annual leave was close to 30 days for all employees. In 1975, the average leave period for the young and the unskilled workers was 20 days, higher income brackets and the older workforce were entitled to 25

Table 7 - Unemployment Rates in the States of West Germany, 1975-1986

	1975	1980	1986	1986:1975
Schleswig-Holstein	5.2	4.2	10.9	2.1
Hamburg	3.7	3.4	13.0	3.5
Lower Saxony	5.5	4.7	11.5	2.1
Bremen	4.5	5.3	15.5	3.4
North Rhine-Westphalia	4.8	4.6	10.9	2.3
Hesse	4.5	2.8	6.8	1.5
Rhineland-Palatinate	5.1	3.8	8.3	1.6
Saar	6.1	6.5	13.3	2.2
Baden-Württemberg	3.5	2.3	5.1	1.5
Bavaria	5.2	3.5	7.0	1.3
Berlin (West)	3.7	4.3	10.5	2.8
West Germany	4.7	3.7	9.0	1.9
Standard deviation (percentage points)	0.8	1.1	3.0	-
Coefficient of variation (percent)	16.7	27.1	29.4	-

Source: Bundesanstalt für Arbeit [1975, 1986].

days on average. Often there is an additional leave remuneration which is paid as a lump-sum, thus raising the employment costs of low income groups more than proportionately.

These levelling tendencies are in marked contrast to the structural employment problems since the mid-1970s:

- Differences in regional unemployment have increased strongly (Table 7), signalling considerable structural problems. Especially the coastal regions with their shipyards (Schleswig-Holstein, Lower Saxony, Hamburg, Bremen) and the regions with a high share of ailing smoke-stack industries (North Rhine-Westphalia, the Saar) have been heavily hit by persistent unemployment.

Table 8 - Degree of Capacity Utilization in the Investment Goods Industry in West Germany, 1970-1985

	1970	1975	1980	1982	1985
Iron, steel	93.7	81.0	85.3	82.0	88.7
Structural, light metal engineering	92.2	78.9	87.5	81.1	76.7
Mechanical engineering	90.1	77.5	86.7	77.7	88.0
Data processing equipment	96.5	80.1	77.4	76.9	91.4
Road vehicles	97.8	80.0	87.0	79.0	84.8
Shipbuilding	90.4	96.5	64.5	66.0	60.7
Electrical engineering	92.7	72.2	83.8	76.9	86.8
Iron, steel, sheet, metal goods	87.0	70.6	81.0	74.2	82.1
Steel forming	90.2	73.8	79.9	68.5	85.2
Precision and optical goods, clocks, watches	90.6	80.6	84.5	75.5	87.5

Source: Ifo-Institut [various issues].

- Differences in capacity utilization and profitability between the different branches of the investment goods industry have widened (shipbuilding, steel, auto industry)(Table 8).

- There has been a growing concentration of unemployment on marginal groups of the labor market (women, migrant workers, and unqualified labor) (1). These problems arising from the diminished wage differentials have been aggravated because of the increase in the labor-force participation of married women and because the baby boom generation entered the labor market (2).

---

(1) The respective unemployment rates in 1985 were: women 10.4, migrant workers 13.9; roughly 50 percent of the unemployed did not have a completed vocational training, 60 percent were classified as unqualified by the employment offices [Bundesanstalt für Arbeit, various issues].

(2) The German labor supply declined during the 1960s until the early 1970s; from 1973 until 1986 it increased by nearly 2,000,000, i.e., 0.5 percent each year [Thon, 1986, pp. 56, 98]. This is roughly the same amount by which total unemployment increased in the same span of time.

204

The pronounced increase, the structure, and the size of unemployment give the impression that supply and demand conditions on West German labor markets are not reflected in relative wages. The bilateral cartel has not pursued a wage policy consistent with changed conditions. Because of the peculiarities of the Collective Bargaining Act there were no competitive forces that could have contested their agreements.

The Collective Bargaining Law has not been altered in essential points during the last thirty years. Thus, any attempt to blame wage rigidity at least to some extent on this law has to come up with an explanation why labor market developments were so favorable up to the early 1970s and have been so unfavorable since then. The mere existence of the bilateral monopoly does not imply that wages cannot reflect the effective scarcities. In principle, the contractors can agree upon wages that take differences between regions, branches, and qualifications into account and, in fact, wage differentials were considerably larger in the 1960s. But unions' wage policies changed fundamentally after the very strong boom-period in 1969/70: the shock of the 1966/67 recession was so deep-seated that unions accepted in 1968 and even in 1969 wage increases that were regarded as "too moderate" [see, e.g., Sachverständigenrat, 1968; 1969]. In 1969, there were widespread wild-cat strikes and the leadership of the unions was at stake. After that experience, unions practised a more aggressive wage policy. They were especially anxious that contracted minimum wages were not allowed to fall significantly short of the wages effectively paid.

The fact that wrong market signals have emerged and have been able to persist since the early 1970s can only be explained if the aforementioned change in the role of government is taken into account: in addition to the macroeconomic targets defined in the Act to Promote Stability and Growth, the federal government assumed far-reaching responsibility at that time for structural policies (sectoral, regional) as well as for active labor market policies. By extending its interventions, the government demonstrated that it was in charge of regulating employment not only at an aggregate level but also in regions and industries. Therefore, the collective moral hazard of both employers' confederations and unions increased substantially. As Calmfors [1985, p. 147] states, it seems plausible to infer that such "fiscal policies aimed at stabilizing employment are likely to steepen the labor-demand schedule perceived by trade unions". The employers did not lean against labor cost-raising agreements for just the same reasons. They implicitly expected monetary and fiscal policies to accommodate. Especially during the second half of the 1970s, an abundance of employment programs was installed, justifying this assumption again and again. However, macropolicies lost credit because of their strong inflationary impact and their obvious ineffectiveness at reducing unemployment.

The analysis so far shows that the behavior of the government and the legal framework of the labor market contributed considerably to the emergence and to the persistence of wage rigidity in West Germany. As the government assumed the responsibility for maintaining full employment, collective bargaining could ignore disequilibria in the labor market. Collective wage agreements were increasingly oriented at improving working conditions for employed workers thus leading to a profound insider-outsider dichotomy.

4. Labor Law, Dismissal Protection, and the Hiring Behavior of the Firm

a. Labor Market Regulation and the Structure of Labor Costs

The freedom of contract is not only limited by the almost waterproof protection against wage competition. Moreover, Parliament has passed a great number of laws which directly affect employment costs by determining or regulating:

- employer's contributions to social security;

- paid sick leave, paid holidays and vacations;

- maternity protection, nursing pauses, and supplements to maternity pay;

- general protection against dismissal, and special protection for distinct groups of employees (works council members, workers in compulsory military service, handicapped persons, apprentices);

- employment protection in the case of takeovers;

- paid time-off for educational vacation and special vacation for youth-oriented work;

- occupational safety and health prescriptions;

- social plan requirements (compulsory severance payments);

- costs to comply with the plant constitution act (meetings, members of the works council);

- special employment protection for the young workers (work time, restricted employment); and

- costs arising from complying with the Vocational Training Act.

In addition to these legally-imposed employment costs, there are those agreed on in collective bargaining contracts:

- paid vacation and sick leave over legal minimum provisions;

- special payments (e.g., Christmas bonus);

- contributions to saving schemes;

- bonuses and extra pay;

- agreements on short-time working;

- agreements on protection against rationalization;

- income protection for elderly workers; and

- other social agreements.

Furthermore, firms usually offer voluntarily:

- provisions for old-age retirement;

- fringe benefits;

- health service;

- housing allowances; and

Table 9 - Structure of Annual Employment Costs in Manufacturing, 1966-1984 (DM)

	1966	1969	1975	1984
(1) Pay for effective work	9,230	11,208	18,582	30,837
(2) Fringe benefits				
- in absolute terms	4,002	5,181	11,661	25,163
- as a percent of (1)	43.4	46.2	62.8	81.6
thereof:				
legally-enforced	19.4	21.3	30.7	34.7
contracted and voluntary	24.0	24.8	32.1	46.9

Source: Statistisches Bundesamt [various issues].

- household and family benefits.

These fringe benefits can change their voluntary character and become compulsory by "common law".

These cost elements - together with costs for old age and health insurance - amount to a considerable and rising share of total earnings. Compared to the remuneration for the time effectively worked, the share of fringe benefits rose from less than one fifth in 1966 to more than one third in 1984. The contracted and voluntary element almost doubled from 24 to 44 percent (1) (Table 9). The total expenditures of the firms for these social purposes were more than six times higher in 1984 than in 1966, while, in the same period, the remuneration for the work effort only tripled (2).

These costs vary considerably with firm size. If a firm increases its labor force from 20 to 21, the additional employee will call forth the following consequences [Watrin, Giebel, 1984, p. 121]:

(1) The voluntarily-agreed fringe benefits amounted to roughly one fifth of total fringe benefits in 1984.
(2) For a detailed study of the cost aspects of these and related social policy measures in firms of different size, see the excellent work of Giebel [1985].

- in case of dismissals of more than 5 employees within 30 days the firm has to give notice to the employment office that has to agree and can delay the dismissals for up to two months after having been informed;

- the number of works council members increases from one to three;

- the firm has to establish a social plan (compulsory severance payments) in case of substantial production and employment changes;

- the firm is obliged to inform the employees at least once in each quarter about the economic situation and development prospects of the enterprise; and

- at least one adviser on work security questions has to be appointed.

The costs of the social policy measures resulting from an increase in the size of the firm make firms reluctant to hire additional labor, thus augmenting the employment problems.

b. Dismissal Protection and Social Plans

The features of the West German employment protection regulations are complex and contained in several laws and contracts. The Dismissal Protection Act (Kündigungsschutzgesetz) covers all employees in firms with more than five employees (excluding apprentices). Each dismissal has to be socially justified. A dismissal is - after a continuous employment of six months - ineffective if it is found to be "socially unfair", i.e., not in agreement with distinct legally-accepted reasons. These can be based on the personality or the behavior of an employee, or on firm-specific reasons.

As regards personal reasons, dismissal because of persistent illness (1) is regarded as socially unfair, if the employer could fill the gap by stand-by personnel, by temporary reorganization, or by the increased work intensity of the remaining staff. Even in cases where a dismissal is unavoidable for firm-specific reasons, the Dismissal Protection Act limits the options of the employer in that he has to follow social criteria in

---

(1) Even dipsomania is recognized as an illness that prevents dismissal.

choosing the employees to be dismissed (1); if these criteria are not met, the dismissal is ineffective. The legal terms are indeterminate and it has been up to the labor courts to define them. The courts have done this in an unforeseeable manner and in a variety of ways - because each case has to be judged individually - and usually in favor of the workers, thereby creating considerable uncertainty for employers. This concerns the firm-specific reasons for the dismissal that have to be observed by firms as well as the social criteria which have to be applied in the case of dismissals (2).

If a dismissal is found to be socially unfair, it is declared ineffective. In such cases, the Dismissal Protection Act stipulates that employment should continue or - if this is not tolerable for the firm - that severance payments should be made. The severance payments can amount to the earnings to twelve months or more (3).

According to §613a BGB (Civil Code), a dismissal following the sale of a firm or of parts of it is ineffective, irrespective of whether it is the buyer of the firm or the seller who comes foward with the dismissal. This applies even in cases of bankruptcy (4). In its decisions, the Federal Labor Court has explicitly put the protection of the individual job over the protection of the firm [Giebel, 1985, p. 177]. The firm incurs a social liability for any dismissal and, according to the rulings of the courts, elderly workers enjoy increased social protection. In addition

---

(1) Among these criteria are: period of employment, age, health, affiliation responsibilities, income of husband, wealth.
(2) For distinct labor market groups that are considered to be in need of special protection, the legislator has set up an even more stringent dismissal protection. To these groups belong especially members of works council and other employees in charge of the shop rules act; draftees (to the army as well as to community services); handicapped employees (even no dismissal for exceptional reasons); apprentices and pregnant women and young mothers. The maternity dismissals protection starts with pregnancy and extends to four months after delivery. In case the female employee opts for maternity leave, the dismissal protection ends two months after the end of the leave. Thus, the duration of this special dismissal protection is 13 months at least and 17 months at most.
(3) For employees older than 50 (55) and with an employment duration of at least 15 (20) years, severance pay is 15 (18) monthly earnings.
(4) This paragraph was implemented in 1972 in the sequel of the Shop Rules Act (Betriebsverfassungsgesetz).

to the legal provisions, there have been collective agreements to protect this group.

Roughly 8 percent of dismissed employees brought their case to court in 1978 [Falke et al., 1981, p. 127]. Statistics are rather poor in this field, but some information on the dynamics of the courts' involvement in dismissal disputes can be derived from the number of finished cases. These statistics, however, do not fully reflect the increase in dismissal disputes because of the capacity constraints of the labor courts (Table 10). Before the recession of 1974/75, less than one percent of all separations were brought to the labor courts. The marked increase thereafter indicates employees' intensified consciousness of their rights. This is enhanced by the fact that unions provide legal aid to their members.

Social plans are collective agreements between the firm and its works council in cases of substantial changes within the firm. Such a change could be a prolonged cut in production (1), a partial or complete closing down of the firm, a change of the firm's site, or an introduction of new technology. The legal basis is the Shop Rules Act of 1972 (2) that applies to firms with more than 20 employees. The social plan can be enforced by the works council. Its basic idea is to reconcile technical progress with social targets, and it is seen in a direct context with the social liability of property (Art. 14 Grundgesetz - West German Constitution). Labor courts have developed the idea of "social property rights" (Sozialer Besitzstand) which would be impaired by substantial changes within the firm and for which the affected employees must be compensated. If the firm is not willing to develop a social plan, the works council can bring the case before the court and usually the firm is forced to pay according to the rules for unfair dismissal.

---

(1) According to highest level jurisdiction, not only large-scale dismissals resulting from structural changes of production and/or of the production program entitle the works council to insist on a social plan, but even dismissals in a cyclical downturn.
(2) Before 1972, social plans were enacted casually in the course of the 1966/67 recession for the mining and the steel industries.

Table 10 - Legal Actions on Dismissal Protection, 1967-1985

	Number of finished cases	
	yearly average	as a percent of total separations
1967-1973	52,044	0.8
1974-1980	113,118	1.8
1981-1985	166,830	3.0

Source: Bundesminister für Arbeit und Sozialordnung [Bundesarbeits-blatt, various issues]; Bundesanstalt für Arbeit [unpublished material]; own calculations.

In cases of bankruptcy, the claims laid down in social plans used to have priority. But after a decision by the Federal Constitutional Court in 1983, the situation is inconclusive. With both, social plan as well as restrictive dismissal protection, more firms are forced into bankruptcy than under normal conditions in a market economy: to avoid insolvency, it is often necessary to dismiss parts of the workforce, but social plan charges may be so high as to drive the firm into bankruptcy (1). The social protection for the redundant part of the work force leads to a situation where the total workforce will become redundant.

c. The Economic Effects of Dismissal Protection and Social Plans

Because of the casuistic rulings of the courts and the high probability for employers to be defeated in dismissal cases, employers often prefer immediate severance payments to pursuing the case in the court. Falke et al. [1981, p. 144] found that in 1978 for nearly one third of all dismissals for firm-specific reasons severance payments were made. In the sample used by Falke et al., the average severance payment amounted to

(1) There was a legal change in 1985: the Employment Promotion Act (Beschäftigungsförderungsgesetz) makes the provision that new firms are excepted from social plan claims for four years.

DM 7,150 (1). In 10 percent of the dismissals, the severance payment was between DM 20,000 and DM 75,000 [ibid., pp. 138-142]. The indemnities in social plans on average seem to be higher than severance payments because of dismissals. Vogt [1981, pp. 131-135] estimated that the average compensation payments in social plans between 1975 and 1980 amounted to roughly DM 12,500 (2). Official statistics on aggregated dismissal compensation payments (including those resulting from social plans) are only available for manufacturing. According to these data, they have increased considerably: in 1972, the dismissal compensation payments in manufacturing were three times higher than in 1966 and in 1982 about ten times higher than in 1972. It has become increasingly expensive to change the workforce via dismissals or simply via restructuring producing facilities.

Theory tells us that the costs of dismissal protection and social plans are included in the employer's calculation whether it is profitable to employ additional labor or even the incumbent workforce. All other things being equal, either the wage paid to the employee must be lower than before or productivity must rise to compensate for this additional cost element if labor demand is not to change. If neither occurs, the employer must reduce employment to restore a profit-maximizing situation [e.g., Nickell, 1979; Schellhaass, 1984]. From this it follows that an increase in dismissal costs will increase productivity requirements for additional labor. Furthermore, it is to be expected that, given volatile demand, employers' caution to take on new workers will become greater as dismissal costs increase (3).

Greater caution on the part of employers means that the probability of the unemployed and of new entrants being hired will decline. Polls among

---

(1) For comparison: net average earnings in 1978 amounted to roughly DM 19,000.
(2) For comparison: on average the net earnings of employees in the West German economy in 1975-1980 (social plan payments are tax free) amounted to DM 18,500.
(3) If uncertainty of future prospects increases, this will contribute to further hesitation. The latter effect and increasing dismissal costs can hardly be disentangled because both have materialized from the 1970s to the present time.

Table 11 - Dismissal   Compensation   Payments   in   Manufacturing,
1966-1984 (a)

	Compensation payments			
	DM mill.	1972=100	per separation, 1972=100 (b)	
			uncorrected	corrected (c)
1966	41.4	26.3	24.8	38.9
1969	67.8	43.0	43.9	59.4
1972	157.7	100.0	100.0	100.0
1975	544.9	345.5	370.9	295.1
1978	657.3	416.8	430.8	291.7
1981	1174.5	744.8	713.3	414.2
1984	2514	1594.2	1973.8	1070.4

(a) Firms with more than 50 employees. - (b) Compensation payments divided by the total number of separations (dismissals and quits) in the economy. - (c) Compensation payments per separation divided by the increase in earnings per employee in the economy.

Source: Statistisches Bundesamt [various issues]; Bundesanstalt für Arbeit [unpublished material]; own calculations.

enterprises show that chances for the unemployed, especially the marginal groups, have permanently and deteriorated, and that the jobs of skilled workers have become more stable while jobs for unskilled labor have become scarce [Daniel, Stilgoe, 1978; Bacot et al., 1977].

In the European Community, employers in manufacturing were asked what sort of measures to enhance flexibility in the labor market would increase employment (1). The answers "Shorter periods of notice for dismissals and simpler procedures at labor courts" and "intensified use of contracts with finite duration" scored the highest ranking. Retailers saw the greatest chances in "lower entry wages for new hires" and "shorter periods ...".

_____

(1) The following references are taken from Nerb [1986, pp. 6-11].

214

Figure 3 - Hirings and Separations, 1960-1984 (a)

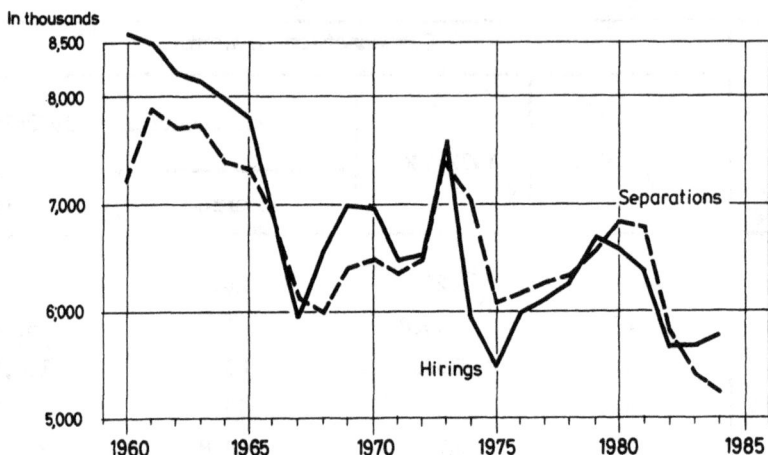

(a) Dismissals and quits.

Source: Bundesanstalt für Arbeit [various issues].

Experience in West Germany shows that both hirings and separations
(quits and dismissals (1)) change in the same direction: declining in
downswings and rising in upswings (Figure 3). It is interesting to note
that, until 1973, there were always more hirings than separations (with
the exception of 1966/67), only after 1973 was the picture reversed. The
absolute number of separations was about 1.5 million higher from 1959 to
1965 than afterwards; and from 1966 to 1973, separations on average
were higher, too, than in the 1974-1984 period. Despite higher separations, the ratio of inflows into registered unemployment to separations
was markedly lower for the 1966-1973 period (2) - on average 30 percent
- than for the time thereafter - on average 50 percent; it increased to
two thirds in the 1980s (Figure 4). The ratio of inflows to total employees has certainly been somewhat higher since 1975 than it was before
but remained astonishingly stable over the following period. From this,
one can infer that it was not the risk of becoming unemployed that was
characteristic for the labor market problem in West Germany; rather it
was the declining chance to come back into employment again. This is

(1) There is no information on inflows prior to 1966.
(2) West German labor statistics do not provide separate information.

Figure 4 - Unemployment in West Germany, 1966-1986

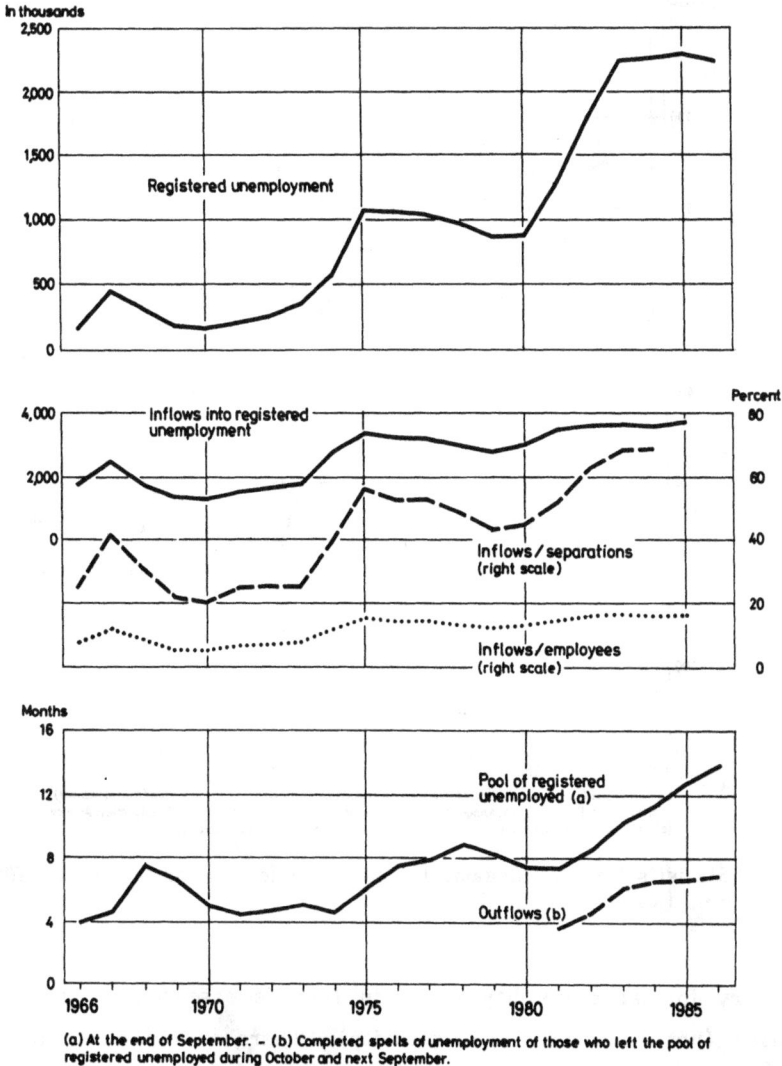

(a) At the end of September. - (b) Completed spells of unemployment of those who left the pool of registered unemployed during October and next September.

Source: Bundesanstalt für Arbeit [various issues].

reflected in the strong increase in the duration of unemployment that points to the sharpened inside-outside dichotomy of the labor market.

In view of this evidence, it is highly questionable whether for the economy as a whole it was a good strategy to foster employment via penalizing dismissals. On the contrary, it seems as if dismissals were

Figure 5 - Migration of Labor (a) and Job Vacancies, 1960-1984 (b)

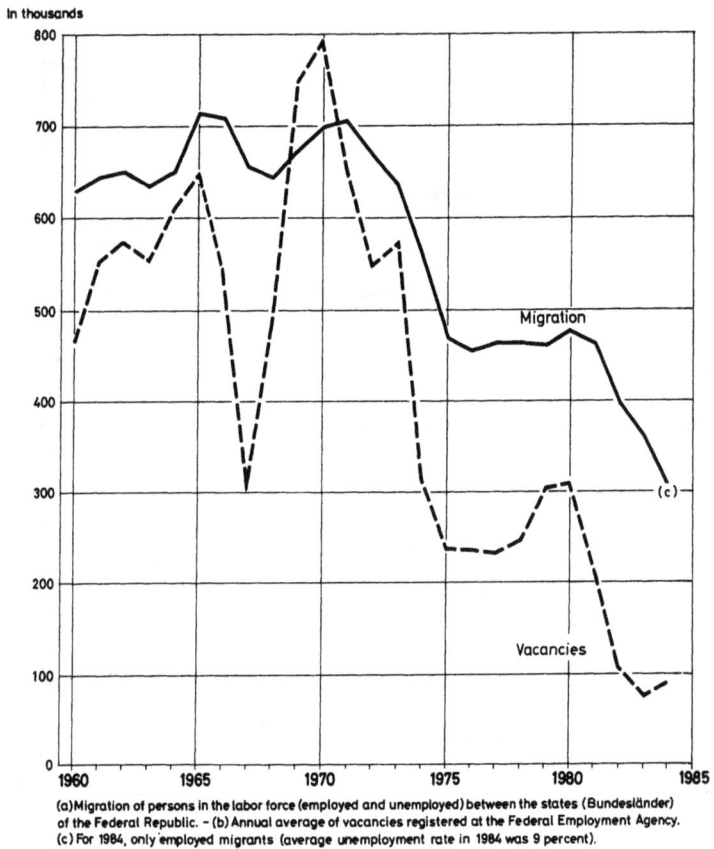

(a)Migration of persons in the labor force (employed and unemployed) between the states (Bundesländer) of the Federal Republic. - (b) Annual average of vacancies registered at the Federal Employment Agency.
(c) For 1984, only employed migrants (average unemployment rate in 1984 was 9 percent).

Source: Statistisches Bundesamt [various issues]; Bundesanstalt für Arbeit [various issues].

necessary for labor mobility which in turn is essential for employment security (not necessarily job security). There is evidence, too, that regional mobility is impaired (Figure 5). The reluctance of entrepreneurs to offer job openings reduces the willingness of job-hoppers or discontented employees to look for other jobs. With higher adjustment costs, there is less impulse for a domino-like process of reshuffling the allocation of labor through a myriad of small individual adjustment processes (chain-mobility process). To discourage individual adjustments means that the whole system is becoming more sclerotic.

Table 12 - The Market for Short-Term Employment, 1973-1981

Year	Total	Placements of the Employment Office		Placements of temporary work firms (a)	
		up to 7 days	more than 7 days up to 3 months		
	1000 (1)	1000 (2)	1000 (3)	1000 (4)	percent of (1) (5)
1973	1522	1011	229	282	18.5
1974	1246	866	192	188	15.1
1975	1083	753	190	140	12.9
1977	1319	858	238	223	14.9
1978	1327	810	239	278	20.9
1979	1447	850	244	353	24.4
1980	1519	784	230	425	28.0
1981 (b)	1244	661	203	380	30.5

(a) Average duration of placement was 19.5 days (1973), 14.4 (1975), 17.7 (1979), 18.6 (1981). - (b) The Statistics were not continued after 1981.

Source: Bundesanstalt für Arbeit [various issues].

The increase in the labor market rigidity can likewise be measured by an intensified utilization of flexibility loopholes which allow a reduction of the high share of fixed labor costs. Such a loophole is temporary work [Walter, Soltwedel, 1984] (1). Temporary work has gained an increasing share in the market for short-term employment (Table 12, col. 5). Companies supplying temporary workers have strongly expanded although they are regulated to a large extent and have to compete with a labor exchange that is heavily subsidized. Because of the extraordinarily high cost differences due to regulations, temporary employment firms must be far more efficient than the labor exchange whose services (2) are free of charge to both employer and unemployed.

---

(1) Unions are opposed to temporary work in West Germany. Their call for a complete ban was partly successful in 1982, when temporary work in construction was forbidden.
(2) After 1981, there was a strong expansion in the activity of temporary work firms even after temporary work was declared illegal in the construction industry in 1982: employment in temporary work firms more than doubled from 1982 to 1985.

218

Government reacted somewhat to the need of the economy for more labor market flexibility by putting the Employment Promotion Act into effect in 1985. This act allows firms to use contracts with finite duration (up to two years) that were heavily regulated before. It also allows the extended use of temporary work - up to six months - which used to be restricted to three months and reduced the compulsory requirements in social plans (new firms are exhibited from social plan requirements for four years). This act seems to be a small a step in the right direction to enhance the flexibility of the labor market [e.g., Kronberger Kreis, 1986], unfortunately it will expire in 1990 unless Parliament agrees to prolong the law. This feature of the law reflects political reasons rather than the belief that flexibility requirements will be significantly lower in the 1990s than at present.

5. Development of Profits and Corporate Investment

The combined effect of social policy, wage policy, and other government intervention has led to a pronounced decline of profits from productive activity. An analysis of the balance sheet data of German corporations reveals that corporate profits have mainly been earned in the nonproduction area over the last years [Dicke, Trapp, 1984; 1985]. Since the beginning of the 1980s, less than one third of corporate profits has originated from production compared to more than two thirds in the early 1970s. The ordinary rate of return - profits from productive activity in relation to the capital invested at replacement costs - declined from about 10 percent at the end of the 1960s to less than 4 percent in the first half of the 1980s (Figure 6). From 1980 to 1985, the rate of return on fixed assets was even lower than the real rate of interest in the domestic bond market. On the other side of the coin there is an increase in financial investments and in direct investment abroad at the expense of domestic investments in plants and machinery. In fact, net corporate investment in real terms declined markedly in the first half of the 1970s and has more or less stagnated since then. The share of investments in productive activities in corporations' overall investments declined from two thirds to about one third in the course of the 1970s. Instead, public

Figure 6 - Return on Fixed Assets, Real Rate of Interest and Net Investment of Private Corporations in West Germany

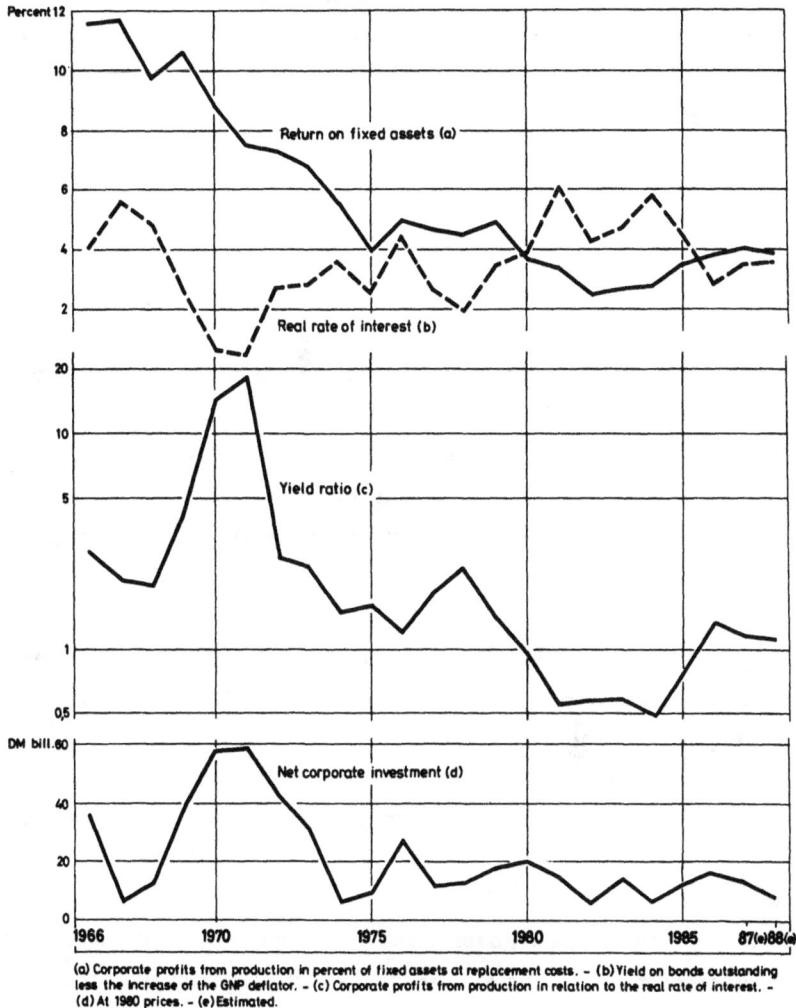

(a) Corporate profits from production in percent of fixed assets at replacement costs. - (b) Yield on bonds outstanding less the increase of the GNP deflator. - (c) Corporate profits from production in relation to the real rate of interest. - (d) At 1980 prices. - (e) Estimated.

Source: Deutsche Bundesbank [various issues]; own calculations.

investment and residential construction gained in importance. Depressed corporate investment has led to slower growth of the productive potential of the economy. During the 1960s, potential production increased at an average annual rate of 4.5 percent; in the 1970s, the growth rate declined to about 3 percent and in the first half of the 1980s, it was 1.5

220

to 2 percent. To revive capital formation, government interventions have to be reduced and more flexibility in wage policy has to be enforced by reducing moral hazard and by allowing fierce outsider competition in the labor market. Lasting progress in this direction requires that the government ultimately withdraws its protection from the bilateral monopoly in the labor market.

6. Summary

Since the early 1970s, the labor market situation in West Germany has deteriorated markedly. In 1986, total employment was about one million (4 percent) lower than in 1973. As the growth of the labor supply accelerated during the 1970s, unemployment increased sharply. The unemployment rate rose from about 1 percent in the early 1970s to 9 percent in the mid-1980s.

The hypothesis underlying this paper is that the West German labor-market problems can be traced back to the change in the policy regime that took place in the late 1960s and which was worked out during the 1970s. The political change in 1982 did not lead to a reversal of the legal and institutional setup that had been developed during the previous two decades.

Since the late 1960s, the government has moved towards more interventionist macroeconomic policies because of the widespread belief that a more active macroeconomic policy was necessary to maintain a high rate of growth and full employment; the market economy was considered to be inherently unstable. In addition, the federal government assumed responsibilities for industrial and regional developments. Furthermore, social reforms were implemented in order to achieve "social justice" and "social peace" which were regarded as preconditions for political stability and for sustained economic growth. An outstanding element of the new policy regime was the unconditional "full employment guarantee" which the Federal Government declared at a time when the unemployment rate was below one percent.

By taking over responsibility for full employment, the government increased collective moral hazard of both employers' associations and
unions. They implicitly expected demand management as well as structural and social policies to take care of any labor-market problems. The
great number of programs supporting growth and employment since the
mid-1970s, the increase in subsidies, and the expansion of labor-market
policies and of welfare benefits have justified this expectation. Governmental interference enabled unions and employers to pursue collectivistic
wage policies that ignored the need for lower real wage increases and for
greater wage differentials in the economy.

The readiness of the government to tackle or to relieve employment
problems combined with the monopolistic features of the wage bargaining
system in West Germany led to a pronounced real wage rigidity. Because
wage settlements were binding for all companies, adjustment to declining
sales and prices was concentrated on employment. Where outsiders were
able to endanger the bilateral cartel on the labor market, the government
stepped in to provide protection against the underbidding of insiders'
wages: in those sectors of the economy covered by collective agreements
only to a relatively small degree, contractual wages and working
conditions were declared compulsory even for outsiders.

Comprehensive social policy measures added substantially to the cost of
labor. The share of fringe benefits in total labor costs increased from
43 percent in 1966 to more than 80 percent in 1984. In order to prevent
companies from reducing employment "arbitrarily" and "unsocially", protection against dismissals was intensified. In addition, labor law has
developed the idea of a "social property right" of employees in their
current jobs. Any significant production change or reduction of employment leads to costly social plans in order to reconcile technical progress
with social targets. So it became increasingly expensive to change the
firms workforce via dismissals or via a restructuring of production
facilities.

Contractual wages are minimum wages and welfare benefits draw the
bottom line for lower-wage groups. By marked increases of welfare benefits relative to earned income, the government has supported unions'

efforts to push for above average wage increases for unskilled workers. The reduction of wage differentials combined with the legal and institutional setup of the labor market has imposed severe barriers to entry for marginal groups of the labor force. This has caused serious problems because of the increase in the labor force. While government interventions helped to enforce contractual wages as minimum wages thus preventing efficient underbidding by outsiders, labor market policies and early retirement schemes deliberately aimed at buying out labor at existing wages in order to reduce the supply of labor. In addition, rather generous income maintenance schemes have implied considerable individual moral hazard.

Due to the increase in government activities, the share of public expenditures has risen from one third to almost half of GNP over the past twenty years. Income tax deductions and social security contributions have risen correspondingly. High marginal tax rates have provided incentives for outsiders not to try too hard by underbidding to find employment in the official sector of the economy but to evade into the shadow economy.

The increase in employment costs and the distorted incentives to work and to invest resulted in a severe economic loss that is mirrored in the depressed yield on fixed productive assets. Firms switched from investments in productive capacities to financial investments and to direct investments. The consequences was a sustained slow-down of the growth rate of the productive potential of the economy.

Bibliography

BACOT, Maryse, et al., La legislation relative à la protection de l'emploi et son impact sur les politiques des entreprises. Paris 1977.

BOSS, Alfred [1986a], "Finanzpolitik seit 1982: Stärker wachstumsorientiert?" Die Weltwirtschaft, 1986, H. 1, pp. 47-54.

BOSS, Alfred [1986b], "Moral hazard als Folge der Lohnfortzahlung im Krankheitsfall - Empirischer Befund und Vorschläge zur Therapie". Schriften des Vereins für Socialpolitik, Gesellschaft für Wirtschaft und Sozialwissenschaften, Neue Folge, Vol. 159, Ökonomie des Gesundheitswesens, Berlin, 1986, pp. 177-188.

--, "Zur Steuerreform in der Bundesrepublik Deutschland". Die Weltwirtschaft, 1987, H. 1, pp. 46-60.

BUNDESANSTALT FÜR ARBEIT, Arbeitsstatistik, Jahreszahlen. Nuremberg, various issues.

CALMFORS, Lars, "Trade Union, Wage Formation and Macroeconomic Stability - An Introduction". The Scandinavian Journal of Economics, Vol. 87, 1985, pp. 143-159.

DANIEL, William Wentworth, Elisabeth STILGOE, The Impact of Employment Protection Laws. Policy Studies Institute, Vol. 44, London 1978.

DEUTSCHE BUNDESBANK, Monatsberichte. Frankfurt, various issues.

DEUTSCHER BUNDESTAG, Bericht der Bundesregierung über die Entwicklung der Finanzhilfen und Steuervergünstigungen gemäß §12 des Gesetzes zur Förderung der Stabilität und des Wachstums der Wirtschaft (StWG) vom 8. Juli 1967, Subventionsberichte. Bonn, various issues.

DICKE, Hugo, Peter TRAPP, Investment Behavior and Yields in Some West German Industries. Institut für Weltwirtschaft, Kiel Working Papers, 205, November 1984.

--, --, "Zur Ertragskraft von öffentlichen und privaten Investitionen". Die Weltwirtschaft, 1985, H. 1, pp. 70-87.

DONGES, Juergen B., Dean SPINANGER, Interventions in Labour Markets - An Overview. Institut für Weltwirtschaft, Kiel Working Papers, 175, May 1983.

--, Klaus-Werner SCHATZ, Staatliche Interventionen in der Bundesrepublik Deutschland. Umfang, Struktur, Wirkungen. Institut für Weltwirtschaft, Discussion Papers, 119/120, May 1986.

FALKE, Josef, Armin HÖLAND, Barbara RHODE, Gabriele ZIMMERMANN, Kündigungspraxis und Kündigungsschutz in der Bundesrepublik Deutschland, Forschungsbericht 47 - Arbeitsrecht - des Bundesministers für Arbeit und Sozialordnung. Bonn 1981.

FRITZSCHE, Bernd, Dietrich von LOEFFELHOLZ, Unbeabsichtigte Einkommensvorteile bei Arbeitslosigkeit. Mitteilungen des Rheinisch-Westfälischen Instituts für Wirtschaftsforschung. Vol. 32, 1981, pp. 13-20.

GIEBEL, Ulrich J., Sozialleistungen und Unternehmensgrößenstruktur. Köln 1985.

GUNDLACH, Erich, "Gibt es genügend Lohndifferenzierung in der Bundesrepublik Deutschland?" Die Weltwirtschaft, 1986, H. 2, pp. 74-88.

HERSCHEL, Wilhelm, Vom Wesen der Allgemeinverbindlichkeitserklärung von Tarifverträgen, Recht der Arbeit, Vol. 36, pp. 162-164.

HUECK, Alfred, Hans Carl NIPPERDAY, E. TOPHOVEN, Tarifvertragsgesetz mit Durchführungs- und Nebenvorschriften. Kommentar, 4th Edition by Eugen Stahlhacke 1964.

IFO-INSTITUT FÜR WIRTSCHAFTSFORSCHUNG, Konjunkturtest - Sonderfragen - Ergebnisse. Munich, various issues.

JÜTTEMEIER, Karl H., Subsidizing the Federal German Economy - Figures and Facts, 1973-1984. Institut für Weltwirtschaft, Kiel Working Papers, 279, February 1987.

KRIEGER, Christiane, Carsten S. THOROE, Wolfgang WESKAMP, Regionales Wirtschaftswachstum und sektoraler Strukturwandel in der Europäischen Gemeinschaft. Kieler Studien, 194, Tübingen 1985.

KRONBERGER KREIS, Mehr Markt im Arbeitsrecht. Schriftenreihe Vol. 10. Bad Homburg 1986.

MINISTERIUM FÜR ARBEIT UND SOZIALORDNUNG, Bundesarbeitsblatt. Bonn, various issues.

NERB, Günter, "Mehr Beschäftigung durch Flexibilisierung des Arbeitsmarktes?" Ifo-Schnelldienst, 1986, H. 24, pp. 6-11.

NICKELL, Stephen J., "Fixed Costs, Employment and Labour Demand over the Cycle". Economica, Vol. 45, 1979, pp. 325-345.

ORGANIZATION FOR ECONOMIC COOPERATION AND DEVELOPMENT (OECD), The Challenge of Unemployment. A Report to Labor Ministers. Paris 1982.

PAQUE, Karl-H., Labour Surplus and Capital Shortage - Unemployment in the First Decade after the Currency Reform. Kiel 1987, mimeo.

SACHVERSTÄNDIGENRAT ZUR BEGUTACHTUNG DER GESAMTWIRTSCHAFTLICHEN ENTWICKLUNG, Jahresgutachten 1968, Bundestagsdrucksache V/3550. Bonn, December 1968.

--, Jahresgutachten 1969, Bundestagsdrucksache VI/100. Bonn, December 1969.

SCHELLHAASS, Horst-M., "Ein ökonomischer Vergleich finanzieller und rechtlicher Kündigungserschwernisse". Zeitschrift für Arbeitsrecht, Vol. 15, 1984, pp. 139-171.

SCHMIDT, Klaus-D., et al., Im Anpassungsprozeß zurückgeworfen. Die deutsche Wirtschaft vor neuen Herausforderungen. Kieler Studien, 185, Tübingen 1984.

SCHMIDT, Klaus-D., Erich GUNDLACH, Das amerikanische Beschäftigungswunder: Was sich daraus lernen läßt. Institut für Weltwirtschaft, Discussion Papers, 109, July 1985.

SOLTWEDEL, Rüdiger, Staatliche Interventionen am Arbeitsmarkt - Eine Kritik. Kiel 1984.

--, "Employment Problems in West Germany - The Role of Institutions, Labor Law and Government Intervention". In: Karl BRUNNER, Allan W. MELTZER (Eds.), Carnegie-Rochester Conference Series on Public Policy, Vol. 27, 1988, forthcoming.

STATISTISCHES BUNDESAMT, Fachserie 16, Arbeitskostenerhebungen, H. 1, Arbeitskosten im Produzierenden Gewerbe. Stuttgart, various issues.

THON, Manfred, Das Erwerbspersonenpotential in der Bundesrepublik Deutschland. Entwicklung seit 1961 und Projektion bis 2000 mit einem Ausblick bis 2030. Beiträge zur Arbeitsmarkt- und Berufsforschung, 105, Nuremberg 1986.

US CONGRESS, JOINT ECONOMIC COMMITTEE, The Economics of Federal Subsidy Programs. A Staff Study prepared for the use of the Joint Economic Committee. Washington 1972.

VOGT, Aloys, Sozialpläne in der betrieblichen Praxis. Köln 1981.

WALTER, Norbert, Rüdiger SOLTWEDEL, Arbeitsmarkt und Zeitarbeit. Bonn 1984.

WATRIN, Christian, Ulrich J. GIEBEL, "Sozialpolitische Hemmnisse für die betriebliche Flexibilität". In: Gerhard FELS, Achim SEFFEN, Otto VOGEL, Soziale Sicherung: Von der Finanzkrise zur Strukturreform. Köln 1984, pp. 114-139.

WITTELER, Doris, "Tarifäre und nichttarifäre Handelshemmnisse in der Bundesrepublik Deutschland. Ausmaß und Ursachen". Die Weltwirtschaft, 1986, H. 1, pp. 136-155.

Martin J. Bailey*

Distortions, Incentives and Growth

1. The Importance of Achieving High Growth Rates

At first glance it might appear that the subject of this paper is of no great practical significance. Although both basic principles and careful accounting show that distortion of incentives, through unsound government intervention in the economy, exerts a drag on growth, the effect looks small. Except for some disastrously misgoverned third-world countries, perhaps, this drag is measured in fractions of a percentage point of annual growth. It would be all too easy to conclude that the effect is negligible. However, one decisive fact leads to the opposite conclusion: small effects that persist eventually add up to big effects.

Although this general point is so straightforward that it might seem to need no further clarification, it is helpful and indeed quite important to distinguish between two types of distortions and consequent growth effects. The first is a change in efficiency that reduces (or increases) per capita output in the long term, but has only a transient effect on the growth rate. The second lowers the long-term growth rate. Both are serious, but the second is by far the more serious.

To see the difference between these two types of distortions, consider two alternative policies by a country. The first would lower total output from given inputs by ten percent, without affecting the long-term growth rate; however, the policy would take effect on resource use gradually, so that its impact is spread over ten years. The second would lower the annual growth rate by one percentage point forever. For the first ten years, the two policies would look alike because the gradual

---

* The views expressed in this paper are the author's own, and do not necessarily reflect those of the US State Department.

impact of the first would imply a reduction of the annual growth rate by about one percentage point during that period. Thereafter, their effects would diverge, as shown in the table.

Output under Alternative Policies

	Year							
	0	10	20	30	40	50	...	100
Base-line path	100	134	181	243	326	438	...	1922
First policy	100	122	164	221	297	399	...	1747
Second policy	100	122	149	181	221	269	...	724

Although the first policy constantly depresses it, output always remains within ten percent of what if would have been without any policy intervention (the base-line path). If the policy were reversed, output would spring back up to the base-line path within, say, ten years. By contrast, output under the second policy drops further and further behind the base-line path, and recovery may not be possible.

The difference between the two cases hinges on whether a policy affects the sources of growth. A policy lowers output if it leads to misallocation of resources, regardless of their role in growth. Agricultural policy, for example, leads to misuse of land, labor, fertilizer and other inputs, and capital. These effects can lower total output without having any appreciable effect on the long-term rate of growth. By contrast, if a policy lowers economy-wide the marginal product of a factor of production whose input is itself growing, it lowers the steady-state growth rate. Consider the standard expression that decomposes growth into its components:

$$g = wdL + rdK + g'$$

where g is the annual growth rate of output, w is the marginal product of labor, dL is the annual growth rate of labor input, r is the marginal product of capital, dK is the annual growth rate of capital input, and g' is the unexplained residual (technological advance). In the major developed economies, population is nearly stable, so that dL drops to zero. In that case, a policy will lower the long-term growth rate only if it lowers the productivity of capital, the rate of capital accumulation, or the rate of technological advance.

The above table shows that small, apparently miniscule differences in growth, if they persist long enough, eventually become dramatic. It is best to illustrate this point with concrete cases. For example, if the data can be trusted, in the 18th century Britain's output grew at a rate of about 0.7 percent per year while its population grew at a rate of just under 0.5 percent; the discrepancy implies that output per capita was rising by just over 0.2 percent; however, due to trade, Britain's standard of living was rising somewhat faster than that. These numbers increased gradually, until by the end of the 19th and early 20th centuries, output per capita was increasing at about 1.3 percent per year. This rise of about one percentage point in the rate of growth of per capita output raised Britain's people out of pre-industrial backwardness and thrust them into an era of comparative affluence. I need hardly belabor the enormous difference both in a typical British family's welfare and in the nation's wealth and influence that went along with this change. The numbers for the rest of Western Europe after 1870, though varying from case to case, were about the same on the average as for Britain [O'Brien, Keyder, 1978, pp. 57-58].

Similarly, a small excess of the US rate of growth of per capita output over that of Western Europe from 1870 to 1950 raised the US to the wealthiest country, overall and per capita, in the world. In those years, per capita output grew at about 2 percent per year, compared to about 1.3 percent in Western Europe [Maddison, 1964, p. 30]. As a result of this apparently small differential, by the early 1950's US real income per person was nearly double that of Western Europe. Thus, a persistent small change in the growth rate eventually makes a large difference.

Through the 1950s and 1960s, Europe seemed to have learned a lesson from past experience. With highly growth-oriented policies and the opportunities presented during reconstruction after World War II, Europe narrowed the gap between its standards of living and that in the US. But this period of excellent performance tapered off, so that a much larger growth differential had the much less dramatic effect of a temporary policy, like the reverse of the first policy shown in the table. Although the temporary losses due to the war were easily made up, the effects of a long-term growth differential were not. The basic elements of the long-term growth equation, just shown, had not been improved.

2. Distortions of Incentives

Output levels and growth rates are sensitive to incentives and to distortions. The effects are usually difficult to measure, but there can be not doubt of their importance. Here is a brief list of policies that distort incentives and interfere with output or growth:

- agricultural programs;
- barriers to international trade;
- subsidized and regulated industries, such as the US merchant marine, and steel and others in Europe;
- costly, excessive environmental, safety, and health programs;
- interference in labor markets.

Agricultural programs distort incentives in several ways. Artificially high prices for agricultural products stimulate overproduction, drawing extra labor, capital, and land into the production of these products. That is, there is an artificial incentive to produce too much, an incentive for too many people to remain in farming, for the use of too much fertilizer and equipment, and so on. The high prices also provide an incentive for consumers to cut back on the consumption of these products. When this policy results in surpluses, and the government disposes of these by exporting them, it must provide an artificial incentive to consumption elsewhere, and a reduction of the incentive to produce elsewhere, by subsidizing the exports and lowering world prices. When this policy results in a reduction of imports, that also lowers world prices and provides an artificial incentive to consumption elsewhere. Other agricultural programs, such as the target price program in the US, operate on the incentive system differently in detail but are similarly distortive.

Barriers to international trade distort incentives by artificially raising the prices of import substitutes and lowering the prices received by exporters. Resources are pushed out of export industries into import substitution.

Subsidized industries generally receive artificially high revenues and thus have an incentive to attract or retain too many resources. Often, without the subsidies, such industries are obsolete and would close down. Regulated industries may have incentives to attract too many or too few resources, depending on the specifics of the regulations. In the case of public utilities, economists in the US have found the incentive effects to be quite complex and to have surprising effects on capital intensity.

Environmental, safety, and health programs create incentives to invest in special equipment that may or may not serve the announced objectives of the programs. In the US, the surprising effect in most cases has been to protect established firms from new competition, and thus to have effects on growth that go beyond the direct, measurable costs of the required investments. Usually the investments involved are quite capital-intensive, and absorb scarce capital that could contribute to growth in other uses.

Interference in labor markets creates incentives to deflect labor away from its most productive uses. Overgenerous unemployment benefits, laws that interfere with dismissals of workers, and so on, tend to increase unemployment. Most modern forms of labor-market intervention have this effect, and some also reduce labor mobility.

3. Some Estimates of Growth Effects

In the interest of presenting concrete examples, I will give some notion of the magnitudes involved in three areas: agriculture, US environmental laws, and labor legislation in Europe. All of these have had their strongest impact in the past ten or fifteen years, and so help to account for the poor growth performance of OECD countries in this period.

Agriculture: Current unpublished estimates show the costs of the various agricultural policies to be about $150 billion in gross cost to consumers and taxpayers per year in OECD countries (1). In round numbers, that is about two percent of OECD's GDP in total. About half of this gross cost is transfers, and about half is an outright reduction of total real incomes. Assuming that nearly all of this cost has built up over a ten-year period from a small base, the reduction of real incomes at the end of the period implies a growth effect of 0.1 percent per year. However, this effect is unlikely to persist. Output will remain lower than it could be, but the growth rate is not permanently lowered, as the discussion in the first section has indicated.

Environmental legislation: A noteworthy feature of environmental legislation in the US is that it has concentrated on new sources of pollution. New plant and equipment must meet costly pollution standards whereas existing plant and equipment need not. Consequently, the old ones have a valuable, cost-saving right to pollute, and continue to operate long past the point at which they would otherwise have been scrapped. Both the extra costs of the standards at the new facilities, and the inefficiencies of the old ones, slow US growth, while in the short run pollution may have been increased rather than reduced. The direct costs of pollution abatement have been estimated by Ed Denison. In the early 1970s they rose to an annual average of about $10 billion per year; their consequent effect on growth worked out at 0.36 percent per year. (Since 1975, however, these costs have been less of a drag on growth, averaging about 0.09 percent [Denison, 1978; 1985].) Moreover, there is an

---

(1) OECD estimates for 1979-1981 updated by members of the staff of the US Council of Economic Advisers.

additional, unmeasured effect of the old, obsolete plants being kept in operation.

It could have been much worse. The Clean Water legislation of 1970 decreed that the US should by 1985 have "zero discharge" of pollutents into its lakes and streams; it also established interim standards for 1983. When the EPA surveyed the states and summed up the investment costs of compliance with the interim standards, the result was some $468 billion in dollars of 1974. That was some 32 percent of a year's GNP at that time. Annual operation and maintainance of the necessary water purification plants and further construction with the growth of the economy would come on top of that. The effect, if this program had ever been carried out, would have been a large permanent reduction of the real standard of living. (And these were just the *interim* standards. The cost of true zero discharge would have been immensely higher, and indeed the goal might not be achievable at any finite cost [US Environmental Protection Agency, unpublished study cited in Kneese and Schultze, 1975, p. 70; US Environmental Protection Agency, 1977].)

Similarly, our passion for eliminating cancer-causing substances from the environment, if applied with equal force to all suspected carcinogens would eat up a big fraction of the real GNP. In 1978 I estimated that the Clean Water Program and the anti-carcinogen programs, taken together, would cost from 17 to 27 percent of the US GNP for the indefinite future; if added without cutting back existing government programs it would lower real private incomes from 25 to 40 percent [Bailey, 1980, pp. 11-14]. But fortunately, our passion in such matters has not yet gone to the extreme of actually applying the relevant laws in full.

Even when not fully implemented, these programs probably lower the long-term growth rate, because they lower the productivity of capital. Both the Clean Water Program and the anti-carcinogen programs require large capital investments for their environmental goals, usually with very low returns in benefits. To that extent, they lower the rate of return to the capital added by the nation's savings, without increasing its amount. Consequently, the growth formula shown in Section 1 would show a reduction.

Labor Legislation: Some specifics of this problem have just been clearly set out in the excellent paper by Soltwedel and Trapp. When I see the data showing growing unemployment in the EEC since 1970, and note the rules concerning the discharge of workers, I am struck by the similarity with Italy in the decade or so just after World War II. Starting in 1946, Italy had massive "structural unemployment", which disappeared in the early 1960s. Two pieces of labor legislation affected it. One affected labor mobility, and the other affected the discharge of workers. Until 1961, a law inherited from the fascist period prevented internal migration of unemployed workers [Hildebrand, 1965, pp. 355-361]. Until 1947, there was also a law prohibiting the discharge of workers; and for years after that, strong labor unions forced high severance payments for discharged workers.

The incentive effects of the latter law and contract provision are clear and drastic. An added worker is a fixed cost like debt service: too much of it can bankrupt a firm [Lutz, 1962, pp. 208-209 and p. 318]. Consequently, firms look for ways to avoid hiring – use of labor-saving equipment, use of overtime to meet peak-load demand, and so on. The result of this set of factors was high unemployment, and their disappearance by the early 1960s contributed to an excellent post-war growth rate in Italy. (I am struck also by the similarity to the effects of tenure legislation for school teachers in some states in the US, which became common in the 1930s.)

For the EEC, the growth of unemployment averaged 0.6 percentage points of the labor force per year, from 1970 to 1985 [OECD, 1986, Table R12, p. 67]. Taking into account the effects of labor-saving equipment on labor productivity, the net effect on GDP was a loss of about 0.33 percent from the average annual growth rate (1).

These effects on employment would surely affect long-term growth if the labor force were to continue growing into the indefinite future. However, population growth in Europe has slowed down as in the US, and will

---

(1) Based on a Cobb-Douglas production function with a labor coefficient of 0.55.

probably taper off to zero in the foreseeable future. In that case, the long-term growth rate is not affected.

For a country with all the above problems, including significant barriers to trade, the effect of these many small insults to output and growth become substantial. Given enough zeal in all these areas, a country could reduce its average annual growth by the greatest part of one percent, or even more. However, not all of these examples are policies that lower the long-term growth rate; some only lower output. Among other things, that means that the damage can be undone fairly quickly if and when the policies are abandoned or their severity is reduced.

Bibliography

BAILEY, Martin J., Reducing Risks to Life: Measurement of the Benefits. Washington 1980.

DENISON, Edward F., "Effects of Selected Changes in the Institutional and Human Environment upon Output per Unit of Input". Survey of Current Business, Vol. 58, 1978, pp. 21-44.

--, Trends in American Economic Growth, 1929-82. The Brookings Institution, Washington 1985.

HILDEBRAND, George, Growth and Structure in the Economy of Modern Italy. Cambridge, Mass., 1965.

KNEESE, Allan V., Charles L. SCHULTZE, Pollution, Prices, and Public Policy. Brookings Institution, Washington 1975.

LUTZ, Vera, Italy: A Study in Economic Development. London 1962.

MADDISON, Angus, Economic Growth in the West. New York 1964.

O'BRIEN, Patrick, Caglar KEYDER, Economic Growth in Britain and France, 1780-1914. London 1978.

ORGANISATION FOR ECONOMIC COOPERATION AND DEVELOPMENT (OECD), Economic Outlook, Vol. 40. Paris, December 1986.

US ENVIRONMENTAL PROTECTION AGENCY, Cost Estimates for Construction of Publicly-Owned Wastewater Treatment Facilities, 1976 Needs Survey. Washington, February 10, 1977.

Comments on Rüdiger Soltwedel and Peter Trapp,"Labor Market Barriers to More Employment: Causes for an Increase of the Natural Rate? The Case of West Germany" and on Martin J. Bailey," Distortions, Incentives, and Growth "

Emil-Maria Claassen

The increasing, if not bewildering, trend of regulations for the German labour market is illustrated by R ü d i g e r S o l t w e d e l and P e t e r T r a p p. After having read their paper, I had the impression that West Germany is unique (compared with other countries) in regard to two institutions: the German Bundesbank and the overregulated German labour market.

It is rather unbelievable that a voluntary wage cut agreed upon by individual employers and workers whose jobs are endangered, is considered as illegal. It is also unbelievable that labour courts protect dismissals even if such a decision leads to bankruptcy and, consequently, to more unemployment. I did not know that there are minimum wages even for qualified workers.

The rise of the German unemployment rate from 1 per cent in the early 1970s to 9 per cent in the mid-1980s is due to a rise in frictional unemployment (e.g., lower labour mobility between regions because of lower wage differentials) and in structural unemployment since the unemployment duration has increased, but also due to a rise in cyclical unemployment, at least for the 1980s. Unfortunately, the authors did not try to evaluate the natural unemployment rate for the mid-1980s compared to the early 1970s. Is it 2 per cent (as in the early 1970s), or 4 per cent, or 6 per cent? It certainly is not 9 per cent.

The phenomenon of over-regulated labour markets is common to nearly all European countries and it must be one of the causes of a higher NAIRU evident all over Europe since the 1970s.

Unemployment Rate, 1980-1985

	1980	1981	1982	1983	1984	1985
US	7.1	7.6	9.7	9.6	7.5	7.2
Europe	5.8	7.7	9.3	10.4	10.9	11.2
West Germany	3.4	4.8	6.9	8.4	8.4	8.4

From the above figures, two interesting features emerge. On the one hand, the evolution of unemployment between the US and Europe is rather similar for 1980-1982 while it diverges considerably for 1983-1985. On the other hand, the West German performance was always better with respect to the average European unemployment rate.

The divergence between the US and Europe may be due to the different policy mixes: fiscal expansion and monetary contraction in the US and fiscal/monetary contraction in Europe. But still the puzzle between West Germany and Europe remains. By looking at the *absolute* figures of unemployment rates, West Germany always did better. However, by considering the *relative* rise of unemployment in 1985 compared to 1980, West Germany's performance was by far worse than that of Europe. Consequently, Soltwedel and Trapp's contention seems to be correct to the extent (or under the hypothesis) that the overwhelming part of the rising unemployment - in West Germany and in Europe - is of the natural-unemployment kind.

M a r t i n   B a i l e y is concerned with the impact of distortions upon the long-term growth rate. I have some difficulty in imagining how the *level* of distortion could influence the *growth rate*. If the author understands distortions in the sense of *rising* distortions, then the causal nexus becomes more plausible.

The issue of why distortions arise is not treated. The paper is only concerned with the approximate quantitative effects of distortions on the long-run growth rate.

The positive theory of regulations provides us with some explanations of the causes. What I should like to discuss is the question of whether the distortions have a chance to be maintained over the very long run, because this very long-run perspective is the horizon the author has chosen in order to demonstrate the devastating effects of distortions on the long-run level of real income.

Thanks to George Stigler, we can use supply and demand analysis to determine regulations. The demand side consists of pressure groups who aim at elevating the price above market pricing via regulations. The supply side consists of the political process in a democratic country. Legislation in terms of regulations can be granted by the parties in power if they receive something valuable in return, i.e., mainly votes for their (re-)election, *and* if these measures do not threaten their position by significantly increasing opposition.

The increasing opposition is important in this respect. The opposition is represented by the consumers who pay the higher prices and by those taxpayers who finance the extra tax in the case of additional subsidies. The increasing opposition is probably the reason for decelerating the continuous regulation process and, at some time in history, for giving rise to measures of deregulations. It is this dynamic aspect of regulations and deregulations (or call it the life cycle of distortions) which is not elaborated in the paper and which should be analysed, since Martin Bailey is concerned with the very long run. However, his quantitative conclusions that a wave of deregulations - at a certain point in history - does not wipe out distortions created by former regulations may remain valid.

Gerhard Fels

Rüdiger Soltwedel and Peter Trapp give us a comprehensive survey of the various labour market regulations in Germany and try to assess their impact on employment. They reveal a permanent deterioration in the institutional framework of the labour market and suggest that this was the main cause of the increase in the natural rate of unemployment. I

238

must confess that I feel much in sympathy with the spirit of the paper. It provides us with convincing examples conducive to teaching politicians what negative effects they can generate if they limit the freedom of contract. It is also important to confront labour courts on the employment implications of their sentences.

The authors never touch upon the question of whether there was an increase in the natural rate. But among economists a wide consensus exists that the NAIRU (non-accelerating inflation rate of unemployment) went up in Germany as in other countries throughout the 1970s and 1980s. A lot of empirical studies, a most recent one by Burda and Sachs (1), suggest this conclusion. There is of course discussion as to how far the actual unemployment rate is away from the natural rate, so that the scope for unconditioned demand stimulation through monetary and fiscal policy is not clearly given. Thus the paper is right to give all its attention to the micro-distortions of the labour market.

I am nevertheless somewhat uneasy with the paper. My objections are not categorical but more analytical in nature. Implicitly, it takes for granted that deficiencies in the legal framework are the main cause of the increase in the natural rate, shifting the whole responsibility to labour-market legislation. They do not check their legal hypothesis against other possible explanations, which may alter the policy conclusions.

At least two other hypotheses should be examined besides the legal-framework hypothesis:

- the one explains the increase in the natural rate with hysteresis in the follow-up to the external shocks in the 1970s and early 1980s.

- the other emphasizes the increase in union power and union militancy as a central cause for the failure of the legal system.

(1) Burda, Michael C., Jeffrey D. Sachs, Institutional Aspects of High Unemployment in the Federal Republic of Germany. National Bureau of Economic Research, Working Papers, 2241, Cambridge, Mass., 1987.

Of course, these three explanations are interwoven. For instance, hysteresis has a lot to do with deficiencies in the institutional framework, and stronger union power also influences labour-market legislation and the interpretation of labour laws by the courts. But, if the two other hypotheses are of significance, a simple reform of legislation affecting the labour market (e.g., lower unemployment compensation, less dismissal protection, more freedom of individual contracts, no declarations of "general binding" for wage agreements) would not be sufficient. The hysteresis argument would perhaps require investment promotion and measures for the rehabilitation of disenfranchised people. The union power argument would call for more legal control of this power (or at least less support of it by the government).

My impression is that the paper correctly assesses the necessity of adjustments in labour-market regulations but understates the importance of increased union power for the malfunctioning of the collective bargaining system. Many inconsistencies in this system have more to do with increased union power than with misguided legislation. This means that a change in the legal framework will not alter the situation as long as unions are as strong as they are.

The authors themselves stress the increased influence of the unions. Figure 2 on page 196 shows a downward trend in the degree of unionisation during the 1950s and 1960s, followed by an upward trend during the 1970s and stabilisation at a high level in the 1980s. The German system of labour-market organisation worked excellently in the 1950s and 1960s but failed to do so afterwards when the degree of unionisation increased again. It is a striking question why unions in Germany have gained more and more influence whilst the unions have been a declining branch in the United States since the early 1970s, and in other Western countries since the late 1970s. I am still looking for a satisfactory answer. Is it the old German inclination to collective solutions and cartelisation? Bruno and Sachs (1) calculated a cross-country index of corporativism which shows Austria and Germany at the top of all Western

(1) Bruno, Michael, Jeffrey D. Sachs, Economics of Worldwide Stagflation. Oxford 1985, pp. 224-227.

countries. As a matter of fact, public opinion moved from anti-union to pro-union at about the end of the 1960s. Today, unions meet a very favourable climate in the mass media and among cultural elites. Only one third of the population believes that unemployment has something to do with unions. Politicians are highly reluctant to remind unions of their responsibility to employment. During the 1984 strike, IG Metall was in a desperate situation until Chancellor Kohl and Norbert Blüm (Minister for Labour and Social Affairs) bailed it out.

The collective bargaining system was regarded as an ingenious way of wage formation for a long time. Its most emphasized merit is that it prevents the government from getting involved in the struggle for higher income shares. But another advantage is that it also protects individual firms from becoming involved in highly emotional negotiations between workers and management. A basic idea is to place the battle on income distribution extra muros. The consequence of this system is a high degree of corporativism. Adherents to the system warn of the danger of syndicalism which may arise when wage negotiations are brought down to the firm level. The experience of other Western European countries with a lower degree of corporativism are not encouraging in this respect. Nevertheless, the German system suffers from a significant lack of downward flexibility. Let me add some observations with respect to this point.

It is doubtful whether relative wages which match relative scarcity of labour can be found in negotiation rounds. They have never been found there. As long as contractual wages were below the equilibrium wage level, the necessary differentiation of wages by industry, region and profession was found within the wage drift. This is the way in which the collective bargaining system works efficiently. But the excessive increase of contractual minimum wages during the 1970s limited the scope for extra payments and thus eroded the system. During the 1980s, there was moderation in the increase of contractual wages, but obviously not enough to allow a wage drift within which the greater need for differentiation could have been covered.

Wage differentiation still exists, especially in effective wage rates, but in many cases wage differences are not in line with scarcity differences. In North Germany, where unemployment is above average, effective wages are, in general, higher than in the prosperous south. The highest wages for workers in the automobile industry are paid not in Baden-Württemberg but in the Saarland, a region with outstanding employment problems.

It must be stated that the wage drift is often highest in depressed industries and regions, for instance in the steel industry in North-Rhine Westphalia. It is not the contractual wages but the extra payments not fixed by collective bargaining which are the impediment to adjustment. One explanation may be that the workers councils are more easily prepared to accept the dismissal of marginal workers than to accept a reduction in privileges for the intra-marginal workers whose jobs are not endangered. The majority/minority problems can thus also be observed on the firm level where union power is strong. This puts the argument that the permission of firm settlements below collective contract wages would increase wage flexibility somewhat in the shade.

To declare collective wage contracts generally binding is a clear violation of the principle that wage settlement should be independent of government influence. But, although the number of contracts declared compulsory has increased, only 20 per cent of the total labour force works under this regime. In all other branches the collectively contracted wages are not binding for employers who are not members of the employers' associations. Only a few cases are known in which these employers pay lower wages than employers who are members. The normal behaviour is that they pay the same or even higher wages. An exciting question is why non-member employers do not use their degree of freedom, and why so many employers are members of the employers' associations although membership is voluntary. My answer is: union power drives employers into the organisations or leads employers to behave as if they were members. It is doubtful whether a change in the legal framework could alter this situation.

My conclusion is that a more sophisticated analysis of the collective bargaining system is necessary. It must be empirical and should account not only for the legal framework but also for the power structure. Economists have not yet found a common ground with politicians. Politicians who think only in distribution categories often have no understanding of the market, and economists who think in efficiency categories often have no understanding of power. How are they to be brought together?

Leland B. Yeager

I learned much from the paper by Rüdiger Soltwedel and Peter Trapp in particular and from the ensuing discussion. All along, I had been vaguely aware that a kind of petty protectionism permeates the German economy; but it was instructive to learn details of the many ways in which German policy impairs the functioning of the labor market, and with the consequences one might expect.

I was surprised that the paper was criticized as likely to be unsuccessful in influencing public opinion because it lacks numerical estimates of the losses of jobs and output inflicted by unwise policy. Even as it stands, the paper makes a great contribution by lucidly organizing a mass of relevant institutional facts; and it seems pointless to criticize its not being decorated with dubious numbers. To come up with valid numbers would be an impressive intellectual achievement; but for precise and credible numbers, it seems to me, one would have to work with data from several dozen otherwise identical countries practicing different labor-market policies. Certainly it is not enough to apply econometric ingenuity to time-series figures from a single country. One reason is that the effects of the policies described by Soltwedel and Trapp occur spread out over time. The figures from each year or each quarter do not constitute a separate data set, a separate observation. It takes time, for example, for people to learn about and act on the attractive alternatives to holding a job that German policy affords; it takes time for new attitudes about the respectability of being unemployed to spread throughout the population.

It would be discouraging to think that market-oriented economists cannot hope to influence public opinion unless they come up with definite numerical estimates of the benefits and costs of each particular policy measure applied on each particular occasion. Such numbers, if offered with any claim to precision, are almost bound not to be credible. They are likely to be more in the nature of decoration than solid argument. Are they what we must nevertheless rely on? Must we treat each specific policy issue arising on each occasion as a separate case to be decided on its own distinct merits? Are there, instead, no generally applicable principles of economics in which we can hope to instruct the public?

Summary of the Discussion by Joachim Scheide

The discussion concentrated on two problems: firstly, how should we measure the effects of various government interventions and regulations in product and labor markets, and secondly, how can the attitudes of the governments and the population (i.e., those who benefit and those who have to pay) possibly be changed? One question related to the measured effects (e.g., in terms of GNP) of government interventions is discussed in Martin Bailey's paper. Should we think of them as one-time reductions in the level, or rather reductions in the growth rate, of GNP? Some of the interventions do not imply permanent reductions in growth but may just be qualified as bad episodes. For example, in the case of agricultural intervention, it was argued that it had led almost completely to a one-time change in the level. The case of environmental legislation may be slightly different, it may have caused more of a permanent drag on growth.

Whatever we may be able to say about the effects of distortions, the fundamental question remains: how much of what we observe is really the revealed preference of the population? Were all these programs not started under the heading of fairness? Did people - at least the majority - not vote for them? Could we say that these interventions continue because the minorities - e.g., the unemployed - have no spokesmen in the political debate? Many of the barriers to entry in the labor market and elsewhere exist simply because they have been supported by those who have the power to take the decisions in the corporativistic society. This may make it difficult to change any of these regulations. There may be, however, some hope, because there are some indications from the United Kingdom, for example, that the opinion of union leaders is not the same as that of other people, including union members.

On the one hand, therefore, one may try to work towards changing the tastes and preferences of the people. On the other hand, economists can try to estimate the costs of various measures. Even if the people wanted all those interventions, they might change their minds if they could be provided with worthwhile information and told how much they are paying in terms of real income for those measures of fairness, income security, job security, and so on.

In this respect, the paper by Rüdiger Soltwedel and Peter Trapp presents a starting point. Some participants of the conference argued that for public policy discussion, it would be helpful if the authors came up with some hard figures; in order to prove to the man in the street how these massive amounts of distortions will actually affect the unemployment rate. Others argued that measuring the effects of interventions in labor and product markets is a very difficult matter.

V

Ronald I. McKinnon*

Money Supply versus Exchange-Rate Targeting: An Asymmetry between the United States and Other Industrial Economies

1. Introduction

For floating exchange rates from the early 1970s to 1985, this paper identifies a fundamental asymmetry in the conduct of monetary policy by the United States on the one hand, and the principal European economies as well as Japan on the other.

Following a changing mix of purely domestic American monetary indicators, the Federal Reserve System, typically, did not adjust US money growth to stabilize the dollar exchange rate before 1985. Indeed, more often than not, American monetary expansion was negatively correlated with the strength of the dollar in the foreign exchange markets: easing when the dollar was weak and tightening when it was strong so as to exaggerate exchange rate fluctuations.

In contrast, from 1971 to 1985 West Germany (representing the continental European bloc) and Japan, on average, adjusted their domestic money growth to be correlated positively with the strength of their currencies against the dollar in the foreign exchanges. In effect, the Bundesbank, other European central banks, and the Bank of Japan opted, although with but limited success, to stabilize their dollar exchange rates: on average, they increased domestic money growth when

---

* I would like to thank Kenichi Ohno of the International Monetary Fund for his great help in completing this paper.

their currencies were appreciating and contracted with exchange depreciation.

This asymmetry has important implications for monetary control within the United States and for the nature of the international business cycle. I shall argue that, by being excessively "nationalistic" in ignoring information contained in the foreign exchanges in the 1970s and early 1980s, the US Federal Reserve System did a rather poorer job of stabilizing the domestic American price level, while needlessly aggravating exchange rate fluctuations and cycles of inflation and deflation in the world economy.

Subsequently, a regime change might have occurred. Starting in 1985 with the Plaza Hotel accord, European central banks and the Bank of Japan kept their money growth rates quite low through 1987 despite the dollar's fall in the foreign exchange. The US Federal Reserve System shifted from high money growth in 1985-1986 to very low growth in 1987 - apparently because of the run on the dollar in that year. Although this 1985-1987 monetary response pattern to floating exchange rates differs substantially from the earlier experience, it is too recent to be analyzed in the body of this paper.

Nevertheless, the earlier experience, where the Fed virtually ignored the strength or weakness of the dollar in the foreign exchanges form 1971 to early 1985 while other central banks did systematically respond, is of great interest in its own right - and could happen again. So let us try to characterize how this asymmetry worked itself out.

2. The International Dollar Standard

As is well known, the Bretton Woods system of fixed exchange rates lasting from 1945 to 1971 was, in reality, a dollar standard. In order to peg their currencies to the dollar within a narrow band, industrial countries other than the United States intervened continually in the foreign exchanges and adjusted their domestic money growth to support their dollar parities. In contrast, the United States (as the "n-th" country) was uniquely free to pursue purely domestic monetary objectives without having to react so directly to pressures in the foreign exchanges - although the gold convertibility constraint occasionally put weak indirect pressure on the American monetary authorities.

With the advent of "floating" exchange rates in the early 1970s, it is rather surprising that asymmetric elements of the old fixed-rate dollar standard persisted. The dollar remained the invoice currency for a high proportion of international trade (particularly in primary commodities) and the important currency of denomination for cross-country capital flows [McKinnon, 1979]. Hence, monetary authorities in other industrial countries, more open than the United States, found that preserving either internal price level stability or international competitiveness required that they try to smooth their dollar exchange rates.

When portfolio disturbances emanated from the United States, other industrial countries behaved as if they were acting collectively: they expanded when the dollar was weak and contracted when it was strong [McKinnon, 1982]. Each was also anxious to offset any domestic portfolio disturbance that would move its dollar exchange rate out of line with those of other industrial competitors.

3. Some Evidence of Monetary Asymmetry

These effects are not easy to measure unambiguously. The more successful central banks are in stabilizing their dollar exchange rates, the less correlation between exchange rates and domestic money growth can one observe. The covariance that remains may be quite sensitive to the choice of time period - weeks, months, or quarters - within which the correlation is measured. There are many definitions of exchange rates, money supplies, and so forth. Hence, the statistical procedures used here are only indicative, and must be interpreted with caution.

248

Figure 1 - US Nominal Effective Exchange Rate (1980=100)

Note: The IMF definition of the dollar exchange rate is "merm" weighted against 17 industrial countries which are trading partners of the United States. Merm means "multilateral exchange rate model" and is close to the concept of trade weighted. The index is foreign currency/dollars.

Source: IMF [various issues].

Figure 1 shows the International Monetary Fund's index of the nominal or "effective" dollar exchange rate, "merm", weighted against 17 other industrial countries. Fluctuations in such a broad measure of the dollar exchange rate are likely dominated by portfolio disturbances in the American financial markets, rather than those in specific foreign countries. What then were (are) the reaction functions of central banks?

Let quarterly percentage rates of change in M1 measure the monetary response of each central bank, and then correlate these with quarterly percentage changes in the IMF's effective dollar exchange rate. It turns out that within-quarter correlations are not high, and become progressively lower as one disaggregates to (noisier) monthly and weekly data. However, using five-quarter moving averages of both changes in the effective dollar exchange and national money-growth rates yields the strikingly negative correlations shown in Figure 2 and Tables 1 or 2.

Figure 2 shows the collective monetary response of the seven principal industrial countries other than the United States: the UK, Canada, France, Germany, Italy, Japan, and the Netherlands. Among convertible-

Figure 2 - Rate of Change for US Effective Exchange Rate and the Rest
of the World (a) Money (percent per year)

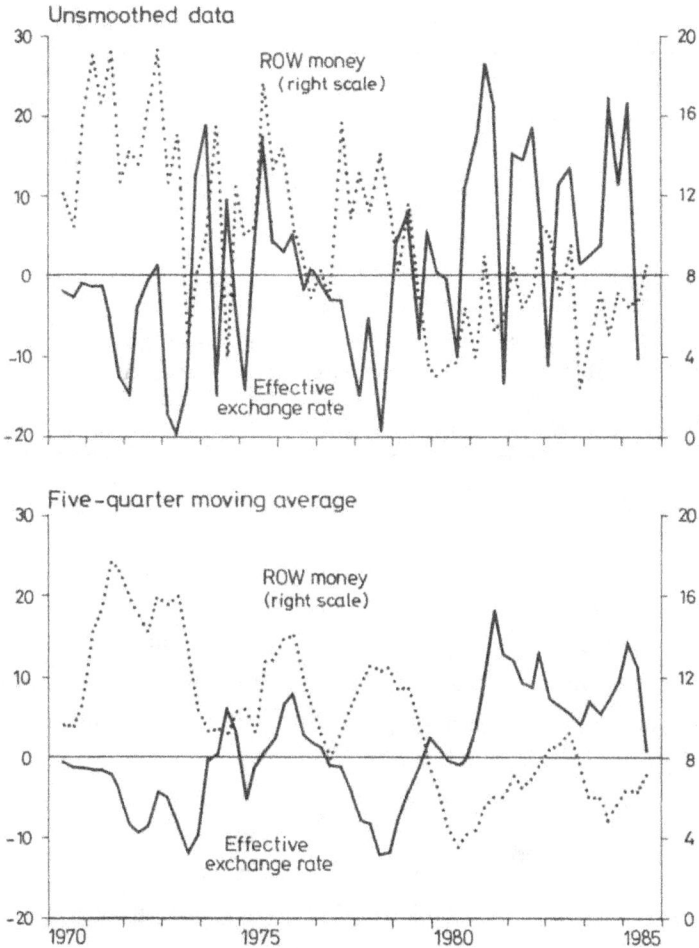

(a) ROW is the rest of the industrial world: Canada, France, Germany,
Italy, Japan, the Netherlands, and the United Kingdom.

Source: IMF [various issues]; Federal Reserve Bank of St. Louis
[various issues].

currency countries providing portfolio alternatives to holding dollar
assets, these seven dominate the stock of transactions balances in the
form of Ml - and thus are simply called the "rest of the world" or ROW.

Table 1 - The Dollar Exchange Rate and Money Growth in the United
States, Japan and Germany: Correlation Matrix for the
1970.IV-1986.II Period

	Not detrended				Detrended			
	E^{US}	M^{US}	M^{JA}	M^{GE}	E^{US}	M^{US}	M^{JA}	M^{GE}
E^{US}	1				1			
M^{US}	-0.417*	1			-0.690*	1		
M^{JA}	-0.405*	-0.245	1		-0.388*	0.486*	1	
M^{GE}	-0.499*	0.112	0.452*	1	-0.455*	0.514*	0.156	1

Note: *Significant at the 5 percent level or better. Data contain 63
observations on quarterly percentage changes smoothed by a five-quarter
moving average. - The E^{US} is the "merm" weighted IMF definition of
changes in the dollar exchange rate against 17 other industrial countries: foreign currency/dollars. The Ms are changes in narrow money
supplies taken from the Federal Reserve Bank of St. Louis.

Source: As for Figure 2.

Without taking relative exchange-rate movements (1) into account, how
can one unambiguously aggregate over the seven countries to calculate
percentage growth in ROW money? For the 1970-1985 period from which
the data are taken, define money growth in the rest of the world to be

[1] $M^{ROW} = \Sigma(w^i M^i)$ i = 1, 2,.....7

where M^i = growth in M1

        w^i = relative weight (GNP for 1977) of ith country such that
        $\Sigma w^i = 1$

The IMF uses a slightly more complicated aggregation procedure to construct its merm-weighted 17-country index of the foreign currency value
of the dollar - call it E^{US}. But virtually any other broad index of the
dollar's foreign-exchange value yields roughly the same results.

---

(1) However, the absolute level of ROW money - as distinct from its percentage rate of change - cannot be unambiguously aggregated without specifying exchange rates at every data point. See McKinnon
[1984] for a discussion of this aggregation problem.

Table 2 - The Dollar Exchange Rate and Money Growth in the United States, Japan and Germany: Correlation Matrix for the 1970.IV-1984.IV Period

	Not detrended				Detrended			
	E^{US}	M^{US}	M^{JA}	M^{GE}	E^{US}	M^{US}	M^{JA}	M^{GE}
E^{US}	1				1			
M^{US}	−0.008	1			−0.519*	1		
M^{JA}	−0.620*	−0.195	1		−0.168	0.338*	1	
M^{GE}	−0.562*	0.102	0.457*	1	−0.341*	0.423*	0.026	1

Note: See Table 1. This time there are only 57 observations.

Source: As for Table 1.

Figure 2 shows this correlation between changes in ROW money and changes in the dollar exchange rate broadly defined. In the upper panel, the simple correlation in unsmoothed quarterly data is -0.280. However, if one smooths the percentage changes in ROW money and the dollar exchange rate over five quarters, this negative correlation increases sharply to -0.599 and is highly visible in the lower panel of Figure 2. When the dollar is strong (rising), ROW central banks cut their collective money growth significantly to resist further increases, and vice versa.

The fundamental asymmetry of the "dollar standard" can be seen in Tables 1 and 2, where Japan and Germany are now separated out - but still representative - of the "rest of the world". The monetary correlations of the United States, Japan and Germany to fluctuations in the IMF's broad index of the dollar exchange rate are displayed.

Depending on whether the smoothed data are detrended or not, Tables 1 and 2 show that US money growth either responds perversely to the dollar exchange rate or not at all. That is, M^{US} is either uncorrelated or negatively correlated with E^{US} - as is visually (barely) evident in Figure 3. Money growth in the United States could well be increasing above normal when the dollar is weak: indeed excessive monetary expansion by the US Federal Reserve System could sometimes be what drives the dollar down, and vice versa.

In contrast, the Bundesbank and the Bank of Japan exhibit a stabilizing response to fluctuations in the dollar exchange rate: M^{GE} or M^{JA} are each also negatively correlated with E^{US}, as one would expect from the analysis of ROW money contained in Figure 2. So they tend to contract when the dollar is strong and expand when it is weak (1).

Because growth in American M1 was unusually high during the great "engineered" fall of the dollar over 1985-1986, I did this same correlation analysis in Table 2 (as in Table 1) but excluded these "extreme" 1985-1986 observations which are so visible in Figure 3. One still gets negative, albeit weaker, correlation between M^{US} and E^{US} in Table 2. It seems fair to conclude that the American monetary authorities were not oriented toward stabilizing the dollar in the foreign exchanges from 1971 through early 1985 - unlike the Bundesbank and the Bank of Japan.

This asymmetry implies that money market disturbances in the United States tended to be amplified in the world economy by the reactions of foreign central banks [Swoboda, 1978]. If unusually strong American monetary expansion incidentally caused the dollar to depreciate, foreign central banks also expanded their money supplies, thus causing inflationary pressure in the world system as a whole. Tables 1 and 2 also indicate some positive correlation between American and foreign money growth - more so for Europe (represented by Germany) than for Japan.

---

(1) In the German and Japanese cases, I have also done these correlations substituting the mark/dollar or yen/dollar exchange rates respectively for E^{US} - and by substituting the German "merm" or the Japanese "merm". The resulting statistical correlations with national money growth using these "own" exchange rates are weaker - although generally of the same sign as in Tables 1 and 2. Because their individual (dollar) exchange rates may be somewhat more influenced by money-market disturbances in Germany and Japan than is E^{US}, they are a less pure reflection of money-market disturbances emanating from the United States which foreign monetary authorities try to smooth.

Figure 3 – Rate of Change for the US Money Supply (M1) and the "Merm" Exchange Rate (percent per year for smoothed data)

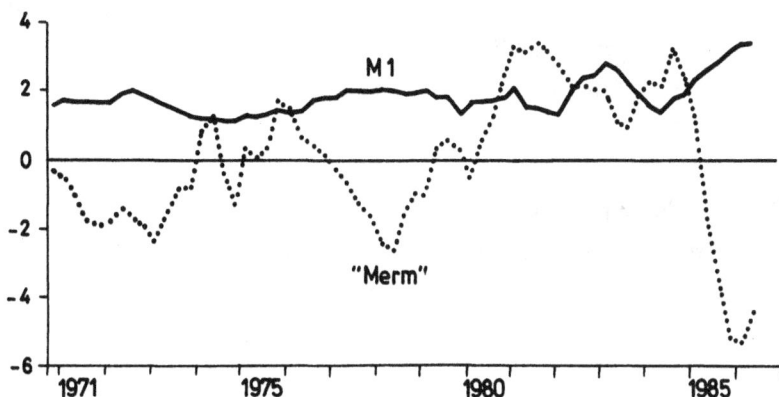

Source: As for Figure 2.

What might be empirically more important, however, is that apparently random fluctuations in the dollar exchange rate also induced collective monetary expansions or contractions abroad, creating an internationally synchronized business cycle. These "random" changes in dollar exchange rates are more associated with shifts in the (international) demand for dollar assets, reflecting future expectations, than with indentifiable concurrent changes in the American money supply [McKinnon, 1982].

4. Monetary Rules for the United States: Money Supply versus the Exchange Rate

Because the Fed (unlike other central banks) has not keyed on stabilizing the dollar exchange rate in any sustained way in the postwar period, domestic American money growth has been independently or "exogenously" determined in this important respect. Did this unique degree of freedom enable the Fed to do a better job of stabilizing the American economy from 1971 to 1985?

For the period of floating exchange rates which began in the early 1970s, I shall argue the converse. Pressure on the dollar exchange rate informed the Fed about unexpected shifts in demand for dollar assets in general, and about effective future changes in the demand for US money in particular. By ignoring this information, the American central bank did a rather worse job of stabilizing the internal American price level (1) than if the Fed had followed a monetary rule requiring it to help other countries stabilize the dollar exchange rate.

To illustrate this hypothesis, let us first test how well purely domestic US money growth predicted future changes in the American price level (P) - measured by changes in either the American WPI (producer price index) or the American GNP deflator. Consider the following equation regressing current quarterly changes in US prices on quarterly changes in American M1 over the preceding three years, i.e., lagged 12 quarters.

$$[2] \quad P = C + \Sigma(a_{-t}M_{-t}) \quad t = 1, 2, \ldots, 12$$

Equation [2] tests the principle of *domestic monetarism*: whether the domestic money supply by itself controls variations in the domestic price level within a three-year time frame.

For the period of fixed exchange rates of the 1960s ending in the first quarter of 1973, Table 3 shows that domestic monetarism worked rather well for the United States. In the regressions on either the American GNP deflator or on the WPI, the sums of the coefficients on the money supply variable were 0.98 and 1.62 respectively, with highly significant

(1) What the central bank's ultimate goals should be are, of course, not fully resolved. However, monetary economists generally agree [see, for example, Friedman, 1968] that the most that can be feasibly accomplished is to ask the central bank to stabilize the purchasing power of the money it issues. In this paper, I interpret this dictum narrowly to mean targeting some broad index of the domestic price level in domestic-currency prices - such as the WPI or GNP deflator. However, because the exchange rate itself defines the purchasing power of domestic money over a broad range of foreign goods whose invoice prices in foreign currencies might be sticky, exchange-rate stabilization *per se* could also plausibly be given a heavy weight in the central bank's objective function. And I have taken this more general approach in other papers [see, for example, McKinnon, 1988].

t-statistics. Serial correlation in the residuals was absent. No wonder American monetarists became convinced that, because the domestic demand for money was sufficiently stable, imposing a constant growth rule for the supply of money would itself smooth major cyclical variations in domestic prices!

However, with the advent of floating exchange rates, the principle of domestic monetarism collapsed. Running exactly the same regression contained in [2] from the second quarter of 1973 to the last quarter of 1984, the first two equations in the middle panel of Table 3 indicate that the coefficients on the US money supply became insignificant - as does the R^2 for the equation as a whole. Furthermore, the residuals now show serial correlation, as if some major explanatory variable had been omitted.

Could the "missing" variable be the dollar exchange rate? Knowing that the exchange rate is a forward-looking asset price [Frenkel, Mussa, 1980], let us include it as a second explanatory variable in our single equation regression:

[3] $P = C + \Sigma(a_{-t}M_{-t}) + \Sigma(b_{-t}E_{-t}) + v$ $t = 1, 2,....., 12$

Because E is defined as foreign currency/dollar, the expected sign for the b-coefficients is negative: a fall in the dollar exchange rate indicates price inflation to come in the American economy. And the middle panel of equations in Table 3 show the sum of the b - coefficients to be significantly negative: -0.34 for the GNP deflator and -1.07 for the WPI. That is, a one percent appreciation in the dollar exchange rate would eventually reduce P^{DEF} by 0.34 percent. Because the WPI consists more of internationally tradable goods, it is even more sensitive eventually increasing virtually one-for-one with the dollar exchange rate.

After any change in E^{US}, the peak impact on the American WPI occurs after about 8 quarters have elapsed (9 or 10 quarters for the GNP deflator). Using smoothed data, Figure 4 shows the strong negative correspondence between movements in the WPI, GNP deflator, and the dollar exchange rate 8 quarters earlier.

Table 3 - The United States: Regressions of Price Levels on Domestic Money and the Dollar Exchange Rate

Dependent variable	M^{US}	E^{US}	$\bar{R}^2$	S.E.R (percentage points)	D.W.	Period
DEF^{US}	0.98 (8.24)		0.61	0.26	2.03	1962.II-1973.I
WPI^{US}	1.62 (5.58)		0.47	0.64	2.07	1962.II-1973.I
DEF^{US}	0.44 (1.12)		0.11	0.58	0.78	1973.II-1984.IV
WPI^{US}	0.81 (0.70)		-0.04	1.73	0.98	1973.II-1984.IV
DEF^{US}	0.57 (1.91)	-0.34 (-4.87)	0.55	0.41	1.33	1973.II 1984.IV
WPI^{US}	1.20 (1.35)	-1.07 (-5.17)	0.49	1.12	2.21	1973.II-1984.IV
DEF^{US}	-0.52 (-1.37)		0.09	0.73	1.32	1973.II-1986.IV
WPI^{US}	-1.13 (-1.24)		0.03	1.77	0.87	1973.II-1986.IV
DEF^{US}	0.20 (0.52)	-0.35 (-4.90)	0.41	0.59	1.96	1973.II-1986.IV
WPI^{US}	0.43 (0.50)	-0.93 (-5.99)	0.48	1.30	1.79	1973.II-1986.IV

Note: Data are quarterly rates of change. OLS regressions run as a 3rd order polynomial distributed lag on right-hand side variables: 12 lagged observations over three years. Regression coefficients are the sum of the 12 estimated coefficients for each lag with t-statistics in parentheses. - DEF^{US} is US GNP deflator and M^{US} is American M1 both taken from the Federal Reserve Bank of St. Louis. - WPI^{US} is the US producer price index and E^{US} is "merm" weighted dollar exchange rate against 17 industrial countries (foreign currency/dollars) both taken from IMF. The "correct" sign for E^{US} is negative.

Source: As for Figure 2.

Even the a-coefficients for the money supply look more sensible (although still not quite significant statistically) once the dollar exchange rate is included as an explanatory variable in Table 3. However, this effect is much less marked once the more "extreme" 1985-1986 observations on US money supply and exchange-rate movements are included in the regressions displayed in Table 3's bottom panel (1).

Changes in the American money supply are just not very good in predicting (cyclical) changes in the American price level over a three-year period. This is not to deny, of course, that money-supply variables dominate the American price level (and exchange rate) over much longer periods.

5. An International Model of American Price Inflation

The effect of the exchange rate on the American price level in [3], and displayed in Figures 4 and 5, seems much greater than what can be explained by direct arbitrage in international commodity markets. American exports and imports together still amount to less than 20 percent of GNP. Just looking at the "pass through" effects of exchange-rate changes on the dollar prices of goods entering American foreign trade - assuming international inflation to be given exogenously - greatly understates the ultimate inflationary impact of, say, a dollar devaluation. There are two additional money-market considerations associated with changes in E^{US} [McKinnon, 1984] that impinge on the American price level.

---

(1) Some readers may be justifiably concerned that the whole analysis so far has relied on M1 to measure "the" money supply. Because of the erratic behavior of the velocity of American M1 in the 1980s in comparison to the 1970s (Figure 5), many American monetarists have switched over to M2 as their preferred aggregate, and, in February 1987, the Fed itself dropped any official target for M1. However, if the regressions in Table 3 are rerun substituting US M2 for US M1, the results (not reported in this paper) are even worse for the domestic monetarist model for the period of floating exchange rates. The regression coefficients on the money supply even have the wrong signs.

258

Figure 4 - US Effective Exchange Rate, PPI and GNP Deflator (percent per year)

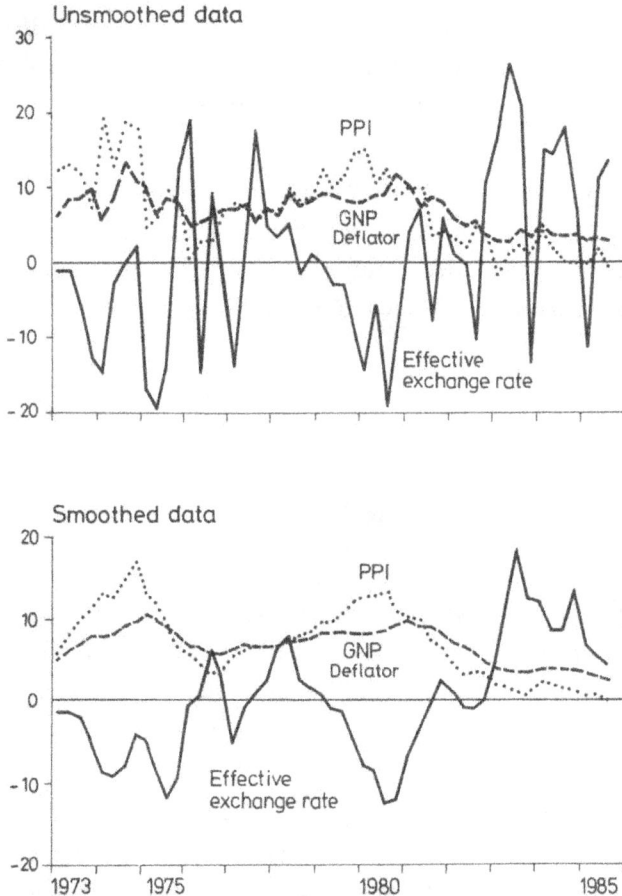

Unsmoothed data

PPI

GNP Deflator

Effective exchange rate

Smoothed data

PPI

GNP Deflator

Effective exchange rate

Note: The correlation between the effective exchange rate and PPI (GNP deflator) is -0.432 (-0.438) in the case of unsmoothed data and -0.785 (-0.784) in the case of smoothed data. - PPI is US producer price index and is commonly called the WPI in the IMF source. - The effective exchange rate is lagged 8 quarters.

Source: As for Figure 2.

First, in the financially more open American economy of the 1970s and 1980s, foreign-exchange assets are the most important portfolio alternative to holding money or bonds denominated in dollars. Because the advent of floating made future exchange rates more uncertain, the demand for dollar assets generally became much more volatile. In moving

Figure 5 - M1 Velocity for the US, Japan and Germany, 1959-1986

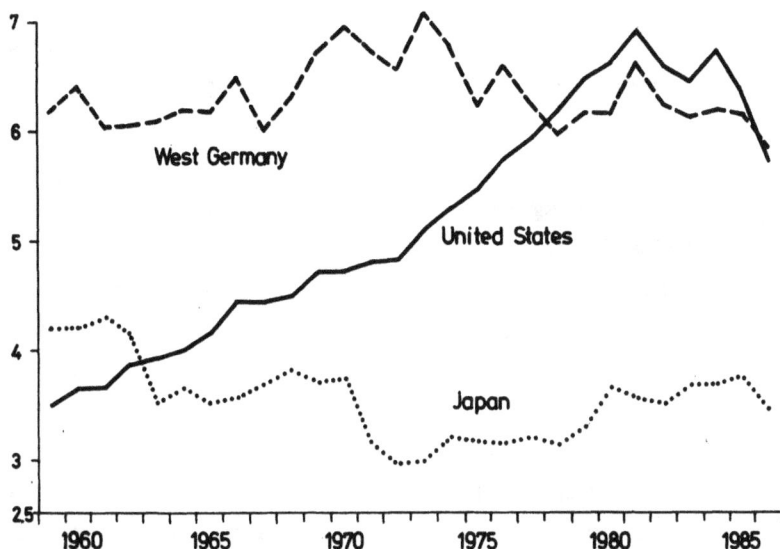

Source: Federal Reserve Bank of St. Louis [various issues].

from the 1950s and 1960s to the 1970s and 1980s, the demand for narrow US money could well have been destabilized - as evidenced by the collapse of the domestic monetarist model of the US economy.

However, the dollar exchange rate in terms of a collection of foreign "hard" monies is a convenient index of when the demand for US M1 is shifting [McKinnon, 1984]: the dollar exchange rate shifts down when the direct and indirect demand for US money falls, and vice versa. Hence, by measuring shifts in money demand, the dollar exchange rate acts as good indicator of inflationary or deflationary pressure to come *within* the American economy (as per [3]).

Second, we know that dollar depreciation generally induces monetary expansion abroad (1) (and vice versa) as shown in Figure 1. In the

_____

(1) The dollar depreciation beginning in March of 1985 could be a partial exception. Because of the unusual "engineered" nature of the dollar's fall, foreign central banks retained tight monetary stances throughout 1985 into early 1986. Rather than resisting the fall by

world economy, this inflationary impact from an increase in ROW money (Figure 1) then reinforces the initiating inflationary impulse in the United States. And the inflationary pressure is distributed across countries depending inversely on whose currencies are appreciated relative to the others.

For the period of floating exchange rates from 1971 to 1985, we have established (Table 3) that the dollar exchange rate is a very good indicator of future inflation or deflation in the United States. Can this proposition then be generalized for other industrial countries? In particular, would the dollar/mark or dollar/yen exchange rates have given good predictions of future price inflation in Germany and Japan?

No, because of the fundamental asymmetry of the world system. Monetary disturbances in either the supply of or demand for dollars originate in American financial markets and then spread out to other industrial countries associated with changes in dollar exchange rates. Hence, the mark or yen tend to be strong against the dollar coinciding with periods of inflationary pressure in the world economy as in the 1970s, and tend to be weak in times of deflationary pressure as in the early 1980s.

Thus a depreciation of the mark or yen generally has not been followed by inflation in the German or Japanese economies. Rerunning regressions in the form of [3] using either German or Japanese data yields inconclusive results for the sign of the dollar/mark exchange rate on the German price level, and for the dollar/yen exchange rate on the Japanese price level. (Some preliminary but not yet fully checked or analyzed data from these regressions are provided in Tables 4 and 5.)

In summary, any effects of changes in the dollar/mark or dollar/yen on future changes in the German and Japanese price levels tend to be offset

---

expanding their money supplies as they did in the past, foreign central banks tried to accommodate the wishes of the American government by staying fairly tight so that their own currencies would appreciate. The result was significant internal deflation in Japan and Germany [McKinnon, 1988], which mitigated the "normal" inflationary pressure in the US that one would expect from such a large devaluation of the dollar.

Table 4 – West Germany: Regression of Price Levels on Domestic Money
and Exchange Rates

Dependent variable	M^{GE}	E^{GE}	$\bar{R}^2$	S.E.R (percentage points)	D.W.	Period
DEF^{GE}	0.11 (0.92)		0.16	0.55	2.06	1973.II-1986.III
WPI^{GE}	0.16 (0.71)		0.26	1.05	1.01	1973.II-1986.IV
DEF^{GE}	-0.20 (-0.99)	MERM 0.34 (2.00)	0.12	0.54	2.25	1973.II-1986.III
WPI^{GE}	-0.48 (-1.39)	MERM 0.71 (2.37)	0.40	0.95	1.34	1973.II-1986.IV
DEF^{GE}	-0.19 (-0.95)	\$/DM 0.12 (2.07)	0.14	0.54	2.23	1973.II-1986.III
WPI^{GE}	-0.19 (-0.64)	\$/DM 0.17 (1.84)	0.47	0.89	1.44	1973.II-1986.IV

Note: DEF^{GE} is Germany GNP deflator and M^{GE} is German M1 both taken from the Federal Reserve Bank of St. Louis. - WPI^{GE} is the Germany producer price index and E^{GE} is "merm" weighted mark exchange rate against 17 industrial countries (foreign currency/marks) both taken from IMF. Note that E^{GE} is also defined alternatively as the dollar/mark exchange rate and that the "correct" sign of its regression coefficient is negative in either case. - For further notes, see Table 3.

Source: As for Table 3.

by inflationary or deflationary pressure from the opposite direction in the world economy (1).

_____

(1) The one significant exception to this offsetting process seems to be the extreme appreciation of the yen and mark since February of 1985. Because this was engineered by maintaining relatively tight money in Europe generally and in Japan, ROW money growth and

Table 5 - Japan: Regressions of Price Levels on Domestic Money and Exchange Rates

Dependent variable	M^{JA}	E^{JA}	$\bar{R}^2$	S.E.R (percentage points)	D.W.	Period
DEF^{JA}	0.82 (11.6)		0.73	0.72	0.88	1973.II-1986.IV
WPI^{JA}	1.25 (5.74)		0.41	2.22	0.88	1973.II-1986.IV
DEF^{JA}	0.85 (11.0)	MERM -0.04 (-0.40)	0.72	0.73	0.95	1973.II-1986.IV
WPI^{JA}	1.06 (5.16)	MERM 0.25 (0.88)	0.54	1.96	1.14	1973.II-1986.IV
DEF^{JA}	0.86 (10.3)	$/YEN -0.05 (-0.68)	0.72	0.74	0.93	1973.II-1986.IV
WPI^{JA}	0.91 (4.26)	$/YEN 0.35 (1.72)	0.58	1.89	1.26	1973.II-1986.IV

Note: DEF^{JA} is Japanese GNP deflator and M^{JA} is Japanese M1 both taken from the Federal Reserve Bank of St. Louis. - WPI^{JA} is the Japanese producer price index and E^{JA} is "merm" weighted dollar exchange rate against 17 industrial countries (foreign currency/yen) both taken from IMF. Note that E^{JA} is defined alternatively as the dollar/yen exchange rate and that the "correct" sign of its regression coefficient is negative in either case. - For further notes see Table 3.

Source: As for Table 3.

inflationary pressure in the world economy has been less than in previous dollar depreciations. Hence, the internal fall in the Japanese and German price levels (WPIs) has been remarkably greater [McKinnon, 1988] than in their previous experience with appreciating currencies.

6. A Concluding Note on Optimal Monetary Policy

From 1971 into 1985, the problem with international monetary instability clearly lay with the failure of the Federal Reserve System to adjust US money growth toward maintaining a more stable dollar exchange rate. With monetary disturbances emanating from the United States, foreign central banks faced a dilemma. Either they allowed their dollar exchange rates to float "cleanly" and thus more violently than even those changes we have observed, or they tried to smooth such exchange-rate fluctuations by expanding their domestic money supplies when the dollar was weak (and vice versa) thus aggravating the international cycle of inflation and deflation.

Even from the narrow point of view of an American monetary nationalist, the domestic US price level would have been better stabilized if the Fed consciously keyed on stabilizing the dollar exchange rate in formulating its domestic monetary strategy. Greater symmetry would then be introduced into the international system: when the dollar tended to be weak, US money growth would contract as foreign money growth expanded. Not only would this more symmetrical response by the Fed smooth fluctuations in the dollar exchange rate and the American price level, but the international cycle of inflation and deflation would also be ameliorated.

Fortunately, the Fed has recently taken some significant steps in this direction. In 1987, US money growth slowed dramatically in response to the run on the dollar - unlike the earlier episodes of a weak dollar in the 1970s. Moreover, The Fed's Vice Chairman Manueal Johnson [1988] recently articulated a new monetary strategy where rates of growth in domestic monetary aggregates were to be deemphasized as monetary indicators. Instead, more weight was to be given to prices determined in forward-looking auction markets - including the dollar exchange rate and the dollar prices of primary commodities, which are also determined in world markets. As of early 1988, the signs are promising that US monetary policy is becoming more internationally oriented.

Bibliography

FEDERAL RESERVE BANK OF ST. LOUIS, International Economic Conditions. St. Louis, Missouri, various issues.

FRIEDMAN, Milton, "The Role of Monetary Policy". The American Economic Review, Vol. 58, 1968, pp. 1-17.

FRENKEL, Jacob, Michael L. MUSSA, "The Efficiency of the Foreign Exchange Market and Measures of Turbulence". The American Economic Review, Vol. 70, 1980, pp. 374-381.

INTERNATIONAL MONETARY FUND (IMF), International Financial Statistics. Washington, various issues.

JOHNSON, Manuel H., Current Perspectives on Monetary Policy. Paper presented at the Conference on Dollars, Deficits and Trade at the CATO Institute, Washington 25th February 1988.

McKINNON, Ronald I., Money in International Exchange: The Convertible Currency System. New York 1979.

--, "Currency Substitution and Instability in the World Dollar Standard". The American Economic Review, Vol. 72, 1982, pp. 320-333.

--, An International Standard for Monetary Stabilization. Institute for International Economics, Washington 1984.

--, "Monetary and Exchange Rate Policies for International Financial Stability: A Proposal". Journal of Economic Perspectives, Vol. 2, Winter 1988, pp. 83-104.

SWOBODA, Alexander K., "Gold, Dollars, Euro-Dollars, and the World Money Stock under Fixed Exchange Rates". The American Economic Review, Vol. 68, 1978, pp. 625-642.

Comments on Ronald I. McKinnon, "Money Supply versus Exchange-Rate Targeting: An Asymmetry between the United States and Other Industrial Economies"

Hermann-Josef Dudler*

Ronald McKinnon's papers on the subject of world-wide monetary policy coordination and exchange-rate stabilisation contain several key elements of which a German central banker can take a positive view. The basic analytical foundations of his writings - a Friedman-type global version of empirical monetarism - are not too far apart from the thinking of those central bankers who have adopted a position of pragmatic monetarism during the past ten years. McKinnon adheres to the widely-accepted traditional monetarist tenet that inflation can, at least in the longer run, essentially be regarded as a monetary phenomenon and therefore prefers non-discretionary monetary policies, with leading central banks, as a group, assuming the task to stabilise the world price level.

Contrary to traditional hard-core monetarist teachings, but in line with many central bankers' views, he recognises unfavourable stylised facts on the actual behaviour of floating exchange rates, which failed to provide the smoothly-functioning, external equilibrating mechanism predicted by early advocates of a flexible exchange rate system. To the disappointment of academics and monetary policy-makers alike the effective real exchange rate of the world's dominant currency as well as key real exchange-rate relationships between the US dollar and other major currencies have exhibited large, medium-run swings. These seemed to correspond rather to random walk patterns than to regular adjustment paths predicted by standard exchange market models. Internationally relevant real and monetary shocks were thus absorbed by the floating rate regime in a socially costly way.

---

* These comments refer not only to McKinnon's conference paper, but also to earlier contributions dealing with the same subject.

Broadly in line with McKinnon's reasoning, major central banks have attempted to dampen excessive real exchange-rate fluctuations and, in this way, have created a "managed" floating-rate system. He correctly draws our attention to the fact that "stop-and-go-type" monetary and fiscal policies in the United States have played a leading role in initiating prolonged real dollar-rate gyrations. These exchange-rate aberrations, in turn, have provoked major central banks outside the United States to tolerate destabilising swings in domestic monetary growth in a defensive effort to reduce an over or undershooting of their national currencies. This "asymmetrical" policy behaviour, in the end, has contributed to synchronised shifts in world-wide monetary management which have exerted a global deflationary or inflationary impact.

Judging from hindsight, a German central banker could hardly deny that the Bundesbank, acting under perceived external constraints and political pressure, has tended to contribute to such global scenarios of monetary instability in the past. During the most recent period of exchange-market turmoil, the Bundesbank has, however, attached increasing weight to international monetary cooperation and global consistency of the direction of monetary policies pursued in major countries. In this context, central bank economists have submitted data on world-wide trends of monetary expansion, international raw material and world stock prices to the Bundesbank's decision-making body in order to relate monetary management in Germany systematically to international monetary conditions and the world price situation.

Does this mean that German monetary policy has begun to follow the cooperation path sketched out in the McKinnon proposals? Certainly not in the sense of the hard policy options contained in McKinnon's recent contributions. Bundesbank representatives have so far rejected plans and suggestions which argue in the direction of nominal dollar-rate pegging, global exchange-rate target zones, joint control by leading central banks of the world money stock or of raw material-price indices, i.e., international policy rules or yardsticks which would subordinate exchange-market intervention and the use of domestic monetary policy instruments to rigid international norms and commitments. The Bundesbank, as a rule, paid tribute to perceived global external constraints by deviating from its announced domestic monetary targets, when real exchange-rate shocks threatened to throw the domestic economy seriously off course and the central bank tended to lose its credibility, because its initial growth or inflation objectives were likely to be missed under the influence of prolonged volatile exchange-rate movements. Depending on initial domestic conditions, the real exchange rate of the Deutsche Mark has thus in most cases been allowed to move quite substantially before the Bundesbank felt compelled to take significant offsetting monetary action.

This apparent reluctance on the part of the German monetary authorities to enter into rigid global exchange rate and "symmetric" monetary policy commitments as proposed by McKinnon and others can be attributed to the fact that views of policy-makers and monetary reformers on hard economic realities differ in important respects. Advocates of more or less stable nominal exchange rates between key currencies tend to take a more pessimistic view of the economic and social efficiency of exchange markets than many central bankers, while the latter have greater doubts than the former as to whether national economic policies and goods, labour and domestic financial markets could be expected to absorb smoothly real and financial shocks and disturbances in the absence of flanking exchange-rate adjustments. In this context, one is struck by the obvious lack of longer-run - as opposed to shorter-run - analyses of how diverse historical shocks would have affected individual industrial economies under fixed-rate regimes in McKinnon's recent writings. The author does, in particular, not discuss the growing wealth of literature where attempts have been made to evaluate alternative monetary policy rules and approaches in medium-sized open economies depending on the kinds of external and internal shocks to which they can be exposed. In fact, he more or less starts from the presumption that exchange-rate rules represent a superior anchor for domestic monetary management, as long as major central banks are able to control collectively the world money stock or world price level.

McKinnon and other proponents of institutionalised tripartite exchange-rate arrangements by the American, Japanese and German central banks seem to assume that such an undertaking could create sufficient credibility so as to convince the general public that a definite return to a pegged exchange-rate regime could be envisaged and begin to be built firmly into market participants' expectations. In this context, McKinnon places some emphasis on the declared political will of the authorities and the existence of small or negligible inflation differentials among the leading economies at the time they create a "quasi-currency union". It almost goes without saying that policy-makers on both sides of the Atlantic - and the Pacific - tend to feel that a number of fundamental obstacles, other than political inertia and measured inflation differentials, appear to stand in the way of formal tripartite exchange-rate arrangements.

The degree of "openness" of goods, labour and financial markets of the three economies in question is significantly different, and trade and financial links between them vary greatly. The structural and dynamic adjustment properties of domestic goods, factor and financial markets in the United States, Japan and Germany are also far from being homogeneous, and their monetary and fiscal policy concepts as well as policy decision-making procedures are hardly compatible. Finally, given the size and political weight of the three countries concerned, there is no independent supranational monetary authority or institution which could enforce policy norms or sanctions upon them in order to ensure that the "rules of the game" will be observed by all participants in a tripolar exchange-rate agreement involving the US dollar, the yen and the Deutsche mark.

This does not rule out broad agreements among bigger countries on desirable exchange-rate patterns and internationally consistent economic policies. The Plaza Statement (of September 1985) and the Louvre Accord (of February 1987) provide examples of such flexible policy commitments. These arrangements, of course, leave an important role for real exchange-rate movements which are to some extent deliberately allowed to provide an international equilibrating mechanism and shock absorber. In this context, critics of the managed floating system should not overlook that pronounced movements in real exchange rates can act as an "invisible hand" which may bring about domestic policy adjustments ex post which formal political coordination efforts fail to generate ex ante.

Manfred J. M. Neumann

1. Introduction

The paper presented by Ronald McKinnon in this conference serves to substantiate his untiring call for a fundamental reform of the international monetary system. The most recent version is McKinnon [1987]. In my comments I will first discuss McKinnon's contribution to this conference, next point out two major problems of his proposal for reform, and finally sketch an alternative.

2. On Monetary Asymmetry

Ronald McKinnon points out a fundamental "asymmetry" in the conduct of monetary policies between the US on the one hand and Europe and Japan on the other. While the central banks of the latter countries appear to behave as prescribed by traditional textbooks, the Federal Reserve System does not. Up to only very recently, the Fed's monetary policy was dominated by domestic considerations. Moreover, as a rule the Fed has automatically sterilized the dollar interventions by the European and Japanese central banks.

Consider the traditional purchasing power parity explanation of the exchange rate as given by the long-run model of the monetary approach. In this framework, a stark fall in the exchange rate of the home currency results from an overly expansionary stance of domestic monetary policy which eventually will raise inflation. Using this interpretation, a declining exchange rate signals that a tightening of domestic money expansion is called for. Consequently, "conservative" central banks will tend to step on the brakes when their currencies devalue.

Why do the central banks of Europe and Japan behave in this way? I see two nonexclusive answers: one is that these authorities adhere to the simple, traditional view of exchange-rate explanation. A second answer is that they apparently believe they must not neglect the exchange rate vis-à-vis the large country for reasons of competitiveness (1).

Clearly, we are still confronted with the n-th country problem, or better still, the large country problem. As a matter of fact, US economic policies give little weight to international considerations, except that negative repercussions for the US are to be expected. The basic philosophy is unchanged: the large country sets the path and the remaining countries may adjust. Though the system of Bretton Woods broke down, the type of policy "coordination" implied by that system is still with us. McKinnon calls it "asymmetric" to highlight that, as a rule, the Fed disregards exchange-rate movements. We may equally well call it "symmetric" to emphasize the quasi-coordinated behavior of monetary policies, inside and outside the US.

McKinnon attacks the Fed on the grounds that it has done a poor job of stabilizing the American price level since the early 1970s. I agree with him. A more responsible conduct of American monetary policy - and fiscal policy, I should like to add - would have helped the rest of the world to stabilize its price level during the past two decades. Moreover, it would have reduced the marked fluctuations of nominal and, more importantly, for real exchange rates vis-à-vis the (US) dollar; compare the stylized facts collected by Mussa [1986]. Had the US avoided the inflationary policies of the seventies and had the US resisted trying the grand experiment of what I call "defonomics" (deficits, deformation and hopefully not default), it is likely that the Western economies would now have been in a better shape today than is the case.

McKinnon presents some evidence on the existence of monetary asymmetry since 1970. Indeed, inspection of simple correlation coefficients and eyeballing the data is sufficient to make the point.

---

(1) Imagine sharing a bed with an elephant. If the elephant moves in your direction, to survive you had better move in the same direction, even if this may result in falling out of the bed.

3. US Price Level versus Dollar Exchange Rate

McKinnon presents in addition regression work designed to support a special conjecture: the Fed has done a poor job of stabilizing the American price level because it has not keyed on stabilizing the dollar exchange rate.

In a way, this conjecture is peculiar as it appears to beg the n-th country problem. If all countries key on stabilizing bilateral exchange rates, their price levels will be indeterminate as the permanent rates of monetary expansion remain unspecified. For exchange-rate movements, it does not matter much which level of monetary expansion the countries choose, provided all of them choose roughly the same rate. But, with respect to price levels it matters very much, of course. McKinnon has to explain why, for the purpose of price-level stabilization, the sort of combination policy he has in mind is superior to a rule which fixes the rate of money expansion.

The regressions McKinnon presents in his Table 3 in support of his hypothesis have to be treated with very great caution. To begin with, it is not clear whether the American price indices have been stationary in first differences during the sample periods examined by McKinnon. It is certainly not the case for the American producer-price index, PPI, (1)(cf., McKinnon's Figure 4). Therefore, I am restricting my comments to McKinnon's estimates of rates of change of the US GNP deflator.

Consider the three regressions reprinted in the following table for convenience. Regression [1] exhibits an elasticity of the rate of inflation with respect to domestic money expansion of unity for the Bretton Woods era. For the following period of floating, however, McKinnon's estimate collapses; see regression [2]. That is what he expected because he believes that, under floating, the development of the American price level will be heavily dependent on movements of the exchange rate. For this reason, McKinnon introduces current and lagged changes in the

---

(1) Note that McKinnon uses the abbreviations PPI and WPI interchangeably.

Selected Regressions

Regression	ΔM^{US}	ΔE^{US}	$\bar{R}^2$	D.W.	Period
[1]	0.98 (8.24)		0.61	2.03	1962.II–1973.I
[2]	0.44 (1.12)		0.11	0.78	1973.II–1984.IV
[3]	0.57 (1.91)	−0.34 (−4.87)	0.55	1.33	1973.II–1984.IV

Note: Dependent variable: quarterly rates of change in the US GNP deflator. - Regression coefficients are summed OLS coefficients of lag 0 to lag 11 with t-statistics in parentheses. M^{US} is M1 and E^{US} is the "merm" weighted dollar exchange rate against 17 industrial countries.

Source: McKinnon [in this volume, Table 3].

dollar exchange rate (foreign currency/dollars) as additional regressors; see regression [3]. If reliable, however, this estimate exhibits again an elasticity of the American rate of inflation with respect to the American rate of M1 growth of close to unity. To see this substitute the exchange-rate equation $\Delta E^{US} = \Delta p^{ROW} - \Delta p^{US} + \Delta E_r^{US}$ into regression [3].

Nonetheless, I doubt that McKinnon's preferred regression [3] constitutes valid evidence. Firstly, the Durbin-Watson statistic indicates significant first-order serial correlation in the estimated residuals. Secondly, and more importantly, regression [3] is not an estimate of a reduced form. The right-hand-side variable ΔE^{US} is neither independent of the left-hand-side variable nor orthogonal to ΔM^{US}. As long as we do not take the interdependence between the exchange rate and the price level into account, we will not arrive at meaningful results. I conclude that it requires a more refined empirical approach really to "establish" McKinnon's conjecture that the dollar exchange rate is a reliable indicator of future inflation or deflation in the US.

4. On McKinnon's Proposal for Reform of the International Monetary System

The proposal consists of two major elements: (i) permanent monetary expansion such that price-level stability is guaranteed in terms of an international basket of tradable goods; (ii) fixed exchange rates among dollar, mark, and yen [McKinnon, 1987]. Given the space limitation, I am restricting my comments to the second element.

If there is anything to learn from the exchange-rate literature it is this: none of the alternative exchange-rate regimes is ideal in the sense that it would permit a minimization of the costs of adjustment to all types of disturbances [Murphy, 1985]. If we differentiate nominal from real shocks, we may conclude from a Poole-type analysis that fixed rates are to be preferred, provided nominal shocks are the dominating source of disturbance. Here, McKinnon's concern about unstable money demands would fit. But, to derive a definite conclusion, we clearly need to know much more because the total costs of adjustment depend sensitively on the variance-covariance matrix of the possible disturbances in the various markets. Moreover, a more interesting differentiation of shocks relates to the aspect of magnitude and persistence. When it comes to large and persistent differential disturbances, flexible exchange rates appear to be better suited to cope with them. They avoid any artificial delaying of the necessary adjustments of real exchange rates, hence relative prices. The stylized fact that the short-run volatility of real exchange rates is smaller in a fixed-rates regime must not be interpreted to imply that here disturbances are elegantly and effectively neutralized [Mussa, 1986]. Rather, they may show up in different ways. Large and persistent real shocks to the supply side are likely to be more distortive under fixed than under flexible rates.

The combination of fixed exchange rates with what McKinnon calls "symmetric" behavior of monetary policies creates a mechanism which is biased towards fiscal expansion. Suppose country A steps up government expenditure and budget deficits such that interest rates tend to rise and currency A to appreciate. Then the McKinnon mechanism will require that country A raise domestic money growth while the remaining countries (ROW) have to contract money growth, in order to keep currency

A from rising. Confronted with a recession forced upon them by the "symmetric" rule of the McKinnon mechanism, the ROW countries will either leave the system or simply compete with country A in stepping up fiscal expansion. I conclude that the McKinnon mechanism - whatever its merits in other respects - is incomplete and, therefore, likely to be untenable should it ever be adopted.

5. An Alternative: International Commitment to Precommitment at Home

Let me finally sketch an alternative approach to international policy coordination. The basic idea is by international agreement to eliminate a major cause of real exchange-rate fluctuation under floating: the uncertainty about the future conduct of differential monetary and fiscal policies. Let the countries sign a treaty by which they commit themselves to

(i) price-level stability at home by writing a monetary rule into the constitution that does away with discretion and inflationary bias,

(ii) limits on the growth of government by writing a fiscal rule into the constitution that excludes a growth of government expenditure above GNP growth.

International commitment to precommitment at home would avoid the dangers of international cooperation pointed out by Vaubel [1983] and Rogoff [1985]. This proposal is clearly not suited to eliminate real exchange-rate fluctuations and the occurrence of current account imbalances. They would continue to occur but likely on a much reduced scale because a major cause of uncertainty, monetary and fiscal experimentation, would be ruled out.

My proposal, in contrast to McKinnon's, arises from the understanding that it has been policies and politicians rather than private agents or "nature" who produced the most harmful disturbances in the past. I find it puzzling, therefore, that McKinnon [1987] relies on the notion of "well-intentioned" politicians who are stymied by doctrinal disputes among economists. Public-choice theory provides us with the more fruitful notion that policymakers are rational economic men who work in their own interest and - given their constraints - in that of specific interest groups rather than in a vague common or public interest. This public-choice notion has great cognitive power. This is one reason why politicians prefer rules which constrain the behavior of the citizen to rules that constrain their policymaking.

To policymakers, all policy rules are nothing but different sorts of straitjackets. If they have to accept one, they will choose the loosest. Therefore, neither McKinnon's mechanism or mine will suit their taste.

Bibliography

McKINNON, Ronald I., Monetary and Exchange Rate Policies for International Financial Stability: A Proposal. Standford, 1987, mimeo.

MURPHY, J. Carter, "Reflections on the Exchange Rate System". The American Economic Review, Papers and Proceedings, Vol. 75, 1985, pp. 68-73.

MUSSA, Michael, "Nominal Exchange Rate Regimes and the Behavior of Real Exchange Rates: Evidence and Implications". In: Karl BRUNNER, Allan H. MELTZER (Eds.), Real Business Cycles, Real Exchange Rates and Actual Policies. Carnegie-Rochester Conference Series on Public Policy, 25, 1986, pp. 117-213.

ROGOFF, Kenneth, "Can International Monetary Policy Cooperation Be Counterproductive?". Journal of International Economics, Vol. 18, 1985, pp. 199-217.

VAUBEL, Roland, "Coordination or Competition among National Macro-Economic Policies?". In: Fritz MACHLUP, Gerhard FELS, Hubertus MÜLLER-GROELING (Eds.), Reflections on a Troubled World Economy. Essays in Honour of Herbert Giersch. London, 1983, pp. 3-28.

Summary of the Discussion by Joachim Scheide

One issue in the discussion was a comparison between Ronald McKinnon's recommendations and the McCallum rule. Can the findings in the McKinnon paper be viewed as either a competing rule or as an improvement of the rule for monetary policy suggested by Bennett McCallum? From the regressions, it seems as if the exchange rate has a strong influence on the price level. However, it was argued that these results do not suggest that a policy of stabilizing the exchange rate could in fact be used to stabilize, for example, the US price level; nor does it follow that fixing the exchange rate would be necessary or helpful in keeping the price level constant. If we want to be able to make any statement we would have to run simulations with a specific model or a system of regressions subjected to shocks actually observed and so on.

Furthermore, the notion of the "inherent instability" of exchange rates was discussed. One may dispute whether the exchange rate always behaves like a random walk. Some hinted at the difficulty of testing that; after all, the graph shown in McKinnon's paper does not - prima facie - provide clear evidence on this proposition. Furthermore, some may view a random walk as a very stable process. Doubts were raised with respect to the recommendation of fixing exchange rates, especially because there was a wide agreement that exchange rates were determined by stock rather than flow variables. Can we really make statements like "a fixed exchange rate is good per se" or even "a fixed exchange rate promotes price level stability"? Does the experience with, for example, the Bretton Woods system really lend support to these hypotheses?

Another way of achieving price level stability within each country when there are different currencies is the concept of currency competition. In this case, there may even be sizable exchange rate changes; if currencies - or, for that matter, central banks - are allowed to compete, the risk of having to restrict capital movements would be reduced. Such policies of interventions or restrictions are always immanent if exchange rates are fixed. Nevertheless, a regime of flexible exchange rates would also allow price level stability, but with a greater amount of freedom for international trade and capital movements than in the case of rigid exchange rates.

Further questions were raised as far as the alleged failure of the present system is concerned. It was argued that a great deal of the exchange-rate fluctuations we could observe in the regime of flexibility over the past 15 years was due to uncertainty with regard to national monetary policies. This instability has created uncertainty with respect to the expectations of the price level within each country. Thus, it seemed obvious to look for another anchor in the system; nevertheless, more predictability and commitment of policy concerning price level stability would also help to stabilize exchange rates because one of the causes for currency substitution may disappear. However, politicians obviously seem to favor action; one example is the Plaza Agreement of September 1985 which implied that the dollar should be brought down. Such activism seems to be part of the politicians' role in convincing the electorate, sometimes overruling the "economic wisdom" shared by many representatives of governments or central banks.

Whatever the advantages of fixed rates may be, the time for fixing exchange rates has obviously not always been chosen with much luck. It was argued that, when the European Monetary System (EMS) was established, the divergencies between the economies were too large to ensure the stability of nominal exchange rates. Countries with high inflation rates should have followed the advice of "bringing their house in order first" and then agreed on some fixed rates. It was also aryued that nowadays one may find it much easier to establish fixed nominal exchange rates between the three blocs - the United States, Japan, and Western Europe - because there have been only minor differences between their inflation rates, and the chances for major real shocks which could create exchange-rate instability have been relatively small.

278

Gilles Oudiz

Macroeconomic Policy Coordination: Where Should We Stand?

1. Introduction

Macroeconomic policy coordination is by no means a recent issue either for policymakers or for academics - economists, political scientists, or historians. The way economists view the problem has, however, evolved markedly since the war. This evolution is twofold. First of all, the confidence in a Keynesian fine tuning of the economy progressively disappeared after the major disturbances of the 1970s. And secondly, a rather simplistic and altruistic view of policy coordination has been rejected first by policymakers and then, with some delay, by its academic proponents.

What is left is certainly not a unified view of policy coordination but rather a separation into two broad conceptions: On the one hand, the proponents of an international "laissez faire" policy advocate more freedom within a flexible exchange-rate system. Market forces are believed to be able to bring about a "natural selection" of the good policies. On the other hand, the proponents of an enhanced international coordination have developed a strategic analysis of policy conflicts and interdependence which emphasizes the costs of counterproductive competition.

The goal of this paper is to expose briefly the basic assumptions of the "strategic approach" of policy coordination in order to discuss their relevance and show their limitations both at the theoretical and at the empirical levels. In the first part of the paper the fundamental results are presented with a minimal specification of a two-country model. The major limitations are then discussed in the second part. The third part of the paper presents an empirical analysis of policy coordination among all western economies and within Europe. At this point, the benefits and the relevance of policy coordination are discussed. Finally, some conclusions on the problems which face the world economy and Europe in the coming years are analyzed within the theoretical framework presented in the paper.

2. The Theoretical Case for Policy Coordination

The game theoretic literature on policy coordination, initiated by Hamada's seminal work [Hamada, 1985], is "almost fashionable" [Vaubel, 1985]. It is thus certainly not useful to dwell extensively on it. It seems however necessary to spell out properly what is and what is not assumed. The basic idea is that the case for coordination must rest on the demonstration that all countries can benefit in terms of their own policy goals from a coordination of policies.

To put this more formally, let us consider a two-country world economy. Each country, i, has m policy targets and ρ policy instruments which are the elements of $T^i = (T_1^i, \ldots, T_m^i)$ and $C^i = (C_1^i, \ldots, C_\rho^i)$. In an interdependent world each country's target vector will be a function of the policy instrument setting of all the countries:

$$T^i = F^i(C^1, C^2)$$

Uncoordinated policymaking is described as a situation in which each country chooses its policy instruments, while taking as given the actions selected by the other country, in order to maximize its utility function $U^i(T^i)$. This Nash-Cournot equilibrium explicitly assumes that each policymaker knows exactly what the other country is doing and that all policymakers know the "true model" of the economy. We shall return to these assumptions later on.

The important fact is that this equilibrium is rarely Pareto optimal. Each country has chosen its optimal policy unilaterally so as to maximize its utility:

$$\partial U^1/\partial C^1 = \partial U^2/\partial C^2 = 0$$

However, in general, the policy instruments of country 2 are not set optimally with respect to country 1's utility:

$$\partial U^1 / \partial C^2 \geq 0$$

Thus, at the margin, a change in the policy of the foreign country can increase welfare at home while not affecting foreign welfare (to a first-order approximation). The whole argument for policy coordination is based on this result. Unilateral policymaking is suboptimal because there are externalities from domestic and foreign policy actions which are not properly priced.

It might however be the case that, at the Nash equilibrium, no gain can be achieved for the home country through a marginal change in the foreign country policy:

$$\partial U^1 / \partial C^2_j = \partial U^1 / \partial T^1 \cdot \partial T^1 / \partial C^2_j = 0$$

This condition might be met for three reasons. Firstly, because $\partial T^1 / \partial C^2_j$ is equal to zero for all the targets of the home country and all the instruments of the foreign country. In other words there is no impact of the foreign country policy instruments on the home country utility.

Secondly, the effects of the foreign country policy instruments on the home country targets are equivalent to the effects of a linear combination of the home country's own policy instruments:

$$\partial T^1 / \partial C^2_j = \sum_{k=1}^{P} \lambda_k (\partial T^1 / \partial C^1_k)$$

then $\partial U^1 / \partial C^2_j = \sum_{k=1}^{P} \lambda_k \partial U^1 / \partial T^1 \cdot \partial T^1 / \partial C^1_k = \sum_{k=1}^{P} \lambda \, \partial U^1 / \partial C^1_k = 0$

In this case the home country can replicate any foreign policy impulse and thus does not need policy coordination.

Finally, the condition might be met because the home country has enough instruments to reach all its targets.

Let us discuss the empirical relevance of these three situations before continuing with our theoretical model. The table presents normalized multipliers from MCM and EPA world econometric models (for a detailed discussion, see Oudiz and Sachs [1984]). Recent comparative studies of world econometric models under the auspices of the Brookings-CEPR program on Macroeconomic Policy Coordination, have shown that the multipliers of these two models are broadly consistent with the multipliers of most other world models. In these tables three policy targets - GNP, inflation and the current account - and two policy instruments: monetary and fiscal policies - are considered. In many cases, cross multipliers are very small especially when Japan and West Germany are considered. For example, according to both models, the impact of a Japanese fiscal expansion on Germany is negligible. Starting from a noncooperative equilibrium, Japan might very well have little to trade with Germany in terms of macroeconomic policy.

In general, it appears that monetary and fiscal expansion both increase inflation and worsen the current account. However, for a given impact on GNP, monetary policies are more inflationary and fiscal policies lead to a larger worsening of the current account. There is thus no combination of one country's instruments which permits to improve simultaneously all three targets. Analysis of the multipliers shows on the contrary that a combination of one foreign country's instruments can do this. For example, according to MCM policy multipliers, "one unit" of fiscal and monetary policy in the US will improve all three targets for Germany or Japan.

In the case of both models it is generally the case that the impact of foreign policies cannot be replicated with home policies alone.

Furthermore, as is shown in Oudiz and Sachs [1984], if one country retains only two targets it can achieve both of its goals and does not need to cooperate to reach a first-best solution.

At this point, it should be clear that the case for or against coordination does not rest on the relative effectiveness of instruments but rather on the fact that the policy instruments of the foreign country can achieve

Normalized Policy Multipliers for Output, Inflation, and the Current Account Ratio (a)

Country acting, and policy	Size of policy	United States			Japan			West Germany		
		GNP	inflation rate	current account ratio	GNP	inflation rate	current account ratio	GNP	inflation rate	current account ratio
		multicountry model								
United States										
monetary	3.64	1.00	0.18	-0.02	0.00	-0.09	0.07	-0.18	-0.18	0.02
fiscal	0.83	1.00	0.12	-0.40	0.17	0.01	0.02	0.29	0.04	0.04
Japan										
monetary	2.67	0.07	0.00	0.03	1.00	0.13	-0.11	-0.07	-0.07	0.00
fiscal	0.71	0.07	0.00	0.03	1.00	0.11	-0.09	0.01	0.00	0.01
West Germany										
monetary	4.44	-0.11	0.00	-0.02	0.11	0.00	0.00	1.00	0.44	-0.04
fiscal	1.03	0.10	0.00	0.04	0.05	0.00	0.03	1.00	0.22	-0.54
		economic planning agency model								
United States										
monetary	4.08	1.00	0.09	-0.08	0.02	-0.22	0.06	-0.54	0.20	0.01
fiscal	0.48	1.00	0.04	-0.16	0.14	0.00	0.04	0.27	0.05	0.06
Japan										
monetary	2.50	-0.11	0.00	0.00	1.00	0.59	-0.02	-0.06	0.00	-0.02
fiscal	0.64	0.00	0.01	0.01	1.00	0.18	-0.13	0.01	0.00	0.00
West Germany										
monetary	1.11	-0.01	-0.01	-0.01	0.01	0.00	0.00	1.00	0.43	-0.05
fiscal	0.51	0.01	0.00	0.00	0.09	0.03	0.02	1.00	0.14	-0.28

(a) The table gives multipliers averaged over two years. Monetary policy is measured by the percentage-point decrease of the discount rate. Fiscal policy is measured by the increase of government spending as a percentage of GNP. The policies are normalized so as to produce 1 percent of GNP increase in the expanding country. GNP is measured as a percentage deviation from a baseline; the inflation rate is measured as a percentage-point deviation from a baseline; and the current account ratio (current account balance as a percent of GNP) is an absolute deviation from a baseline.

Source: Oudiz, Sachs [1985].

results unattainable solely with the home country's instruments. Thus, it is established that starting from a noncooperative equilibrium, it is generally the case that some Pareto superior equilibrium can be achieved. The question is then: how far can the cooperating countries go?

This benchmark, the cooperative equilibrium, is characterized as the point on the contract curve which corresponds to the "Nash bargaining" solution [cf., Roth, 1979]. This formal choice of a precise point on the contract curve is partially arbitrary even though the Nash bargaining solution is relatively general. The real question is, however, to discuss its enforceability.

The cooperative equilibrium is not a Nash equilibrium. There is thus a clear incentive for either country to move unilaterally and renege on its commitments. The policy commitments would have to be enforced either by a supranational authority which could impose sanctions' on violators or by a set of rules, within which the countries could act freely, or even by the need for the policymakers to maintain a reputation. We will come back later to these issues.

It is important to note that the formal cooperative process outlined here does not imply any bargaining on the actual objectives, or more generally, on the utility functions of each country. Nor is there a logical need for any kind of convergence of the objectives of each country. Starting from a noncooperative equilibrium, each country can objectively improve its own welfare without either modifying its objectives or accepting to take into account its partner's targets.

In the case of a very simple two-country model [Oudiz, 1985], it can be shown that the choice of this "ideal" cooperative policy can be separated into two problems. Firstly, the determination of the average level of economic policies given an average model of the world economy which is formally equivalent to a closed economy; this implies choosing the average level of macroeconomic variables. Secondly, the determination of policy differentials given a model of differential variables which is formally equivalent to an open economy: This essentially implies the choice of an exchange-rate policy. It should be noted that coordination in no way implies the choice of a fixed exchange rate but rather an optimal management of exchange rates according to differences among countries.

This simple setting clarifies the gains from coordination. The "ideal" decisionmaker takes into account the externalities generated by foreign policy actions and acts accordingly. This remains partially true in a different strategic setting where one of the national policymakers acts as a Stackelberg leader vis-à-vis the other policymaker. Knowing that the

284

follower will want to engage in competitive policies, the leader will avoid going too far in deflation or inflation. Even though the outcomes of different strategic settings cannot be directly compared, it is generally the case that, in terms of welfare for both countries, the Stackelberg equilibrium will be better than the Nash noncooperative equilibrium.

3. The Major Limitations to the Strategic Analysis of Policy Coordination

The strategic analysis of policy coordination has the advantage of clarifying the problem and first of all of getting rid of the altruistic view which was behind, for example, the "locomotive theory". It needs, however, to be largely qualified in many respects. We shall discuss here the more important problems which arise when trying to apply this theory to "real life".

a. How Can the Cooperative Equilibrium Be Achieved?

As we have seen above, the cooperative equilibrium is not sustainable as a Nash equilibrium. Its enforceability is thus problematic.

As a benchmark, the cooperative equilibrium sets the goals of policy. It could theoretically be achieved either by a supranational authority or by continuous joint decisionmaking. The discussion of the institutional arrangements which could bring the world or groups of countries closer to this ideal situation is clearly a topic of research for economists and political scientists.

International policy rules - for example, fixed exchange rates or a fixed rate of money growth - can and should provide a realistic substitute for centralized decisionmaking. There remains only to find rules which lead independent policymakers to an intermediary equilibrium Pareto superior to the noncooperative equilibrium.

As the experiences of the Bretton Woods system or of the European snake show such rules are far from being easy to design or implement. Too much rigidity eventually leads some of the participants to withdraw from the agreement. On the contrary, too much flexibility does not allow them to get closer to the cooperative equilibrium. In this respect, the Williamson proposal of target zones for real exchange rates with a 10 percent margin of fluctuation on each side of the target rate does seem much too flexible in order to yield a significant improvement of the present situation [Williamson, 1985].

b. Model Uncertainty

The most important limit of the strategic analysis of policy coordination is certainly the problem of model uncertainty. The simple theoretical model assumes that each policymaker knows the "true model" of the world economy. Recent empirical papers by Frankel and Rocket [1986] and Holtham and Hughes-Hallet [1987] explore the implications of both uncertainty on the true model and disagreement among policymakers. These papers show that, in many instances, choosing the wrong models can lead to counterproductive cooperation. In other words, the coordinated policy would lead to an equilibrium Pareto inferior to the noncooperative outcome.

This is potentially a devastating argument. What could be said against it? First of all, model uncertainty definitely applies to macroeconomic policy in general rather than solely to macroeconomic policy coordination. At worst, if there is no information whatsoever on the "true model" of the economy no economic policy should be implemented.

Economic analysis does provide us with some information on the nature and the relative magnitudes of the effects of macroeconomic policies on the domestic and foreign economies. There is a relative consensus among economists on the medium-run impact of tight monetary and fiscal policies on inflation and growth which could be sufficient to outline what cooperative policies should look like. Even such unambitious considerations could help resolve some of the problems of the world economy or of the European community.

It nevertheless remains true that the derivation of cooperative policies is far from being robust and that it implies both an agreement and an actual knowledge of the relevant economic mechanisms.

c. Flexibility of Policy Instruments

Many of the recent papers on policy coordination, be they empirical or analytical consider that the governments have two policy instruments at their disposal: monetary and fiscal policy.

The experience of the recent years in the United States and Europe has definitely shown that fiscal policy is far from being a flexible instrument. Thus, the possible trading of fiscal policies among interdependent countries needs to be treated as a medium to long-run issue. This stands in sharp contrast to the negotiation on monetary policy and the actual attempts at coordination which we have observed in the last months.

The discussion of policy coordination definitely needs to take into account this essential feature of fiscal policy in order to reach realistic conclusions.

d. Credibility and the "Rogoff Paradox"

In a widely quoted paper, Rogoff [1985] has shown that policy coordination can be counterproductive if it alters the credibility of the governments. The argument is as follows. Consider an economy where the private sector sets wages according to its inflation expectations. If it believes that its government will want to inflate away its wages, then policy coordination will, by alleviating the exchange rate constraint on inflationary policies, increase expectations of inflation. It will thus lead to higher wage settlements and to a more inflationary equilibrium. By undermining the credibility of the governments, cooperation will thus have worsened the situation.

The paper is in its author's view definitely an ad hoc counterexample which aimed at showing the complexity of the issue of coordination. The general result that cooperation among all players will lead to Pareto improvement remains nonetheless true.

In Rogoff's model, two of the players, the private sectors of both countries, are left out of the game. The general result need not hold necessarily.

It can also be the case that coordination among national governments would increase the credibility of these governments and thus lead to *less* inflationary outcomes. The working of the EMS up to now provides a good example of this type of situation. Within a system of partially adjustable exchange rates, the French and Italian governments have succeeded in importing some of the Bundesbank's credibility. In other words, the rules of the EMS have been perceived by the public as limiting the magnitudes of discretionary policies.

e. Collusion of Governments

This line of arguments largely developed by Vaubel [1985] goes further than the credibility problem. It assumes that governments' objectives differ markedly from the collective or social objectives of their constituents. The direct counterpart of this assumption is that market forces - i.e., competition - should be used to sort out the good governments.

Coordination in Vaubel's view is nothing but an attempt at building a cartel of the incumbents solely interested with their short-run electoral problem. This argument has its own logic and it is clear that in purely formal terms if governments have different or simply more short-run

288

objectives than their public sectors, coordination can be counterproductive [cf., Oudiz, Sachs, 1985, for a numerical example].

What seems less convincing is the existence of a "market for government, or policies' which will let the good governments survive and the bad ones disappear by natural selection".

4. The Empirical Issue

The strategic approach of policy coordination has definitely helped to sort out the issue in more rigorous terms. Numerous empirical studies of expansionary packages for the world economy [EEC, 1984; Bergsten, Klein, 1983] did nothing but present the advantages of joint fiscal or monetary expansion of the western economies.

These simulations were based on a set of irrelevant assumptions:

- the package was identical for each country;
- the welfare analysis, instead of being made on each country's own terms - i.e., own objective functions - was reduced to the evaluation of the growth potential of the world economy;
- strategic considerations were totally ignored. In particular, nothing was said about the means of enforcing these policies.

Empirical applications of the strategic approach of policy coordination have tried to get rid of these irrelevant assumptions. All the limitations we have seen in the second part of this paper remain, however, true.

First of all, there is uncertainty about the model of the world economy. There is, thus, a need to replicate simulation experiences with various models. As we have seen above, the issue becomes complicated if one starts considering situations where different policymakers use different empirical models.

A second point of importance is the choice of objective functions for the governments. Imposing a priori utility functions for each government can potentially lead to any kind of conclusion. There is consequently a need for some assumptions in order to try and reveal the preferences of the governments under study [Oudiz, Sachs, 1984]. Holtham and Hughes-Hallet [1987] have shown that this can be impossible when one does not assume that the "true model" of the world economy is common knowledge. This is a clear limitation to empirical analysis. In principal, this problem could be solved either by interviewing policymakers or by "revealing" their preferences with the econometric models actually used by national administrations.

Finally, it must be stressed that the econometric models used for the various simulation studies of policy coordination are very unsatisfactory as far as the determination of exchange rates is concerned. This last consideration unfortunately applies to any evaluation of macroeconomic policy. An alternative solution is to rely upon ad hoc simulation models [cf., for example, Currie, Levine, 1986; McKibbin, Sachs, 1987] which are more satisfactory as far as their theoretical foundations are concerned but lack empirical estimation.

Notwithstanding all these problems, the empirical analysis of policy coordination has allowed us to sort out some of the issues. Some rather stable conclusions emerge which we will summarize.

There is large consensus among the various studies that coordination among the United States, Japan and Europe yields dissappointingly small results [Canzoneri, Minford, 1987; Oudiz, Sachs, 1984; Carlozzi, Taylor, 1985]. The reasons for this seem to be the limited degree of direct interdependence between these three blocks of the world economy. Even though this conclusion is not inconsistent with our empirical knowledge of policy spillovers it needs to be qualified.

The impact of exchange-rate instability and the evolution of the third-world debt are not taken into account by standard econometric models. A crucial aspect of the problem of world economic coordination is thus left out of the picture.

Simulation of policy coordination at the European level yields moderately more satisfactory results. The larger degree of interdependence among European countries no doubt explains this result [Oudiz, 1985].

It must, however, be stressed that even then the gains remain modest. The essential impediment to more expansionary growth in Europe seems to be the very large weight put on inflation targets by the European governments. Thus, any significant move seems to be so costly as to preclude any real agreement for expansion.

5. Conclusion

The issue of policy coordination is far from having been sorted out. It is clear that a simplistic application of game theoretic results to international interaction in no way solves the problem. It is also clear that fundamental questions about the nature and the effectiveness of macroeconomic policies need to be agreed upon in order to be able to discuss the issue of coordination. Until some agreement has been reached and some progress has been made both in theoretical and in empirical model building, the evaluation of the gains from policy coordination will be flawed.

However, the development of a strategic approach to policy coordination has definitely helped to set the problem in more proper terms.

Bibliography

BERGSTEN, C. Fred, Lawrence KLEIN, article in The Economist, 23-30 April 1983.

CANZONERI, Matthew, Patrick MINFORD, Policy Interdependence: Does Strategic Behavior Pay? An Empirical Investigation Using the Liverpool World Model. Centre For Economic Policy Research, Discussion Paper Series, 201, October 1987.

CARLOZZI, Nicholas, John B. TAYLOR, "International Capital Mobility and the Coordination of Monetary Rules". In: Jagdeep S. BHANDARI (Ed.), Exchange Rate Management under Uncertainty. Cambridge, Mass., 1985, pp. 186-211.

EUROPEAN ECONOMIC COMMUNITY (EEC), "Bilan Economique Annuel 1984-1985 de la CEE". Economie Européenne, Vol. 22, November 1984.

FRANKEL, Jeffrey A., Katharine ROCKETT, International Macroeconomic Coordination when Policy-Makers Disagree on the Model. Department of Economics, University of California, June 1986, mimeo.

HAMADA, Koichi, The Economic Policy of Interdependence. Cambridge, Mass., 1985.

HOLTHAM, Gerald, Andrew HUGHES-HALLET, International Policy Co-operation and Model Uncertainty. Centre for Economic Policy Research, Discussion Paper Series, 190, July 1987.

LEVINE, Paul, David CURRIE, The Sustainability of Optimal Cooperative Macroeconomic Policies in a Two-Country World. Centre for Economic Policy Research, Discussion Paper Series, 102, April 1986.

McKIBBIN, Warwick, Jeffrey SACHS, "Coordination of Monetary and Fiscal Policies in the OECD". In: Jacob A. FRENKEL (Ed.), International Aspects of Fiscal Policies. Cambridge, Mass., 1987.

OUDIZ, Gilles, "European Policy Coordination: An Evaluation". Recherches Economiques de Louvain, Vol. 51, 1985, pp. 301-339.

--, Jeffrey SACHS, "Macroeconomic Policy Coordination among the Industrial Economies". Brookings Papers on Economic Activity, 1984, pp. 1-64.

--, --, "Macroeconomic Policy Coordination in Dynamic Macroeconomic Models". In: Willem BUITER, Richard MARSTON (Eds.), International Economic Policy Coordination. Cambridge 1985.

ROGOFF, Kenneth, "Can International Monetary Policy Cooperation Be Counterproductive?". Journal of International Economics, Vol. 18, 1985, pp. 199-217.

ROTH, Alvin E., Axiomatic Model of Bargaining. Lecture Notes in Economics and Mathematical Systems, 170, Berlin 1979.

VAUBEL, Roland, "Coordination or Competition among National Macroeconomic Policies?". In: Fritz MACHLUP, Gerhard FELS, Hubertus MÜLLER-GROELING (Eds.), Reflections on a Troubled World Economy. Essays in Honour of Herbert Giersch. London 1983, pp. 3-28.

WILLIAMSON, John, The Exchange Rate System. Institute for International Economics, Washington 1985.

Comments on Gilles Oudiz, "Macroeconomic Policy Coordination: Where Should We Stand?"

Pascal Salin

Gilles Oudiz uses the traditional instruments of microeconomics to discuss the problem of cooperation in macroeconomic policies. According to him, the main justification for policy coordination is the existence of externalities, since the decisions of government 1 (or individual 1) influence government 2 (or individual 2) and vice versa. Since his approach is of a microeconomic nature, it is justifiable to ask whether the coordination of decisions between governments is different from the coordination of activities between individuals.

Let us first take the case where a society is composed of two individuals. The welfare of each depends on the decisions of the other. As an example: if one offers a commodity and demands another commodity, the price he can get - and, therefore, his welfare - depends on the conditions under which the other is willing to do the symmetrical sale-purchase operation. In such a case, it seems meaningless to speak of an externality: there is interdependence, no externality. However, one may wonder in which other situations externalities could exist.

In fact, the existence of externalities is mainly called for by people who would like others to behave as they wish. If property rights are clearly defined, which means that one does know what each individual has the right to do and not to do, externalities do not exist. The word "externalities" is misleading, we ought to speak rather of the absence of property rights and of legitimizing coercion. When property rights are well defined, there are interactions between people, but no externalities. For instance, if individual A wants individual B to produce more of the commodity i he offers a higher price for i.

Coordination between individual A and individual B means that an exchange of information between A and B about their future decisions may be useful to one and/or the other, since there is interdependence between them. But, as for any good, "usefulness" cannot be defined in an absolute sense. We have to compare the utility of the information and its cost. If my neighbour has the right to build anything on his own lot, his decisions may have adverse effects on me and I may want to know them in advance in order to decide which trees to grow or how to decide upon the orientation of my house. However, if he is entitled to do whatever he wishes, because there were no restrictions on his property rights once he has got his property, I cannot make him give me free information, but I may buy the relevant information (not only by giving money, but, for instance, by making efforts to be kind to him and helping him when necessary ...).

If society is composed of a great number of individuals, the welfare of everyone depends even more on others, since his environment may be more affected by the decisions of others than by those he makes himself. In that sense, it would seem that there is a higher need for coordination. But, at the same time, it is more difficult to coordinate a great number of people. In such a case, one knows that the price system is the most efficient way of bringing information to the members of society and of coordinating their decisions. However, prices can exist only for goods which are appropriated.

Let us now assume that society is composed of n individuals and two "big" individuals (which are called governments). It may be apparently easy to coordinate the decisions of the two governments since they are not numerous. In fact, neither of them has a total control on what it is assumed to coordinate and, in that sense, coordination between governments is different from coordination between individuals whose acts and decisions concern what they own. In his model, where the only decisions considered are those of governments, Gilles Oudiz seems to forget that individuals *also* exist. The consequences on country 1 of policies decided by the government of country 2 cannot be directly known by the government of country 1 when designing its policy, since the consequences depend on the reactions of the whole system - namely the individuals in countries 1 and 2 - to the policy decisions. "Perfect" coordination of decisions between governments could only exist in "perfect" slavery societies, in which the governments decide the activity of any individual at any time. It is certainly not desirable, and even inconceivable: governments cannot be the owners of the citizens.

Any decision taken by any individual has consequences on some other individuals, which means that all the members of society are interdependent. But the fact that activities are interdependent does not mean that there are externalities. One cannot assume that externalities exist without having first determined who has the right to do what. If I am doing something which I have the right to do and if it is not agreeable to someone else, it does not mean that there is an externality. It does, however, mean that I am using my rights to act.

What about the decisions of governments? Let us assume, for instance, that government 1 decides to increase the quantity of money. It has consequences not only on the possible decisions of government 2 but, what is more important, on the decisions of individuals in country 1 and country 2. Before discussing the need for coordination between both governments, one may wonder whether the decisions of the government in one country has consequences on individuals in both countries and in which respect it has the right to make these decisions. If, for instance, there were rules to the game for monetary creation, there would not be any need for coordination. The problem of coordination arises when the governments give themselves the right to act in a completely discretionary way, which means that they are not working under the rule of law. Once more, the problem is not one of externalities but one of the absence of rules and precise definition of rights. In that sense coordination could be considered as a "second-best solution". Whenever there is such a lack of law, coordination might be better than the absence of coordination, but it would be better to be in a system in which coordination were not necessary (for instance, to take the monetary example again, rules of the game as in the gold standard, or currency competition, where there is no need for coordination).

In this second-best world, the problem to be solved is to decide whether it is better to exchange directly information between governments about the decisions of both, or to let the market produce the necessary signals when it is informed of the decisions taken by the governments. There is, in fact, a major objection against coordination: the governments do not have the necessary information to coordinate, which means that they cannot determine in which cases there are externalities. Therefore, the case discussed by Gilles Oudiz is a purely hypothetical one, without any possible practical consequence.

In fact, the market is producing ever-changing signals due to changes in preferences, in information, in technology. Instead of discretionary coordination, it would be preferable that the two governments either announced permanent rules, or announced what they could do if the market were to give such or such signal. Thus, there would be an improvement in the coordination of decisions not only between governments but also between governments and individuals and between the individuals themselves.

The lack of information on the working of the system, the preferences and targets of individuals, also means that governments can take decisions only on the basis of a very simplified model of society. They choose arbitrarily some quantitative targets, which they pretend to reach. From this simplified view of the world, it may appear, for instance, that international coordination implies an increase in taxes in country 1. Thus, under the pretext of maximizing the world welfare by taking account of possible externalities, a government may deprive an individual of part of his property! More generally, if one considers - as we do (1) - that governments are unable to pursue a stabilization policy, it is evidently a waste of time to speak of coordination of policies. The coordination of illusory activities is an illusion.

---

(1) Compare Pascal Salin, "Macro-Stabilization Policies and the Market Process". In: K. Groenveld, J. Muysken, J.A.H. Maks (Eds.), Economic Policy of the Welfare State and the Market Process, Success or Failure. Amsterdam, forthcoming.

Roland Vaubel

This is an unusually sober and balanced analysis of international policy coordination (also by its author's own standards).

I agree with Oudiz that "the development of a strategic approach to policy coordination has definitely helped to set the problem in more proper terms" (p. 290). I see three main achievements:

(i) Contrary to some previous studies, the game-theoretic approach does not claim that uncoordinated policies tend to be inconsistent but merely that they are likely to be Pareto-inferior to cooperation.

(ii) Contrary to some previous studies, the game-theoretic approach does not view international economic interdependence as a sufficient condition for the desirability of cooperation; it is merely a necessary condition. An additional necessary condition is that policymakers pursue more targets than they have instruments. Increasing international market interdependence alone reduces the need for international intergovernmental coordination because more market interdependence means more competition and a smaller role for the government.

(iii) Contrary to previous perceptions, the game-theoretic approach does not rely on international altruism (as Oudiz emphasizes on p. 284).

While these are the achievements, there are also serious defects which, in my view, render this approach more likely to mislead than to enlighten. I shall focus on two of them: the uncertainty problem and the "left-out-players problem". To some extent, these are recognized in Oudiz's paper but they need to be spelt out more fully.

Uncertainty about the values which the variables, parameters, and disturbance terms of the model take, undermine the case for internationally-negotiated coordination of macroeconomic policies more severely than the case for domestic macroeconomic policies. This is because international policy diversification is an efficient way of dealing with macroeconomic policy risk. Independent national macroeconomic policymaking is more likely to stabilize the world real interest rate or the world business cycle than internationally-negotiated macroeconomic policymaking. Moreover, as Hayek has emphasized, independent and diverse decisionmaking is likely to be a more effective mechanism of discovery, i.e., of finding out which policies perform best.

As for the *"left-out-players* problem", two versions ought to be distinguished. The first is the "Rogoff Paradox" which Oudiz mentions. In this case, the players who are left out of the game are the market participants, in particular wage and price setters. The game-theoretic conclusion breaks down because there is no enforceable contract between politicians and the market. Since politicians are not credible, international policy competition is required as a substitute for credibility. It is important to recognize that the Rogoff Paradox is consistent with the public interest view of government. Politicians may be well-meaning but they are not believed. This is a second-best world, and the second-best solution is "no cooperation".

The other version of the "left-out players problem" is the "public choice critique". In this case, the voters are the left-out players. Again we are in a second-best world but this time the imperfection is the absence of an enforceable contract between politicians and voters. There is a principal-agent problem. In this case, politicians are not assumed to be well-meaning altruists but self-interested utility maximizers. This has two implications:

(i)   In order to mitigate the principal-agent problem, it is desirable to reduce the cost of monitoring and to increase the scope for corrective sanctions. This can be attained by assigning clear responsibilities to each policymaker, i.e., clear targets to each policy instrument. This requires that the number of targets should not exceed the number of policy instruments. However, in these circumstances, the game-theoretic case for international policy coordination is no longer valid. Most likely candidates for elimination are such international targets as the current account balance, the level of foreign exchange reserves, the exchange rate and the world real interest rate. Politicians, it is true, tend to pursue such aims. But is it the proper task of the economic adviser simply to take their targets as given and to limit himself to the instrumental aspect (the "your obedient servant" view), or can he also play a useful role in advising them on the proper choice of (intermediate) policy targets?

(ii)   Even if the number of targets is not reduced to the number of instruments, international macroeconomic policy coordination may be detrimental because it enables politicians (the suppliers of public goods, natural monopoly goods, and others) to collude at the expense of demanders, the citizens. The game-theoretic message that contracts and cooperation improve welfare has intuitive appeal to economists. But we also know that contracts and cooperation can be detrimental if they are designed to establish a cartel at the expense of third parties.

Germany's recent history seems to provide two outstanding examples of such international policy collusion. It had the purpose of generating a political business cycle and, therefore, was not in the interest of voters.

The first example is the Bonn Summit of 1978 - according to Cooper [1985, p. 370] "the most successful summit". While the American President, Jimmy Carter, promised measures to reduce US imports of petroleum, the German Chancellor, Helmut Schmidt, committed his government to an additional fiscal stimulus of up to one percent of GNP. The increase in the German budget deficit (especially in the cyclically-adjusted federal deficit) became effective in the boom year 1979. It was ill-timed from a cyclical point of view and contributed to the severe budgetary problems of the 1980s. During the 1980 election campaign, Schmidt himself attributed them to concessions he had to make at the Bonn Summit. But students of this episode emphasize that he had "welcomed being pushed onto a more expansionist course" and that "all [his advisers] were aware of his domestic political needs, including the need to plan now for an adequate economic growth in the approach to the 1980 elections" [Putnam, 1983, p. 82; Putnam, Bayne, 1984, p. 87].

The second example is the monetary policy collusion that took place at about the same time. In the first quarter of 1978, the German Chancellor launched the first moves towards the European Monetary System (EMS).

which finally came into effect in the spring of 1979. Schmidt's initiative was not popular with the German central bank and among German economists. Since the power to adjust the Deutsche Mark parity rests with the federal government (and the other members of the EC Council), the EMS enabled the German government to prevent the (formally autonomous) Bundesbank from following a significantly more restrictive monetary course than the (nonautonomous) central banks of the other member countries. In retrospect, the EMS has not prevented the Bundesbank from returning to price level stability by 1986. In the long run, the Bundesbank managed to assert itself as the price leader of the EMS money supply cartel. But as various studies [e.g., de Grauwe, 1987; Collins, 1987] show, the average inflation rate of the EMS countries fell less and more slowly than the average inflation rate of the other OECD countries.

Oudiz admits that "coordination can be counterproductive" but he adds: "What seems to be less convincing is the existence of a 'market for government, or policies' which will let the good governments survive and the bad ones disappear by natural selection" (p. 288). In my view, the process of selection and imitation is improved by policy competition in the following ways (1):

(i)   *"Exit"*: international asset substitution puts pressure on the exchange rate if the domestic central bank unilaterally pursues an inflationary monetary policy. This tends to serve as a corrective feedback mechanism (United States 1977/78, United Kingdom 1978/79, France 1983).

(ii) *"Voice"*: policy competition activates the protest of voters as a corrective feedback mechanism:
      - voters in the inflation-ridden countries can point to the example of superior foreign central banks,
      - the causal nexus between monetary policy and inflation becomes more transparent [Johnson, 1970, p. 105]; the price level reacts

---

(1) The distinction between "exit" and "voice" is due to Hirschman [1970].

300

faster because the currency depreciates immediately vis-à-vis the currencies of competing central banks.

The vote mechanism is less efficient than the price mechanism but it is a competitive mechanism and superior to cartelization.

Bibliography

COLLINS, Susan M., PPP and the Peso Problem: Exchange Rates in the EMS. Paper presented at the Workshop on the International Monetary System, the European Monetary System, the ECU and Plans for World Monetary Reform, European University Institute, Florence, April 1987.

COOPER, Richard N., "Panel Discussion: The Prospects for International Economic Policy Coordination". In: Willem H. BUITER, Richard C. MARSTON (Eds.), International Economic Policy Coordination. Cambridge 1985, pp. 366-372.

de GRAUWE, Paul, Fiscal Policies in the EMS: A Strategic Analysis. Paper presented at the Workshop on the International Monetary System, the European Monetary System, the ECU and Plans for World Monetary Reform, European University Institute, Florence, April 1987.

HIRSCHMAN, Albert O., Exit, Voice and Loyalty. Cambridge, Mass., 1970.

JOHNSON, Harry G., "The Case for Flexible Exchange Rates, 1969". In: Georg N. HALM (Ed.), Approaches to Greater Flexibility of Exchange Rates. Princeton 1970, pp. 91-111.

PUTNAM, Robert, "The Western Economic Summits: A Political Interpretation". In: Cesare MERLINI (Ed.), Economic Summits and Western Decision Making, London 1983, pp. 43-88.

--, Nicholas BAYNE, Hanging Together: The Seven Power Summits. Cambridge, Mass., 1984.

Manfred Willms

In his paper, Gilles Oudiz presents a clear analysis of the theoretical underpinnings and of some economic implications of international policy coordination. Oudiz builds his case in favour of policy coordination within a framework of a simple two-country model. The argument is based on the assumption that a change in the monetary and fiscal policies of the foreign country can increase welfare in the home country while not affecting foreign welfare. The foreign country has an incentive to carry out such policies only under a regime of coordination because it would benefit from respective measures of the home country. Thus, coordination leads to an increase in world welfare.

What Oudiz has in mind is obviously a situation where the goals of the policy-makers are disturbed by a real shock such as the oil price hike. The non-cooperative reaction is an expansionary monetary and fiscal policy to the point where the marginal costs of this policy in the form of monetary devaluation and domestic inflation are equal to the marginal benefits in the form of additional employment. Further expansionary measures are not introduced because every country expects to experience more inflation whereas the benefits from this policy, in the form of higher production and higher employment, are transferred to the foreign country. Thus in a non-cooperative situation unemployment remains high in all countries, while through cooperation at least one country would be better off and no country worse off.

The background for this type of argument is the Keynesian theory of demand management. It is implicitly assumed that output and employment can be permanently increased by a combination of monetary and fiscal policy. Empirical evidence for individual countries, as well as for the world economy as a whole, shows, however, that stimulation of demand does not have long-lasting effects on real economic activity. In the long run, countries cannot overcome real shocks and world welfare cannot be increased by demand management, neither within a cooperative regime nor within a non-cooperative system. A weakness of most coordination models is that they do not include the long-run implications of inflationary effects on economic activity, and this model is no exception.

Furthermore, the outcome that cooperation leads to greater world welfare than do unilateral decisions rests basically on the characteristics of the utility function. In most models, the utility function is a function of politicians who want to maintain the macro-economic performance on a desired level despite an exogenous shock from the world economy. If policies are not coordinated, this assumption leads to a suboptimal Nash equilibrium. If, however, the utility function is not sticky, but adjusts to the new economic situation, the case for policy coordination no longer applies.

A fundamental disadvantage of the Oudiz approach is its lack of any type of micro-economic foundation. Accordingly, the impact of policy coordination on consumer welfare cannot be shown. However, from an economic point of view, it is more important to acquire information on the effect of policy coordination on the household's consumption of domestic and foreign goods, its labour supply and its real money balances than on the utility function of politicians.

A further problem of policy coordination which is also discussed by Oudiz is the credibility problem. The question is whether international policy coordination or a competitive decision-making process gives governments a higher incentive to levy a surprise inflation tax on the private sector of the economy. In the literature it is often argued that within a regime of coordination, a built-in inflation incentive exists because if both governments agree to increase their money supply, no depreciation of the real exchange rate occurs. In a non-cooperative system a unilateral acceleration of monetary growth leads to a depreciation of the real exchange rate and imposes the inflation costs on the country which started the excessive monetary growth. Thus, the incentive to inflate should be much smaller in a non-cooperative system.

Oudiz criticizes this conclusion. Referring to the European Monetary System, he points out that policy coordination can also increase the credibility of governments and lead to a reduction of inflation. Unfortunately, the EMS is not a good example for lower inflation rates and more government credibility. It can be shown empirically that most non-

EMS countries have been much more successful in their disinflation policy than the member countries of the EMS.

A final remark is necessary with respect to the derivation of time-consistent policies for the evaluation of the benefits of international policy coordination. Most of the models, including the Oudiz model, only discuss appropriate adjustment policies induced by an exogenous shock. What, however, is the optimal long-run coordination strategy between countries? If the first-best solution cannot be realized, what is the ranking of alternative policies with respect to consumer welfare? For example: is coordination without government precommitment better than competitive decision-making with precommitment? Or is coordination with government precommitment better? The paper by Oudiz does not give an answer to these important questions.

Summary of the Discussion by Joachim Scheide

It was stressed that most empirical models indeed come up with only small gains from coordination, especially when the three blocs (United States, Japan, Western Europe) are considered. So the interdependence with respect to trade seems to be small which is surprising in light of the enormous interdependence in the financial area. In some models, the scope for gains from coordination seems to depend also on the initial conditions: if unemployment is high, the gains estimated in the models can also be relatively high, possibly because – in such a case – the output effects dominate the inflation effects.

One issue raised in the paper by Gilles Oudiz was the problem of the scarcity of instruments; gains from coordination could be expected if the number of targets exceeded the number of policy instruments in a system without coordination. Most models imply such a scarcity mainly in the short run, because in the longer run the objectives hardly differ between countries (e.g., zero inflation, output at the natural rate, compatible current account balances, and so on). The possible benefits from coordination are large because of the incompatibility of short-run objectives.

The presumed scarcity of instruments relative to targets relies, of course, also on the choice of targets for government policy. What can coordination really replace? One may argue that current account balances or market shares are meaningful policy objectives; given this, coordination is necessary in order to make the targets compatible, simply because both sides are affected by any change in these variables. However, some expressed the view that these external variables were outcomes determined by *markets*. If exchange rates are flexible, these targets are no longer legitimate objectives for governments. Now, the fact is that governments obviously do consider themselves as being responsible; but economists should then make it clear that these targets are to be given up. If this were the case, the scarcity of instruments may no longer exist - there are fewer targets - and therefore coordination would no longer be necessary on these grounds.

Some argued that coordination very often leads to cartels. It was mentioned, for example, that the EMS could be viewed as a cartel among central bankers to protect themselves against national politicians. This allowed France and Italy to reduce their inflation rates relatively fast. Political leaders may establish a cartel to protect themselves against their voters. Whether such cartels are good or bad may be an empirical matter. But also theoretical considerations, such as the "Rogoff paradox" mentioned in Oudiz's paper, can illuminate some problems; in this particular example, it is shown that coordination can be counterproductive. A cartel with positive effects for the world economy could be an institution like the GATT if it succeeds in reducing barriers to trade and if it protects politicians from the protectionist pressures of interest groups in their countries.

VI

Willem H. Buiter*

The Right Combination of Demand and Supply Policies: The Case for a Two-Handed Approach

1. Introduction

The title of this paper was chosen *for* me, *not by* me. Its ring of open-mindedness, evenhandedness and balance all but compels an author to parade as a man of the extreme center, a fanatical moderate in analysis and policy prescription. I identify with such a characterization only reluctantly.

My uneasiness with the title of this paper is, however, due to something more fundamental than an innate inability to try and please both sides of an argument. The usefulness of the very concepts of "demand-side" and "supply-side" should be questioned for a number of reasons.

Firstly, even where in individual markets demand and supply can be distinguished conceptually (i.e., in traditional competitive analysis), the uses of these concepts are at times confused and confusing. The demand for labor is part of the aggregate supply side. The supply of credit is part of aggregate demand. However, in working capital models of production (or in any model involving input-output lags) interest rates and/or the availability of credit affect aggregate supply (cf., e.g.,

---

* This paper was written while I was an academic visitor at the University of Groningen during May and June 1987. I would like to thank Klaus-Werner Schatz, Christian Seidl, Alan Blinder and Bennett McCallum for helpful comments on the first version of this paper.

Blinder [1987]). In any model with endogenous capital formation, financial market conditions affect aggregate supply in the long run.

Secondly, every nontrivial policy action (monetary, fiscal, financial, regulatory, incomes-policy etc.) influences both aggregate demand and aggregate supply (whenever these concepts are well-defined). We therefore cannot speak of demand policies and supply policies but only of the demand effects and the supply effects of given policies, which will always have both kinds of effects.

Thirdly, and most fundamentally, modern theoretical developments which are only just entering the stage of being the subject of systematic econometric testing, suggest that demand and supply may not even conceptually be separated. The best-known of these developments are those concerning efficiency wage and those related to hysteresis or path-dependence.

While I believe it to be important and even essential for progress in our understanding of how mature industrial economies work and how to improve their performance, to escape from the clutches of an intellectually moribund conventional competitive analysis (1) I cannot offer an integrated, coherent alternative "Weltanschauung". I shall however list a few of the many promising developments that may become the bricks and mortar of the economics of the 21st century. Enough has been achieved already to suggest the need for major changes in our view of how modern mixed economies work and in our appreciation of the scope for and limits to what policy can achieve.

If the demand-side versus supply-side dichotomy is no longer very useful, the distinction between *stabilization policy* and *structural* or *allocative* policy may still have some limited taxonomic usefulness. Stabilization policy aims to influence (and, one hopes, to minimize) deviations of the actual equilibrium (in general a non-Walrasian and possibly

---

(1) I include in this the quasi-competitive fix-price analysis of Barro, Grossmann [1971], Malinvaud [1977] and the French School. The occasional replacement of competitive agents by a conventional monopolist does not represent a great gain in insight either.

a quantity-constrained, rationing equilibrium), which will in general not be (constrained) Pareto-efficient, from the (or a) (constrained) Pareto-efficient equilibrium. In the context of the aggregate labor market, stabilization policy aims at deviations of actual employment from full employment or from a (presumed stabilization policy-invariant) "natural" level of employment. As regards aggregate output, stabilization policy is concerned with the gap between actual output and its full employment capacity value or some other appropriate notion of the "natural" level of output. Sometimes stabilization policy is defined more broadly to include the stability of the internal and external values of the currency and the achievement of "sustainable" financial deficits and surpluses for the public and private sectors (and by implication for the external sector).

Structural or allocative policy aims to influence the nature of (constrained) Pareto-efficient equilibria in labor, product and financial markets. In the labor market, such policies aim to influence the (presumed stabilization policy-invariant) natural rate of unemployment. In the aggregate product market, it seeks to modify the capacity or full-employment level of output.

The dichotomy is not neat but can be helpful in focussing policy debate. It is again true, however, that any nontrivial monetary, financial, fiscal, regulatory, and such like policy action will almost always have both allocative and stabilization consequences (see Buiter [1983]).

The plan of the paper is as follows. In Section 2, I review the role of stabilization policy in New Classical macroeconomic models. I reproduce a result of Marini [1985] that in all New Classical models which have (i) signal extraction and (ii) a non-predetermined intertemporal speculation term (somewhere in the model), monetary policy (and by direct extension fiscal policy) is very effective as a stabilization instrument in the sense that it can eliminate entirely the gap between actual and "full information" output or employment even when the policy authority is no better (or even less) informed than the private sector.

In Section 3, the efficiency wage hypothesis and the hysteresis or path-dependence hypothesis are shown to blur or eliminate entirely the

distinction between the demand and supply side. The far-reaching implications for policy are sketched briefly. Section 4 sums up and touches
briefly on some other important policy issues that could not be addressed
in the body of the paper for reasons of space. It also contains some
forthright policy recommendations aimed at challenging prevalent Euro-
pessimistic complacency.

2. The Role of Stabilization Policy in New Classical Macroeconomic Models

New Classical macroeconomic models are sequential competitive equilibrium
models where market participants have symmetric information and (Muth)-
rational expectations. This discussion relates only to the monetary
variant of the New Classical School, associated with the names of Lucas,
Sargent, Wallace and Barro. It ignores the real business cycle models
developed by Kydland and Prescott [1982], Long and Plosser [1983] and
others.

Since markets clear continuously, with equilibrium prices determined by
the equality of competitive supply and demand, stabilization policy in
New Classical models has a much more restricted meaning than in
Keynesian or neo-Keynesian models.

Because of incomplete (albeit symmetric) information, markets may clear
at the "wrong" prices and quantities: actual prices and quantities may
differ from what they would be under full current or contemporaneous
information. Policy rules might therefore influence (and indeed eliminate)
the gap between the actual competitive equilibrium and the "full information" competitive equilibrium.

On reading recent contributions to this literature, the conclusion is in-
escapable that Marini's [1985] powerful and general result about policy
effectiveness in New Classical macromodels has not yet permeated a large
part of the professional economic awareness. I shall therefore reproduce
it very briefly, using Marini's example of Barro's [1976] well-known
model.

Leaving out some unimportant intercept terms, Barro's model is given in equations [1]-[7]. Equation [8] is a generalization of his policy rule. The (self-explanatory) notation is as in Barro [1976](1).

[1] $\quad y_t^s(z) = \alpha_s(P_t(z) - E(P_{t+1}|\Omega_t(z))) - \beta_s(M_t + E(\Delta M_{t+1}|\Omega_t(z))$

$$- E(P_{t+1}|\Omega_t(z))) + u_t^s + \epsilon_t^s(z)$$

[2] $\quad y_t^d(z) = -\alpha_d(P_t(z) - E(P_{t+1}|\Omega_t(z))) + \beta_d(M_t + E\{\Delta M_{t+1}|\Omega_t(z))$

$$- E(P_{t+1}|\Omega_t(z))) + u_t^d + \epsilon_t^d(z)$$

[3] $\quad y_t^s(z) = y_t^d(z) = y_t(z) \quad$ for all z, t

[4a] $\quad \alpha \equiv \alpha_d + \alpha_s$

[4b] $\quad \beta \equiv \beta_d + \beta_s$

[4c] $\quad \epsilon_t(z) \equiv \epsilon_t^d(z) - \epsilon_t^s(z)$

[4d] $\quad u_t \equiv u_t^d - u_t^s$

[4e] $\quad P_t \equiv \frac{1}{N}(\sum_z P_t(z))$

[4f] $\quad y_t \equiv \sum_z y_t(z)$

[5] $\quad \sum_z \epsilon_t(z) = 0$

[6] $\quad u_t = u_{t-1} + v_t$

---

(1) The occurrence of M_t in the local demand and supply functions even though it does not belong to the information set at time t if there are monetary disturbances is rather awkward.

[7a] $E(\epsilon_t, v_t, m_t) = 0$

[7b] $E[\begin{pmatrix} \epsilon_t \\ v_t \\ m_t \end{pmatrix} (\epsilon_s \; v_s \; m_s)] = 0; \quad t \neq s$

$$= \begin{bmatrix} \sigma_\epsilon^2 & 0 & 0 \\ 0 & \sigma_v^2 & 0 \\ 0 & 0 & \sigma_m^2 \end{bmatrix} ; \quad t = s$$

[8] $\Delta M_t \equiv M_t - M_{t-1} = m_t + \sum_{j=1}^{\infty} \gamma_j v_{t-j} + \sum_{j=1}^{\infty} \delta_j m_{t-j}$

E is the mathematical expectation operator and $\Omega(z)$ the information set conditioning expectations formed at time t in local market z. N is the (large) number of local markets. $\Omega_t(z)$ contains the model [equations [1] - [8]], lagged values of all exogenous and endogenous aggregate variables $\{P_{t-1}, P_{t-2}, \ldots; M_{t-1}, M_{t-2}, \ldots; v_{t-1}, v_{t-2}, \ldots; m_{t-1}, m_{t-2}, \ldots\}$ and $P_t(z)$, the current local price. It does not contain $\epsilon_t(z)$, v_t, m_t, M_t or P_t. v_t is the aggregate real shock, $\epsilon_t(z)$ the local real shock and m_t the monetary shock. Note that the policy feedback rule contains a response to past (white noise) monetary shocks, m_{t-j}. The past shocks are all white noise and are in the information set of the private sector.

The actual solution values $P_t(z)$, P_t and y_t will, in general, be different from the full-information solution values $P_t^*(z)$, P_t^* and y_t^*. These are the solution values that would prevail if there were full contemporaneous information; i.e., with information set $\Omega_t = \Omega_t(z) \cup \{m_t, M_t, \epsilon_t(z), v_t, P_t\}$. Using, for example, the method of undetermined coefficients, it is easily checked that the difference between the actual intertemporal substitution term $P_t(z) - E(P_{t+1}|\Omega_t(z))$ and the "full-information" intertemporal substitution term $P_t^*(z) - E(P_{t+1}^*|\Omega_t)$ can be written as (1):

[9] $D_t \equiv P_t(z) - E(P_{t+1}|\Omega_t(z)) - [P_t^*(z) - E(P_{t+1}^*|\Omega_t)] = \frac{\beta}{\alpha} [m_t -$

$E(m_t|\Omega_t(z))] + \frac{1}{\alpha} [v_t - E(v_t|\Omega_t(z))]$

---

(1) Bubble solutions are ruled out and $|\frac{\alpha - \beta}{\alpha}| < 1$.

$$- \frac{\beta}{\alpha} \sum_{i=1}^{\infty} [(\alpha-\beta)/\alpha]^{i-1} [E(\Delta M_{t+1+i}|\Omega_t(z)) - E(\Delta M^*_{t+1+i}|\Omega_t)]$$

D_t therefore depends on the "inference errors" concerning the current monetary shock $(m_t - E(m_t|\Omega_t(z)))$ and the current aggregate shock $(v_t - E(v_t|\Omega_t(z)))$, and on the differences between current estimates of future monetary growth based on actual information and estimates based on full current information:

$$E(\Delta M_{t+1+i}|\Omega_t(z)) - E(\Delta M^*_{t+1+i}|\Omega_t); \quad i = 1, 2, \ldots$$

Note that, through some idiosyncrasy of the (ad-hoc) model, only monetary growth estimates for periods t+2 and beyond (i.e., not for period t+1) matter. This is the source of Barro's erroneous generalization [Barro, 1976, p. 20] from his policy rule $\Delta M_t = m_t + \gamma_1 v_{t-1}$, a special case of our general rule. For the general rule, [9] becomes:

$$[9'] \quad D_t = \frac{\beta}{\alpha} (1+ \sum_{i=1}^{\infty} [(\alpha-\beta)/\alpha]^{i-1} \delta_{i+1}) (m_t - E(m_t|\Omega_t(z)))$$

$$+ \frac{1}{\alpha} (1+ \beta \sum_{i=1}^{\infty} [(\alpha-\beta)/\alpha]^{i-1} \gamma_{i+1}) (v_t - E(v_t|\Omega_t(z)))$$

The δ_{i+1} and γ_{i+1} are policy-choice parameters. Clearly we can set $D_t \equiv 0$ by choosing any values of δ_{i+1} and γ_{i+1} such that $1 + \Sigma_{i=1}^{\infty} [(\alpha-\beta)/\alpha]^{i-1} \delta_{i+1} = 0$ and $1 + \beta \Sigma_{i=1}^{\infty} [(\alpha-\beta)/\alpha]^{i-1} \gamma_{i+1} = 0$ (1).

With $D_t \equiv 0$, it follows immediately that actual output y_t is also equal to full-information output y_t^*. Three points should be noted.

Firstly, Barro's rule $\Delta M_t = m_t + \gamma_1 v_{t-1}$ is indeed ineffective. While he deserves credit for having found the only lagged feedback rule to yield ineffectiveness, that result clearly lacks any generality. Feeding back in a deterministic manner (i.e., with known δ_{i+1} and γ_{i+1}) from aggregate

---

(1) Since Barro's model does not exhibit superneutrality of money, even different constant and known proportional rates of growth of money will alter both the actual and the full-information equilibrium. Models with "surprise" supply functions will not have this property.

information arbitrarily far in the past, monetary policy can eliminate the gap between actual and full-information output. Note also that both the conditional and unconditional variances of output can be set at any value, including zero.

Secondly, this perfect stabilization can be achieved even when the monetary authorities have an informational disadvantage vis-à-vis the private sector, in the sense that the authorities could, in period t, use only information older than the most recent information available to the private sector. For example, with $\Delta M_t = m_t + \gamma_{375} v_{t-375} + \delta_{375} m_{t-375}$, the authorities can achieve $D_t \equiv 0$, provided $1 + [(\alpha-\beta)/\alpha]^{373} \delta_{375} = 1 + \beta [(\alpha-\beta)/\alpha]^{373} \gamma_{375} = 0$. This contradicts, for example, King [1983].

Thirdly, it doesn't matter if the monetary authority randomizes its policy $(\sigma_m^2 > 0)$, as long as it responds appropriately to one or more past monetary shocks (through the δ_j) so as to undo the effects of its own unpredictability!

Intuitively, what makes for effectiveness, is that the lagged feedback rules act like contingent forward contracts by the policy authority, which complete the incomplete set of contingent private markets implicit in this model. Private agents at time t are (implicitly) prevented from making future actions contingent on the future revelation of the as yet unkown realizations of m_t and v_t. The policymaker, through its lagged rule, can do this, because the presence of a (nonpredetermined) intertemporal substitution term means that current endogenous variables are functions of current expectations of all future values of the policy instrument(s). Through the lagged feedback rule, these *future* instrument values can be made functions of the (currently unknown) *current* realizations of the exogenous variables. By adopting such a rule and, with rational expectations, by being known to be doing so, the policymaker can change the information content of the currently observed local price and indeed make it fully revealing. In the ad-hoc models of Barro [1976; 1980; 1981] and others, the reason for this asymmetry in private and public opportunity sets isn't clear. In optimizing models, a finite-horizon OLG structure might explain the asymmetry [e.g., Lucas, 1972].

It is easily checked (but left as an exercise for the reader) that policy effectiveness remains if we replace the intertemporal substitution term in the supply and demand functions (1) and (2) by a real interest rate term such as $i_t + (P_t(z) - E(P_{t+1}|\Omega_t(z)))$ where i_t is the nominal interest rate. (We must of course ensure that if i_t belongs to $\Omega_t(z)$, say because it is set in an economy-wide capital market, a signal extraction problem remains. This will require adding another independent source of noise to the system.) Replacing the intertemporal substitution term in the supply function by a "surprise" term such as $P_t(z) - E(P_t|\Omega_t(z))$ also does not affect Marini's policy effectiveness result. Only if there is no signal extraction problem, i.e., either because P_t is known or because there is no current (period t) information in $\Omega_t(z)$, will there be policy ineffectiveness. Sargent and Wallace [1975] fall into this category with a model that can be summarized as follows:

$$y_t = \alpha(P_t - E(P_t A]_{t-1})) + u_t^y \qquad \text{(Aggregate supply)}$$

$$y_t = -\beta(i_t - E((P_{t+1} - P_t)|\Omega_{t-1})) + u_t^d \qquad \text{(IS)}$$

$$M_t - P_t = -\lambda i_t + k y_t + u_t^m \qquad \text{(LM)}$$

Where u_t^y, u_t^d and u_t^m are white noise and Ω_{t-1} contains the model and aggregate information dated period t-1 and earlier. The intertemporal substitution term is predetermined and there is no policy effectiveness. Policy effectiveness is restored if, as in Sargent [1973] the term $E((P_{t+1}-P_t)|\Omega_{t-1})$ in the IS curve is replaced by $E((P_{t+1}-P_t)|\Omega_t)$. This makes the intertemporal substitution term nonpredetermined. Marini's result can be summarized as follows:

Proposition: Signal extraction + (nonpretermined) intertemporal substitution (somewhere in the model) → policy effectiveness

Marini's result about stabilization-policy effectiveness in New Classical macromodels is important from the perspective of the intellectual developments in our discipline. It corrected a pervasive logical error in a wide range of policy analyses. I do not consider it equally important for practical policy design, because the object of New Classical stabilization policy (the gap between symmetric actual and full-information equilibria) is, practically, a side-show. If markets do indeed clear in traditional competitive fashion, stabilization policy based on signal extraction problems is a second-order affair. With efficient competitive markets (conditional on the symmetric information held by the private agents), the gains in welfare to be gained by informing private agents more promptly of the current value of the aggregate money stock (or by pursuing feedback policies that have the same effect) are bound to be trivial. This literature also has the information problem exactly backwards: private agents are assumed to know (or to act as if they know) the true structure of the model (the values of all the parameters of the model, the behavioral parameters of the government included) but to be badly informed about the current realization of the money stock. In practice the money stock can be known very quickly and at very little cost, while neither the private agents nor the policy authorities have much of a clue about the true structure of the model.

To have nontrivial scope for stabilization policy, the actual equilibrium must be a non-Walrasian one. Marini's policy effectiveness result has very little to do, therefore, with Keynesian or neo-Keynesian stabilization policy concerns, which are motivated (even if only informally) by non-Walrasian equilibria.

One point of practical importance brought out by Marini's analysis is the distinction between *asymmetries in information sets* between the public and the private sector and *asymmetries in opportunity sets*, as a source of policy effectiveness. Even with equal or inferior public sector information, policy effectiveness will emerge because there are things the authorities can and will do that the private sector cannot do or chooses not to do. The power to tax and to regulate, the monopoly of legal tender and the longevity of the *institutions* of government (even if not of individual administrations) are some of the obvious "deep" sources of such asymmetries between public and private opportunity sets.

Finally, as shown by Marini [1985], it is easily checked for Barro's model and similar ones, that the feedback rules that influence (and possibly eliminate) the gap between the actual and the full-information equilibrium also affect the full-information equilibrium itself. Stabilization policy and structural or allocative policy in this model are inextricably intertwined.

3. The Dependence of Demand on Supply (and vice versa): Efficiency Wages and Hysteresis

To conduct one's analysis and to specify one's policy recommendations in terms of demand and supply betrays old-fashioned competitive thinking. The crucial issue is whether this represents a robust, felicitous shortcut or a misleading or indeed dangerous focus on a rather uninteresting special case.

It may no longer be correct that the way to make a good economist is to teach a parrot the two words "supply" and "demand". This possibility is apparent even in conventional noncompetitive analysis where we teach our first-year students that there is no monopolist's supply schedule. Recent developments have undermined the primacy of the law of supply and demand from at least two different perspectives. The *efficiency wage hypothesis* with its new asymmetric information microfoundations destroys the conventional distinction between demand and supply even in competitive markets. It has implications for labor markets, insurance markets, credit markets and heterogeneous product markets in general. The *"hysteresis"* or *"path-dependence"* hypothesis, based on human capital or insider-outsider microfoundations suggests that today's actual unemployment rate may be tomorrow's "natural" unemployment rate. It destroys the distinction between aggregate demand and aggregate supply outside the very short run. I now turn to these two developments in turn.

a. Efficiency Wages and the Death of the Law of Demand and Supply

In a conventional competitive market, equilibrium price and quantity are determined by the intersection of competitive demand and supply

316

schedules derived from the utility maximizing behavior of price-taking households and the profit maximizing behavior of price-taking firms. Both parties to a transaction have identical (symmetric) information.

In order not to be unnecessarily awkward, it will be assumed in what follows that the (uncompensated) competitive demand schedule is downward-sloping, that the competitive supply schedule is upward-sloping and that a unique equilibrium exists.

Consider, for example, the familiair competitive aggregate labor market. The representative firm, i, maximizes profits π_i:

[10] $\pi_i = PY_i - W(1+\tau_p)L_i$

P is the parametric price of output, W the parametric money wage paid to workers, τ_p the proportional payroll tax rate, Y_i output (and sales) of firm i and L_i the employment of homogeneous labor by firm i. The production function is given by

[11] $Y_i = f(Q_iL_i);$ $f' > 0;$ $f'' < 0;$ $Q_i > 0$

Q_i is the quality, efficiency or productivity of labor, assumed to be exogenous to the firm. Taking p, W, τ_p and Q_i as given, the firm optimally chooses its level of employment L_i^d according to

[12] $Q_if'(Q_iL_i^d) = (W/P)(1+\tau_p)$

Competitive supply of homogeneous labor is assumed to be an increasing function of the after-tax real wage, $w(1-\tau_w)$, where τ_w is the proportional labor income tax rate and $w = W/P$.

[13] $L_i^S = s(w(1-\tau_w));$ $s' > 0$

Competitive equilibrium prevails when

[14] $L_i^d = L_i^S = L$

Policy analysis in this simple static model is the comparative static analysis of the effects of changes in the two tax rates on the equilibrium real wage and level of employment. This amounts to determining the "reduced form multipliers", i.e., the partial derivatives of equations [15] and [16] below, which are obtained by solving equations [12], [13], and [14] for w and L.

[15] $\quad w = h(Q_i; \tau_p, \tau_w); \quad h_{Q_i} > 0; \quad h_{\tau_p} < 0; \quad h_{\tau_w} > 0$

[16] $\quad L = j(Q_i; \tau_p, \tau_w); \quad j_{Q_i} > 0; \quad j_{\tau_p} < 0; \quad j_{\tau_w} < 0$

This comparative static analysis can always, often in an illuminating way, be decomposed in terms of the shifts in the demand schedule and/or the supply schedule, drawn in w-L space, as one or more parameters change. Figure 1 shows as an example the effect of a higher payroll tax rate on real wages and employment.

This analysis can be fancied up considerably, e.g., by introducing labor adjustment costs, many factors of production and rational expectations. Comparative statics become comparative dynamics. The actual and anticipated nature of the policy changes becomes important (when were changes first anticipated? How permanent, transitory or reversible are they perceived to be? How confidently are these expectations held and so on?). But this is not important for our purposes. What matters here is that demand functions and demand shocks are conceptually and (subject to the standard identification caveats) also operationally distinct from supply functions and supply shocks. The intersection of the two schedules determines the Walrasian, competitive, market-clearing price and quantity.

This picture changes dramatically when efficiency-wage considerations are permitted. In the context of our simple example this means that labor is no longer viewed as homogeneous. Different workers have different levels of productivity or efficiency, but employers cannot (perfectly) discriminate between workers of different qualities. The average quality

318

Figure 1 - The Effect of a Higher Payroll Tax Rate in a Conventional Competitive Labor Market

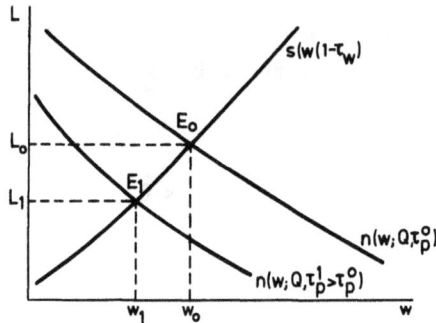

(or efficiency level) of the workforce is, however, an increasing function of the real wage (other versions make it an increasing function of the firm's wage relative to the wage of its competitors). The literature suggests a whole range of possible mechanisms for this positive dependence of Q_i on w (for recent surveys see Katz [1986] and Stiglitz [1987]). Most of those that are relevant to a mature industrial economy rely on asymmetric information between workers and employers and resulting adverse selection or moral hazard problems. In the adverse selection model of Weiss [1980], for example, employers do not know the quality of the individual worker and a worker's reservation wage is an increasing function of his/her quality (a more efficient worker is also better at painting his/her home). In other models with imperfect monitoring of workers by employers and consequent incentives to shirk, a higher wage increases the worker's opportunity cost of being found shirking. Other models rely on labor turnover costs or on morale effects.

For the efficiency wage hypothesis to bite, Q_i should be an increasing function of w_i and there should be initially a region of "increasing returns" in which a higher wage induces a more than proportionate increase in labor quality. η denotes the elasticity of quality with respect to the real wage, i.e., $\eta \equiv \partial Q_i / \partial w_i \cdot w_i / Q_i$. For simplicity, I assume that for any given value of the parameter vector θ, which contains all exogenous factors and policy instruments affecting the price-quality relationship, there exists a unique $\bar{w}_i(\theta)$ such that for all $w_i \leq \bar{w}_i$ we have $\eta > 1$ and for all $w_i > \bar{w}_i$ we have $\eta < 1$. Thus

[17] $Q_i = Q(w_i, \theta)$; $Q_{w_i} > 0$; $\eta(w_i, \theta) \gtrless 1 <=> w_i \lessgtr \bar{w}_i$

It is easy to generate reasonable models with this property (see, for example, Stiglitz [1987] and the references contained therein).

The representative firm now maximizes [10] with respect to L_i and W_i, subject to both [11] and [17]. For the moment, the "availability constraint", i.e., the ability of the firm to obtain the labor it demands, is ignored. The first-order conditions can be written as in [12] and [19].

[18] $\eta(w_i, \theta) = 1$ or $w_i = \bar{w}_i(\theta)$

$\bar{w}_i$ is called the efficiency wage. It minimizes the cost of employing an effective (quality-adjusted) unit of labor w_i/Q_i. The quantity of labor demanded $\tilde{L}_i^d$ is solved for from

[19] $Q(\bar{w}_i(\theta), \theta)$ $f'(Q(\bar{w}_i(\theta), \theta) \tilde{L}_i^d = \bar{w}_i(\theta)(1+\tau_p)$

The availability constraint for the firm (often called the individual rationality constraint) is that V, the utility of the representative worker selling to the firm an amount of labor L_i of quality Q at a wage w_i should be at least as high as the utility obtainable in the next best alternative use V^*, that is to say

[20] $V(w_i, L_i, Q(w_i, \theta), \theta') \geq V^*(\theta'')$

θ' and θ'' are vectors of parameters. Reasonable restrictions on V would be $V_{w_i} > 0$, $V_{L_i} < 0$, $V_Q < 0$. When [20] holds with equality we can solve for the labor supply schedule

[21] $\tilde{L}_i^s = s(w_i, Q(w_i, \theta), \theta', V^*(\theta'')); \quad s_{w_i} > 0; \quad s_Q < 0, \quad s_{V^*} < 0$

Note that it is possible (though not necessary) that at the efficiency wage $w_i = \bar{w}_i(\theta)$, $\tilde{L}_i^d < \tilde{L}_i^s$. The firm's optimizing demand for labor can be met without the constraint [20] being binding. If at the efficiency wage there is excess supply of labor, there is no "disequilibrium" downward pressure on wages. Labor costs per efficiency unit of labor are minimized at a real wage in excess of the market-clearing wage. Not also that the demand function and the quantity of labor demanded by the firm $\tilde{L}_i^d$ are crucially dependent on supply parameters. Q is part of the "supply side" of the labor market. We can see this clearly by considering the case where θ contains the wage income tax rate, i.e., by assuming, in the spirit of the model of Weiss [1980], that average quality depends on the after-tax wage $Q = Q(w_i(1-\tau_w))$. In that case, the efficiency wage increases and the quantity of labor demanded decreases as the tax on labor income increases. A supply-side parameter shifts labor demand! The old language clearly is less than helpful here.

The possibility (*not* the inevitability) of quantity-constrained, rationing equilibria and other non-Walrasian equilibria is complemented by comparative statics that may be very different form those of traditional symmetric information competitive analysis. Apart from explaining real wage rigidity in the face of persistent (equilibrium!) excess supply, these models can generate, in rationing equilibria, quantity responses with multiplier properties in response to exogenous shocks, with little or no (or even perverse) adjustment in the real wage.

It can similarly explain persistent excess demand in credit markets and the "non-Walrasian" response of credit and interest rates to changes in monetary and fiscal policy. It cannot, however, motivate any form of *nominal* rigidity in wages, prices or interest rates. "Rigid" real wages and real interest rates can be equilibrium outcomes in the efficiency wage universe. Nominal inertia of any kind still awaits another explanation.

When the efficiency wage model of the labor market is combined with imperfect competition in the product market, the scope for demand management becomes more transparent. I first summarize an interesting model of Akerlof and Yellen [1985]. Blanchard and Kiyotaki [1985] and Ball and Romer [1987] are in the same spirit as Akerlof and Yellen. They rationalize nominal inertia through the rather arbitrary device of assigning a lumpy real cost to nominal price adjustment. The availability constraint is assumed nonbinding. Let there be $N > 1$ firms selling similar but nonidentical products. Each firm i faces the following demand curve for its product (1):

[22] $y_i^d = (Y/N) (P_i/P)^{-\epsilon}; \quad \epsilon > 1$

Y is aggregate demand and P the general price level, defined as the geometric mean of the P_i

[23] $P = \left[\prod_{j=1}^{N} P_j \right]^{1/N}$

Each firm has the identical production function $Y_i = f(Q(W_i/P)L_i)$ and maximizes profits $\pi_i = P_i Y_i - W_i L_i$ by optimally choosing W_i and P_i, taking as given P and Y. The first-order conditions are:

[24] $\eta(W_i/P) = [Q'(W_i/P)/Q(W_i/P)] (W_i/P) = 1$

[25] $Q(W_i/P) f'(Q(W_i/P)L_i) (1-\frac{1}{\epsilon}) = W_i/P$

Equation [24] reproduces the fixed efficiency wage. In a symmetric equilibrium, $P_i = P$ and $W_i = W$ for all i. The real wage and aggregate employment are therefore given by:

[26a] $\eta(w) = 1$

[26b] $Q(w) f'(Q(w) \frac{L}{N}) (1-\frac{1}{\epsilon}) = w$

[26c] $L \leq L^*$

L^* is the aggregate supply of (physical) units of labor, assumed to be independent of the real wage for simplicity.

---

(1) ϵ could be a function of N.

α. Akerlof-Yellen "Near-Rationality"

As in Akerlof and Yellen [1985], aggregate demand is given by the constant velocity quantity equation [27], the production function is Cobb-Douglas as in [28] and Q_i takes the form given in [29].

[27] $\quad Y = M/P$

[28] $\quad Y_i = (Q_i L_i)^{\alpha}; \quad 0 < \alpha < 1$

[29] $\quad Q(w_i) = -a + bw_i^{\gamma}; \quad 0 < \gamma < 1; \quad a > 0; \quad b > 0$

It follows that, for an initial money stock M_o, the general price level P_o is given by equations [30] and [31] where w_o is the initial (real) efficiency wage.

[30] $\quad P_o = kM_o$

[31] $\quad k = (\varepsilon w_o / \alpha(\varepsilon-1)Q(w_o))^{\alpha/1-\alpha}$

Equations [26]-[31] characterize a full, long-run, optimizing equilibrium in which all firms are Bertrand maximizers. Assume that, at this long-run equilibrium, a perturbation in the form of an increase in the nominal money stock from M_o to $M_o(1+v)$ leads to a short-run optimizing response by only a fraction $1-\beta$ of the total number of firms. The remaining fraction of firms β, keeps its money wage and nominal output price unchanged. For small shocks, this suboptimal behavior is *near-rational*, in the sense that the profit loss resulting from the suboptimal behavior is an order of magnitude smaller than the shock. The reason for the second-order nature of the profit loss is that the imperfectly competitive firm's profit function is differentiable in its two controls: own price and own wage. As regards own price, this follows immediately from the monopolistically competitive Bertrand behavior. As regards own wage, the efficiency wage hypothesis does the work. In other words, at a full, long-run equilibrium, a failure optimally to adjust the own price and wage has no first-order effect on profits because the envelope theorem strikes for the individual firm. The effect of the nominal money shock on real demand and employment, however, has the same order of magnitude as the shock.

Let the superscript n denote variables pertaining to near-maximizing firms and the superscript m variables pertaining to maximizing firms. It is easily shown [Akerlof, Yellen, 1985] that

[32a] $P^n = P_o$

[32b] $P^m = P_o(1+v)^\lambda$

[32c] $P = P_o(1+v)^{(1-\beta)\lambda}$

[32d] $w^n = w_o(1+v)^{-(1-\beta)\lambda}$

[32e] $w^m = w_o$

Where

[33] $\lambda = (1-\alpha)\alpha^{-1}[\beta(\varepsilon\alpha^{-1}-\varepsilon+1) + (1-\beta)(1-\alpha)\alpha^{-1}]^{-1}; \quad 0 < \lambda \leq 1$

The near-maximizing firms increase their demand for labor because the relative price of their output has declined and because real money balances have increased. Their reduction in profits as a result of their failure to optimize fully in response to the shock is simply the difference between the profit of a fully optimizing firm Π^m and that of a near-optimizing firm Π^n. Some arithmetic shows that

[34] $\left.\dfrac{d(\Pi^m - \Pi^n)}{dv}\right|_{v=0} = 0$

The response of aggregate employment is given by

[35] $\left.\dfrac{d(N/No)}{dv}\right|_{v=0} = \dfrac{1}{\alpha}(1-(1-\beta)\lambda) + \beta(1-\beta)\lambda$

Only when $\beta = 0$ (which implies $\lambda=1$) is the employment effect zero. For $\beta > 0$ there is a first-order employment effect.

β. A Kinked Demand Curve (1)

With the demand function [22], the price elasticity $-\epsilon$ is independent of aggregate demand. In general, however, the price elasticity will depend both on Y and on P_i/P, that is

[36] $\quad \epsilon = \epsilon(Y, P_i/P)$

In a fully optimizing symmetric equilibrium, $P_i = P$ and real aggregate demand will have a positive (negative) effect on the employment of an individual firm if ϵ_Y is positive (negative). Note however, that since aggregate demand, Y, must equal aggregate supply, the equilibrium conditions will still generate unique equilibrium values for L and Y as long as there is a unique value of ϵ for any given Y (and for any given P_i/P). This is obvious from equations [37] and [38] below.

[37] $\quad Q(w) f'(Q(w)\frac{L}{N}) (1 - \frac{1}{\epsilon(Y,1)}) = w$

[38] $\quad Y = Nf(Q(w)\frac{L}{N})$

An interesting model that permits one to escape from this box (effectively by making equation [37] nonbinding for a range of Y values) is the piecewise-linear kinked demand curve given in [39] and shown in Figure 2.

[39] $\quad Y_i^d = \min \left(\frac{1}{N} Y - \alpha(\frac{P_i}{P}-1), \frac{1}{N} Y -\beta(\frac{P_i}{P}-1)\right); \quad \alpha > \beta > 0$

---

(1) Van Ees [1987] independently developed the idea of combining the efficiency wage hypothesis in the labor market and the kinked demand curve in the product market in order to create scope for a potential influence of aggregate demand on employment. His paper contains a much more elaborate and thorough development of these ideas.

The greater responsiveness of sales to increases in P_i relative to P compared to decreases can be rationalized using search-theoretic "shopping models". An increase in P_i relative to P discourages potential new customers that visit the firm in the same way that a decrease P_i-P attracts potential new customers. An increase in P_i-P in addition causes the existing clientele of the firm to leave in order to search for a lower price elsewhere. A reduction in P_i-P does not have a corresponding sales-boosting effect on the firm's current customers.

Figure 2 - The Kinked Demand Curve and Aggregate Demand

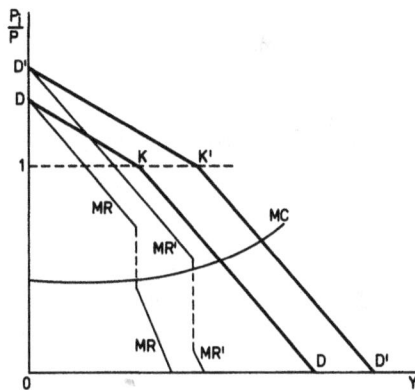

In Figure 2, an increase in real aggregate demand shifts the demand schedule from DKD to D'K'D'. The firm's marginal cost curve is given by $MC((W_i/P), Y_i) = (W_i/P) \cdot [1/(Q(W_i/P)f'(Q(W_i/P)L_i))]$ where L_i is, given Q, an increasing function of Y_i through the production function given in [11] or [28]. Figure 2 shows the case where the upward-sloping marginal cost-curve MC intersects the marginal revenue correspondences MR and MR' of both demand curves in their vertical segments. A higher level of real aggregate demand in this case generates a higher level of supply and employment. Each firm sets P_i=P (even before the assumption of a symmetric equilibrium is imposed). "At the kink", output demanded and supplied is therefore given by $Y_i = Y_i^d = \frac{1}{N} Y$.

The real wage, output and employment are therefore given as functions of real aggregate demand by:

[40] $\eta(w) = 1$

[41] $f(Q(w)\frac{L}{N}) = \frac{Y}{N}$

A symmetric equilibrium exists in this model for real demand values in the range $\underline{Y} \leq Y \leq \overline{Y}$. $\underline{Y}$ is the level of real demand for which marginal cost (MC) equals $-\beta^{-1}(Y/N)+1$, the lowest value of marginal revenue "at the kink". $\overline{Y}$ is the level of real demand for which MC equals $-\alpha^{-1}(Y/N)+1$, the highest value of marginal revenue "at the kink". Note that at the kink, $MC(Y_i) = MC(Y/N)$. $\overline{Y}$ can be below the level of output corresponding to full employment of the labor force.

γ. An Ad-Hoc Model of Real Demand and Nominal Prices

Can the authorities influence real aggregate demand and if so, can they do this systematically or only through policy surprises? Consider the following standard ad-hoc model of aggregate demand and of the determination of nominal prices and wages. M is the nominal money stock, B the stock of government bonds, G exhaustive public spending, T taxes net of transfers. The aggregate demand schedule is given in equation [42]. Two alternative nominal wage-price blocks are given. The first, represented in equations [44], [47], and [48], has a sticky general price level and a flexible money wage. The second, represented in equations [45], [46], [47], and [48], has a sticky money wage and a flexible general price level. Following McCallum [1980] P_t^* is the general price level that would prevail at full employment, W_t^* the money wage that would prevail at full employment and w^* is the labor market-clearing real wage.

[42] $Y = y(G,T,M/P,B/P);$ $\quad y_G > 0;$ $\quad y_T \leq 0;$ $\quad y_m > 0;$ $\quad y_b \geq 0$

[43] $w \equiv W/P$

[44] $P_t = \delta p_t^* + (1-\delta)p_{t-1};$ $\quad 0 \leq \delta \leq 1;$ or

[45] $W_t^* = w^* P_t^*$ and

[46] $W_t = \delta'W_t^* + (1-\delta')W_{t-1};$ $\quad 0 \leq \delta' \leq 1$

where p_t^* is defined by:

[47] $Y^* = y(G_t, T_t, M_t/P_t^*, B_t/P_t^*)$

[48] $Y^* = f[Q(w^*)L^*]$

With the addition of the government budget identity given in [49], where i is the nominal interest rate, we now have a sample of a wider class of dynamic macromodels with the potential for persistent equilibrium unemployment.

[49] $(\Delta M + \Delta B)P \equiv G + i(B/P) - T$

The scope for demand management to influence Y is transitory in these models unless there is complete nominal rigidity, i.e., $\delta = 0$ in the version with equation [44] or $\delta' = 0$ in the version with equations [45] and [46]. I consider an exogenously given money wage or nominal price level to be quite acceptable in a model such as this. There seems to be no good reason for the money wage (nominal price level) to be driven towards the full employment equilibrium money wage (nominal price level) when that full employment equilibrium need never be reached. The further analysis of the determination of the exogenous nominal anchor by history, convention, habit or accident is beyond the scope of this paper. What matters for our purposes is that there are no obvious disequilibrium forces within the model, no perceived free lunches, that will tend to move the nominal anchor from any arbitrarily-assigned value.

This model and many like it suggest that aggregate demand expansion can expand employment without the need for a reduction in real wages (or more generally in real marginal labor costs). The conventional competitive model rules out this possibility. If, as I believe, the imperfect competition-efficiency wage model is a better parable for Europe today than the conventional competitive parable or other real wage-constrained employment parables, the case against a demand stimulus is weakened considerably. The authorities must of course be able to influence real aggregate demand. In a monetary model, this ability hinges on the behavior of money wages and prices, something about which the real efficiency wage-imperfect competition model has nothing to say.

b. Hysteresis and the Footloose NAIRU

Hysteresis is a property of dynamic systems. If it is present, the steady-state or long-run equilibrium position of the system will not be a function only of the long-run values of the exogenous variables but also of the initial condition of the state variables and of the values assumed by the exogenous variables outside the steady state. Hysteretic or path-dependent systems are therefore "historical" systems: how you get there determines where you get to. In discrete time linear systems for predetermined variables hysteresis is present when there are one or more unit roots in the characteristic equation of the state matrix (1).

Hysteresis in the natural rate of unemployment is present when today's natural rate of unemployment is a function of past actual unemployment rates. Consider, for example, the simple first-order partial adjustment mechanism used in Buiter and Gersovitz [1981], Hargreaves-Heap [1980] and Buiter and Miller [1985]. u is the actual unemployment rate and u^* the natural rate:

[50] $\quad u_t^* = \alpha u_{t-1}^* + (1-\alpha)u_{t-1}; \quad 0 \leq \alpha \leq 1; \quad 0 \leq u \leq 1$

Equation [50] specifies the natural rate as moving average of past actual unemployment rates with geometrically declining weights, since

[51] $\quad u_t^* = (1-\alpha) \sum_{i=0}^{\infty} \alpha^i u_{t-1-i}$

---

(1) For non-predetermined state variables a unit root indicates quite the opposite of persistence; the unit root for consumption generated by certain life cycle models and the unit root for stocks generated by certain efficient asset pricing models are examples. David Begg has on many occasions emphasized the different interpretation of unit roots for backward-looking and forward-looking variables.

The idea of hysteresis in the natural rate is not a new one [Phelps, 1972; Tobin, 1980]. The two most popular economic mechanisms for generating hysteresis are the "human capital" hypothesis and the "insider-outsider" hypothesis. According to the human capital hypothesis the experience of unemployment destroys the human capital of the unemployed by having a negative effect both on their attitudes towards working (the "culture of unemployment and dependence" and so on) and on their aptitudes (skills, knowledge and so on) for work.

The effective labor supply represented by a given number of unemployed workers therefore declines over time with the duration of the unemployment spell. Empirical evidence that the long-term unemployed do not have any explanatory power in Phillips-curve type equations when the shorter-term unemployed are also included as an argument [see, for example, Layard, Nickell, 1986] is consistent with this view. Insider-outsider theory (1) attributes very different influences on the firm's wage bargain to those currently employed (the "insiders") and to the unemployed, both previous employees of the firm and new job candidates (the "outsiders"). In the limit, the unemployed are disenfranchised completely and the wage bargain is conducted solely in the interests of the firm and those currently employed. A range of explanations of varying degrees of plausibility is offered for the inability of the outsiders to undercut the insiders either by offering to work for less than the insiders in the existing firm or by seeking employment in new firms that might be able to undercut the insider-controlled firm. In this model too, the unemployed are, gradually or immediately, effectively excluded from the bargaining process in the labor market.

As it stands, equation [50] is clearly too strong. The notion that the natural rate can be anywhere between zero and one hundred percent is most implausible. The concept of *local* hysteresis, as opposed to the *global* hysteresis of equation [50], would be much more acceptable. The

---

(1) Compare, e.g., Gregory [1982; 1983; 1986], Lindbeck and Snower [1984; 1986a; 1986b; 1986c], Solow [1985] and Blanchard and Summers [1986]. For some empirical tests of the insider-outsider hypothesis, see Blanchflower et al. [1988].

kinked demand curve model just analyzed has such local hysteresis properties.

Equation [50] suggests that, by keeping u at any given level for long enough, the natural rate u^* can be made to approach that level and reach it (asymptotically). Physical capital formation theories of prolonged and persistent unemployment do not quite generate that very strong property [e.g., Modigliani et al., 1986]. These theories suggest that the kinds of shocks that produce unemployment also produce low physical capital formation. Either because of real wage rigidity and real wage-constrained employment or because of strong physical complementarity and limited substitutability between physical capital and labor (fixed coefficients are the extreme example), employment will fall or rise with the physical capital stock. Declining rates of capital formation will therefore have a long-lasting effect on unemployment. Unless there is hysteresis in the capital stock itself, however, this mechanism will not generate hysteresis in unemployment. The roots may be close to but will not be equal to unity. For practical purposes, it may of course not matter very much whether we have unit roots or merely roots close to unity, hysteresis or near-hysteresis. If the natural rate returns to its invariant long-run equilibrium level only very slowly after being per-turbed by a movement in the actual rate, the economy will exhibit near-hysteretic behavior for long periods of time.

To obtain the implications of hysteresis for the existence of an unem-ployment-inflation trade-off, we must consider the remainder of the wage-price mechanism. I will short-cut most of this mechanism and consider the simple augmented price Phillips curve given in [52]. P is the logarithm of the price level, π the augmentation term and $\Delta P_t \equiv P_t - P_{t-1}$.

[52] $\quad \Delta P_{t+1} = -\beta (u_t - u_t^*) + \pi_{t+1}; \quad \beta > 0$

Equations [50] and [52] imply that

[53a] $\quad u_t^* = u_{t-1}^* + (1-\alpha)\beta^{-1}(\pi_t - \Delta P_t)$

$$[53b] \quad u_t = u_{t-1} - \beta^{-1}(\Delta P_{t+1} - \pi_{t+1}) + \alpha\beta^{-1}(\Delta P_t - \pi_t)$$

It should be noted that, hysteresis or not, the old debate about the presence and nature of nominal inertia or stickiness in wage and price formation and about the backward-looking or forward-looking nature of the augmentation term π is still relevant if we are to evaluate policy options [compare, e.g., Taylor, 1980; Buiter, Jewitt, 1981; Buiter, Miller, 1985]. In other words, equation [50] tells us that, depending on the behavior of the actual unemployment rate, the natural rate can assume any value. The remainder of the wage-price mechanism (i.e., equations such as [52] and [53a] or [53b]) determines whether actual unemployment (or real demand) can be influenced systematically through policy or only through policy surprises. Blanchard and Summers [1986], perhaps surprisingly, choose what translates into a "surprise supply function" specification of π_{t+1}, i.e., in their model

$$[54a] \quad \pi_{t+1} = E_t(P_{t+1} - P_t)$$

where E_t is the expectation operator conditional on information in period t. If only unanticipated inflation can drive a wedge between the natural and the actual rate, the natural rate becomes a random walk, since $\pi_t - \Delta P_t = E_{t-1}(P_t) - P_t$ which is white noise when expectations are rational. The change in the actual unemployment rate will be an MA1 process. With [54a], only *unanticipated* expansionary (contractionary) shocks can lower (increase) the natural rate. Bad luck (OPEC) or bad management (unexpected contractionary fiscal or monetary policy) caused the rise in unemployment since the late 1970s. Only good luck or expansionary-policy surprises will get it back down.

Neither the theoretical nor the empirical foundations of the "surprise supply function" are terribly robust, however. With some inertia in the inflation process, anticipated, systematic policy too can drive the natural and actual unemployment rate to more desirable levels. Buiter and Miller [1985] consider the familiar partly backward-looking adaptive process for core inflation π, given in [54b].

$$[54b] \quad \pi_{t+1} = \gamma\pi_t + (1-\gamma)E_t\Delta P_{t+1}; \quad 0 \le \gamma \le 1$$

With this specification we have

$$u_t^* = u_{t-1}^* + (1-\alpha)\beta^{-1}[E_{t-1}(\Delta P_t) - P_t] - (1-\alpha)\beta^{-1}\gamma\ (E_{t-1}\Delta P_t - \pi_{t-1})$$

Systematic policy keeping expected (and actual) inflation ahead of core inflation will lower the natural rate. With rational expectations and any constant rate of inflation, actual unemployment will, in the long run, equal the natural rate. The "long run" Phillips curve is vertical but it can be located at any unemployment rate. Similar results can be derived using staggered, overlapping nominal contracting models as in Taylor [1980], Buiter and Jewitt [1981] or Buiter and Miller [1985]. Nominal inertia of the kind considered by McCallum [1978; 1980] does not permit systematic policy to influence the mean level of unemployment or real demand.

With hysteresis, the case for a boost to demand in current economic conditions is irresistible. With core inflation given by [54b] and $\gamma > 0$, the sacrifice ratio is infinite; i.e., the cumulative undiscounted unemployment cost of achieving a one percentage point sustained and sustainable reduction in the rate of inflation is infinite. That also means that the permanent inflation cost of achieving any lasting reduction in unemployment is zero. In the "surprise supply function" case, we can only hope that the authorities will succeed in surprising us. Even in economies that are merely near-hysteretic, the case for expansionary demand policy is overwhelming. We would be as far removed as we could possibly be from the prevailing Euro-pessimist perception that the supply side constrains everything.

I believe that the case for the existence of a high degree of hysteresis in Europe is strong enough and that the European unemployment situation is desperate enough for us to "have a go" at a significant (supply-side-friendly) boost to aggregate demand. The risk exists that the situation has been diagnosed wrongly, but it is dwarfed by the cost of not seizing the opportunity that may be there.

4. Conclusion

Unemployment in Europe is very high and shows no signs of coming down significantly in the next few years. Under current policies, the growth of real demand is barely sufficient to keep pace with the trend growth rate of productive potential, leaving the existing reservoir of unused and underutilized labor power untouched. Three kinds of responses to this situation are possible. The first response (or nonresponse) is to accept the situation, if not as a God-given punishment for our past sins, in any case as beyond the scope of the existing policy instruments and/or beyond the existing capacities and institutions for formulating and implementing policy. This, by revealed preference, seems to be the approach of many European governments, including those of the United Kingdom, West Germany, France, Belgium and the Netherlands.

The second response blames policy-induced "supply-side" failures for much of the deterioration of the employment situation and recommends "supply-side" measures to remedy the situation. Among the past policy measures that are in the dock are the following: socalled employment protection policies that raise the cost of hiring and firing; policies providing rights, privileges and immunities for organized labor; minimum wage laws; laws and regulations limiting relative wage flexibility; laws and regulations limiting regional, occupational and industrial mobility of labor; taxes that raise the nonwage component of marginal labor costs, such as employers' social security contributions; high marginal income tax rates on wage income; high marginal benefit rates for the unemployed and lax administration of eligibility requirements for unemployment benefits and medical disability payments. Growth of the public sector in any of its dimensions ("exhaustive" public spending, employment, total spending, total revenue, scope of regulatory interventions in the market sector, public sector production of marketable commodities, and so forth) is viewed as synonymous with waste and inefficiency. In the short run, such expansion of public sector activity may appear to improve the employment picture (in terms of a simple "body count"), but ultimately the "real" jobs that finance and sustain these unproductive public sector activities will suffer, the "wealth-creating" sector will shrink and with it, in due course, the public sector activities and employment it can no longer support.

Large public sector deficits, probably causally connected with the growing scope of public sector activities (because of a tendency for the political mechanism to try and avoid paying with current taxes for current outlays) are either monetized, causing high inflation, or financed by borrowing, thus crowding out interest-sensitive private spending. Both the inflation tax and borrowing are viewed as inimical to private capital formation, which further weakens the supply side.

The policy prescription following from this diagnosis is self-evident; reverse all these developments to the maximum possible extent. This explanation is at best incomplete and exaggerated and at worst simply wrong. While many intelligent "supply-side" measures can and should be implemented to improve both efficiency and equity in the European economies, a good case can be made that adverse policy-induced supply-side developments did not cause the bulk of the deterioration of the European employment performance, and that "supply-side" measures will not be sufficient even or necessary, if the hysteresis view is valid, to remove much of the existing labor slack.

Much of the increase in European unemployment since the mid-1970s can reasonably be attributed to the two massive adverse supply shocks of OPEC I and II and to the deliberate global demand deflation, never reversed in Europe, of the early 1980s. With the recent decline in the real price of oil and related energy products, the adverse supply shocks are being reversed. It will take years for this to take its full effect, however, because the scrapping of productive capacity and low rates of capital formation following OPEC I and II have resulted in a secularly low path of the physical capital stock.

This suggests the need for the third response: a significant, sustained, supply-side-friendly, coordinated expansion of aggregate demand through monetary and fiscal stimuli. Both the efficiency wage view and the Blanchard-Summers version of the insider-outsider model suggest that an expansion of demand can result in a sustainable increase in employment and production without significant upward pressure on real wages and without permanently higher inflation. The near-hysteretic behavior of the unemployment rate in Europe indeed suggests that any adverse inflationary consequences of a demand stimulus will be temporary, while the output and employment effects will be lasting. The parallel with the rapid, noninflationary recovery of employment and output in Britain and other European countries in the late 1930s, under the impetus of rearmament spending, comes to mind.

Even if it were agreed that a boost to demand could solve many of the European problems, it would not automatically follow that the authorities could actually engineer such a stimulus (1). I will consider briefly the following obstacles to expansionary monetary and fiscal policy. As regards monetary policy, firstly the absence of *nominal inertia* and secondly the threat of inflation. As regards fiscal policy, the threats of financial crowding out and of government insolvency. As regards both, the threats of adverse exchange rate or current account consequences. The issue of government *credibility* will be seen to be central in determining the ability of the government to stimulate aggregate demand. In what follows, I shall concentrate on anticipated or perceived government policy since, except in the hysteresis-cum-"surprise"-supply-function view of the world (given in equations [50], [52], and [54a]), unanticipated or unperceived policy actions are unlikely to be welfare-increasing, even if they were feasible in a systematic manner.

As stated in Section 2, the effectiveness of anticipated or perceived policy requires either superior public sector information or a public sector opportunity set that is superior to the private sector's opportunity set in at least one dimension. While some of those responsible for the design and implementation of economic policy may have a (temporary) information advantage over at least some private sector agents, for

---

(1) It is noteworthy that a demand stimulus from abroad (or from a boom in private domestic capital formation) is often welcomed (or even sought) by some of the most ardent opponents of a public sector-led expansion of demand: the source of the demand stimulus determines its desirability.

example, as regards the behavior of the monetary aggregates, international reserves and - most importantly - as regards the future intentions of the policy authorities, it would seem unwise to base the case for stabilization policy on that slim foundation. *Pace* Fischer's "benevolent dissembling government" [Fischer, 1980] it is hard to see how in practice a government could do better as a rule than by devulging both its privileged information and its future intentions (1).

The existence of a public sector opportunity set which in some ways dominates that of the private sector is very plausible indeed. The proximate reason for stabilization policy effectiveness is the government's superior access to the capital markets. Governments can borrow on terms not generally available to private agents (at any rate in the main industrial countries). This is reflected both in lower required rates of return on government debt compared with private debt of the same maturity, currency denomination and so on, and in the ability of governments to continue borrowing when private agents encounter credit rationing. The fundamental reason for this public sector financial clout is that the government's collateral consists of the maximal stream of current and future resources it can appropriate through taxation and seigniorage. (The binding constraints that define the maximum tax revenue are likely to be political rather than narrowly economic or administrative in character.) The government's monopoly of the power to exact legitimate unrequited transfers of purchasing power both at a point in time and over time may also account for the private sector's willingness to hold noninterest-bearing nominal government debt (high-powered money). In addition, restrictions on what constitutes legal tender and reserve requirements may generate a private sector demand for base money. The absence of perfect private sector substitutes for base money, for whatever reasons, creates the tax base for the seigniorage tax.

The asymmetry between public and private opportunity sets in financial markets is sometimes formalized by attributing finite horizons (in OLG

---

(1) Note that in the "thousand islands" literature, the private sector is assumed to possess local information ($P_t(z)$) that the authorities do not possess. It is clearly realistic to assume that private agents have superior firm-specific information.

models without operative intergenerational gift and bequest motives) or uncertain lifetimes to households, while governments are treated as having effectively infinite lifetimes (1). Note that it is not the lifetime of individual administrations that matters here, but the lifetime of the institution of government. More precisely what matters is that successive governments are expected to assume the debt they inherit from their predecessors or, as in the case of balanced-budget intergenerational redistributions, that they are expected to implement the schemes initiated by their predecessors. The implication is that debt neutrality is absent: given the exhaustive spending program, the substitution of current borrowing for current lump-sum taxes by a solvent government will not leave the path of private consumption unchanged. The substitution of seigniorage revenue for either explicit lump-sum taxes or borrowing will also in general have real effects (2). Given these basic considerations, I now turn to the main instruments of stabilization policy.

As a revenue-raiser, seigniorage is now of very limited actual and potential importance in most industrial countries (3). For monetary policy to be an effective stabilization instrument, other channels of influence must therefore be present.

Ignoring as empirically unimportant the ability of the authorities to influence the inflation rate and through it the real interest rate (via the Tobin effect) even in an economy with flexible money wages and prices, and ignoring for the same reason the ability of systematic monetary feedback rules to influence the variance of real output and employment even in flexprice "surprise" supply models (cf., Section 2 of this paper and Buiter [1981]), monetary policy can only be an effective instrument for aggregate demand management if there is some form of nominal inertia or

---

(1) As shown in Buiter [1988], finite or uncertain lifetimes are not sufficient for absence of debt neutrality in OLG models without operative intergenerational gift and bequest motives. A positive birth rate is sufficient.

(2) Distortionary taxes will introduce a further reason for absence of debt neutrality.

(3) Note that seigniorage is defined as $(\Delta H)/P$, where H is the high-powered money stock. Unanticipated changes in the price level will of course reduce the real value of the government's nominally-denominated debt and thus provide another source of revenue.

338

stickiness: money wages and/or prices must be predetermined (1). Recent empirical evidence suggesting that the degree of nominal inertia is low in Europe (in contrast to the US) (see, e.g., Bruno and Sachs [1985]) would therefore put into question the ability of monetary policy in Europe to be an important instrument of demand expansion. The empirical evidence on this issue is, however, by no means clear-cut (2), and as long as there is some nominal inertia, monetary policy can play a supporting role in a coordinated expansion of demand.

The monetary expansion required for a demand stimulus is of the nature of a once-off increase in the *level* of the path of the nominal money stock, not a sustained increase in the *rate of growth* of the nominal money stock. In due course such a level shift will only raise the level of the price path without any long-run effect on the inflation rate. In "real time", the process of moving from a lower to a higher price-level path will in practice involve a *temporary* increase in the inflation rate (3). With imperfect information, nonrational expectations or mechanical indexation procedures, this temporary increase in the inflation rate may trigger a wage-price spiral that will prolong the bout of higher inflation. Provided the money stock is not permitted to respond endogenously to this further inflationary twist, the process will be damped and the long-run rate of inflation will not be affected.

Convincing the private players in the labor markets, the product markets and the financial markets that the increase in the money stock they are witnessing is a once-off level shift rather than the first step in a repeated process of ever-increasing monetary injections, requires a credible government (4), i.e., a government with a strong, proven record of anti-inflationary preferences and actions. The three conservative administrations in London, Bonn and Paris have such credibility as do the Japanese and, to a lesser extent, the US governments. For most of

---

(1) McCallum [1977; 1980] shows that while this is necessary, it is not sufficient for policy effectiveness.
(2) The theoretical foundations of nominal stickiness are fortunately virtually nonexistent.
(3) With a flexible price level, there could be a once-off discrete jump in the price-level path.
(4) The central bank is, for our purposes, part of the government.

the important players, the desirable monetary policy is actually likely to be time-consistent.

Even in the absence of debt neutrality, fiscal policy may fail to stimulate aggregate demand because of complete financial crowding-out. A variable velocity of circulation of money and/or accommodating monetary policy will prevent full crowding-out (in the presence of idle real resources) unless current fiscal expansion creates expectations of continued future expansion leading to an ever-increasing debt burden and, ultimately, the threat of *de jure* or *de facto* partial or complete repudiation of the public debt. Again the *credibility* of the temporary nature of the fiscal stimulus and the limited increase in the debt-GNP ratio it entails is crucial for the success of expansionary fiscal measures. If the financial markets panic, complete crowding-out is likely (1).

The current conservative administrations in the larger OECD countries (with the exception of Italy) are uniquely well-placed to provide a credible temporary fiscal stimulus. Their reputations for fiscal prudence again make the right policy time-consistent. Table 1 gives the general government financial balances for some of the OECD countries.

Combined with the public debt figures of Table 2, these figures suggest that, with the exception of Italy, the debt-deficit situation in the major European countries is well under control. Even the much-maligned US budgetary deficit is much less dramatic than has been suggested. With the US General Government public debt at 30 percent of GNP and a modest 8 percent growth of nominal GNP, the public sector deficit could be almost 2.4 percent of GNP without this adding to the debt-GNP ratio. The actual US general government deficit of 3.5 percent of GNP in 1986 is only one percentage point of GDP higher than the deficit that would stabilize the low debt-GDP ratio. A US fiscal correction is required in due course, but there is no need to be panicked into one right now.

A fiscal stimulus in an economy with idle resources need not crowd out private investment even if interest rates rise. The positive response of

---

(1) For a more extended discussion, see Buiter [1985].

340

Table 1 - General Government Financial Deficit as a Percentage of Nominal GNP/GDP

	1984	1985	1986
US	2.8	3.3	3.5
Japan	2.1	0.8	1.1
West Germany	1.9	1.1	1.2
France	2.7	2.9	2.9
UK	3.9	2.9	2.7
Italy	11.7	12.6	11.6
Canada	6.6	7.0	5.5
Total smaller OECD countries	4.1	4.0	3.4

Source: OECD [1986, Table 4].

Table 2 - Net Debt of General Government as a Percentage of GNP/GDP

	1974	1981	1982	1983	1984	1985	1986
US	22.0	18.8	21.4	24.0	25.1	26.8	28.8
UK	54.9	47.2	46.4	47.1	48.5	46.9	46.9
Italy	49.2	66.8	73.4	80.6	87.8	96.3	99.2
France	8.8	9.9	11.3	13.4	15.2	16.7	18.5
West Germany	-4.7	17.4	19.8	21.4	21.7	22.1	22.2
Japan	-5.4	20.7	23.2	26.2	26.9	26.5	26.2

Source: OECD [1987, Table 15].

investment to the higher future profits stream permitted by higher demand will mitigate and may even overcome the negative effect of higher interest rates. Such a positive response is even more likely if the composition of the fiscal stimulus is investment and supply-side-friendly.

This implies such actions as temporary investment tax credits and temporary investment subsidies. Reductions in marginal payroll tax rates should also be part of the package as would be increases in public sector investment in Europe's crumbling infrastructure. The stimulus should be modulated across countries to take account of their differing budgetary and debt conditions. On average for Europe, a modest proposal would be a three or four-year boost equal to 2 percent of GDP per year, with sufficient monetary accommodation to prevent a significant increase in short nominal interest rates or an appreciation of the ecu against the US dollar and the yen.

In an open economy with a fixed exchange rate, part of any expansion of demand will "leak" abroad through increased demand for imports. With a floating exchange rate and a high degree of capital mobility, a fiscal expansion will be partly or even completely crowded-out by an appreciation of the currency. Even if an accommodating monetary policy succeeds in keeping the nominal exchange rate constant, the problem of a worsening current account still exists. This calls for a coordinated expansion, involving at least the major European economies and preferably also Japan. The US should ensure that any attempt to restore its fiscal equilibrium does not lead to a recession (cf., e.g., Blanchard et al. [1986]). This would be an interesting first challenge for the new chairman of the Federal Reserve Board.

With a modicum of common sense and a bit of luck this kind of coordinated, supply-side-friendly, temporary expansion, differentiated by country according to its internal and external circumstances will contribute to the resolution of the European unemployment problem and the restoration of its prosperity. Under present circumstances, "two-handed" rules out "tight-fisted".

Bibliography

AKERLOF, George A., "The Market for 'Lemons': Qualitative Uncertainty and the Market Mechanism". The Quarterly Journal of Economics, Vol. 24, 1970, pp. 488-500.

AKERLOF, G. A., Janet YELLEN, "A Near Rational Model of the Business Cycle, with Wage and Price Inertia". The Quarterly Journal of Economics, Vol. 100, 1985, pp. 823-838.

BALL, Laurence, David ROMER, "Are Prices Too Sticky?" NBER Working Papers, 2171, Cambridge, Mass., February 1987.

BARRO, Robert J., "Rational Expectations and the Role of Monetary Policy". Journal of Monetary Economics, Vol. 2, 1976, pp. 1-32.

--, "A Capital Market in an Equilibrium Business Cycle Model". Econometrica, Vol. 48, 1980, pp. 1393-1417.

--, "Intertemporal Substitution and the Business Cycle". Carnegie-Rochester Conference Series on Public Policy, Vol. 14, 1981, pp. 237-268.

--, Herschel I. GROSSMAN, "A General Disequilibrium Model of Income and Employment". The American Economic Review, Vol. 61, 1971, pp. 82-93.

BLANCHARD, Olivier, "Debt, Deficits and Finite Horizons". Journal of Political Economy, Vol. 93, 1985, pp. 223-247.

--, Rudiger DORNBUSCH, Richard LAYARD (Eds.), Restoring Europe's Prosperity. Cambridge, Mass., 1986.

--, Lawrence H. SUMMERS, "Hysteresis and the European Unemployment Problem". In: Stanley FISCHER (Ed.), NBER Macroeconomics Annual 1986. Cambridge, Mass., 1986, pp. 15-78.

--, Nobuhiro KIYOTAKI, Monopolistic Competition, Aggregate Demand Externalities, and Real Effects of Nominal Money. NBER Working Papers, 1770, December 1985.

BLINDER, Alan S., "Credit-Rationing and Effective Supply Failures". The Economic Journal, Vol. 97, 1987, pp. 327-352.

BRUNO, Michael, Jeffrey SACHS, The Economics of Worldwide Stagflation. New Haven, Conn., 1985.

BUITER, Willem H., "The Superiority of Contingent Rules over Fixed Rules in Models with Rational Expectations". The Economic Journal, Vol. 91, 1981, pp. 647-670.

--, "Allocative and Stabilization Aspects of Budgetary and Financial Policy". Centre for Economic Policy Research Working Papers, 2, January 1983.

--, "A Guide to Public Sector Debt and Deficits". Economic Policy, Vol. 1, 1985, pp. 13-60.

--, "Death, Birth, Productivity Growth and Debt Neutrality". The Economic Journal, Vol. 98, 1988, pp. 279-293.

343

BUITER, Willem H., Mark GERSOVITZ, "Issues in Controllability and the Theory of Economic Policy". Journal of Public Economics, Vol. 88, 1981, pp. 33-43.

--, Ian JEWITT, "Staggered Wage Setting with Real Wage Relativities: Variations on a Theme of Taylor". The Manchester School of Economic and Social Studies, Vol. 49, 1981, pp. 221-228.

--, Marcus H. MILLER, "Costs and Benefits of an Anti-Inflationary Policy: Questions and Issues". In: Victor ARGY, John NEVILE (Eds.), Inflation and Unemployment: Theory, Experience and Policy Making. London 1985, pp. 11-38.

van EES, Hans, An Explanation of Unemployment through an Integration of the Efficiency Wage Theory and the Kinked Demand Curve Approach. University of Groningen, October 1987, mimeo.

FISCHER, Stanley, "Dynamic Inconsistency, Cooperation and the Benevolent Dissembling Government". Journal of Economic Dynamics and Control, Vol. 2, 1980, pp. 93-107.

GREGORY, R. G., "Work and Welfare in the Years ahead". Australian Economic Papers, Vol. 21, 1982, pp. 219-243.

--, The Slide into Mass Unemployment. Labour Market Theories, Facts and Policies. The Academy of Social Science, Annual Lectures, Canberra 1983.

--, "Wages Policy and Unemployment in Australia". Economica, Vol. 53, 1986, Supplement.

HARGREAVES-HEAP, Shaun P., "Choosing the Wrong Natural Rate, Accelerating Inflation or Decelerating Unemployment and Growth". The Economic Journal, Vol. 90, 1980, pp. 611-620.

KATZ, Larry F., "Efficiency Wage Theories: A Partial Evaluation". In: Stanley FISCHER (Ed.), NBER Macroeconomics Annual 1986. Cambridge, Mass., 1986, pp. 235-276.

KING, Robert G., "Interest Rates, Aggregate Information and Monetary Policy". Journal of Monetary Economics, Vol. 12, 1983, pp.199-234.

KYDLAND, Fynn, Edward PRESCOTT, "Time to Build and Aggregate Fluctuations". Econometrica, Vol. 50, 1982, pp. 1345-1370.

LAYARD, Richard, Stephen NICKELL, "Unemployment in Britain". Economica, Vol. 53, 1986, Supplement, pp. S 121-170.

LINDBECK, Assar, Dennis SNOWER, "Labor Turnover, Insider Morale and Involuntary Unemployment". Institue for International Economic Studies, Seminar Papers, 310, Stockholm 1984.

--, -- [1986a], "Wage Rigidity, Union Activity and Unemployment". In: Wilfred BECKERMAN (Ed.), Wage Rigidity and Unemployment. Oxford 1986, pp. 97-125.

LINDBECK, Assar, Dennis SNOWER [1986b], "Explanations of Unemployment". Oxford Review of Economic Policy, Vol. 1, 1986, pp. 34-59.

--, -- [1986c], "Wage Setting, Unemployment and Insider-Outsider Relations". The American Economic Review, Vol. 76, 1986, pp. 235-239.

LONG, J., C. PLOSSER, "Real Business Cycles". Journal of Political Economy, Vol. 91, 1983, pp. 1345-1370.

LUCAS, Robert E., "Expectations and the Neutrality of Money". Journal of Economic Theory, Vol. 4, 1972, pp. 103-124.

MALINVAUD, Edmund, The Theory of Unemployment Reconsidered. Oxford 1977.

McCALLUM, Bennett T., "The Current State of the Policy Ineffectiveness Debate". The American Economic Review, Vol. 69, 1978, pp. 240-245.

--, "Rational Expectations and Macroeconomic Stabilization Policy: An Overview". Journal of Money, Credit and Banking, Vol. 12, 1980, pp. 716-746.

MARINI, Giancarlo, "Intertemporal Substitution and the Role of Monetary Policy". The Economic Journal, Vol. 95, 1985, pp. 87-100.

--, "Employment Fluctuations and Demand Management". Economica, Vol. 53, 1986, pp. 209-218.

MODIGLIANI, Franco, et al., Reducing Unemployment in Europe: The Role of Capital Formation. CEPS Papers, 28, Brussels 1986.

ORGANIZATION FOR ECONOMIC COOPERATION AND DEVELOPMENT (OECD), Economic Outlook. Paris, June 1987 and June 1988.

PHELPS, Edmund, Inflation Policy and Unemployment Theory. New York 1972.

SARGENT, Thomas J., "Rational Expectations, the Real Rate of Interest, and the Natural Rate of Unemployment". Brookings Papers on Economic Activity, 1973, pp. 429-472.

--, Neil WALLACE, "Rational Expectations, the Optimal Monetary Instrument, and the Optimal Money Supply Rule". Journal of Political Economy, Vol. 83, 1975, pp. 241-254.

SOLOW, Robert, "Insiders and Outsiders in Wage Determination". Scandinavian Journal of Economics, Vol. 87, 1985, pp. 411-428.

STIGLITZ, Joseph, "The Causes and Consequences of the Dependence of Quality on Price". The Journal of Economic Literature, Vol. 25, 1987, pp. 1-48.

TAYLOR, John B., "Aggregate Dynamics and Staggered Contracts". Journal of Political Economy, Vol. 88, 1980, pp. 1-23.

TOBIN, James, "Stabilization Policy Ten Years After". Brookings Papers on Economic Activity, 1980, pp. 19-71.

WEISS, Andrew, "Job Queues and Layoffs in Labor Markets with Flexible Wages". Journal of Political Economy, Vol. 88, 1980, pp. 526-538.

Comments on Willem H. Buiter, "The Right Combination of Demand and Supply Policies: The Case for a Two-Handed Approach"

Klaus-Werner Schatz

Willem H. Buiter's paper consists of 4 sections. In his introduction he states that the "demand-side versus supply-side dichotomy" is no longer very useful, his most powerful argument being that "modern theoretical developments ... suggest that demand and supply may not even conceptually be separated" (p. 306). Instead of utilizing the term demand-side policy, he prefers speaking of stabilization policy, which - among others - is to smoothen actual employment or to avoid deviations from full employment or a "natural" level of employment. And instead of using the term supply-side policy, he wishes the term structural or allocative policy to be applied which aims at, among others, reducing the natural rate of unemployment. While I will return to his case against the possibility of separating demand from supply later on, for the time being let me mention only that Willem Buiter himself does not refrain from talking of demand and supply, both in the analytical parts of his paper and in discussing policy advice.

For reasons of space, I shall not comment on his second section, which is about "the role of stabilization policy in new classical macroeconomic models", but shall concentrate on the third and the fourth sections. The latter is to draw the conclusions, above all from Section 3; but both sections in my view have relatively little to do with one another, and, moreover, the insights gained in Section 3 may even allow one to draw just the opposite conclusions from those at which Buiter arrives.

Section 3 deals with efficiency wages and hysteresis. It is designed, firstly, to shed light on the nature of the increase in unemployment in Europe, and secondly, to destroy the distinction between demand and supply. The efficiency wage hypothesis maintains that, at least initially, the productivity of labour and, hence, the efficiency and the output of a firm increase more than proportionately when labour is paid higher wages. This implies that the supply and/or demand schedule in the labour market is not independent of the price labour is paid. For example, if a higher wage raises the productivity of labour more than proportionately, the firms' demand-for-labour curve will be shifted upwards. Or, an example given by Buiter, if the government reduces the wage income tax rate, the take-home pay of workers increases inducing higher productivity and, again, shifting labour demand. Accepting the efficiency wage hypothesis for the time being, does it destroy the distinction between demand and supply in the labour market as Buiter claims? I doubt this proposition. For, what has been induced with the parameter change - the increase in wages paid to the worker by the individual firm or the reduction of the tax rate - is an adjustment of the firms' labour demand according to its new production function, one with higher labour efficiency. Why should this render the distinction between demand and supply meaningless? Buiter argues: "the old language clearly is less than helpful here", because "a supply-side parameter shifts labour demand!" (p. 320). But what is new with such an observation or our understanding of it? Do we not know that, e.g., reducing barriers to vertical mobility within a given firm, a clear supply-side measure is likely to increase productivity of workers as it opens up opportunities to achieve higher income levels, and that in turn the demand for labour of this firm may increase?

What seems to be new with the efficiency wage hypothesis is the proposition that a profit-maximizing firm may even in a competitive labour and product market pay more than market clearing wages. One common explanation is that workers, as opposed to machinery, suffer from working, and, hence, do not really like to give their best - that is to be as productive or efficient as they could be. They try to shirk. Like other human beings, workers are individuals, and, hence, they shirk to differing extents. As the employer cannot be fully informed about shirking either on average or in each individual case, he has to bear monitoring costs if he wants to reduce shirking. Taking these monitoring costs into account, it may be cheaper for the employer to pay more than market-clearing wages if he can trade higher wages (minus lower monitoring costs) for more than proportionate productivity increases. Reasons for the increase in productivity may lie, for instance, with the rise in opportunity costs if a worker is found shirking, or with the unions' willingness to reduce labour unrest in the firm that increases wages above market clearing levels. Hence, granting the higher wage, the efficiency wage may both be in the interest of the firm and the workers employed. As the efficiency wage cannot be lower than the market clearing wage, it is highly probable that unemployment will result. And, as Buiter states, "if at the efficiency wage there is excess supply of labor, there is no ... downward pressure on wages" (p. 320). The pressure is lacking because the firm would suffer more from the reduction in efficiency than it would gain from the reduction in wages.

At first glance, this seems to explain plausibly why real wages are rigid downwards preventing unemployment from being reduced. However, a number of questions come to mind at a second glance. The efficiency wage hypothesis should apply best in times and in regions where the opportunity costs from being found shirking are low. These are times and regions with a high degree of employment and where, therefore, it is not difficult to find a new and often even better-paid job. Examples may be West Germany in the 1960s and some southern German regions or Switzerland at present. So one may wonder why the efficiency wage hypothesis may be particularly valuable in explaining unemployment when and where it is high. A quite different and more fundamental problem is: how can efficiency wages above market-clearing wages persist? Given a situation where unemployment exists, the unemployed would be willing to work at wages at the market-clearing level or temporarily even below, as their opportunity costs are lower, and they would be willing to offer the same productivity as those employed. Yet, the proponents of the efficiency wage hypothesis argue that, because of asymmetric information, firms will not employ the unemployed, because the lower wage signals that the productivity they buy will also be lower.

This proposition, however, suggests that firms will not be willing to undertake experiments or, in other words, to explore whether the labour market does not offer opportunities to hire cheaper labour. Such behaviour would strictly contradict their behaviour in product markets where efforts at seizing opportunities are not only quite normal, but are even a prerequisite for commercial success. Also, the firms do not refute buying cheaper inputs like raw materials, if they are offered, fearing that the quality is poor. Rather, they will try to find out the quality through tests and then take this quality into account when formulating the contracts. Therefore, similar behaviour towards lower-priced labour seems to be more likely than the assumption on which the efficiency wage hypothesis rests. Of course, the wage claims of the unemployed would have to be lower than those of the employed, as the employers would impose on them - rightly or wrongly - the costs for more intensive monitoring plus a premium covering the risk of getting less productive labour than anticipated. But there is always a wage rate for the unemployed which meets their productivity minus higher monitoring costs. Moreover, if existing firms do not seize the opportunity of hiring cheaper labour, why should newly-established firms not do so? Or, if the hours worked and efficiency are two different features, why will a second price for efficiency not evolve in addition to the price for the hours worked, treating shirking as shirking? There is a strong incentive for the profit-maximizing firm to differentiate wages in this way and to reduce monitoring costs, if they are really as important as the efficiency wage hypothesis postulates. Or to put it differently, the efficiency wage hypothesis rests on the unproven assumption that market-clearing wage rates do not already incorporate all efficiency considerations, in the sense of the theory of rational behaviour which suggests that people make the best use of information available to them.

Not contradicting what has been said, there is of course a reason to argue that those who are employed receive an extra premium for working efficiently and that the efficiency wage hypothesis may therefore contribute to the explanation of today's unemployment. But what is needed to make the hypothesis a valuable explanation lies on the supply side: there are - among other things - legal provisions which - as, e.g., in Germany - prohibit the unemployed from undercutting their happier, employed companions' wages; there are regulations that forbid employers form hiring labour at lower costs than for those who are already employed. And there are numerous other barriers to entry bott for labour and for firms. The Soltwedel and Trapp paper is full of examples. And last, but not least, there are the unions which can successfully press for higher wages for the insiders by threatening with labour unrest. Hence, there are restrictions on the supply side - and I am not sure whether Willem Buiter would not finally share my view - which could make the efficiency wage hypothesis a relevant explanation for the high unemployment in Europe and the relatively low unemployment in the United States.

The hysteresis argument for the labour market tries to explain why unemployment, once it has emerged (maybe through a shock like that of OPEC II in the late 1970s), may remain high or even increase, although real wages may have not increased. It departs from the empirical observation that with the continuation of unemployment the average duration of unemployment increases. Given this increase in the duration, the unemployed become less and less qualified because of lacking experience gained otherwise from employment. Hence, at given real wages, unemployment tends to increase. The crucial issue, of course, is: why does unemployment continue? And once more, why don't the unemployed accept lower real wages? All in all, the hysteresis argument also has to take recourse to barriers on the supply side, which may mean that the interests of the unemployed are not taken fully into consideration in the bargaining process, or, not to forget that unemployment insurance together with welfare payments are too high, creating disincentives to work. Hysteresis means, in Buiter's sense, that the natural rate of unemployment, for whatever reasons, is higher than it could be (p. 328). Reducing the natural rate of unemployment then would require - in the words of Buiter - the application of structural or allocative policies, and it is, in his own understanding, no case for stabilization policy, the term which he prefers to demand policy (p. 306).

At this point, I should like to draw attention to Buiter's conclusions, the fourth and last section in the paper. Both the efficiency wage and the hysteresis hypotheses must attribute unemployment to some real wage stickiness: workers will reduce shirking only if they are granted higher real wages than the market-clearing real rates, and companies will pay them; and hysteresis exists because the unions and others do not allow real wages for the unemployed to fall to their marginal productivity level. What strikes me now is that, from these two explanations, Buiter draws the conclusion that Europe suffers from a lack of real demand and

recommends demand stimulation as the appropriate way to achieve higher
employment rates (pp. 334 f.). It is true he also lists an impressive
number of examples (p. 333), explaining unemployment and poor growth
by supply-side deficiencies; but he states "that adverse policy-induced
supply-side developments did not cause the bulk of the deterioration of
the European employment performance, and that "supply-side" measures
will not be sufficient even or necessary, if the hysteresis view is valid,
to remove most of the existing labour slack" (p. 334). As quickly as he
rejects the supply-side considerations without presenting any empirical
evidence, he accepts the hypothesis of demand shortages, which does
not convincingly follow from his previous analysis.

But even if lack of demand was not the cause for the emergence of the
European malaise, one could ask whether this malaise could not be treated by boosting demand, what Buiter recommends. With regard to monetary policy, he wants a one-off increase in the nominal money stock,
not a sustained increase in its rate of growth (p. 338). For this monetary shock to be successful there must be "some form of nominal inertia
or stickiness: money wages and/or prices must be predetermined"
(pp. 337/8) Buiter views this precondition of nominal prices as given, so
his recommendation for the monetary stimulus follows. Yet, is it not real
wage stickiness on which both the efficiency wage and the hysteresis
hypotheses draw? How can real wages be reduced, accepting the attitudes of workers, firms and unions in the efficiency wage and hysteresis
world, in which money illusion is not cultivated? Moreover, if the unions
perceive that the monetary authorities are willing to conduct accommodating policies, will they not even claim higher real wages causing even
larger damages for employment and growth? One could argue that real
wages must not be reduced in order to achieve higher employment, provided that the monetary stimulus leads to higher real demand in the first
phase, and higher prices only in the later phase. In this case, money
illusion must first rest with the firms and later on with the workers and
the unions. Given the experience of the late 1970s, it seems to me but a
hope that this time - unlike that of the locomotive strategy - monetary
expansion would not end up with accelerating inflation and finally
require the monetary stop which means recession. The danger of such a
development seems the greater, as, e.g., in West Germany capacity

utilization rates are at present close to the rates in the peak of the preceding upswing.

Buiter argues that an acceleration of inflation to permanently higher rates (and the costs of breaking this upward trend) can be avoided if the government enjoys credibility in the sense that the private agents in labour, product and capital markets are convinced that the increase in money stock, which will be pre-announced, is a one-off level shift. It may be that three benevolent dictators, being responsible for the labour, the product, the capital markets respectively, could be persuaded to refrain from increasing prices and wages in the required manner, following the advice of a fourth benevolent dictator, the government. That could make the proposed monetary strategy a success. But since we do not live in such a world, I doubt that Buiter's proposal can provide us with the benefits he promises.

Buiter also recommends a fiscal stimulus, his argument being that "the current conservative administrations in the larger OECD countries ... are uniquely well-placed to provide a credible temporary fiscal stimulus" (p. 339). This is the case - according to Buiter - because in these countries public deficits are low. Again, he wisely places the emphasis on credibility. I agree that larger deficits would not be undesirable per se. Yet, in the conservatively governed countries, the reduction of deficits has been achieved by cutting public expenditure growth. This makes up for the credibility of their governments. I doubt whether their reputation would remain the same if they started increasing public expanditures at previous growth rates again. I strongly recommend, however, that governments cut taxes with the commitment to cut expenditure growth equivalently. The reason why I support such a strategy is that the message to private agents is different from the one they would receive if the government increased expenditures. The message from cutting tax rates and other obstacles to growth on the supply side will certainly induce an increase in capacities and potential output hence reducing hysteresis and simultaneously leading to higher demand.

While going through Buiter's paper, I was sometimes not sure where he stands with his diagnosis and with his policy recommendations. Has it been lacking demand or shortcomings on the supply side which he makes responsible for the high unemployment in Europe? The last section of his paper makes his position clear (or may I say even more unclear?). He votes for supply-side-friendly demand policies - whatever that means.

Christian Seidl

1. Introduction

Willem Buiter has launched two rather forceful attacks at accepted traditions and has taken up the cudgels for demand management to supplement the prevailing supply-side economic policy as the proper policy mix for European economic policy.

(i) Using Barro's model and drawing on work by Marini, Buiter denies the hypothesis regarding the ineffectiveness of economic policy as put forward by many rational expectations theorists. Instead, he contends that economic policy is effective even if the policy-makers are worse informed than the economic agents in the private sector.

(ii) Drawing on work in the fields of asymmetric information and path-dependent economic processes (hysteresis), Buiter argues that conventional demand and supply analysis is completely outdated, as these new theories reveal the mutual dependence of demand and supply forces that cannot be separated.

(iii) As to the appropriate economic policy for Europe, Buiter rejects the laissez-faire solution as well as a purely supply-side oriented economic policy to remedy the present high unemployment in Europe. Instead he recommends as the third way "a significant, sustained, supply-side-friendly, co-ordinated *expansion of aggregate demand* through monetary and fiscal stimuli" (p. 334).

My comment follows this structure of Buiter's paper. I shall first deal with the two attacks and then with Willem Buiter's recommended economic policy that should be pursued for Europe.

2. Is Economic Policy Effective?

Buiter presents the Marini version of the Barro model and acquaints the reader with Marini's policy effectiveness result. Economic policy is effective in the sense that it can achieve any stabilization goal, even if the policy-makers are less informed than the other economic agents.

This outcome is accomplished through some crucial characteristics of the Barro-Marini model. As soon as policy-makers are informed about economic data, they react in a precisely predictable way that is generally known to all private agents. Through such a lagged feedback rule, future values of instrument variables become functions of the yet unknown current values of the exogenous variables. If this feedback rule is known to all private agents, the policy-maker can change the information content of the currently observed prices, and can make them, therefore, fully revealing. Any agent can anticipate the future economic policy and its consequences, and will react in a way aimed at by economic policy.

Let me first pose a more technical question: what about the question of *feasibility* of the realizations of the instruments of economic policy in equation [9]? Imagine that in order to make D_t equal to zero we need a negative nominal rate of interest or an absurdly high growth rate of the money supply. I suppose that situations may arise that require, in a technical sense, realizations of economic instruments that are beyond all limits of economic realizability.

Secondly, what guarantees the expectation that the policy-makers will react in some precisely predictable way? Policy-makers typically do not have long time horizons. They may be tempted to make some perhaps short-sighted use of an economic situation that will violate the usual lagged feedback rule. I agree that the Barro-Marini model conveys some important theoretical insights as to how economic policy could be designed to become effective, but I think that the conditions for effective economic policy, as stated in this model, are so exacting that they render the model impotent in designing an applicable economic policy. In particular, I can see hardly any relevance for the solution of the economic problems of contemporary Europe.

Willem Buiter himself notes somes rather strange requirements of the Barro-Marini model which renders it unsuitable for practical policy design. These requirements include the provision that all economic agents are perfectly informed of the policy-makers' true economic model and true reaction functions, but are badly informed about the current values of economic data, e.g., the size of the money stock. Strangely enough, this information is in the real world much more easily accessible than information on the true economic model and the true reaction functions of economic policy.

Therefore, the question arises, what exactly does the Barro-Marini model contribute to practical policy design? Is economic policy, as we need it to cope with imminent economic problems, effective or ineffective? What is the importance of the lesson to be learned from Section 3 for Section 5 of this paper? It is somewhat difficult to see the connection between these two sections.

3. Is Demand and Supply Outdated?

Willem Buiter illustrates the death of supply and demand with the efficiency wage theory on the one hand, and with path-dependence (hysteresis) on the other.

Efficiency wage theory descibes an Akerlof-type stable disequilibrium on the labour market. Employers cannot make distinctions between employees according to their quality, but must pay them according to the *average* employee quality. It is, furthermore, essential for this class of models that the average employee quality is an increasing function of the wage rate. Furthermore, Buiter persuades us to accept the assumption that the elasticity of the average employee quality with respect to the wage rate is initially greater than one, but falls to values less than one for higher wage rates. These, as well as other components of the efficiency wage model, show that a stable efficiency wage disequilibrium on the labour market may exist. Uncertainty as to employee qualification and, simultaneously, wages being equal to the average productivity of labour induces a poorly-qualified work force into the labour market. This forces down average employee quality and prohibits employers from demanding more workers. Although they would gladly employ higher-quality staff at the going wages, they could not distinguish high-quality from poor-quality job applicants, and therefore demand only that amount of the labour force which corresponds to average employee quality. Any outside underbidding of a firm's wages would be ineffective, because lower wages, then paid to all workers in a firm, would induce high quality staff to leave. But only average quality staff is recruited. In such a disequilibrium on the labour market, wage reductions (in terms of the efficiency wage model) would not help, as they lead to an over-proportional reduction in average employee quality (here the above-mentioned elasticity assumption becomes essential) that reduces, rather than increases, labour demand.

I think that models of this kind provide us with much insight and we should be glad to have our reservoir of disposable economic models enriched by them. But do these models really mean the death of supply and demand theory? This can only be the case if the assumptions of the efficiency wage models do indeed apply.

Concerning the crucial assumption that employers cannot distinguish among employees according to their qualifications, we may note the existence of a rich set of devices to improve the information situation. Employers have a lot of *screening devices* at their disposal and employees may use a lot of different *signals* to reveal their respective qualification. Moreover, employees may be dismissed, downgraded, or else upgraded once information on their true qualification emerges.

Notice also that conventional models assume that employee quality is constant in the short run. Is it really true, however, that average employee quality is a function of the wage rate? Could it not also be the other way round, viz. that high average employee quality enables employers to pay higher wages? It comes very much into question whether the chicken came before the egg, or vice versa.

Labour patterns in Switzerland and Germany show us, of course, that high labour quality is concomitant with high wages, but this is a result of a rather long development. Quality cannot be elicited in the short run by high wages; it presupposes a long period of human capital formation. On the other hand, high quality is not frustrated by low wages if the general economic situation is bad. Recall the rapid reconstruction of the West German economy after World War II. Quality reacts much slower than wages. These observations on employee quality translate readily into average employee quality. But if average employee quality is either assumed to be constant or to be moving rather slowly in the short run, the proposition that wage cuts increase unemployment is no longer tenable. Instead, this proposition presupposes a rather sharp decrease in average employee quality as a reaction to wage cuts.

If we go one step further and recognize that employee quality may be discerned by employers to a sufficient degree of accuracy, and assume in addition, that the qualification structure remains fixed in the short run, we are once again back at our traditional concepts of supply and demand with wage rates doing the equilibrating job.

I am far from disputing the significance of the efficiency wage theory; but I doubt whether this is the new general paradigm that makes demand and supply analysis really obsolete. Also the insider-outsider theory contributes much to the explanation of unemployment. But is the insider-outsider situation actually just another deadlock that may be escaped only through policy-driven capital formation, e.g., by way of an expansionary monetary of fiscal policy? Another escape may be the *political change of institutions*, such as the recent union legislation in the United Kingdom. An institutional policy change may in fact be much cheaper than monetary or fiscal policy stimuli. Of course, this is also a matter of political power. But no economic policy may be put into force without political power.

4. An Appropriate Economic Policy For Europe?

Willem Buiter rightly objects to an economic policy of laissez-faire for
Europe, as this would not solve the present unemployment problem. But
he rejects the sole reliance on "supply-side" economic policy as well. He
expressed the conviction that just the repeal of policy-induced "supply-
side" failures would not remedy the present unemployment situation. And
he remarks that supply-side measures would neither be sufficient nor
necessary to remove most of the existing labour slack (p. 334).

Instead, Buiter recommends a "supply-side-friendly, coordinated expansion of aggregate demand through monetary and fiscal stimuli"
(p. 334). He argues that both the efficiency wage view as well as the
insider-outsider model suggest that an expansion of demand can result in
a sustained increase in employment and production without significant
upward pressure on real wages. The near-hysteretic behaviour of the
unemployment rate in Europe should also suggest that any adverse in-
flatory consequences of a demand stimulus would be temporary, while the
output and employment effects would be lasting (p. 335).

The gist of Buiter's economic policy recommendations for Europe is an
extra once-and-for-all boost to the money supply, which is presented in
the garb of the innocent word *"seigniorage"*. Of course, Buiter refers to
the possible inflationary dangers of a policy such as this that may only
be effective if there is nominal inertia, or stickiness, in money wages
and prices (pp. 337/8). He also sees the danger of triggering a wage-
price spiral in the case of governments which show insufficient deter-
minedness to combat inflation (p. 338). But he is confident that the preconditions for a success of a seigniorage policy can be met. However, I
do not find the argument particularly convincing that these preconditions
hold true because "the empirical evidence on this issue is
... by no means clear-cut" (p. 338). Quite the contrary, if we were
actually to embark on such a dangerous adventure, we must dispose of
the significant empirical evidence that there is, indeed, wage and price
inertia and that people can be persuaded that a boost to money supply is
a definite one. Several governments have only recently gained credibility
with respect to the determination of their monetary policy. Should they

again hazard this newly acquired public confidence for the sake of the uncertain consequences of a boost to money supply?

Now let me raise another problem: how is this additional money supply dissipated to create a higher level of demand? If it is only spent by governments, this would inevitably incur heavy follow-up costs that would necessarily frustrate any attempts to control the money supply further. Inflation would be inevitable.

Buiter suggests that this increase in the money supply should be used to elicit more private investment. But by what means to be precise? By a policy of cheap money? The interest rates in West Germany and Japan are presently so low that this would hardly have any significant effect. Investment subsidies would impinge on economic efficiency and would create firms and industries that could not survive without routine subsidies. These would call for more and more seigniorage. Increasing social security benefits, furthermore, impose heavy mortgages on the future.

I think the recommendation of a policy of seigniorage is a rather hazardous game. On the contrary, I consider supply-side policy measures to be more promising instruments to overcome our present difficulties. These should be sustained by a rigid anti-privilege policy against vested institutions. This would mitigate insider-outsider hardships on the labour market.

Willem Buiter was uneasy with the title of his paper that was chosen *for* him and not *by* him. This had obviously induced him to prepare a rather provocative paper, which he successfully accomplished.

Summary of the Discussion by Joachim Scheide

The discussion focused first on the model presented in Willem Buiter's paper, especially on equations [52]-[54b]. The implication of this part was that positive output effects can be created by price surprises;

according to equation [54b], where expected inflation is postulated to be a weighted average of past inflation, it would be possible to keep unemployment below its natural rate if inflation is higher than expected. To some, this implication was highly implausible; in fact, this version of the original natural rate model led Robert Lucas - and others - to adopt rational expectations. These new models then entirely dismissed the implication that you can enrich a country forever in real terms by printing money.

The view expressed in Buiter's paper also led to a comparison of the policy implications with those of the McCallum paper. His rule aimed at zero inflation in the long run. Should we conclude from Buiter's paper that on average the economies would have fared better in the past with respect to employment if they had produced more inflation? Whether this was the case or not, could we also make a statement concerning the future, i.e., allowing more inflation will imply permanently lower unemployment? While the answer by some participants was negative, the alternative view was that, under certain conditions, the answer could be positive. To those holding this view, demand stimulation was appropriate in situations when there was slack in the economy, whether "actual or hysteretic"; in the same way, they would suggest restrictive policies in situations in which they could identify excess demand. Furthermore, they argued if the efficiency-wage hypothesis were correct, the demand stimulus would work even if it did not come as a surprise.

Those who were in favor of a demand push could also not agree with the notion that the demand expansion since 1982 had simply passed the labor market, i.e., had not reduced unemployment in Europe. In their opinion, there simply was no major stimulus, demand expanded only with the rate of potential output without reducing the existing slack.

It was further argued by the sceptics that the demand stimulation would not work under certain conditions, even if hysteresis existed: deficiencies on the supply side, like immobility of labor or lack of qualification, simply could not be resolved by a demand push. Also, permanent reductions of unemployment could not be expected because hysteresis had to do with a learning effect: some argued that people had learned how to work the system of unemployment benefits, the black economy, and so on. This could not be reversed.

Major problems concerning the demand push were would it really deliver the stimulus, could the authorities produce a "time-inconsistent surprise"? The way economic policy works seems to suggest that when the policymakers start to discuss the measures, economic agents will anticipate them. But if, we could have this surprise, would it really be worth it, because the effect would be the loss of the credibility of policymakers ("what's the sense of building up credibility and then blowing it?"). It was argued that it would be very difficult to restore credibility again. The counterargument was that a demand stimulus would not necessarily destroy credibility at all; in fact, it might even be enhanced if, for example, fiscal policy became expansionary for a while and then, as announced, return to the old path. In this sense, credibility could really be "used for something", rather than being built up "for its own sake". According to this view the crucial issue at stake was how to weight the risk of doing nothing - and thus achieving nothing - against the possibility of having the positive effect of a permanent reduction of unemployment induced by demand stimulation. The efficiency wage hypothesis would, in this case, provide a basis for demand policy.

VII

Juergen B. Donges

Lessons for Europe

The issues we had to face in this conference are protracted problems as far as slow and erratic growth and high unemployment in Europe (in contrast of the United States) is concerned; they have afflicted most economies since the mid-1970s. The agenda included also more recent problems, such as sharp short-term exchange-rate volatility, longer-lasting overvaluation and undervaluation of key currencies, and un-sustainable trade and current account imbalances. The papers and the discussions were expected to provide new answers to these problems and, in particular, to settle the controversy over policy paradigms, diagnoses and therapies, with the ultimate aim to enlighten policymakers.

The stimulating papers and a lively debate have helped a lot to come close to these expectations. If I had to admit to feeling somewhat uneasy about anything, I should summarise this unease in the following four points: firstly, there was a sensible supply of formal (and rhetorical) elegance, but this was perhaps not as clearly matched by relevance as desired. Secondly, we have carefully focused on the best methodology to produce persuasive numbers, but the empirical evidence presented on specific issues has nevertheless turned out to be quite ambiguous. Thirdly, results have become a matter of controversy on the ground that everyone's model (or computer) "tells a different story", even if more or less the same data base was used. Fourthly, a great emphasis has been laid on macroeconomic aspects (i.e., stabilization concerns), whereas much less attention has been paid to the microeconomic dimensions of the observed problems.

The interaction of macro and micro is crucial in the European context because, should governments embark upon reflationary policies, the additional demand expansion would soon come up against supply constraints. The explanation for this is the many rigidities built into the system. West Germany is a case in point, but deep-seated structural rigidities are said to afflict also other European countries. These rigidities have not emerged by chance. They reflect to a considerable degree the outcome of creeping trade protectionism, of open-ended and industry-specific (if not firm-specific) subsidies and the countless regulations of economic activities (in particular services) and markets (in particular labor markets). Some of these government interventions are rooted in history; but most of them developed during the 1970s and 1980s. Whatever the origin, their impact is much greater now than it was 15 or 20 years ago because they have made our economies too rigid just at a time in which far-reaching shocks and challenges require more flexibility and efficiency, not less. These events, well-documented in the literature, weaken the case for a "controlled" demand boost, as called for by Willem Buiter in his paper (in addition to the damage done on the credibility of governments if the experiment fails or inflation accelerates, as Patrick Minford has pointed out).

The core of microeconomic distortions in most European economies is the labor market. As the paper by Rüdiger Soltwedel and Peter Trapp has shown for Germany, and as other papers (had they been commissioned) would have shown for Belgium, the Netherlands, France or Spain, the labor market can hardly function in an adequate manner. The true problems are not captured by looking only at the average real wage (supplements and payroll taxes included). Wage moderation, which would keep the increase of hourly real wages behind the trend productivity growth over a period of time, may be necessary; in fact, the EC Commission has been promulgating such wage moderation since 1985 under the label of "a cooperative growth strategy for more employment" (recently with some renaming). Such wage moderation could become a means for stimulating capital formation which is required for the creation for more jobs which are productive (i.e., internationally competitive) in the medium run.

However, it is the structure of wages by skills and regions which decisively matters and, by the way, reflects best the "insider-outsider" problem. Almost everywhere there is a trend towards a nation-wide binding of wage contracts; and it has become a common practice in collective bargaining to increase the wages of low-skilled workers at more than average and in excess of their marginal product. Hence, it is almost impossible for workers in declining industries (regions) to bid down wages with a view to keeping a job which they would otherwise have lost; and it is hard for unemployed young or low-skilled (or wrongly-skilled) workers to price themselves into the market, what they sometimes try (in contrast to what the "efficiency wage" models state). Furthermore, structurally weak regions find themselves at a disadvantage when competing with the more prosperous ones for attracting fresh investment, dynamic entrepreneurship and qualified manpower; their "exchange-rate" appreciates in real terms vis-à-vis the "currencies" of the more prosperous regions.

If this diagnosis is correct (and it was not refuted by this conference), Europe's severe unemployment problems will not automatically disappear, not even by means of expansionary demand policies, whatever output gaps are econometrically measured (incidentally, we should not count every job and installed capacity as being available to meet aggregate demand expansion; they are often economically obsolete to some degree due to previous labor cost increases, technology changes and/or stiffer import competition). In a "two-handed approach", which seems to be favored by many at this conference (and elsewhere), the overhaul of the labor market institutional set-ups must be a cornerstone, accomplished hopefully by the active participation of trade unions. Whether or not governments should intensify active labor market policies as Gerhard Fels and others have advocated in light of the hysteresis argument for unemployment is an open question. It seems to make sense that vocational training and retraining programs should be provided for the unemployed and that firms should obtain some wage subsidies for that. And yet, evidence does not suggest that these policies have been as effective as expected in redeploying and/or reintegrating labor. Moreover, there may be the temptation for the unemployed to raise their "reservation wage" and for employers to feign the need to employ an unemployed person (to get the wage subsidy). Also, there is a possibility that governments regard active labor-market policies as a substitute to the deregulation of labor markets, which they are not.

This said, micro policies are more widely needed in order to strengthen the system of relative price incentives as a necessary condition for new investment and technological innovations to flourish in Europe over the longer run. Important measures include (i) tax cuts and tax reform, (ii) the scaling down of public subsidies, (iii) the removal of the unusually restrictive market - entry regulation for new firms (especially in transportation, insurance services, and telecommunications), and (iv) trade liberalization. As to the latter, the Kiel position on trade liberalization must not be identified with seeking free trade, as some participants at this conference stated. The primary objective to be achieved is to restore the principle of nondiscrimination, transparency and predictability for trade policy measures. In this sense, liberal trade is fine, it need not be free trade. As to the gains which can be expected from internal and external liberalization, a recent analysis undertaken at the Kiel Institute for France, Italy, the United Kingdom and West Germany has shown that they would be considerable indeed. The annual rate of growth of GDP per capita in the 1984-1995 period could be two and more percentage points higher than it would have been the case if existing subsidization, protection and regulation were maintained (1).

Unfortunately, in most European countries, and certainly in Germany, there is no comprehensive and coherent macro and micro strategy geared towards strengthening the growth potential and restoring full employment. Governments do not eschew reflationary policies in favor of improving the supply side of the economy first because they don't want to rekindle inflationary pressures. To be sure, our politicians are meanwhile aware of the many distortions. They also deplore those distortions time and time again (particularly loudly when they belong to the Op-

---

(1) For details, see Juergen B. Donges and Hans Hinrich Glismann, Industrial Adjustment in Western Europe - Retrospect and Prospect. Institut für Weltwirtschaft, Kiel Working Papers, 280, March 1987, pp. 47-58.

position in parliament). But our politicians also find it difficult in reality to transform this recognition into appropriate policy changes.

In Germany, for instance, the Government which came into power in 1982 promised comprehensive liberalization and the deregulation of product and factor markets. Some measures have been taken, but on balance, progress has been quite slow. Probably the export-driven upswing of 1983-1985 gave politicians the impression that the situation was improving, i.e., that the structural rigidities had been overcome. This perception was wrong, and a good indicator of this is that public subsidies have not been reduced, as announced, but increased (1). One is tempted to invite American critics of Germany's allegedly austere (or inappropriate) macroeconomic policy stance that they should call less for conventional expansionary remedies and insist more on the Federal Government to do the unfinished homework with regard to micro policies.

In retrospect, it turns out to be a disadvantage that what was (and still is) at stake was (and is) left to the government's discretion in Germany (and other European countries). I wonder whether Alan Blinder would regard the continuance of discretionary policies as justified on the grounds that the markets were working inefficiently at that time (and keep on doing so); after all, this inefficiency is self-inflicted to a large extent, i.e., it reflects government failure in the first place. But I submit that had the government stuck its reform ideas to rules, this would not only have protected the government against pressures from organized interest-groups to maintain, or even tighten, protective and regulatory devices. Rules would also have made provision for predictability of the policy course, improving the probability that the economy would have been in a better shape than it actually is. By a rule-oriented strategy I mean the precommitment by the government to specific and publicly-announced micro policies, which are sensible and credible and unambiguously inform economic agents about the rules of the game.

---

(1) For details, see Juergen B. Donges, Klaus-D. Schmidt, Hugo Dicke, Erich Gundlach, Karl-H. Jüttemeier, Henning Klodt, Frank D. Weiss, Mehr Strukturwandel für Wachstum und Beschäftigung: Die deutsche Wirtschaft im Anpassungsstau. Kieler Studien, 216, Tübingen 1988.

Whenever microeconomic reforms are to be enacted discretionarily, the question of timing arises. Should reforms be implemented abruptly or gradually? A gradual approach may appear as more feasible from a political point of view and seems to provide everybody with a fair chance to adjust. But it also allows counterpressure to be formed effectively, unless there is strong political leadership (which typically is an extremely scarce factor in public affairs). Abrupt actions may be more promising on this count.

Which ever approach is chosen, however, the crucial parts of microeconomic reforms have to be dealt with at the beginning of a legislative period, and they should be complemented by accommodating macro policies. The longer a newly elected government waits, the greater the danger is that other issues will emerge, policy priorities change and the whole project suffers the same fate as earlier "attempts". As election dates differ from country to country, there is almost no scope for an international coordination of micro policies. In fact, such a coordination is not needed for these policies to be effective, and it would have its limitations here as in other policy areas anyway (as Roland Vaubel has reminded us and the reality plainly shows). Perhaps with the exception of trade liberalization, each country can unilaterally take the required steps to bring his house in order. Your can argue, of course, that unilateral actions is the least one can expect in a world in which mercantilist sentiments prevail and reciprocity as a general rule in the conduct of international negotiations has a much greater public appeal. If this is the case, I am afraid that the general economic situation in Europe is unlikely to improve significantly in the medium run; we then shall also have to keep on living with the labor market malaise.

List of Contributors

Prof. Martin J. Bailey, Ph.D.	United States Department of State, Washington; University of Maryland
Prof. Alan S. Blinder	Princeton University
Prof. Willem H. Buiter	Yale University, New Haven
Prof. Dr.Dr. Emil-Maria Claassen	Europäisches Hochschulinstitut, Italy, Florence
Prof. Dr. Juergen B. Donges	Institut für Weltwirtschaft, Kiel
Dr. Hermann-Josef Dudler	Deutsche Bundesbank, Frankfurt/M.
Prof. Dr. Gerhard Fels	Institut der deutschen Wirtschaft, Cologne
Prof. Dr. Drs.h.c. Herbert Giersch	Institut für Weltwirtschaft, Kiel
Prof. Robert J. Gordon, Ph.D.	Northwestern University, Evanston
Prof. Dr. Gerd Hansen	Universität Kiel
Dr. Sean Holly	London Business School
Prof. Bennett T. McCallum	Carnegie-Mellon University, Pittsburgh
Prof. Ronald I. McKinnon, Ph.D.	Stanford University
Prof. Patrick Minford, Ph.D.	University of Liverpool
Prof. Dr. Manfred J.M. Neumann	Universität Bonn
Prof. William A. Niskanen, Ph.D.	CATO Institute, Washington
Prof. Gilles Oudiz	Ecole Polytechnique, Paris
Prof. Dr. Pascal Salin	Université de Paris-IX-Dauphine, Paris
Prof. Dr. Klaus-Werner Schatz	Institut für Weltwirtschaft, Kiel
Dr. Joachim Scheide	Institut für Weltwirtschaft, Kiel
Prof. Dr. Christian Seidl	Universität Kiel
Dr. Peter N. Smith	London Business School
Dr. Rüdiger Soltwedel	Institut für Weltwirtschaft, Kiel

Dr. Peter Trapp	Institut für Weltwirtschaft, Kiel
Prof. Dr. Roland Vaubel	Universität Mannheim
Prof. Dr. Jean Waelbroeck, Ph.D.	Université Libre de Bruxelles
Prof. Dr. Manfred Willms	Universität Kiel
Prof. Leland B. Yeager, Ph.D.	Auburn University

Weltwirtschaftliches Archiv

Review of World Economics

Zeitschrift des Instituts für Weltwirtschaft Kiel
Journal of the Kiel Institute of World Economics

Herausgegeben von Herbert Giersch
in Zusammenarbeit mit Mitgliedern der Wirtschafts- und Sozialwissen-
schaftlichen Fakultät der Christian-Albrechts-Universität Kiel

Schriftleitung: Hubertus Müller-Groeling

Band 124	**1988**	**Heft 2**

AUFSÄTZE – ARTICLES

Intra-Industry Trade: An "Untidy" Phenomenon *H. Peter Gray*

Effects of Knowledge and Service Intensities on Domestic and Export Performance
Seev Hirsch, Shlomo Kalish, and Shauli Katznelson

Time Series Properties of Comparative Advantage Indices
Ingeborg Menzler-Hokkanen

The Game-Theoretic Approach to International Policy Coordination: Assessing the
Role of Targets *Juan Carlos Martinez Oliva and Stefan Sinn*

The Macroeconomic Implications of Wage Indexation in a Two-Sector Open Economy
Rogério L. Zandamela

Stock Prices and Merger Movements: Interactive Relations
John J. Clark, Alok K. Chakrabarti, and Thomas C. Chiang

The Economic Effects of Agricultural Policy in West Germany
Hugo Dicke, Juergen B. Donges, Egbert Gerken, and Grant Kirkpatrick

Exchange-Rate Uncertainty and Foreign Direct Investment in the United States
David O. Cushman

KÜRZERE AUFSÄTZE & KOMMENTARE – SHORTER PAPERS & COMMENTS

Inter- versus Intra-Industry Trade: A Note on U.S. Trends, 1963–1980
Farhang Niroomand

BERICHTE – REPORTS

Some Neglected Issues in Factor Proportions and Ownership: An Indonesian Case
Study *Hal Hill*

LITERATUR – LITERATURE

Discrimination in International Trade – A Review *Alfred Tovias*

Rezensionen (Verzeichnis siehe nächste Seite) – Book Reviews (list see next page)

Erhaltene Bücher – Books Received

Das »Weltwirtschaftliche Archiv« erscheint vierteljährlich. Das Jahresabonnement kostet DM 130,-,
das einzelne Heft DM 36,-. (The »Weltwirtschaftliches Archiv« appears quarterly. The subscription
price for one year is DM 130.-; the price for a single issue DM 36.-).

J. C. B. Mohr (Paul Siebeck) Tübingen

Postfach 2040, D-7400 Tübingen
ISSN 0043 – 2636

Institut für Weltwirtschaft an der Universität Kiel

Symposien- und Konferenzbände

Herausgegeben von Herbert Giersch

The Economic Integration of Israel in the EEC
Tel Aviv Conference
Tübingen 1980. V, 316 S. Broschiert *DM* 84,-. Leinen *DM* 98,-.

Macroeconomic Policies for Growth and Stability:
A European Perspective
Symposium 1979
Tübingen 1981. V, 255 S. Broschiert *DM* 55,-. Leinen *DM* 71,-.

Towards an Explanation of Economic Growth
Symposium 1980
Tübingen 1981. VI, 476 S. Broschiert *DM* 119,-. Leinen *DM* 139,-.

Emerging Technologies: Consequences for Economic Growth,
Structural Change, and Employment
Symposium 1981
Tübingen 1982. VI, 480 S. Broschiert *DM* 98,-. Leinen *DM* 123,-.

Reassessing the Role of Government in the Mixed Economy
Symposium 1982
Tübingen 1983. VIII, 292 . Broschiert *DM* 72,-. Leinen *DM* 92,-.

New Opportunities for Entrepreneurship
Symposium 1983
Tübingen 1984. VI, 266 S. Broschiert *DM* 62,-. Leinen *DM* 84,-.

The International Debt Problem - Lessons for the Future
Symposium 1985
Tübingen 1986. VI, 193 S. Broschiert *DM* 49,-. Leinen *DM* 69,-.

Free Trade in the World Economy: Towards an Opening of Markets
Symposium 1986
Tübingen 1987. VI, 624 S. Broschiert *DM* 90,-. Leinen *DM* 110,-.

Macro and Micro Policies for More Growth and Employment
Symposium 1987
Tübingen 1988. VII, 369 S. Broschiert *DM* 70,-. Leinen *DM* 90,-.

J. C. B. Mohr (Paul Siebeck) Tübingen